ANDRE THE GIANT
LIFE AND LEGEND

BOX BROWN

:01
First Second
New York

Thanks to my wife and family,
Josh B., Pat A., Ian H., Tom H., James K., Bill O.,
and all my other pals and supporters.

First Second

New York

Text and art copyright © 2014 by Brian Brown

Published by First Second
First Second is an imprint of Roaring Brook Press, a division of Holtzbrinck
Publishing Holdings Limited Partnership
175 Fifth Avenue, New York, New York 10010

Cataloging-in-Publication Data is on file at the Library of Congress.

ISBN 978-1-59643-851-4

First Second books may be purchased for business or promotional use.
For information on bulk purchases please contact Macmillan Corporate
and Premium Sales Department at (800) 221-7945 x5442 or by email
at specialmarkets@macmillan.com.

First edition 2014
Book design by Rob Steen

Printed in the United States of America

10 9 8 7 6 5 4 3 2 1

Isn't It Fake? A Note about the Nature of Professional Wrestling and Comics

It would be difficult to discuss the life of Andre the Giant without a small foundational discussion of the world he lived in. The culture of professional wrestling is, in some ways, built upon mass deception. It's no wonder it's often a misunderstood business.

The world of professional wrestling has been fascinating to me ever since my friend Bill started bringing wrestling magazines to school in fourth grade. He had a lot of wrestling on VHS and would order the pay-per-view events. After I watched *WrestleMania VI* at his house in 1990, I was in for life. I started consuming all the wrestling-related media I could. Back in the days before the Internet, there were a wealth of wrestling magazines sold at the supermarket. I would take wrestling any way I could get it. I'd search the TV Guide for anything that even sounded like wrestling. Late at night you could even catch local wrestling on weird cable access channels.

Yes. It's "fake." The outcomes are predetermined. I like to compare it to psychic mediums. Magicians are not really performing magic. They are using certain methods to make you believe they are levitating or sawing someone in half. Most people know this. But when magicians are really good at what they do they'll have the audience, at least for a moment, believing. This is what wrestling was like for a long time. The notion that the audience believes that wrestling is real is called "kayfabe." For a wrestler to come out and admit that wrestling is actually not a real fight would be breaking this social contract. There was a time when this was simply not done. A performer would be drummed out of the business, if not beaten or killed, for admitting that wrestling was staged. It was seen at one time to be essential to the business to never reveal to anyone that wrestling was staged—that information existed on a need-to-know basis. I'm sure there are many people who worked in wrestling who were never "smartened up" to the business.

At some point in the 1990s things started to change. The reason they changed is debatable but people often cite Vince McMahon of the WWE admitting that wrestling was staged to avoid paying sports licensing fees in my home state of New Jersey (pride!). Certainly though, the Internet changed things a lot. People had greater access to information about professional wrestling and sooner or later, for better or worse, the audience was in on the "work." This led to a lot of former performers coming out and telling their stories about the business without worrying about breaking kayfabe. This act of pulling back the curtain is endlessly fascinating to me. I'd like to take the time to thank two companies, Highspots and RF Video, for committing these stories to video.

Because of the nature of kayfabe it's hard to believe anything a wrestler says. Sometimes wrestlers will hide things from each other; they'll "work" even each other. So the idea that wrestlers would exaggerate stories to make themselves look better, and make their friends look better, make their actual enemies look worse, even in so-called "real" shoot interviews, is not unheard of.

The idea of truth in professional wrestling is certainly elastic and is connected to the idea of the wrestler as a product. Wrestlers are acutely aware that they are products to be sold. For most of professional wrestling's history wrestlers were paid for work as independent contractors. They were forced to take care of all of their own expenses, including medical bills, and could be disposed of at any time. At the same time, they were told to put the company above all else. If the company made money everyone made money. Money is the only morality in professional wrestling. Things that make money are good. Period. The end. Truth? Who needs it?

The fuzzy line between truth and fiction in professional wrestling matches extends to the stories wrestlers tell about each other outside of the ring—and stories about Andre the Giant can be especially hard to judge. In researching this book, I used my best judgment on the truth of what I was watching or reading. There were cases where it was one man's word against another and I had to make a subjective judgment on which I should believe. Additionally, Andre the Giant was truly a legendary figure. Stories about him were unbelievable just due to the extraordinary circumstances of his life.

I took some unavoidable liberties—and used some artistic license—in the storytelling of this book. Certain kinds of information that are needed to create a comic are just not included in the stories people tell. Where was Andre sitting in the bus? What did the bus actually look like? What kinds of pleasantries were exchanged? Because of the nature of comic storytelling this information needs to be in the comic story. And beyond the purely practical side of the craft, there's the art of it: the story has to move along to be readable. A writer presents his or her information in an artful, entertaining way. That's why we're interested in that writer's work, perhaps. All of which is to say: there are some parts in the story where dialogue and events were improvised (see the notes at the end of the book).

For me, creating this book was a scholarly pursuit. I wanted to tell Andre's story as best I could. Andre the Giant represents all that is good in professional wrestling. People all around the world loved him. The professional wrestling industry respected him. In his time he made more money than any other wrestler. In a world where money is the only morality he was the best. He was a man who was given a death sentence at a very young age. He was a disabled person who had difficulty with the activities of everyday life. He was an inspiring figure to countless people in all walks of life, a real hero! Still, he was as imperfect as we all are. He was 7'4" and 500 pounds. He was a human with human complexities and desires. He was Andre Roussimoff.

He was Andre the Giant.

TERRY
"HULK HOGAN"
BOLLEA
TAMPA, FL, 2010

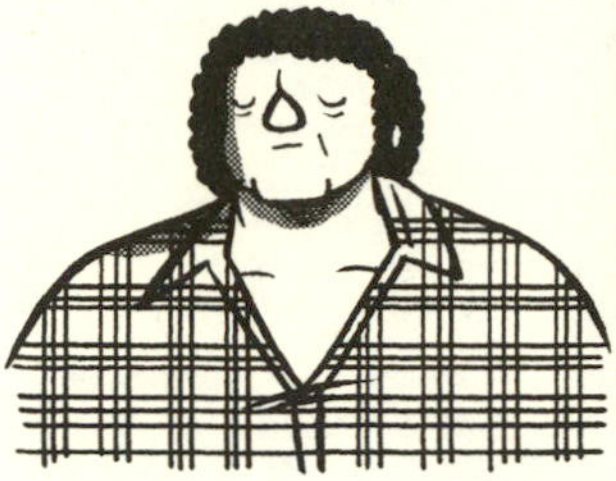

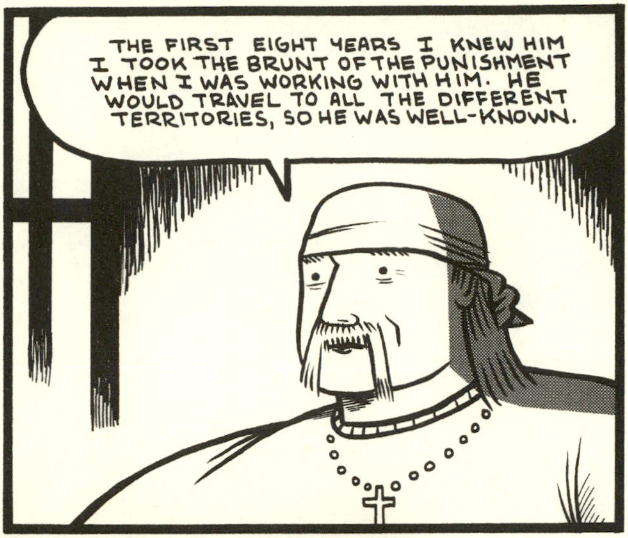
THE FIRST EIGHT YEARS I KNEW HIM I TOOK THE BRUNT OF THE PUNISHMENT WHEN I WAS WORKING WITH HIM. HE WOULD TRAVEL TO ALL THE DIFFERENT TERRITORIES, SO HE WAS WELL-KNOWN.

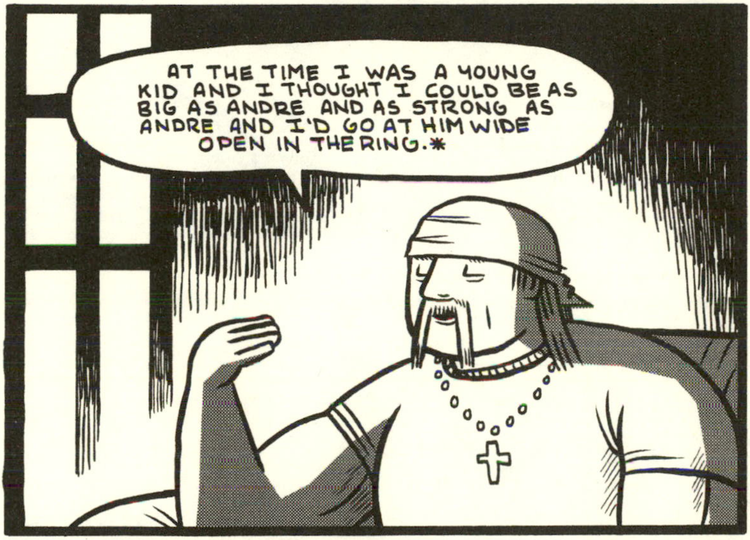
AT THE TIME I WAS A YOUNG KID AND I THOUGHT I COULD BE AS BIG AS ANDRE AND AS STRONG AS ANDRE AND I'D GO AT HIM WIDE OPEN IN THE RING.*

* USING AGGRESSION AND STRENGTH TO MAKE SURE A MATCH GOES THE WAY A WRESTLER WANTS IT TO GO

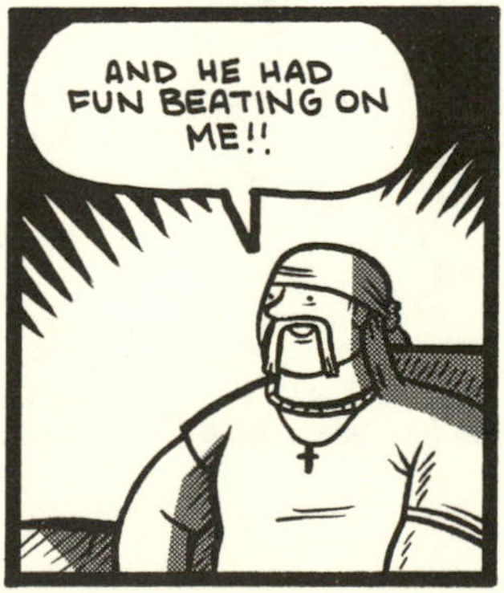
AND HE HAD FUN BEATING ON ME!!

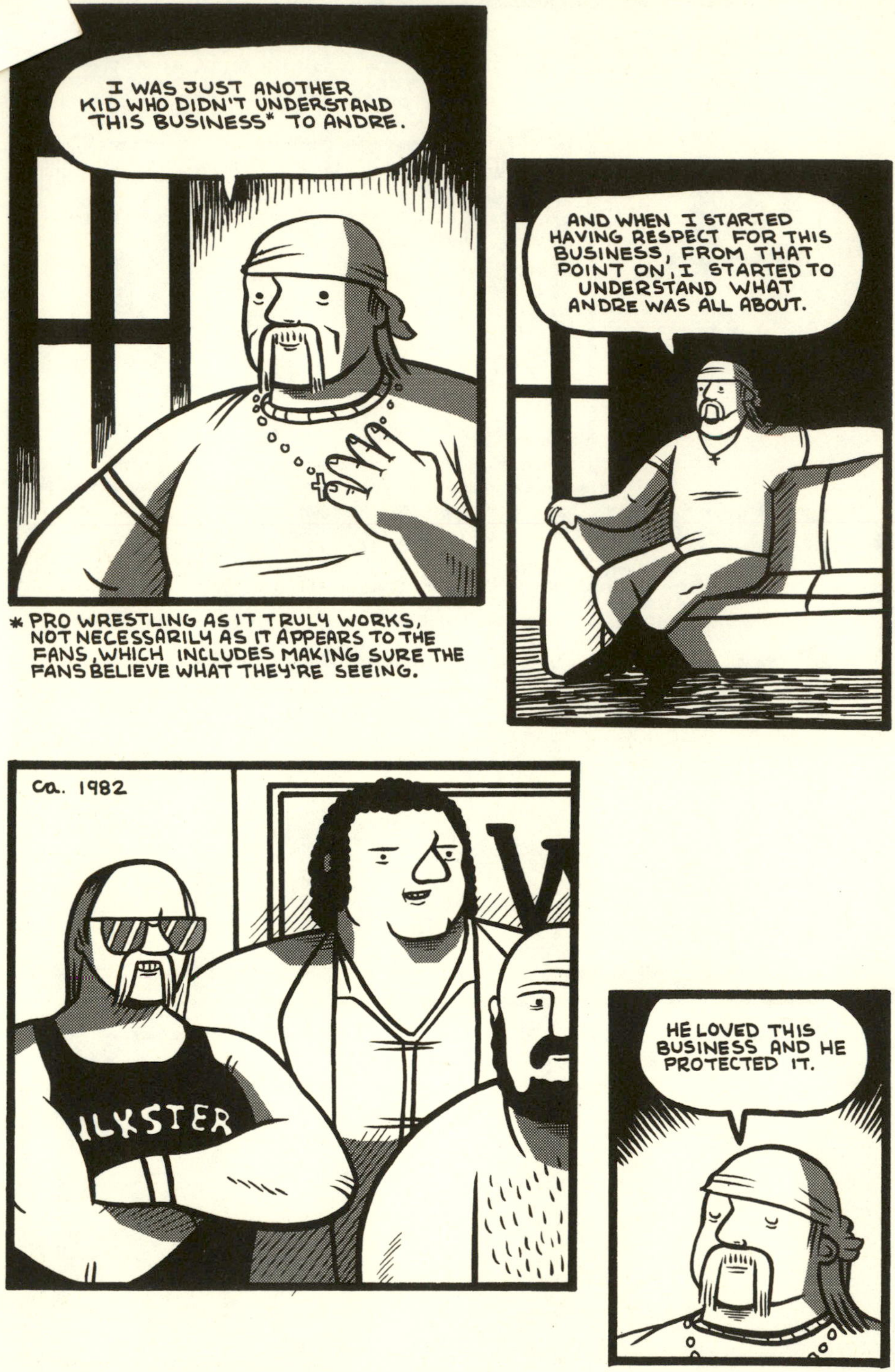
I WAS JUST ANOTHER KID WHO DIDN'T UNDERSTAND THIS BUSINESS* TO ANDRE.
* PRO WRESTLING AS IT TRULY WORKS, NOT NECESSARILY AS IT APPEARS TO THE FANS, WHICH INCLUDES MAKING SURE THE FANS BELIEVE WHAT THEY'RE SEEING.
AND WHEN I STARTED HAVING RESPECT FOR THIS BUSINESS, FROM THAT POINT ON, I STARTED TO UNDERSTAND WHAT ANDRE WAS ALL ABOUT.
ca. 1982
ILKSTER
HE LOVED THIS BUSINESS AND HE PROTECTED IT.

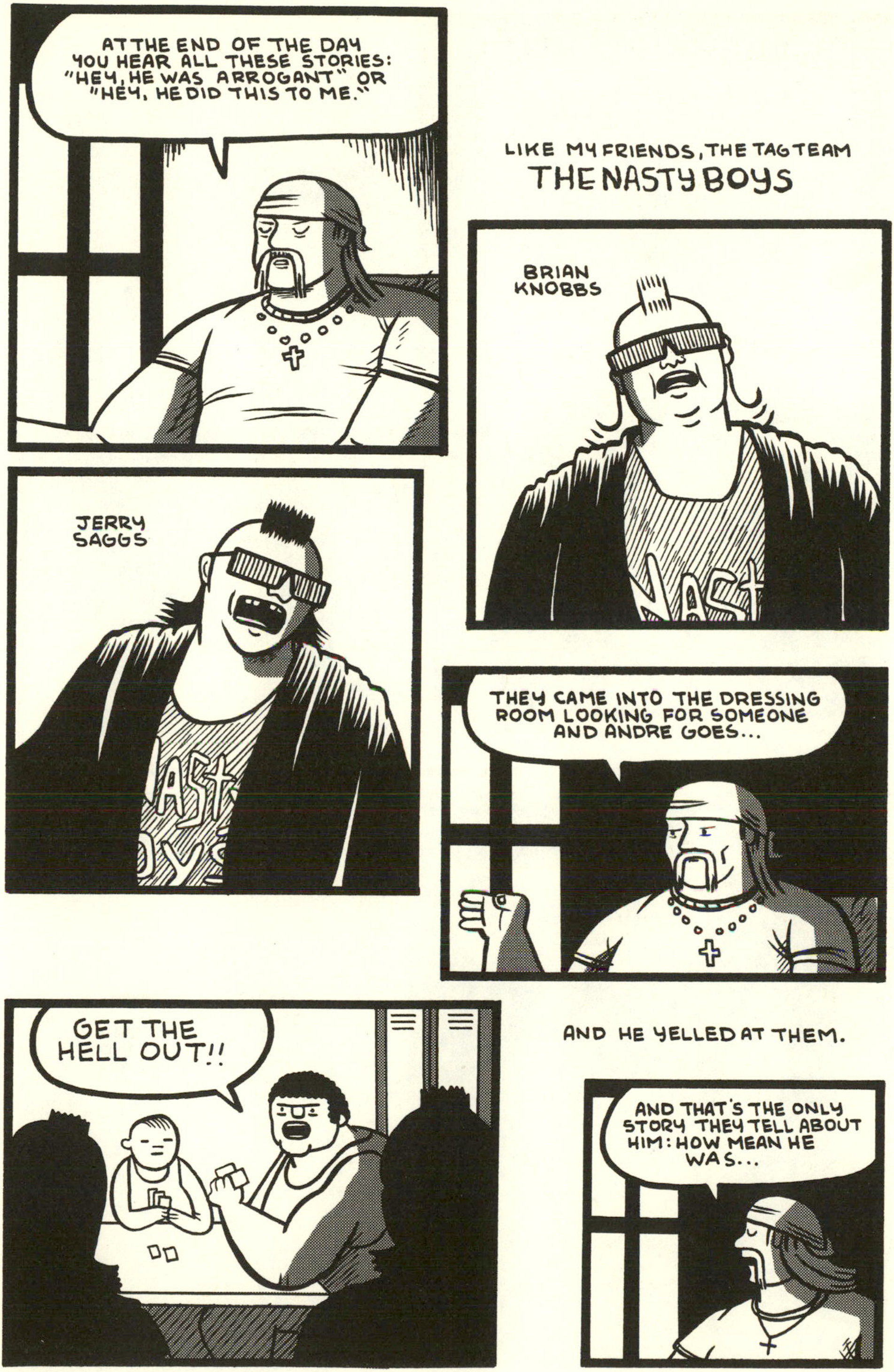
AT THE END OF THE DAY YOU HEAR ALL THESE STORIES: "HEY, HE WAS ARROGANT" OR "HEY, HE DID THIS TO ME."
LIKE MY FRIENDS, THE TAG TEAM
THE NASTY BOYS
BRIAN KNOBBS
JERRY SAGGS
THEY CAME INTO THE DRESSING ROOM LOOKING FOR SOMEONE AND ANDRE GOES...
GET THE HELL OUT!!
AND HE YELLED AT THEM.
AND THAT'S THE ONLY STORY THEY TELL ABOUT HIM: HOW MEAN HE WAS...

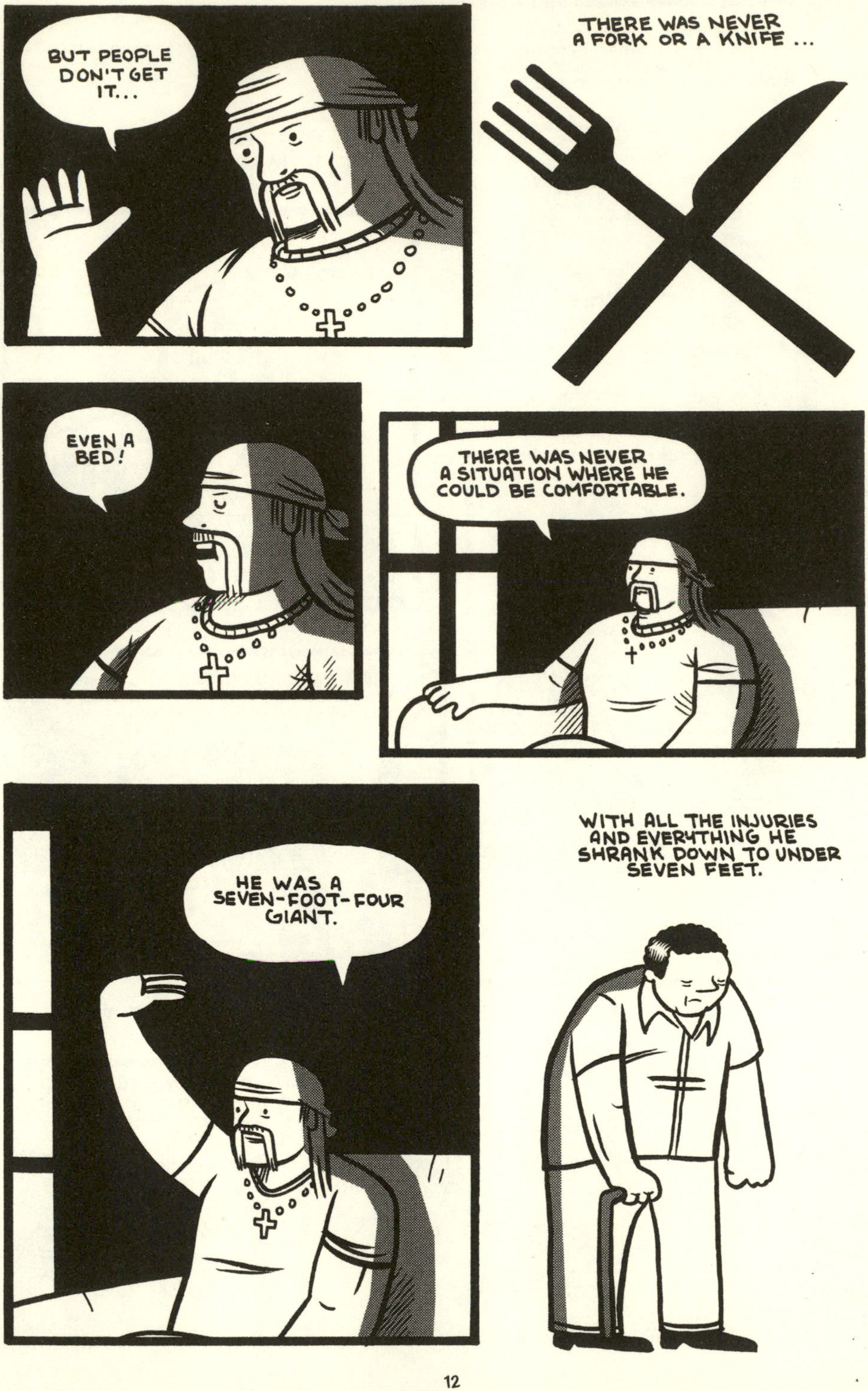
BUT PEOPLE DON'T GET IT...
THERE WAS NEVER A FORK OR A KNIFE ...
EVEN A BED!
THERE WAS NEVER A SITUATION WHERE HE COULD BE COMFORTABLE.
HE WAS A SEVEN-FOOT-FOUR GIANT.
WITH ALL THE INJURIES AND EVERYTHING HE SHRANK DOWN TO UNDER SEVEN FEET.

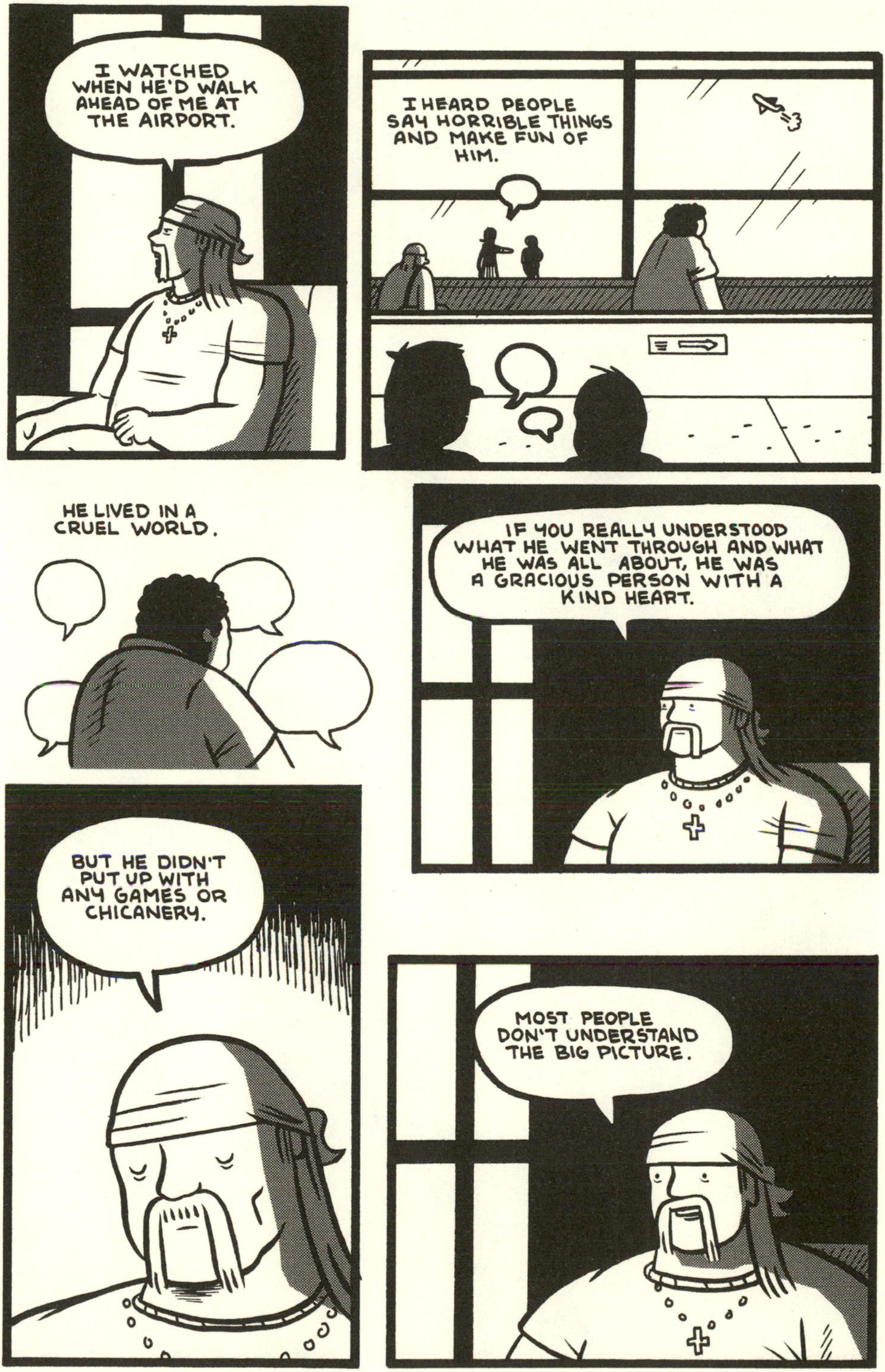
I WATCHED WHEN HE'D WALK AHEAD OF ME AT THE AIRPORT.
I HEARD PEOPLE SAY HORRIBLE THINGS AND MAKE FUN OF HIM.
HE LIVED IN A CRUEL WORLD.
IF YOU REALLY UNDERSTOOD WHAT HE WENT THROUGH AND WHAT HE WAS ALL ABOUT, HE WAS A GRACIOUS PERSON WITH A KIND HEART.
BUT HE DIDN'T PUT UP WITH ANY GAMES OR CHICANERY.
MOST PEOPLE DON'T UNDERSTAND THE BIG PICTURE.

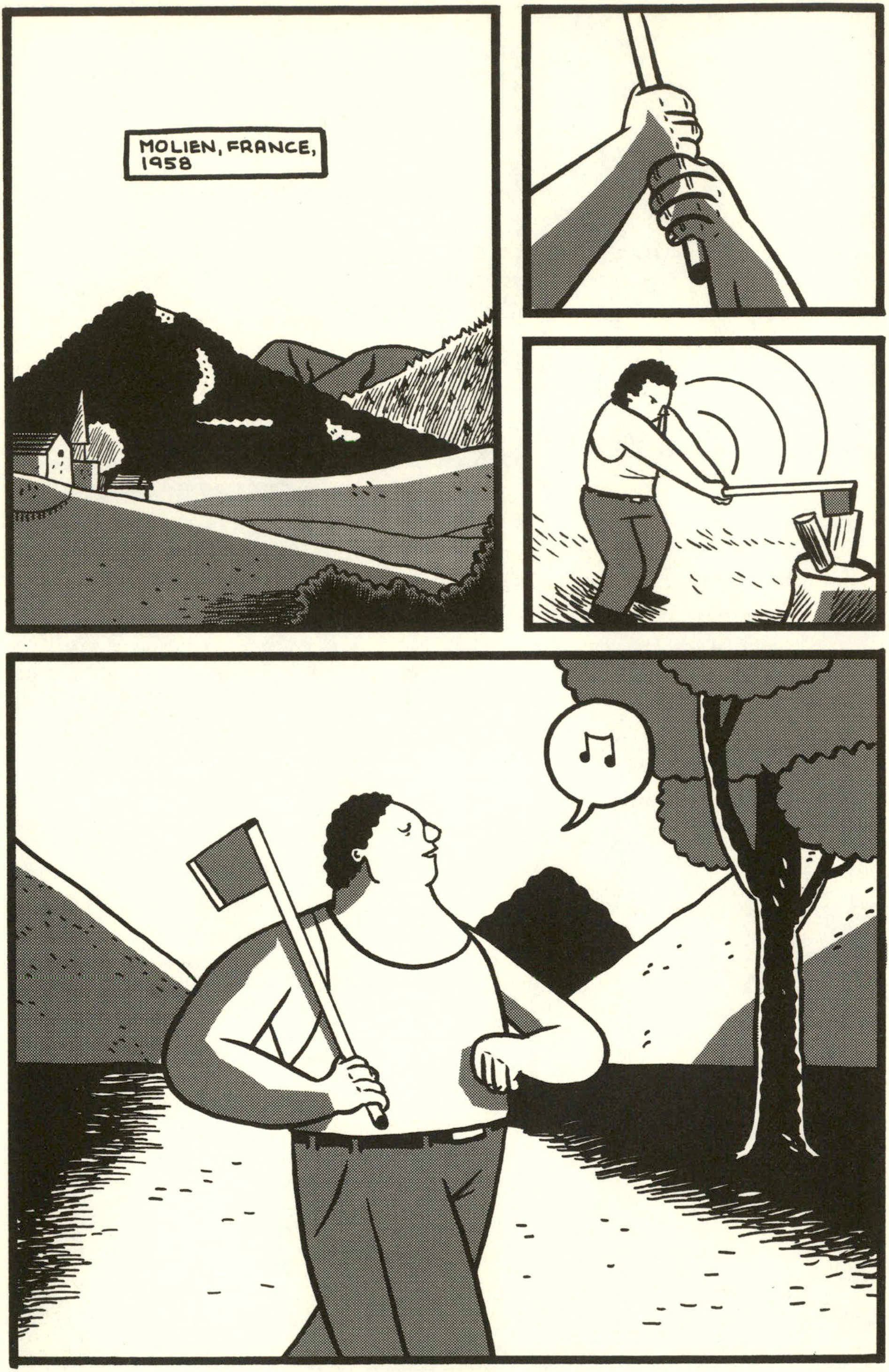
MOLIEN, FRANCE, 1958
♫

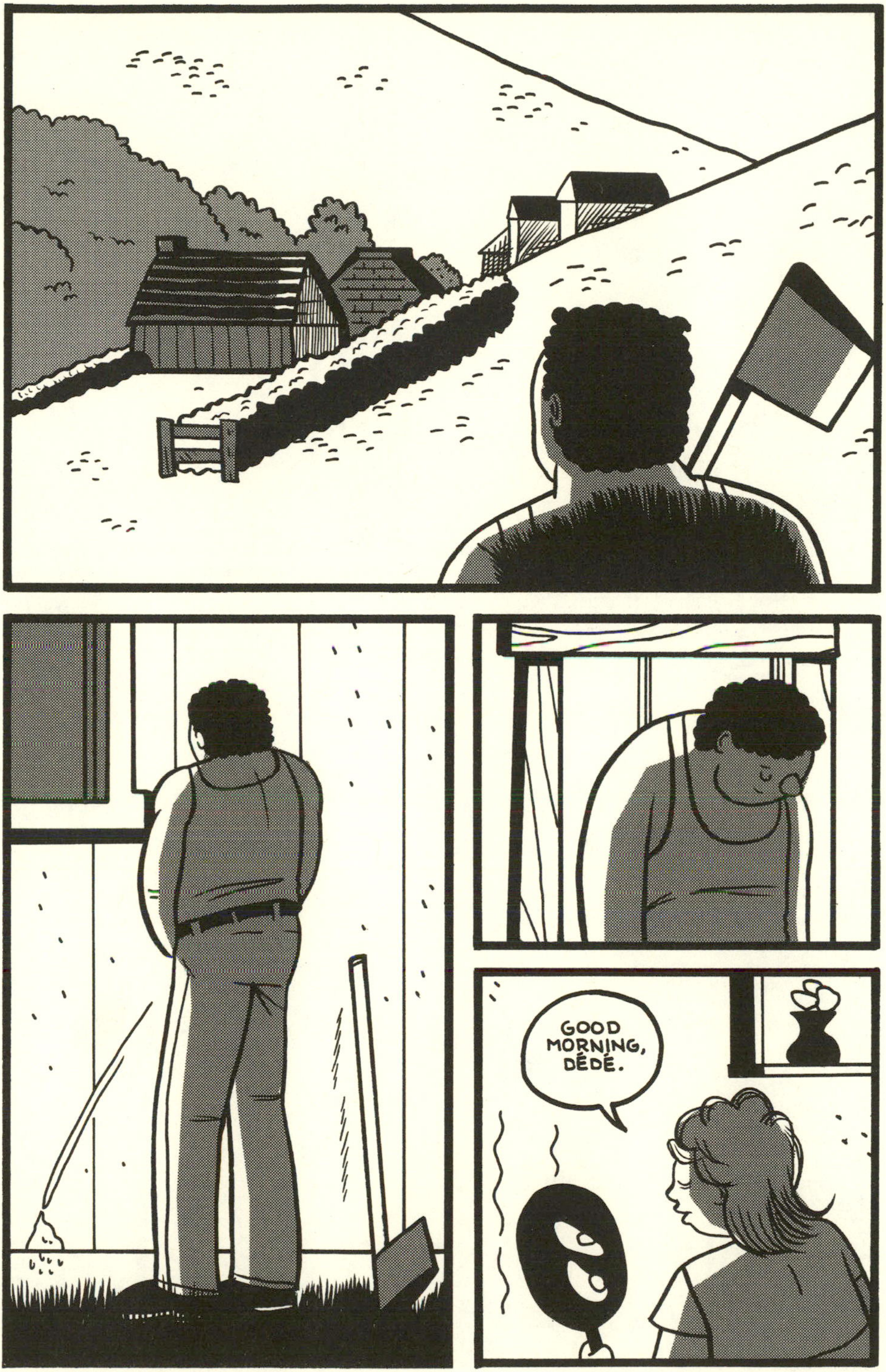
GOOD MORNING, DÉDÉ.

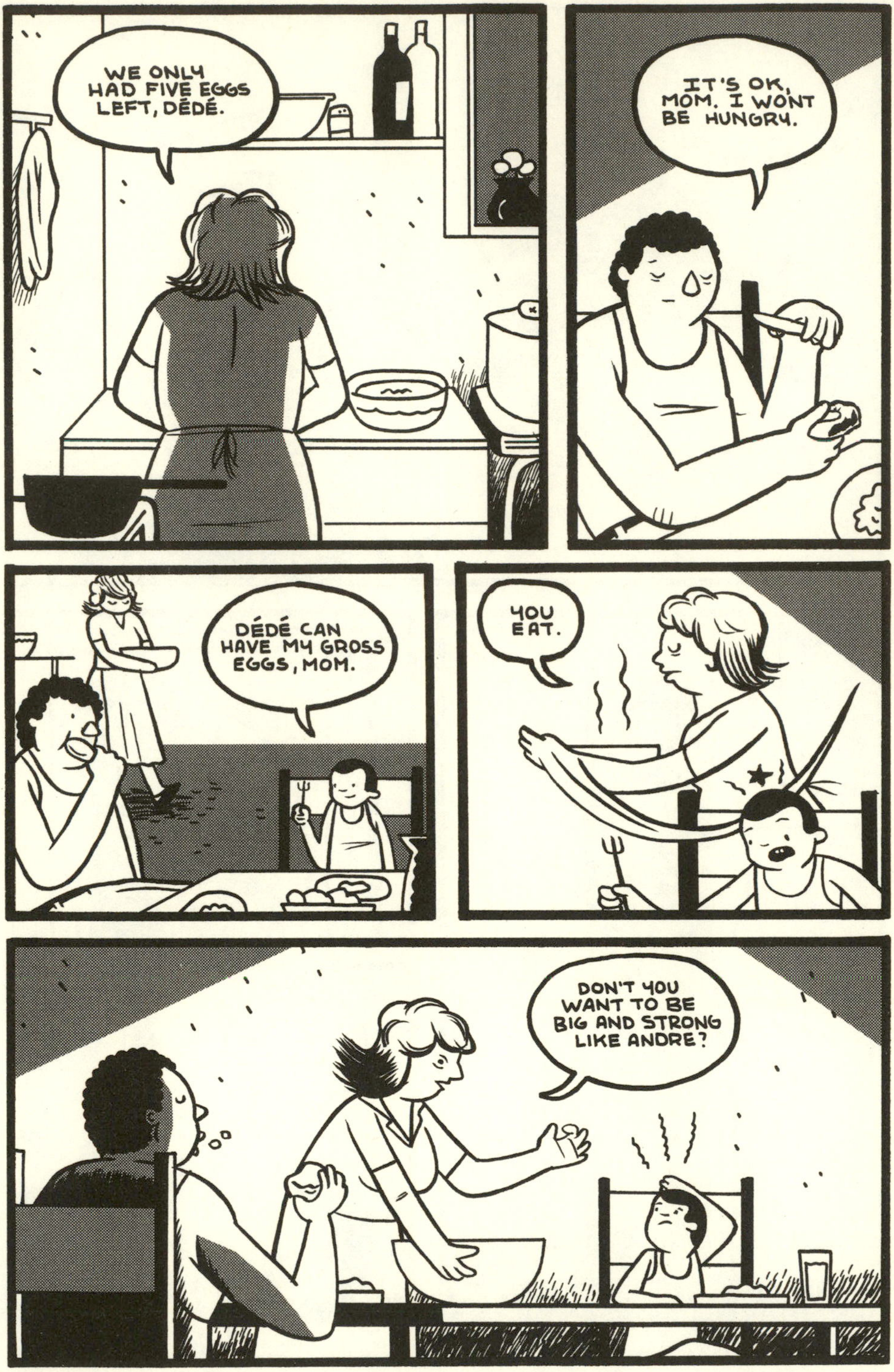
WE ONLY HAD FIVE EGGS LEFT, DÉDÉ.
IT'S OK, MOM. I WON'T BE HUNGRY.
DÉDÉ CAN HAVE MY GROSS EGGS, MOM.
YOU EAT.
DON'T YOU WANT TO BE BIG AND STRONG LIKE ANDRE?

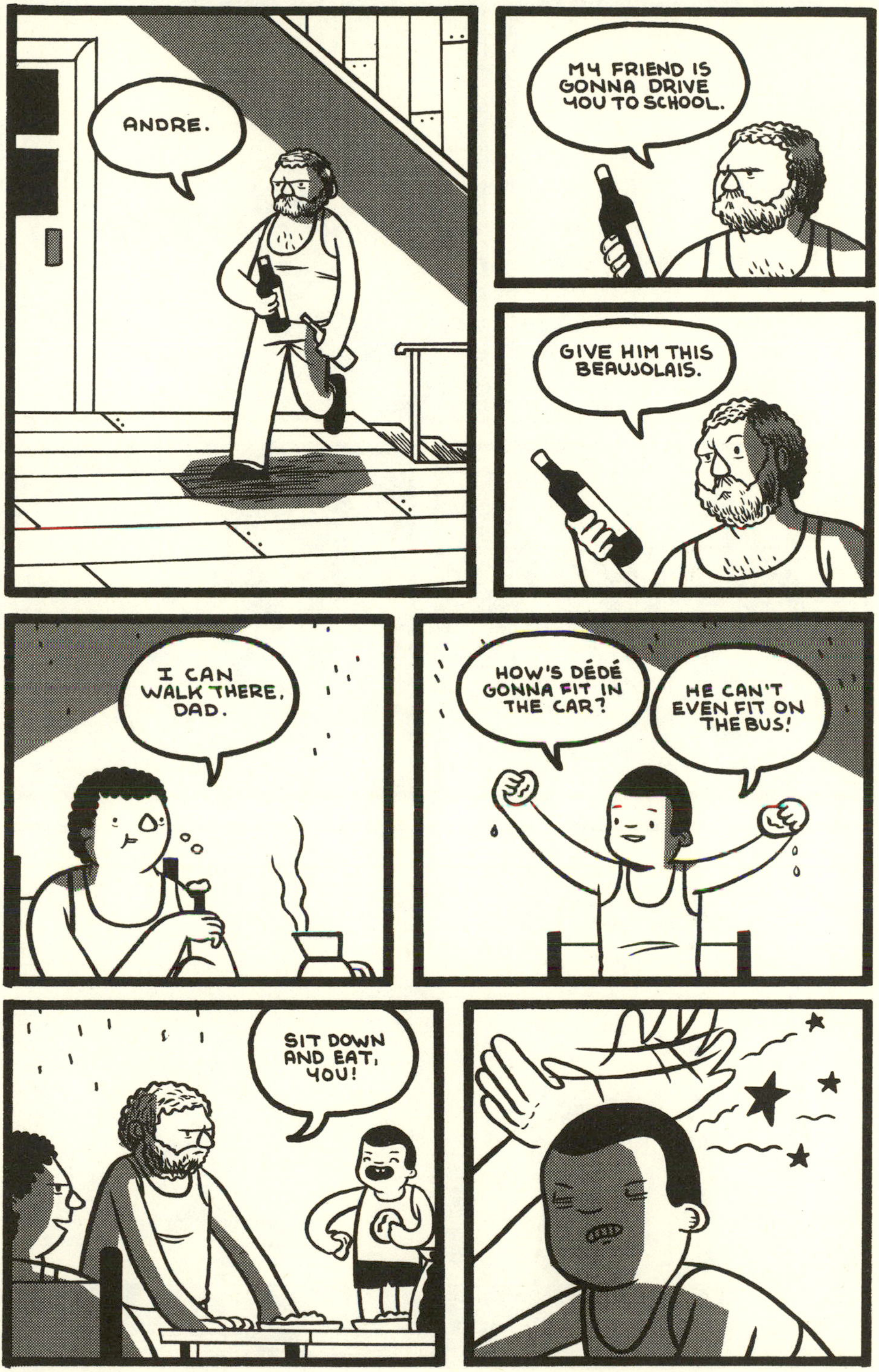
ANDRE.
MY FRIEND IS GONNA DRIVE YOU TO SCHOOL.
GIVE HIM THIS BEAUJOLAIS.
I CAN WALK THERE, DAD.
HOW'S DÉDÉ GONNA FIT IN THE CAR?
HE CAN'T EVEN FIT ON THE BUS!
SIT DOWN AND EAT, YOU!

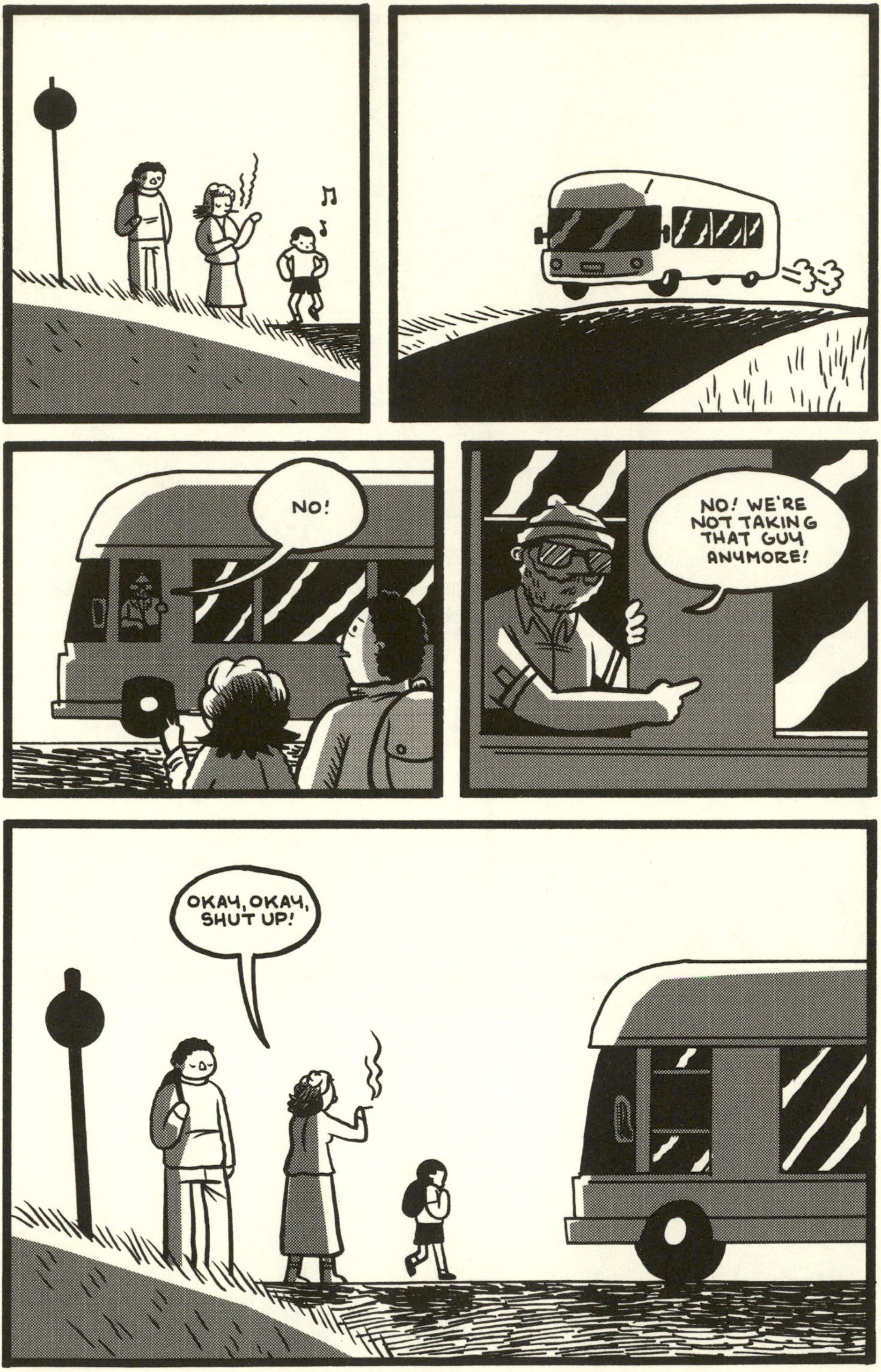
NO!
NO! WE'RE NOT TAKING THAT GUY ANYMORE!
OKAY, OKAY, SHUT UP!

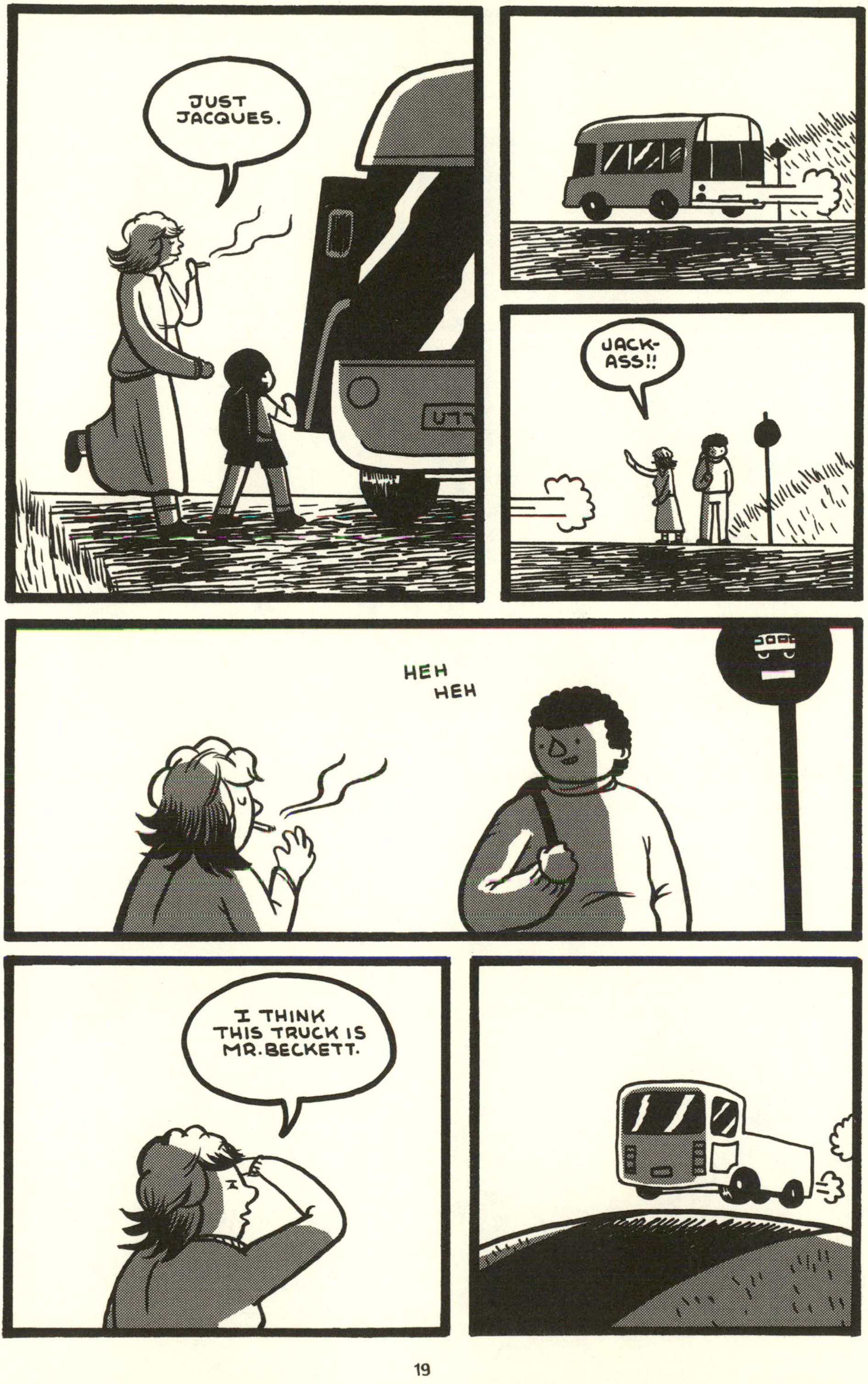
JUST JACQUES.
JACK-ASS!!
HEH HEH
I THINK THIS TRUCK IS MR. BECKETT.

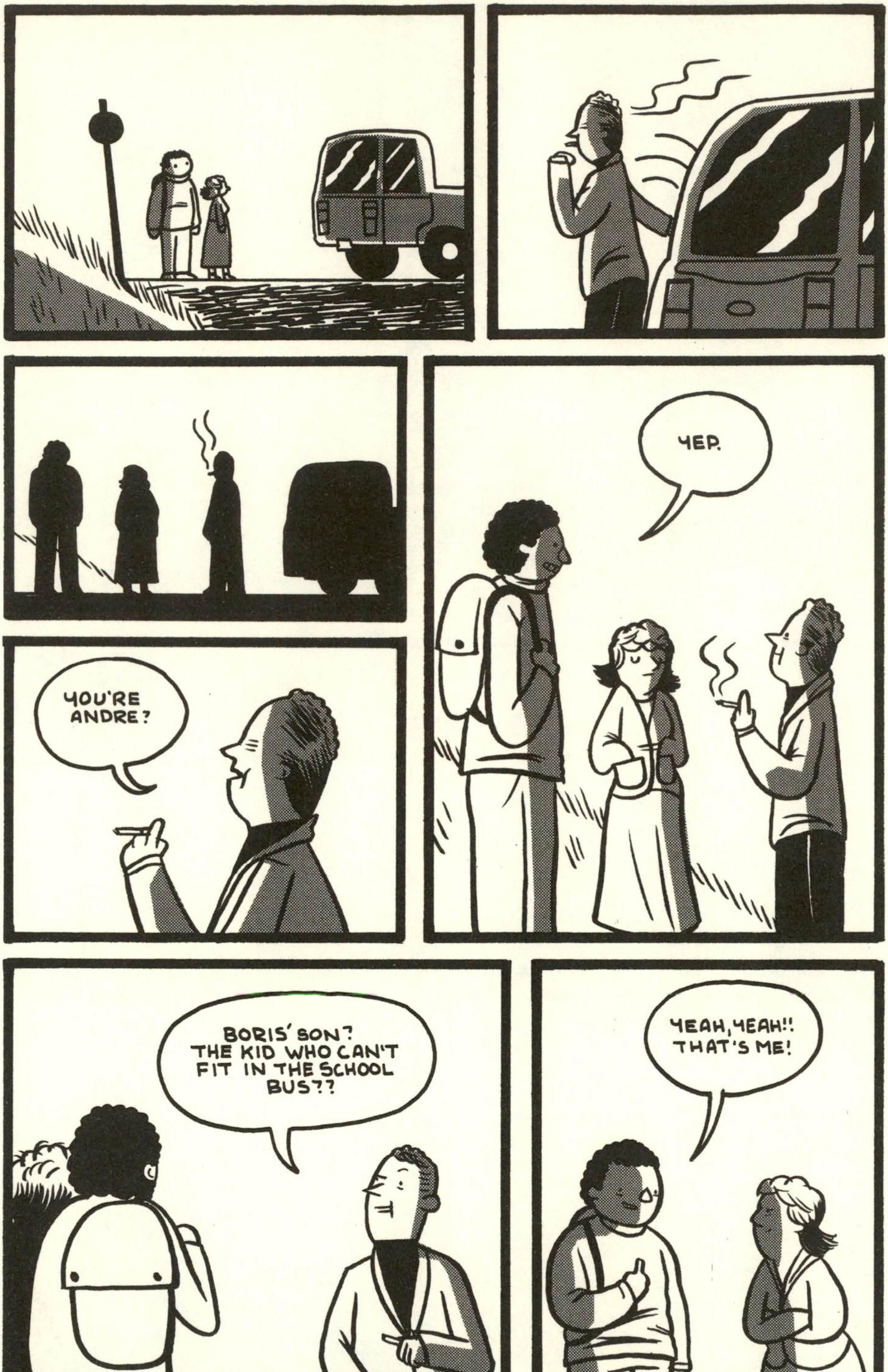
YOU'RE ANDRE?
YEP.
BORIS' SON? THE KID WHO CAN'T FIT IN THE SCHOOL BUS??
YEAH, YEAH!! THAT'S ME!

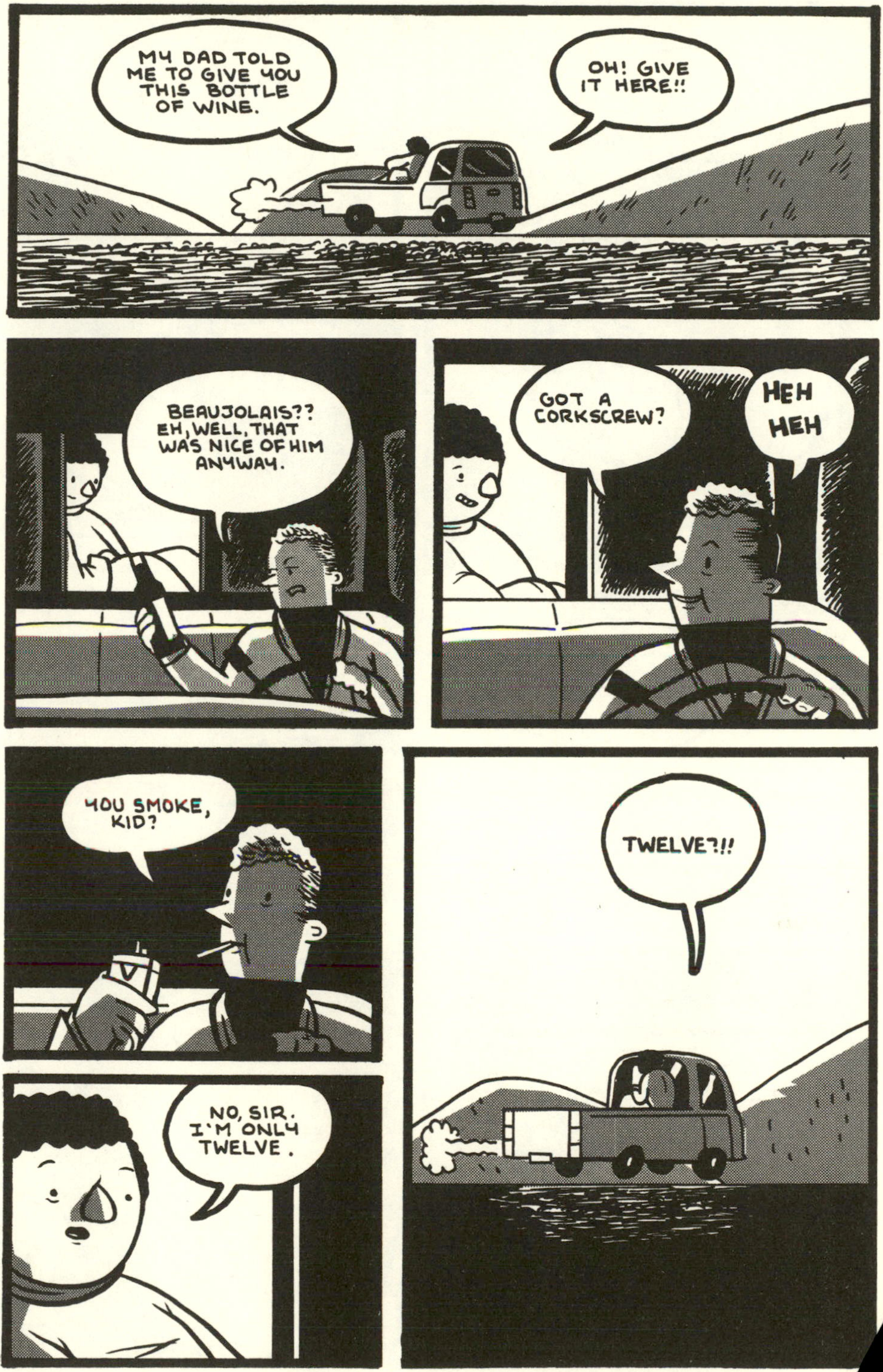
MY DAD TOLD ME TO GIVE YOU THIS BOTTLE OF WINE.
OH! GIVE IT HERE!!
BEAUJOLAIS?? EH, WELL, THAT WAS NICE OF HIM ANYWAY.
GOT A CORKSCREW?
HEH HEH
YOU SMOKE, KID?
NO, SIR. I'M ONLY TWELVE.
TWELVE?!!

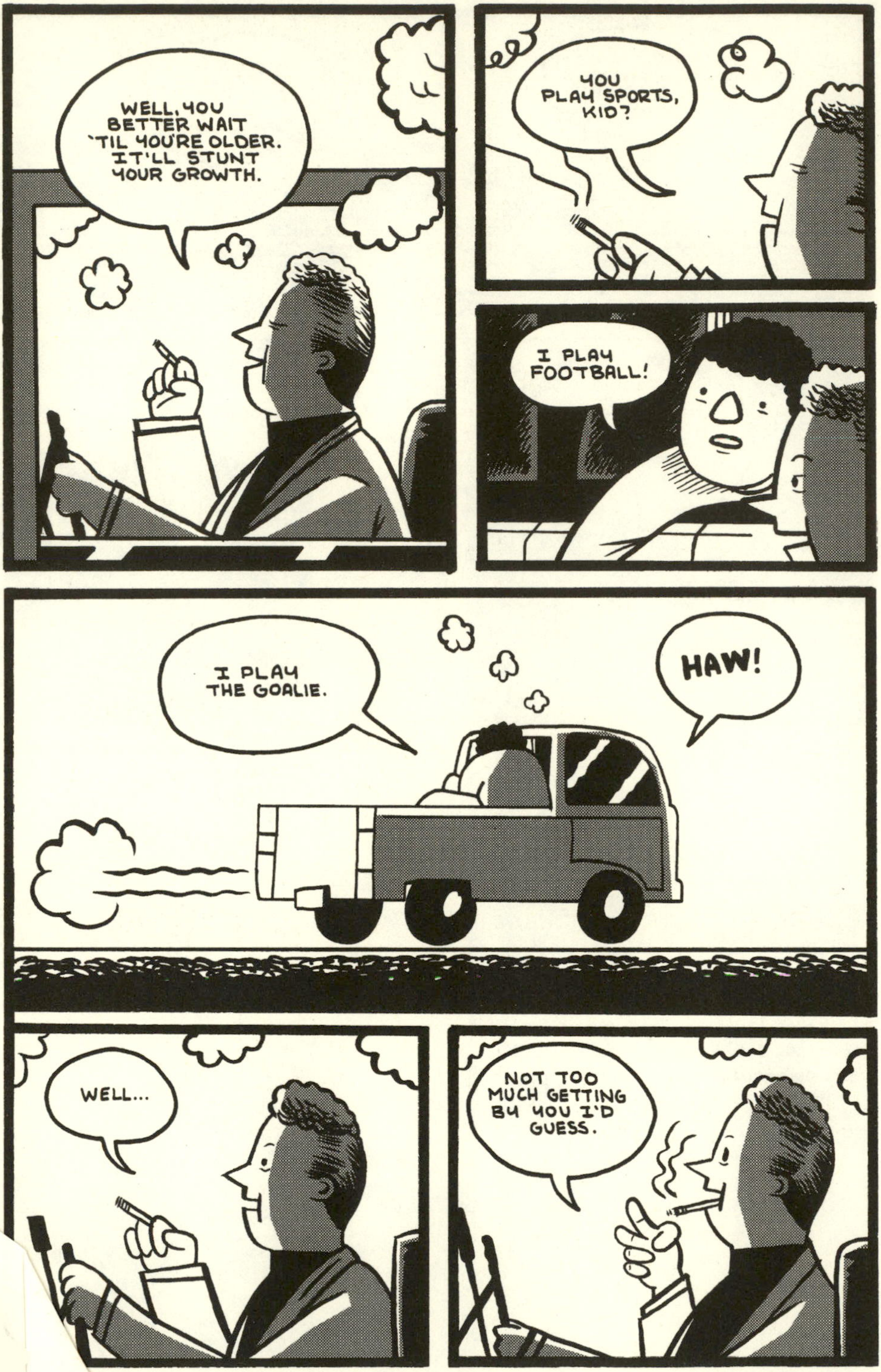
WELL, YOU BETTER WAIT `TIL YOU'RE OLDER. IT'LL STUNT YOUR GROWTH.
YOU PLAY SPORTS, KID?
I PLAY FOOTBALL!
I PLAY THE GOALIE.
HAW!
WELL...
NOT TOO MUCH GETTING BY YOU I'D GUESS.

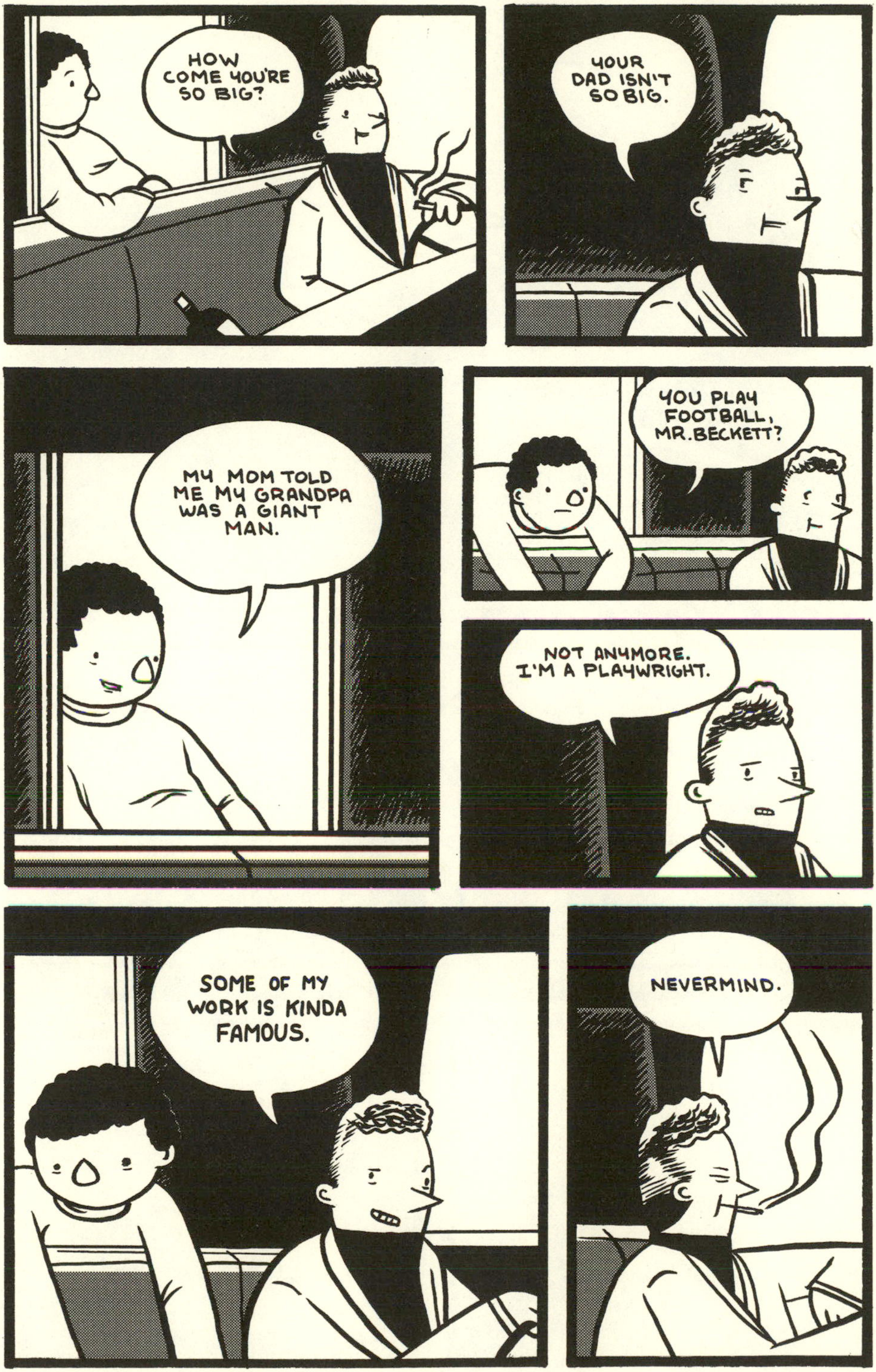
HOW COME YOU'RE SO BIG?
YOUR DAD ISN'T SO BIG.
MY MOM TOLD ME MY GRANDPA WAS A GIANT MAN.
YOU PLAY FOOTBALL, MR. BECKETT?
NOT ANYMORE. I'M A PLAYWRIGHT.
SOME OF MY WORK IS KINDA FAMOUS.
NEVERMIND.

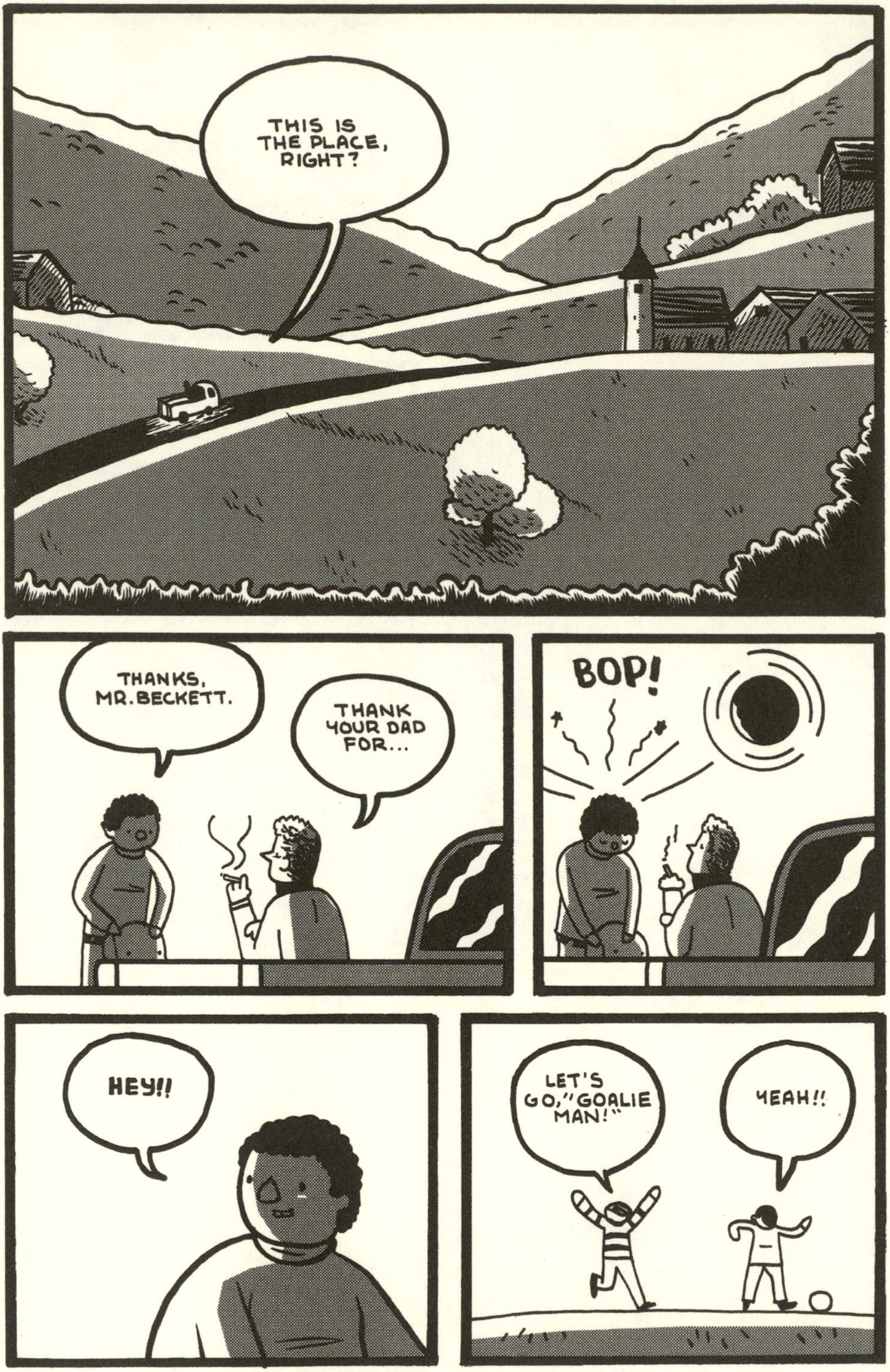
THIS IS THE PLACE, RIGHT?
THANKS, MR. BECKETT.
THANK YOUR DAD FOR...
BOP!
HEY!!
LET'S GO, "GOALIE MAN!"
YEAH!!

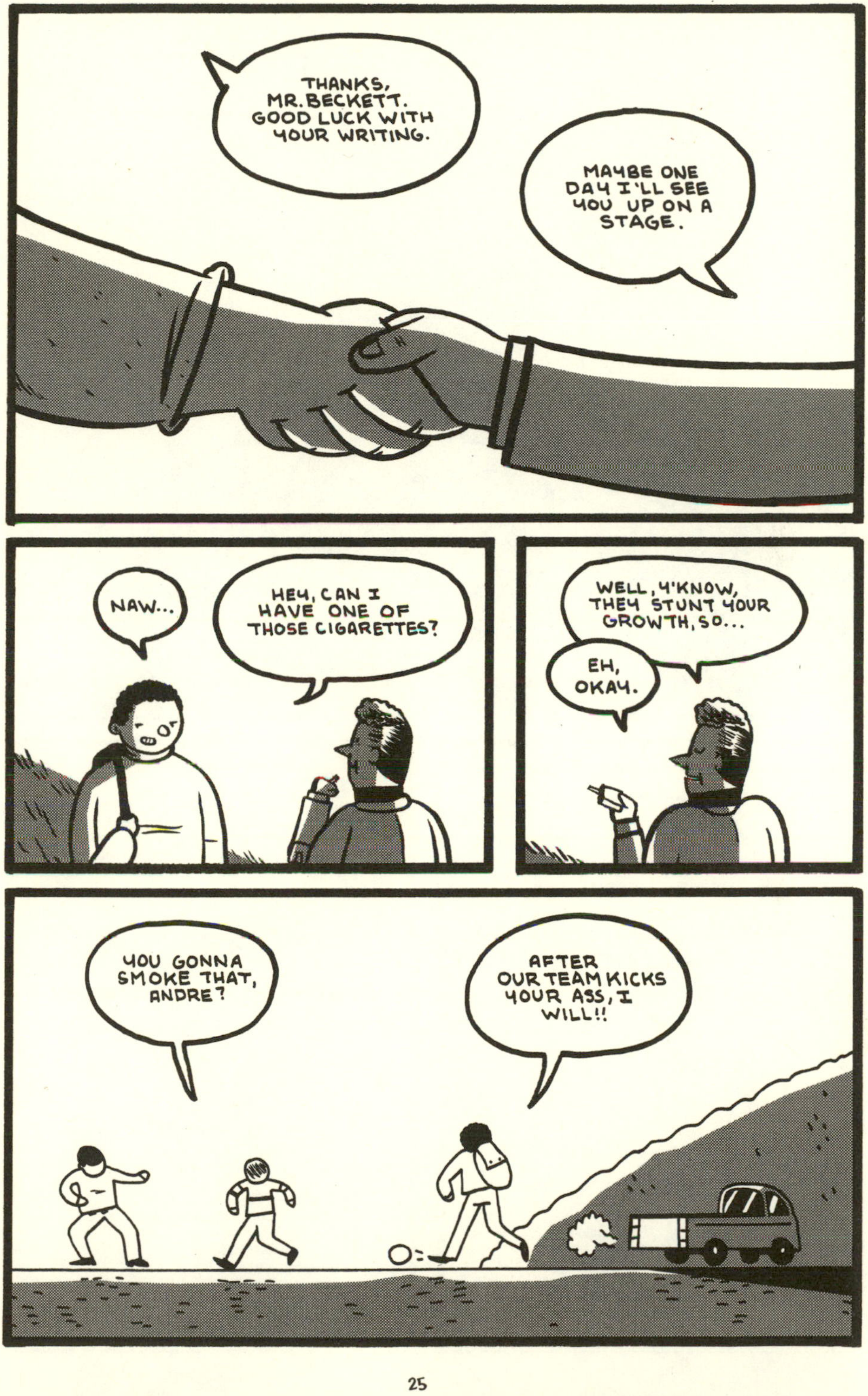
THANKS, MR. BECKETT. GOOD LUCK WITH YOUR WRITING.
MAYBE ONE DAY I'LL SEE YOU UP ON A STAGE.
NAW...
HEY, CAN I HAVE ONE OF THOSE CIGARETTES?
WELL, Y'KNOW, THEY STUNT YOUR GROWTH, SO...
EH, OKAY.
YOU GONNA SMOKE THAT, ANDRE?
AFTER OUR TEAM KICKS YOUR ASS, I WILL!!

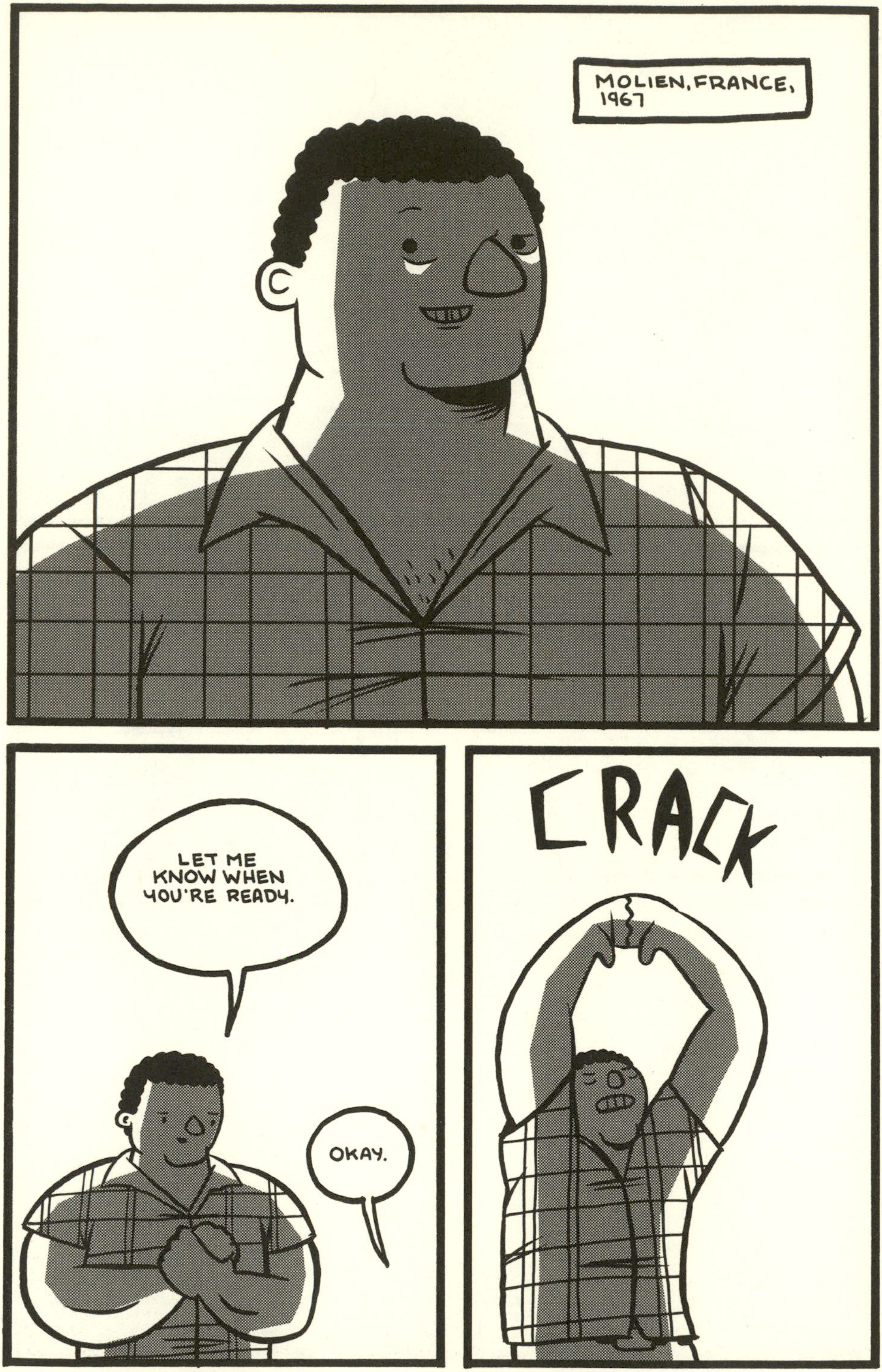
MOLIEN, FRANCE, 1967
LET ME KNOW WHEN YOU'RE READY.
OKAY.
CRACK

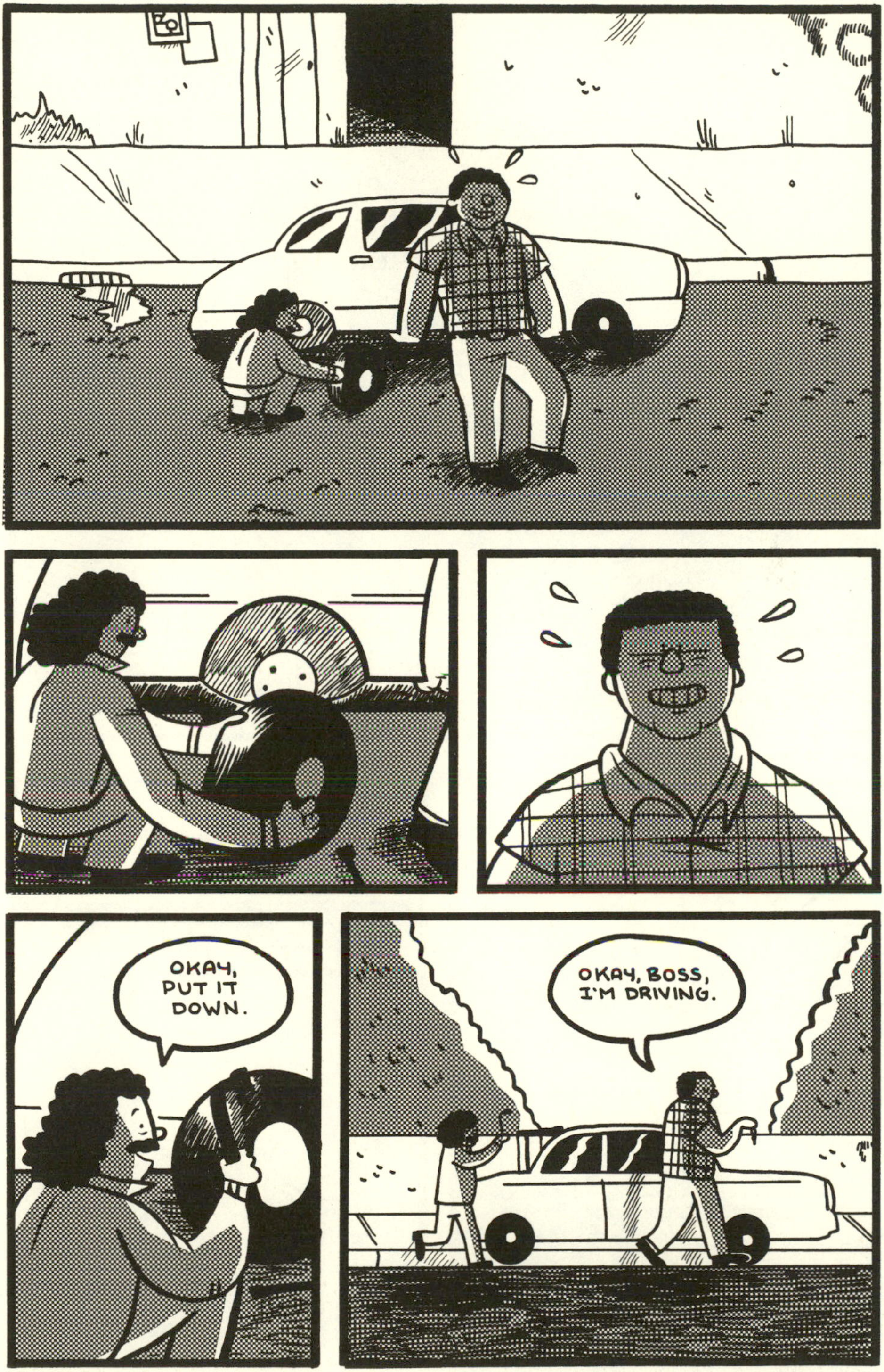
OKAY, PUT IT DOWN.
OKAY, BOSS, I'M DRIVING.

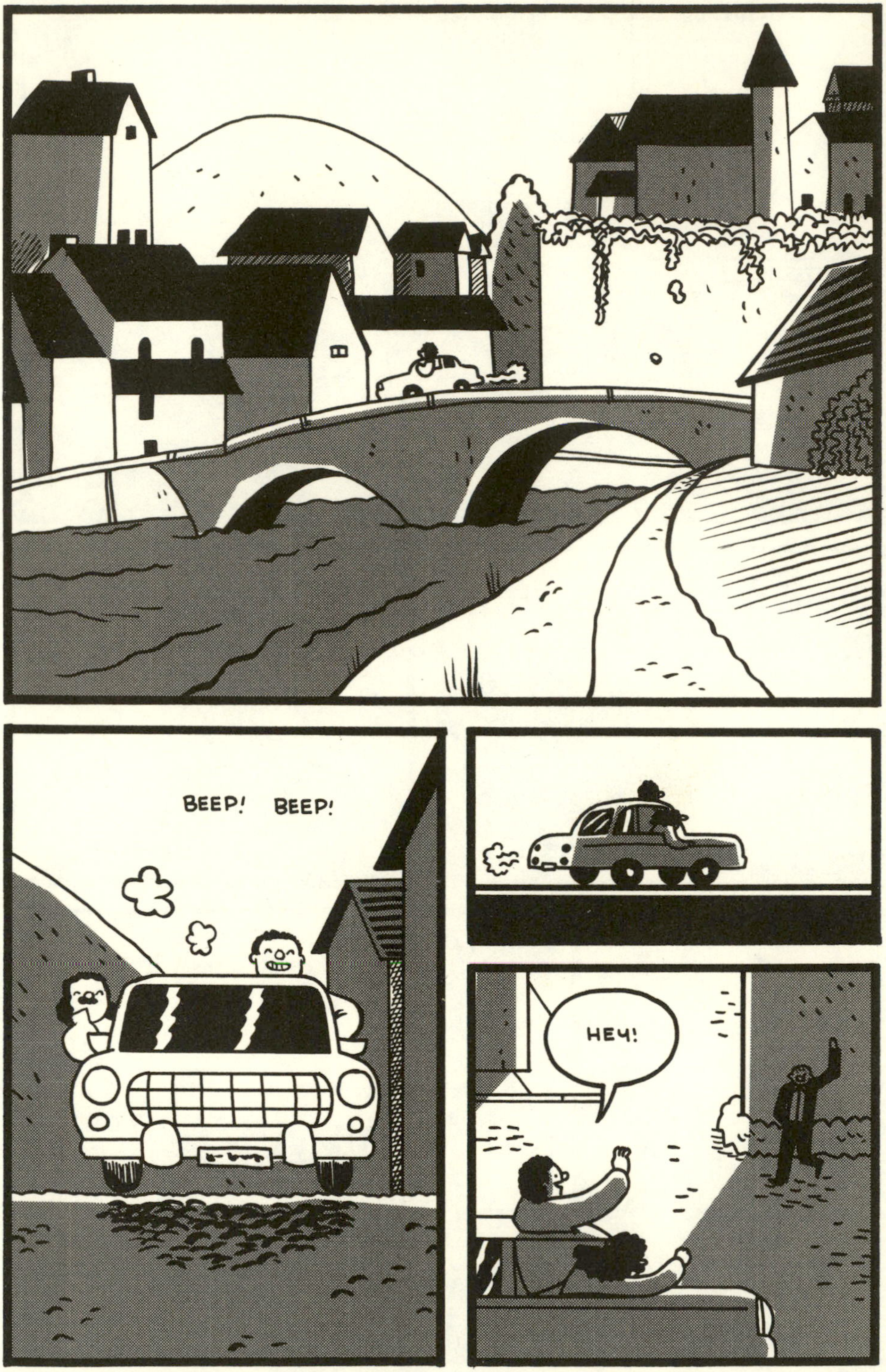
BEEP! BEEP!
HEY!

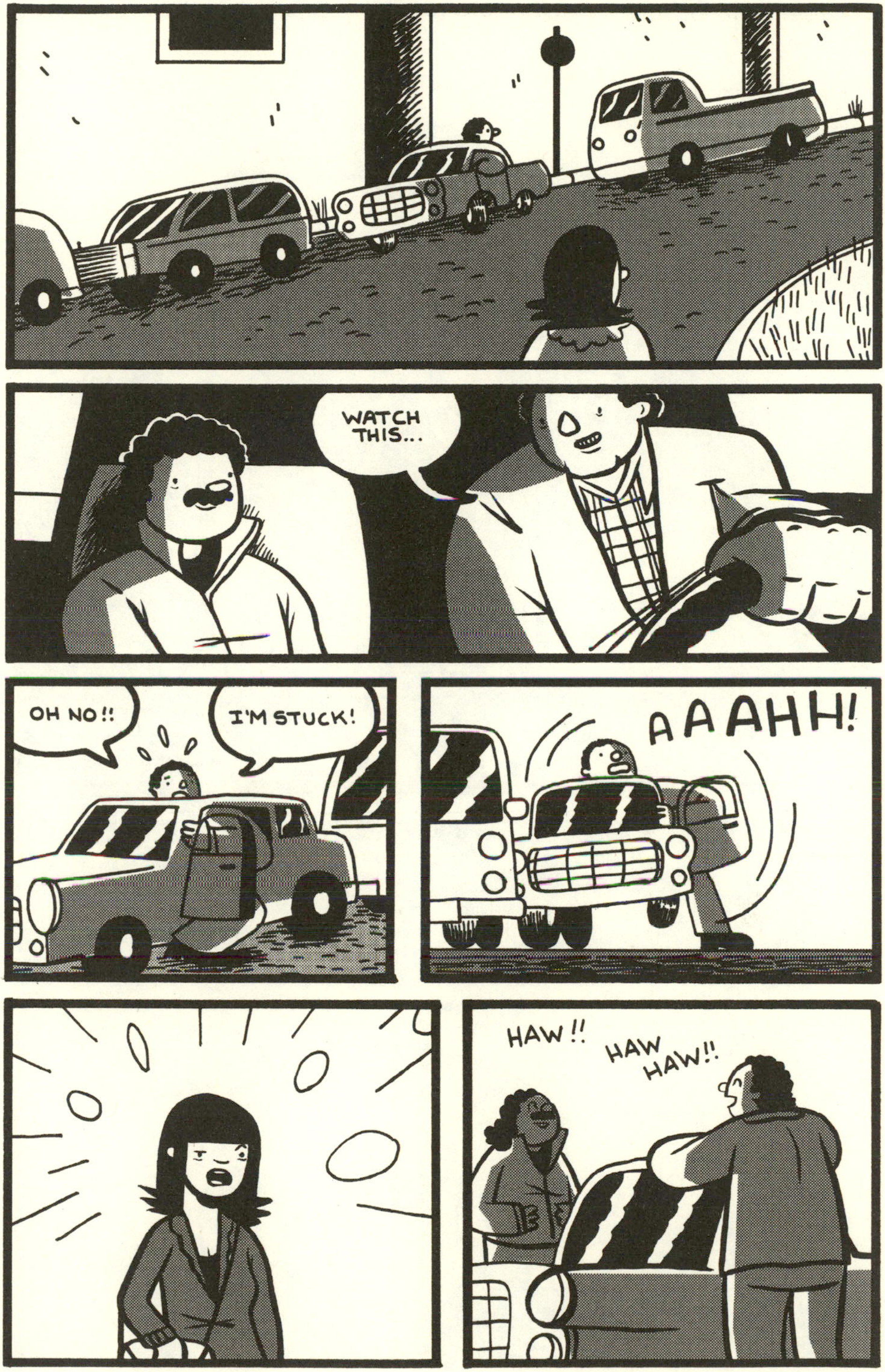
WATCH THIS...
OH NO!!
I'M STUCK!
AAAHH!
HAW!!
HAW HAW!!

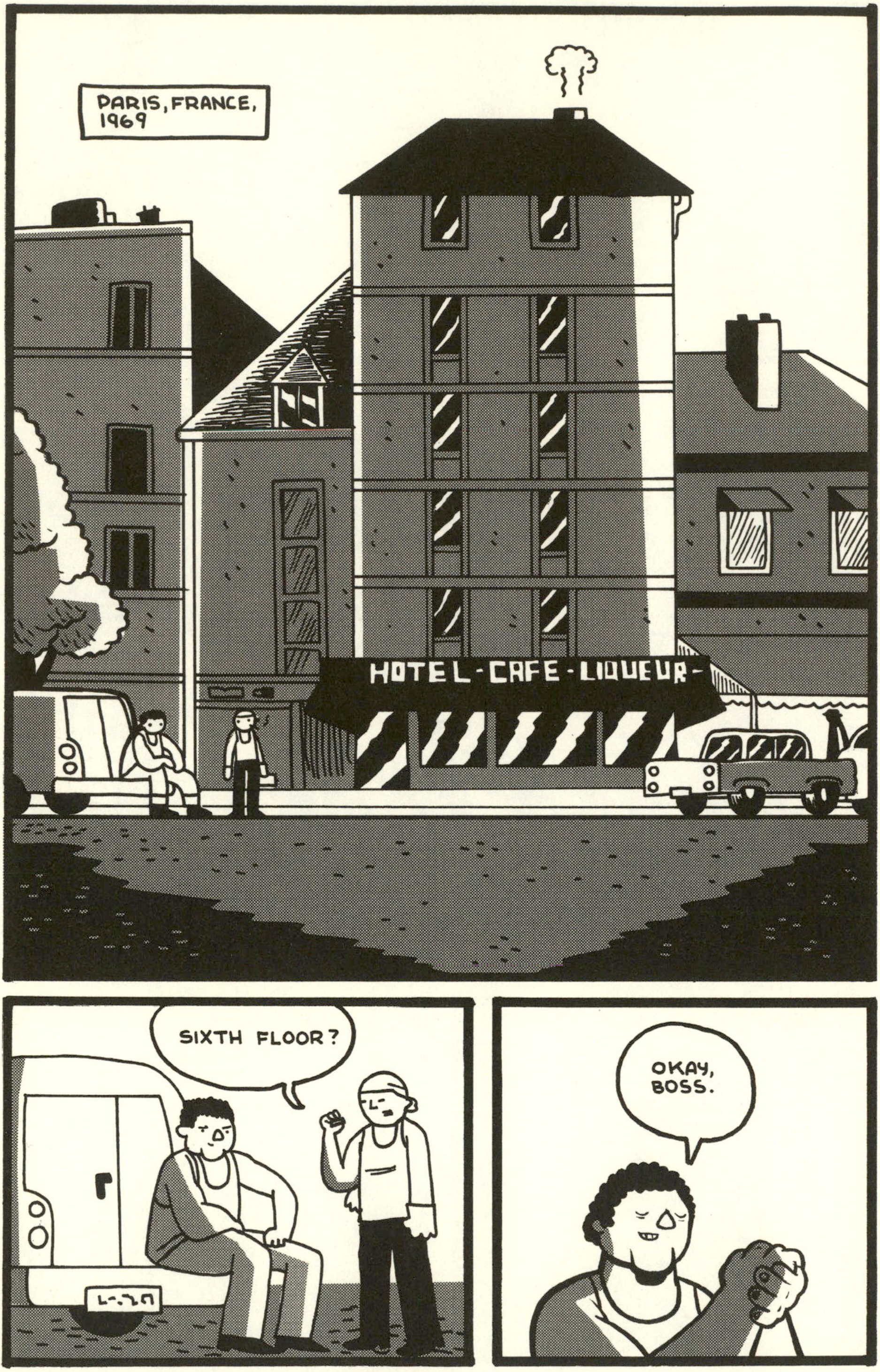
PARIS, FRANCE, 1969
HOTEL - CAFE - LIQUEUR -
SIXTH FLOOR?
OKAY, BOSS.

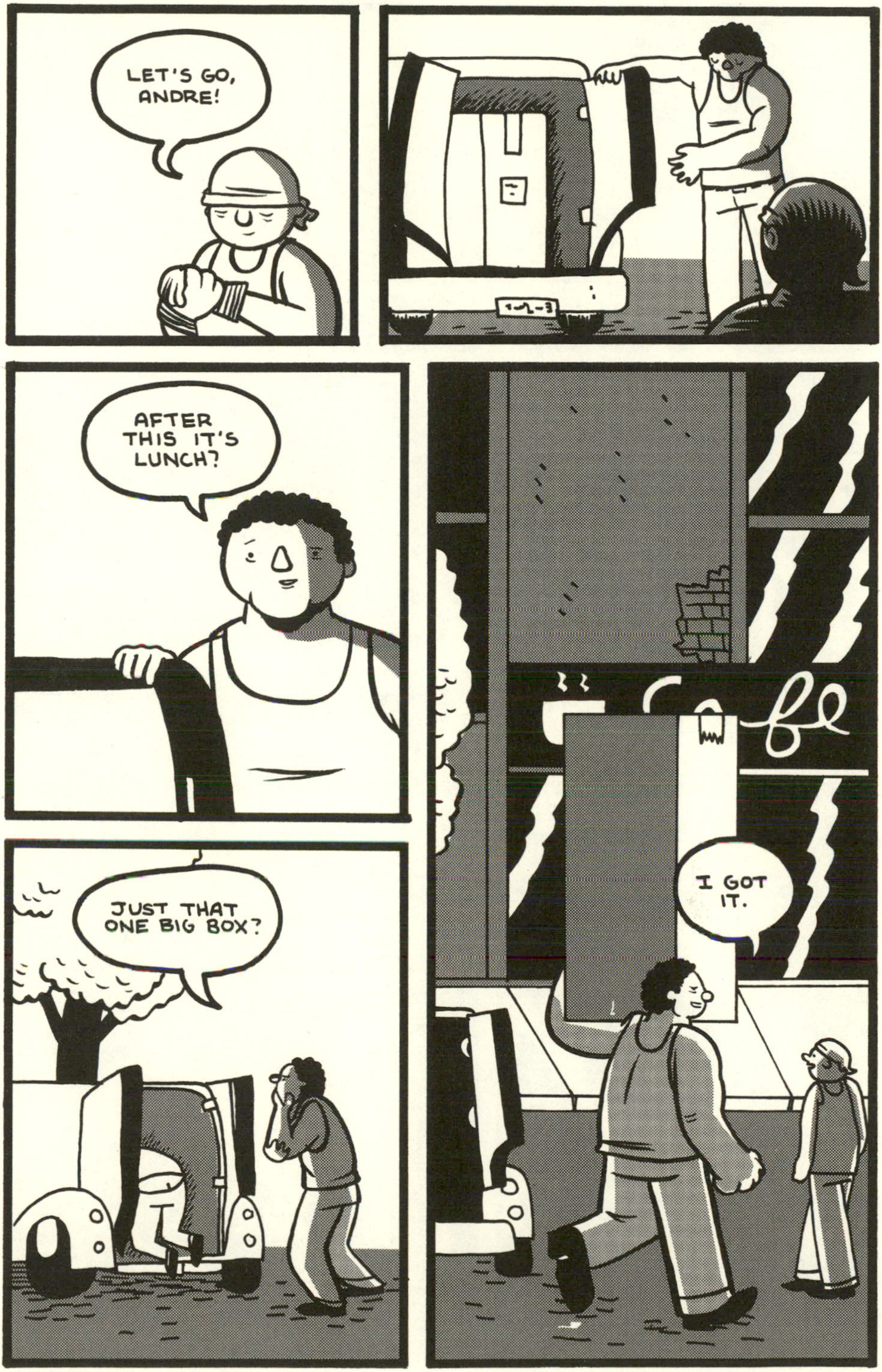
LET'S GO, ANDRE!
AFTER THIS IT'S LUNCH?
JUST THAT ONE BIG BOX?
I GOT IT.

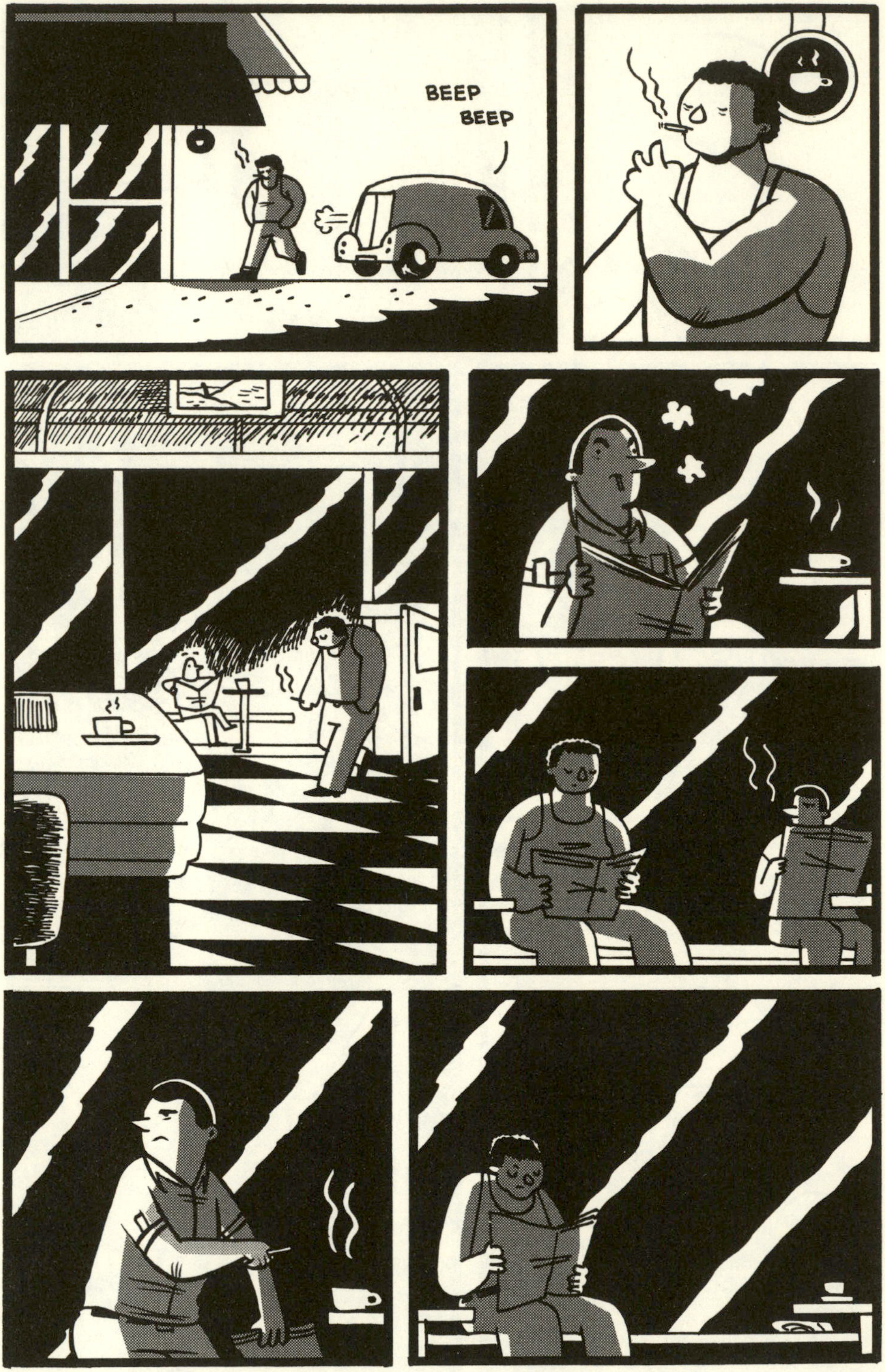
BEEP
BEEP

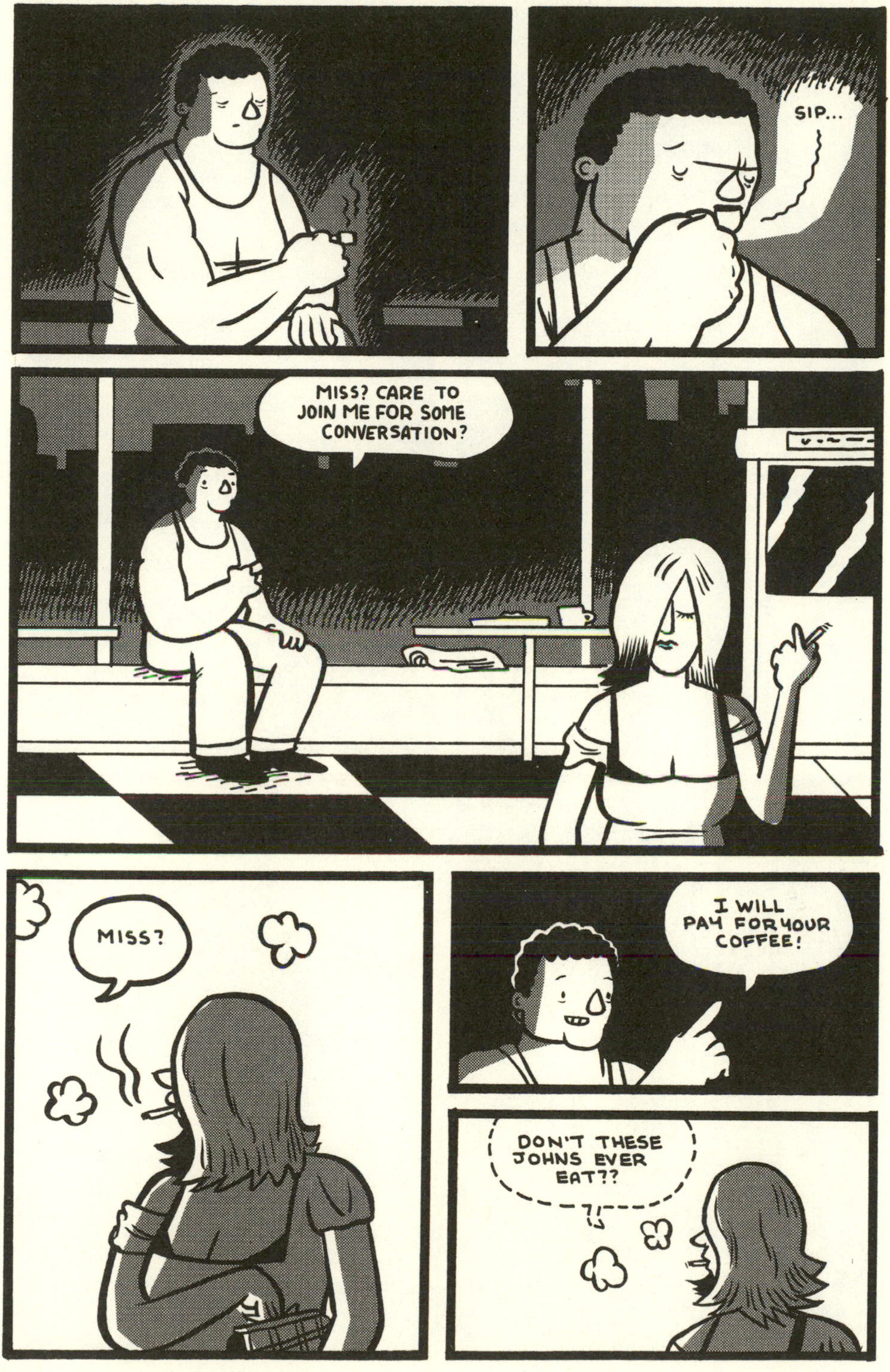
SIP...
MISS? CARE TO JOIN ME FOR SOME CONVERSATION?
MISS?
I WILL PAY FOR YOUR COFFEE!
DON'T THESE JOHNS EVER EAT??

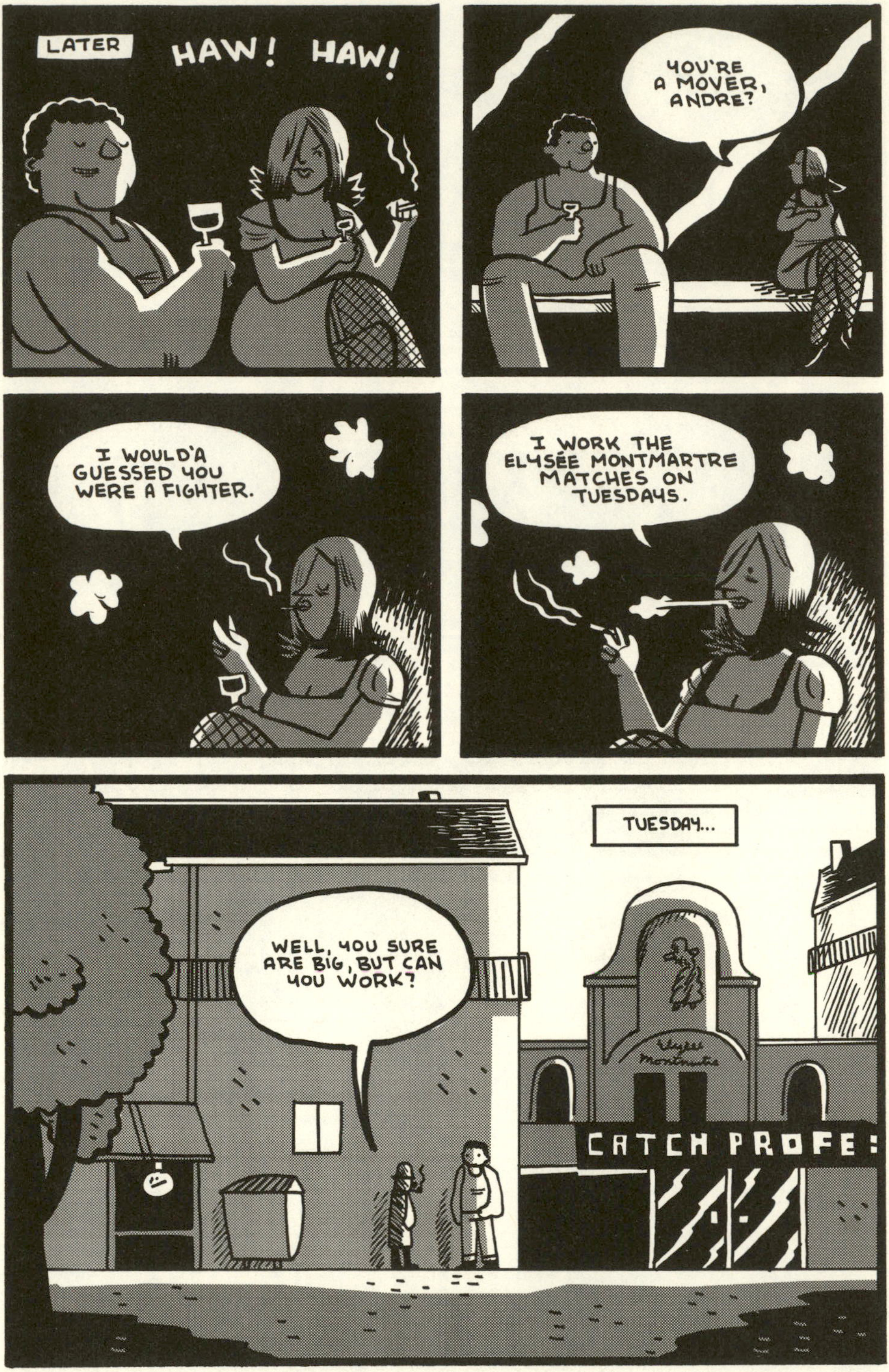
LATER
HAW! HAW!
YOU'RE A MOVER, ANDRE?
I WOULD'A GUESSED YOU WERE A FIGHTER.
I WORK THE ELYSÉE MONTMARTRE MATCHES ON TUESDAYS.
TUESDAY...
WELL, YOU SURE ARE BIG, BUT CAN YOU WORK?
CATCH PROFE:

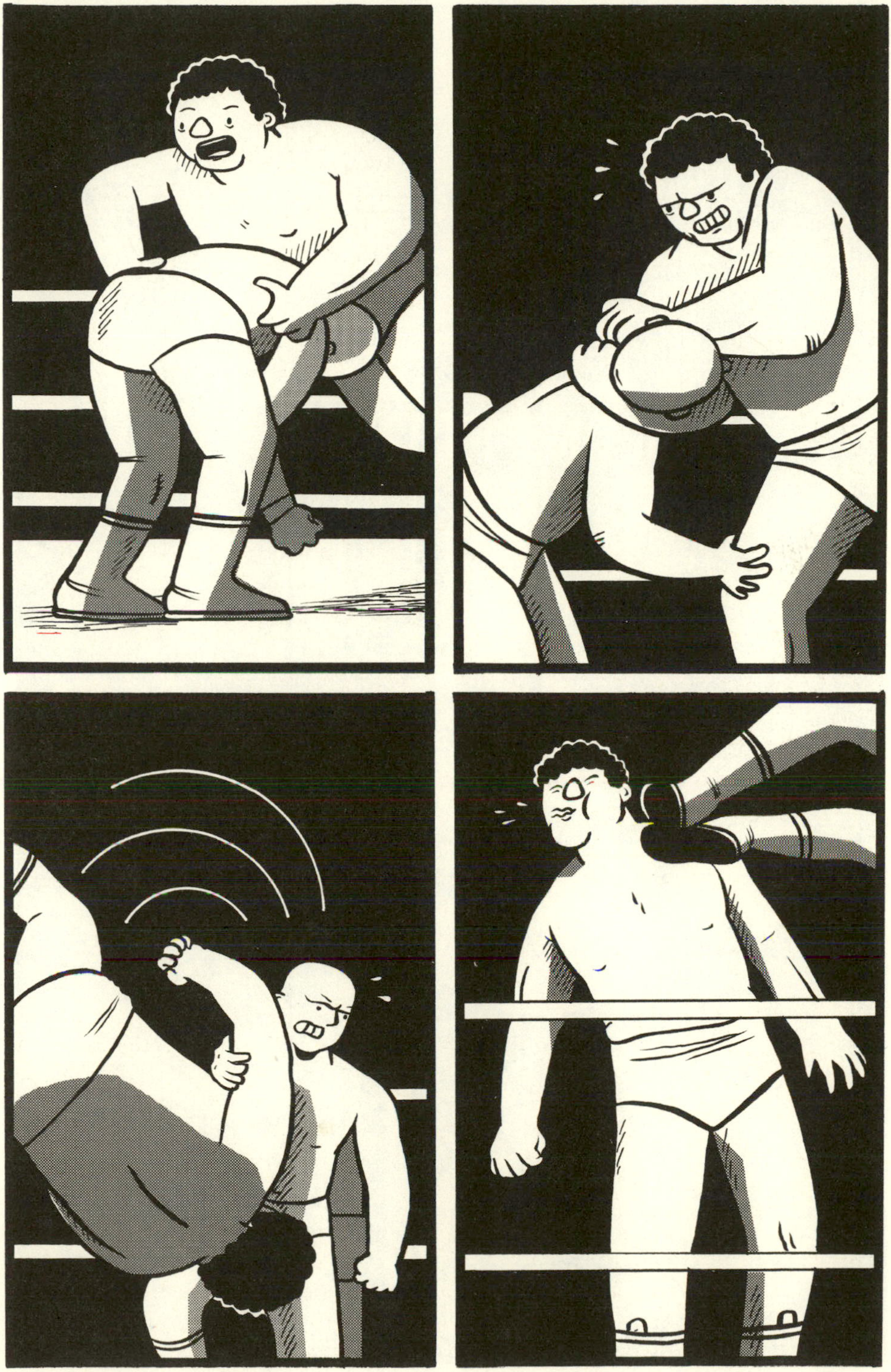

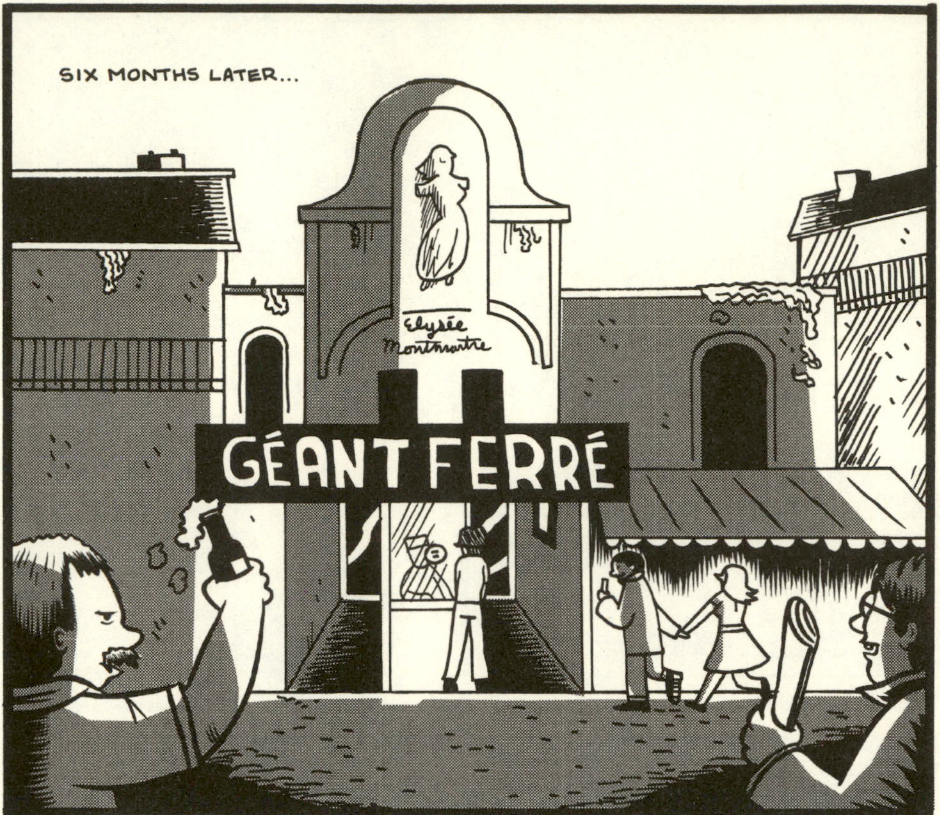
SIX MONTHS LATER...
Elysée Montmartre
GÉANT FERRÉ

*GÉANT FERRÉ IS A MYTHICAL FRENCH GIANT AKIN TO PAUL BUNYAN

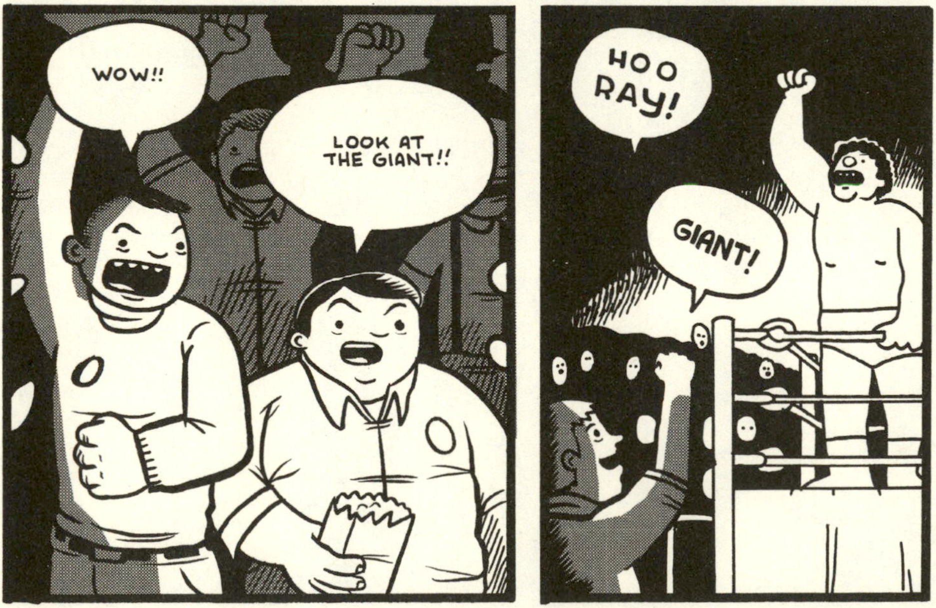
WOW!!
LOOK AT THE GIANT!!
HOO RAY!
GIANT!

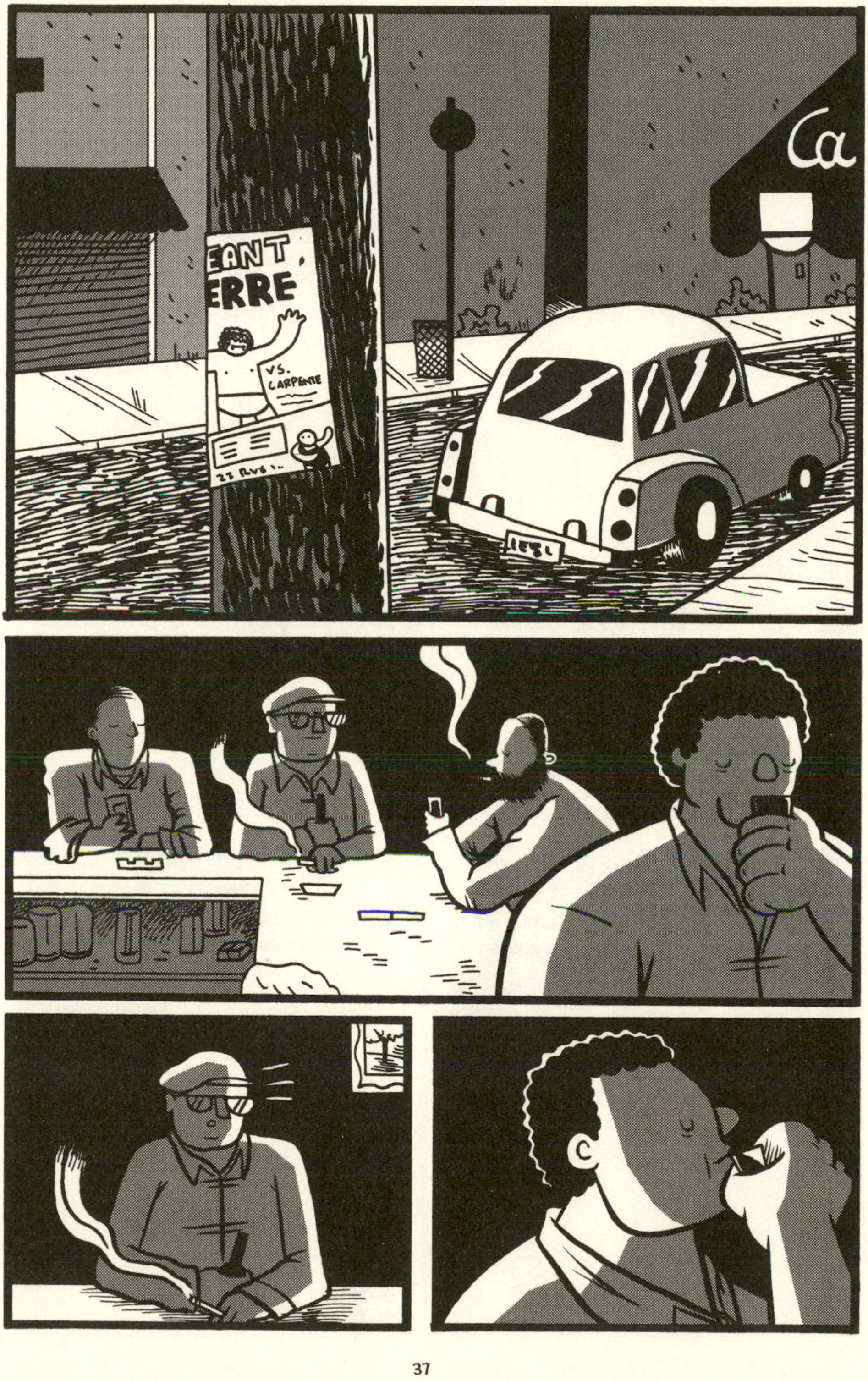
EANT,
ERRE
VS.
CARPENTE
Ca

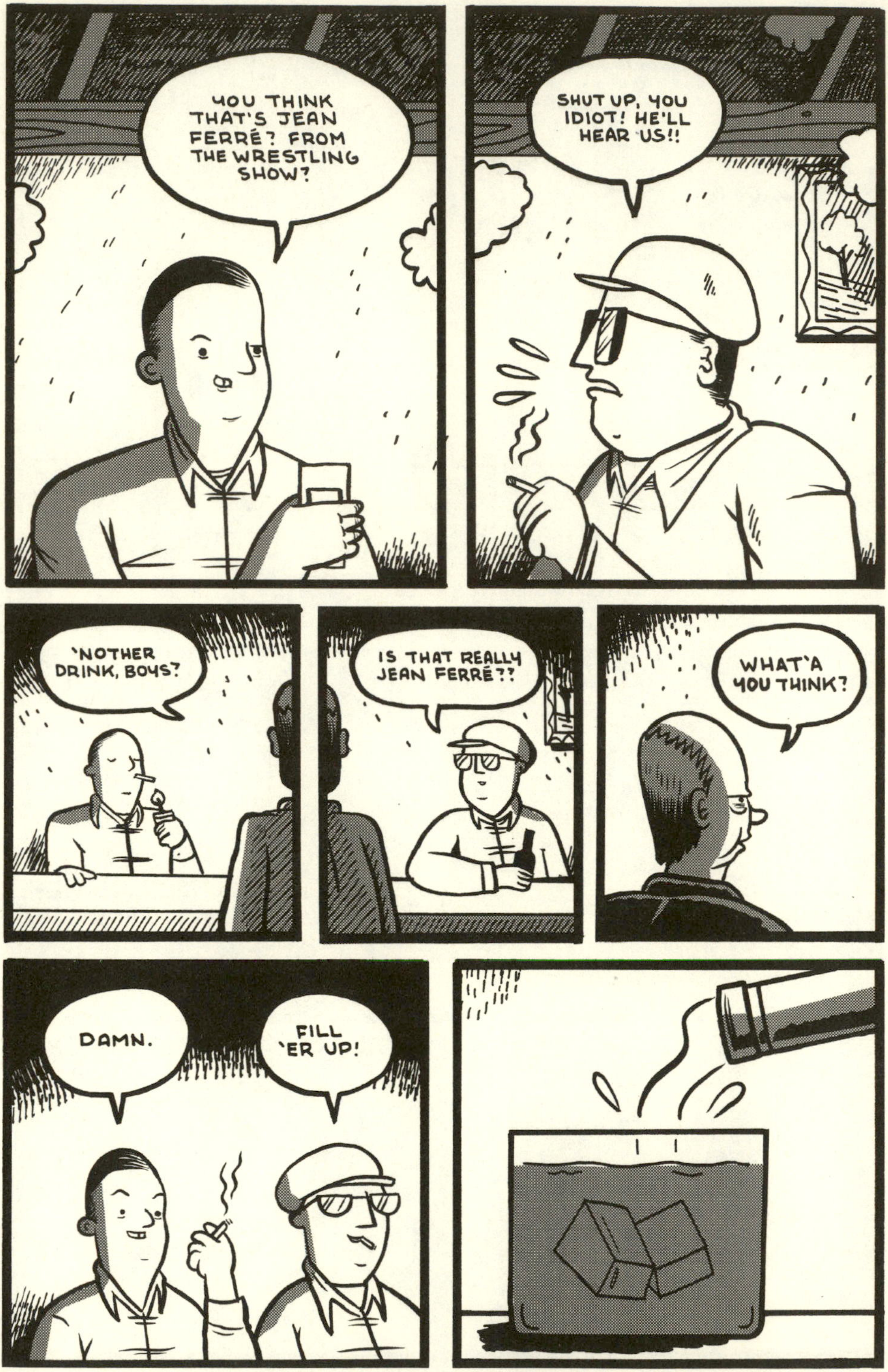
YOU THINK THAT'S JEAN FERRÉ? FROM THE WRESTLING SHOW?
SHUT UP, YOU IDIOT! HE'LL HEAR US!!
'NOTHER DRINK, BOYS?
IS THAT REALLY JEAN FERRÉ??
WHAT'A YOU THINK?
DAMN.
FILL 'ER UP!

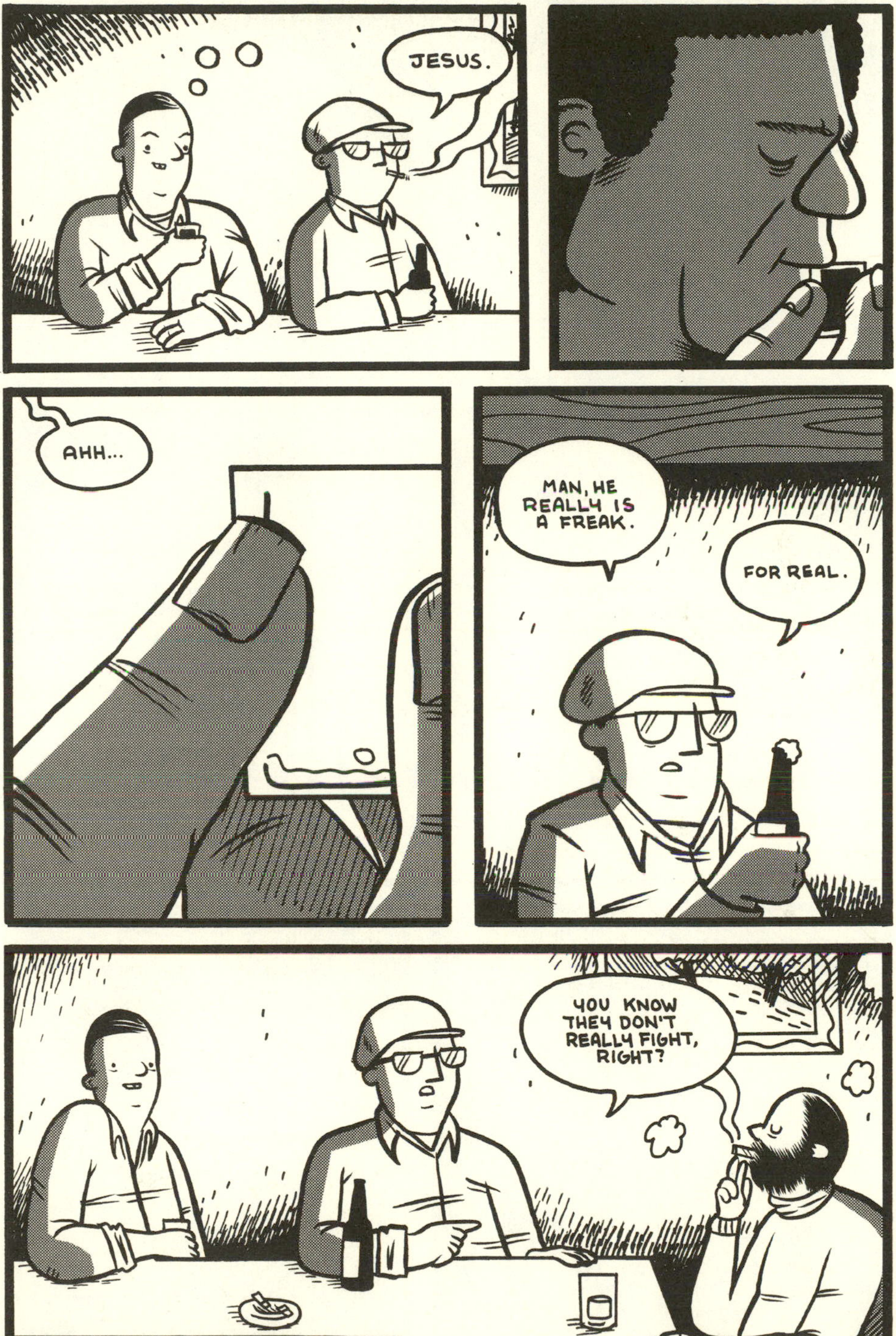
JESUS.
AHH...
MAN, HE REALLY IS A FREAK.
FOR REAL.
YOU KNOW THEY DON'T REALLY FIGHT, RIGHT?

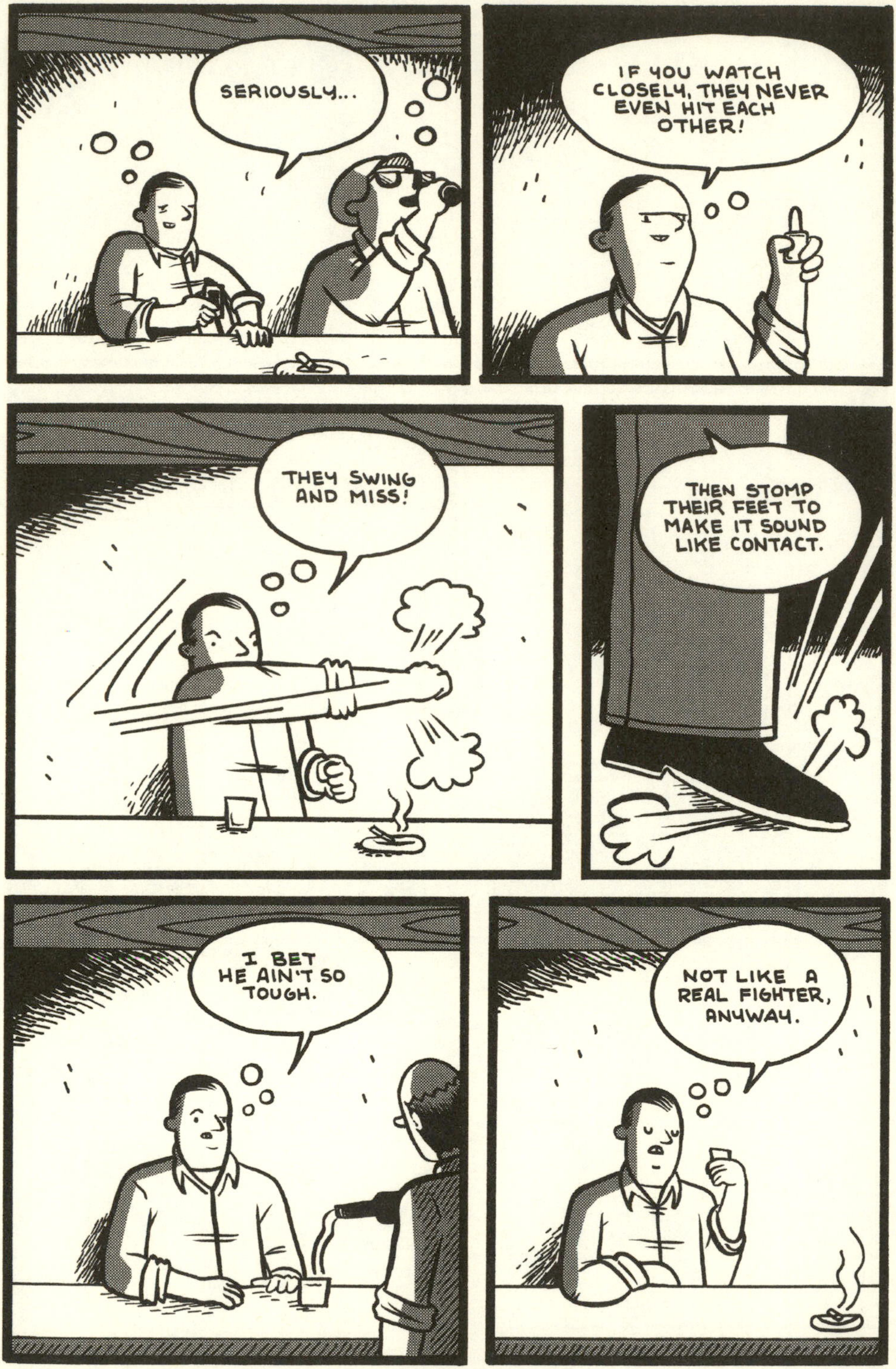
SERIOUSLY...
IF YOU WATCH CLOSELY, THEY NEVER EVEN HIT EACH OTHER!
THEY SWING AND MISS!
THEN STOMP THEIR FEET TO MAKE IT SOUND LIKE CONTACT.
I BET HE AIN'T SO TOUGH.
NOT LIKE A REAL FIGHTER, ANYWAY.

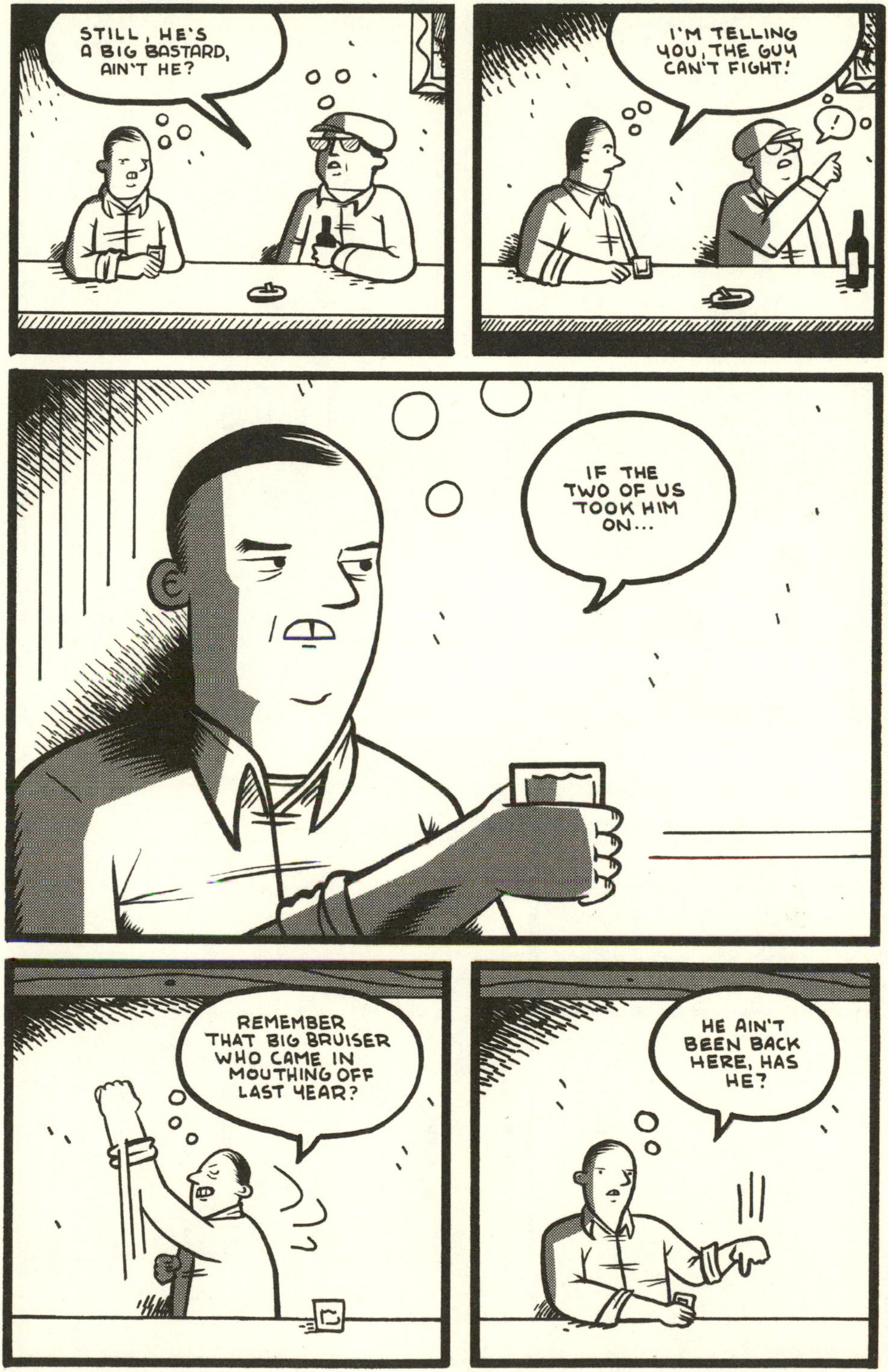
STILL, HE'S A BIG BASTARD, AIN'T HE?
I'M TELLING YOU, THE GUY CAN'T FIGHT!
!
IF THE TWO OF US TOOK HIM ON...
REMEMBER THAT BIG BRUISER WHO CAME IN MOUTHING OFF LAST YEAR?
HE AIN'T BEEN BACK HERE, HAS HE?

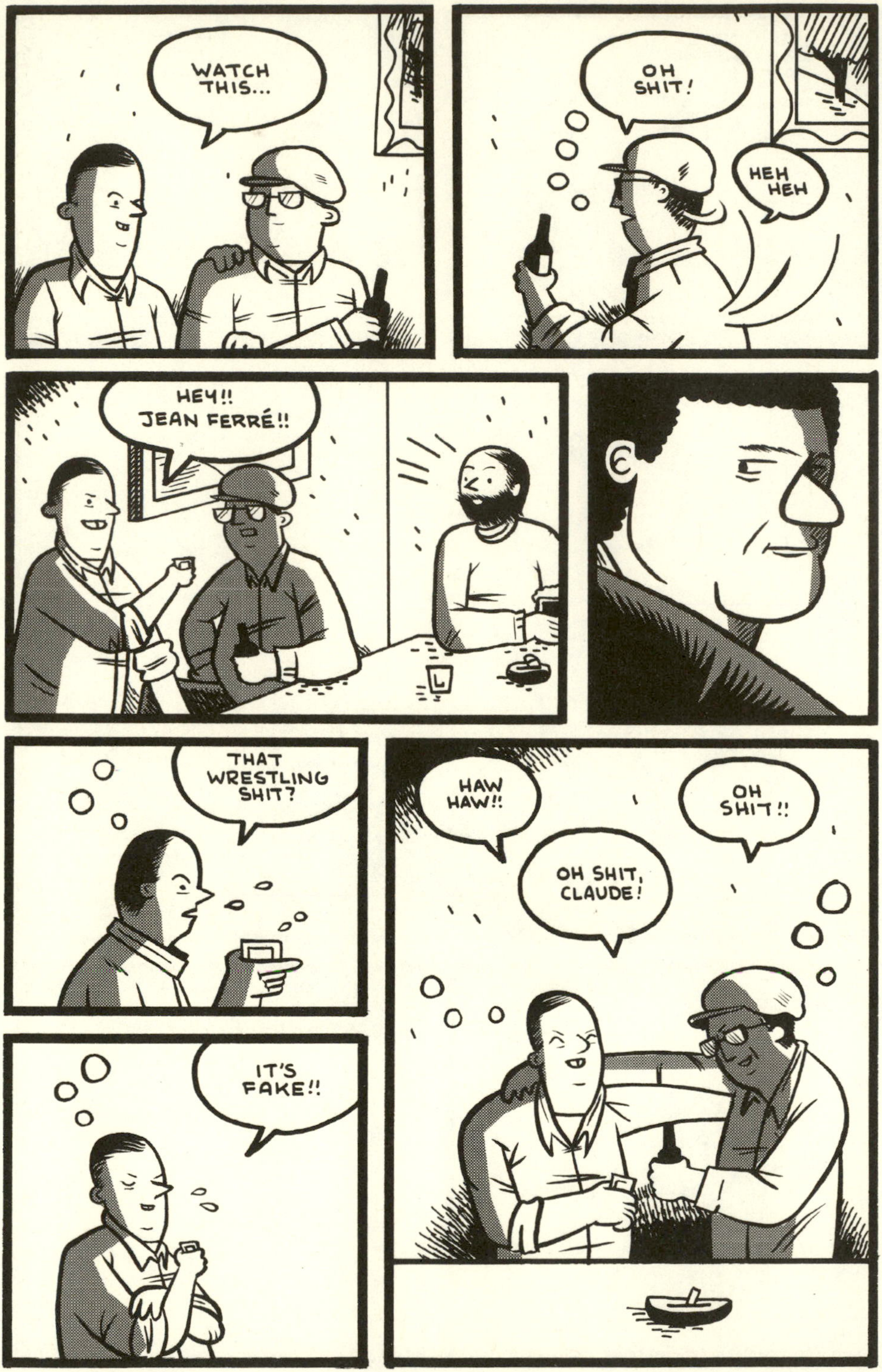
WATCH THIS...
OH SHIT!
HEH HEH
HEY!! JEAN FERRÉ!!
THAT WRESTLING SHIT?
IT'S FAKE!!
HAW HAW!!
OH SHIT!!
OH SHIT, CLAUDE!

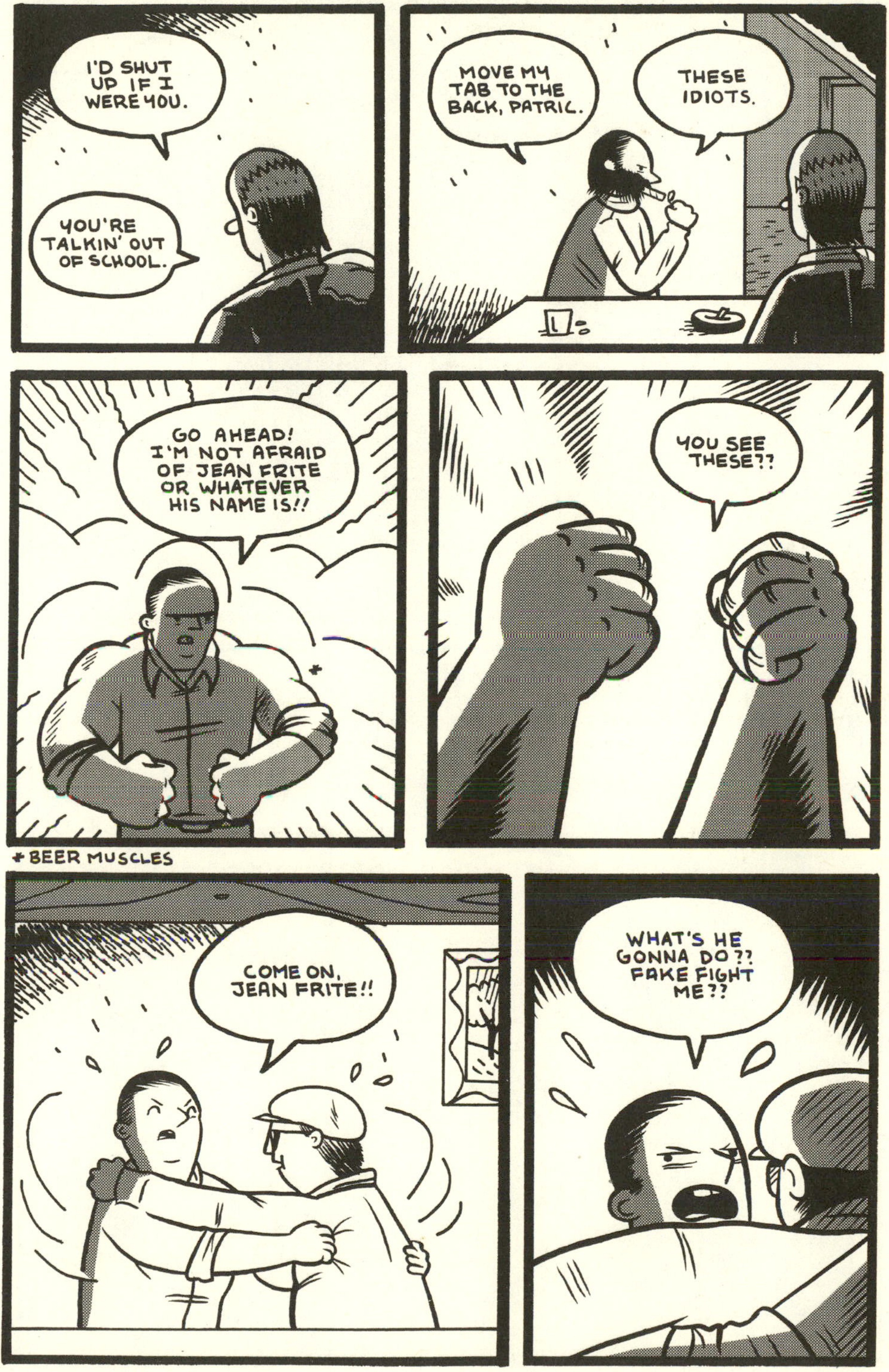
I'D SHUT UP IF I WERE YOU.
YOU'RE TALKIN' OUT OF SCHOOL.
MOVE MY TAB TO THE BACK, PATRIC.
THESE IDIOTS.
GO AHEAD! I'M NOT AFRAID OF JEAN FRITE OR WHATEVER HIS NAME IS!!
*
YOU SEE THESE??
* BEER MUSCLES
COME ON, JEAN FRITE!!
WHAT'S HE GONNA DO?? FAKE FIGHT ME??

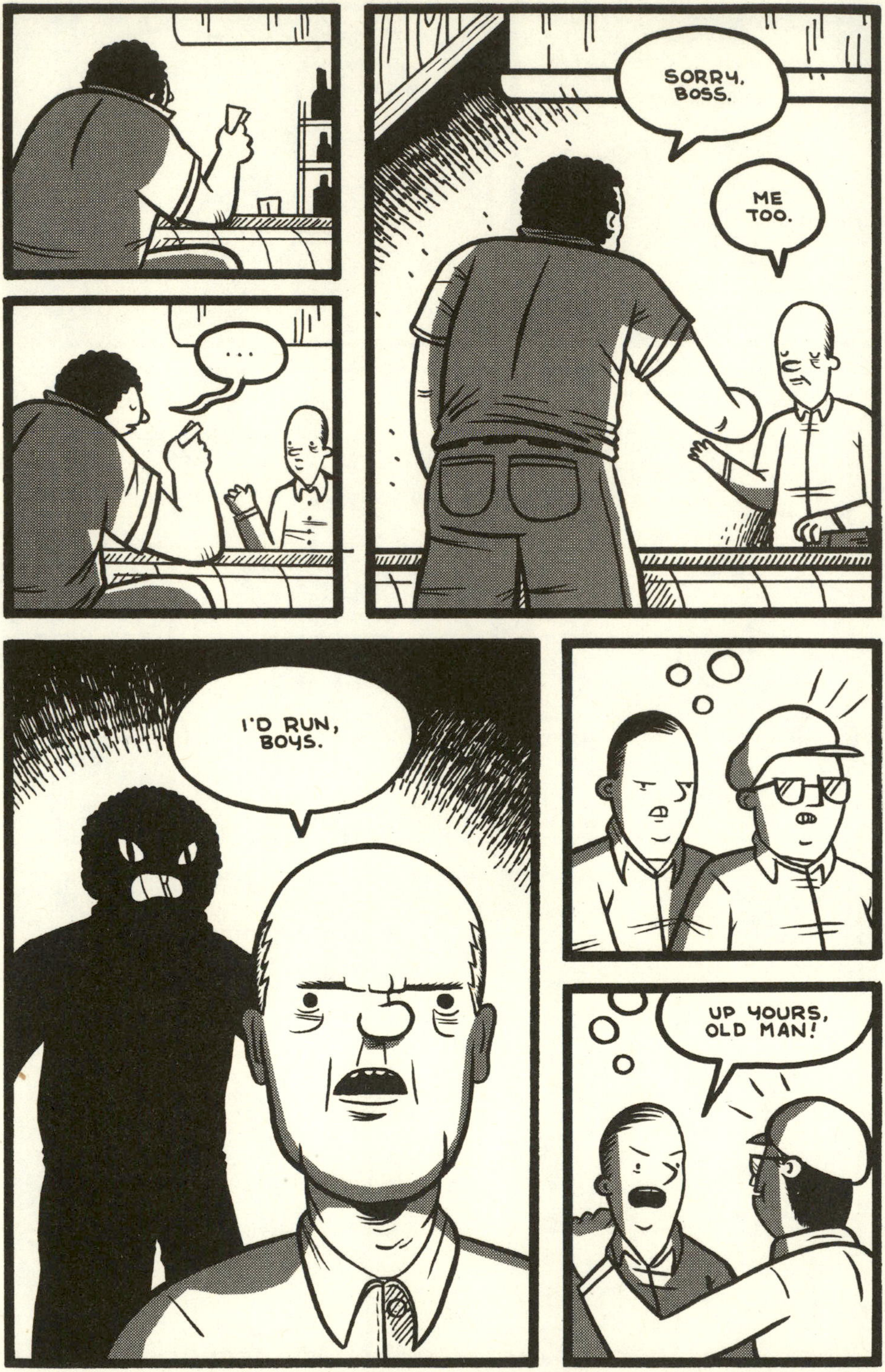
...
SORRY, BOSS.
ME TOO.
I'D RUN, BOYS.
UP YOURS, OLD MAN!

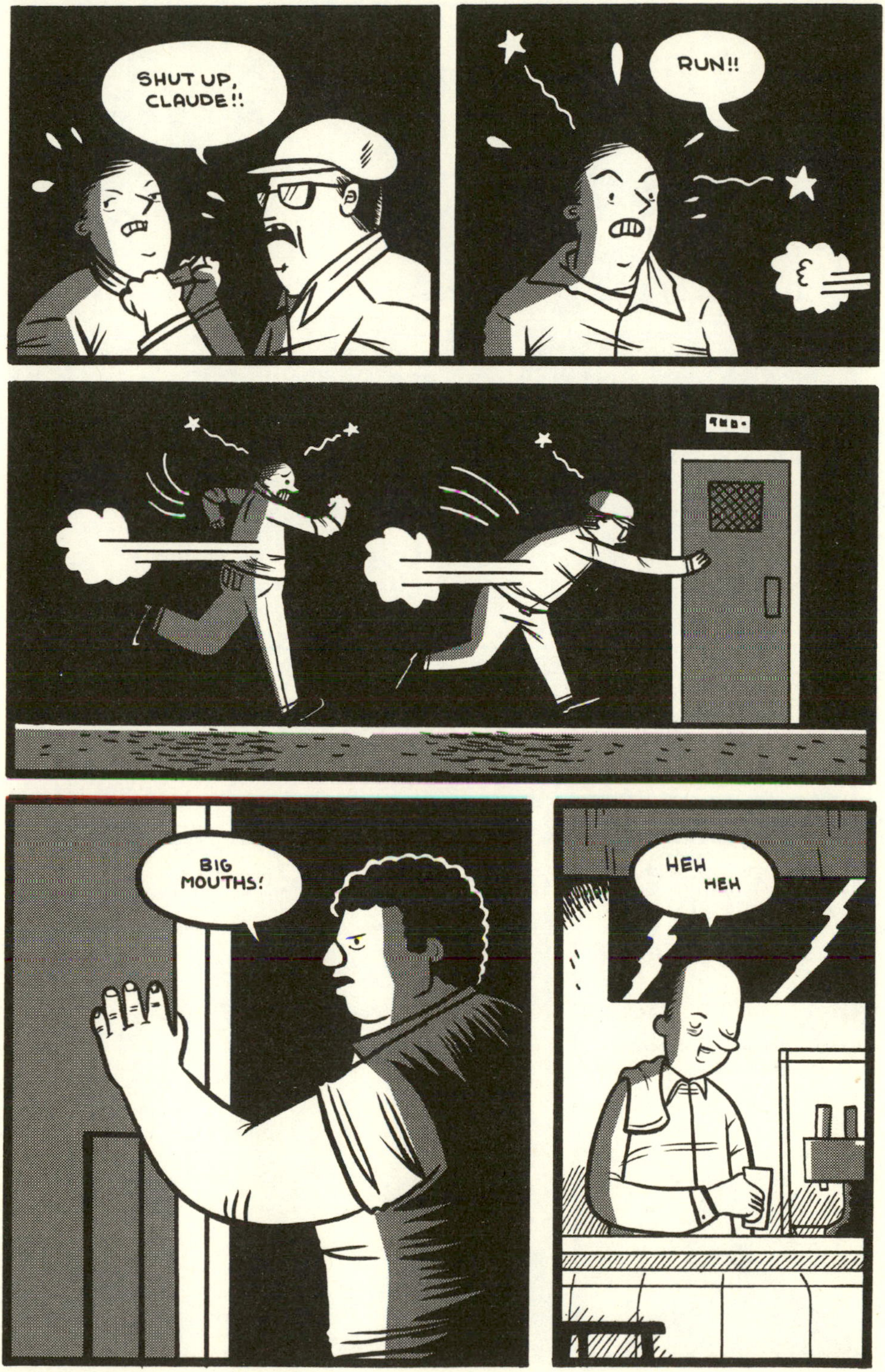
SHUT UP, CLAUDE!!
RUN!!
BIG MOUTHS!
HEH HEH

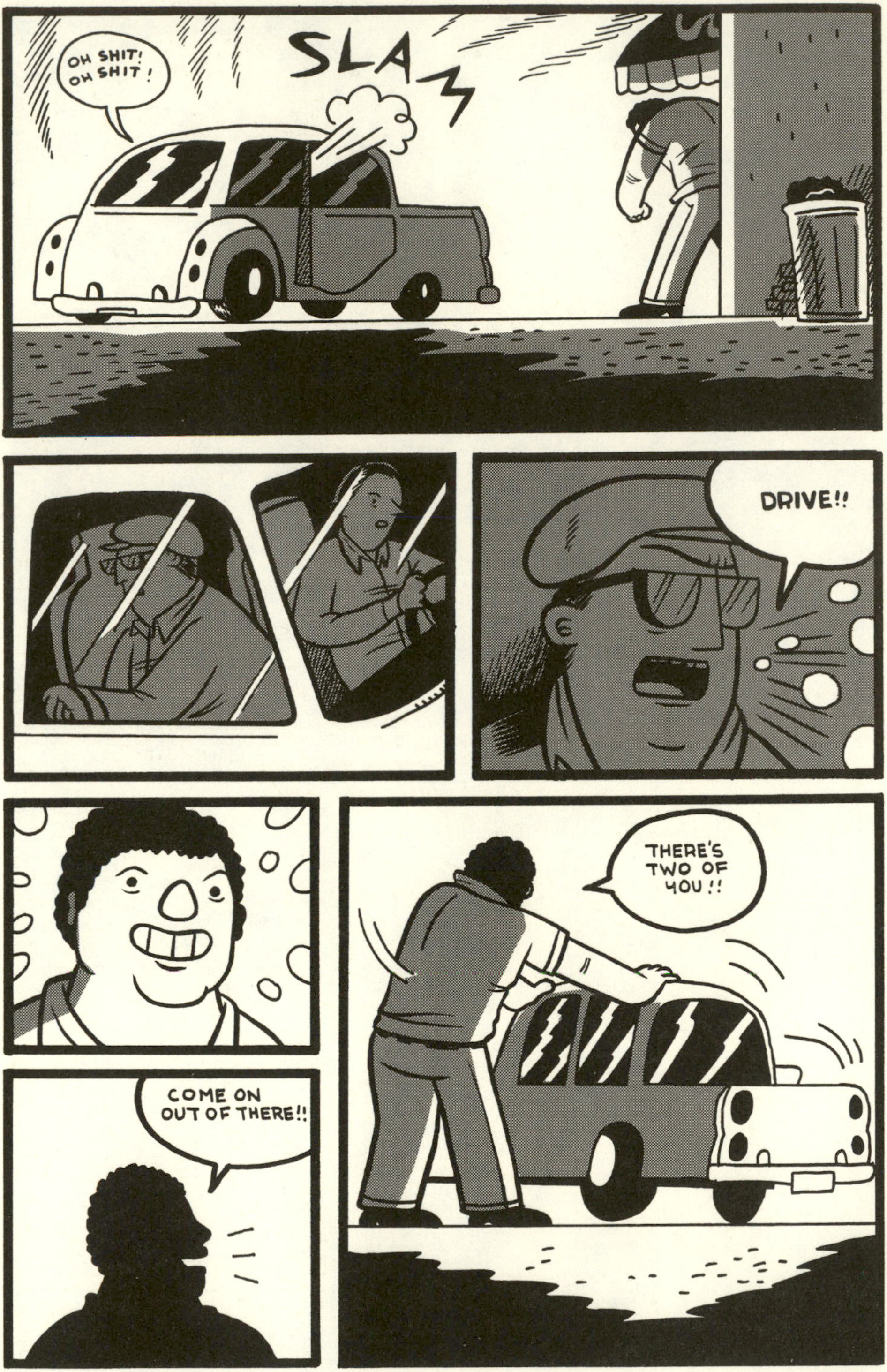
OH SHIT! OH SHIT!
SLAM
DRIVE!!
THERE'S TWO OF YOU!!
COME ON OUT OF THERE!!

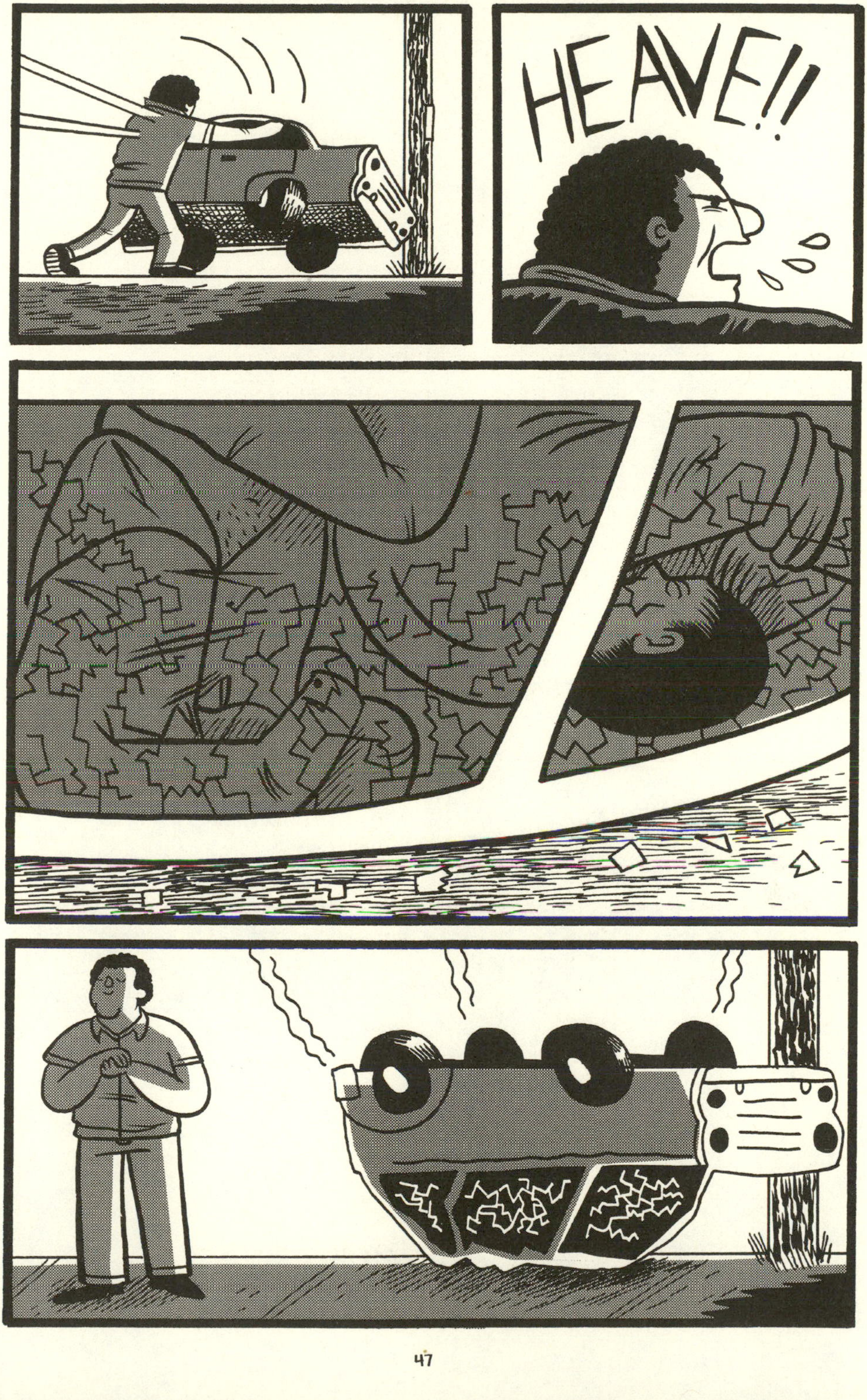
HEAVE!!

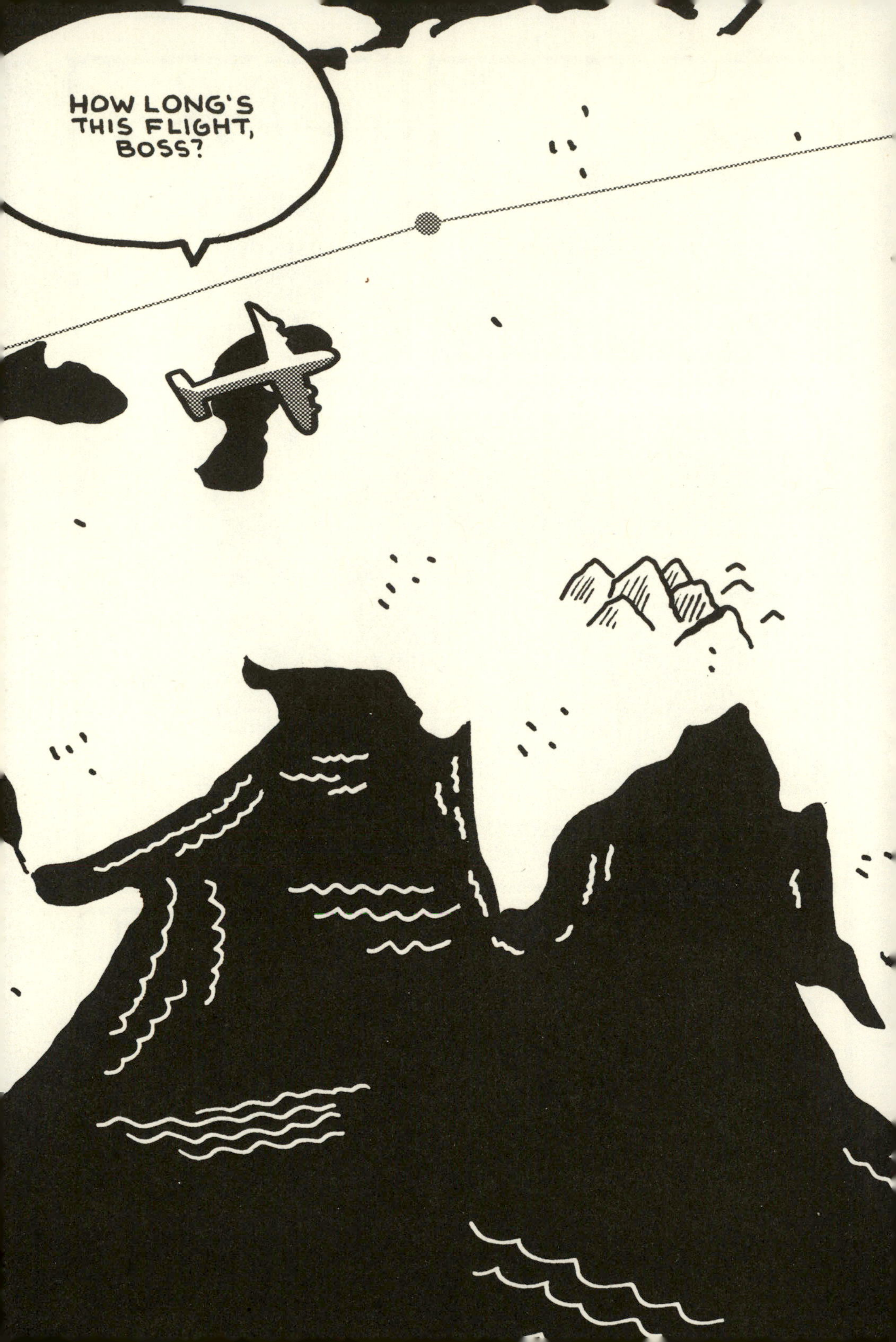
HOW LONG'S THIS FLIGHT, BOSS?

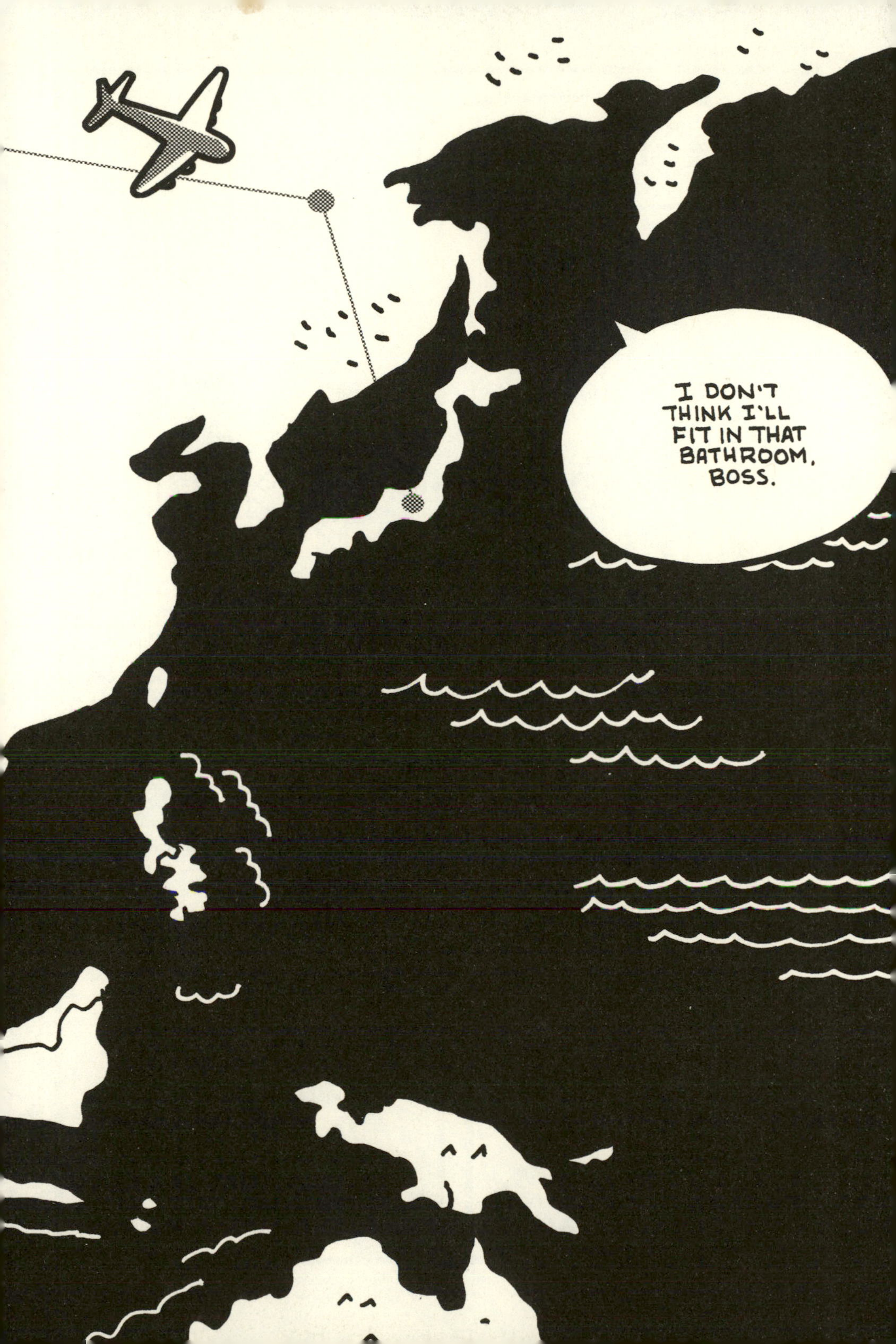
I DON'T THINK I'LL FIT IN THAT BATHROOM, BOSS.

TOKYO, JAPAN, 1970

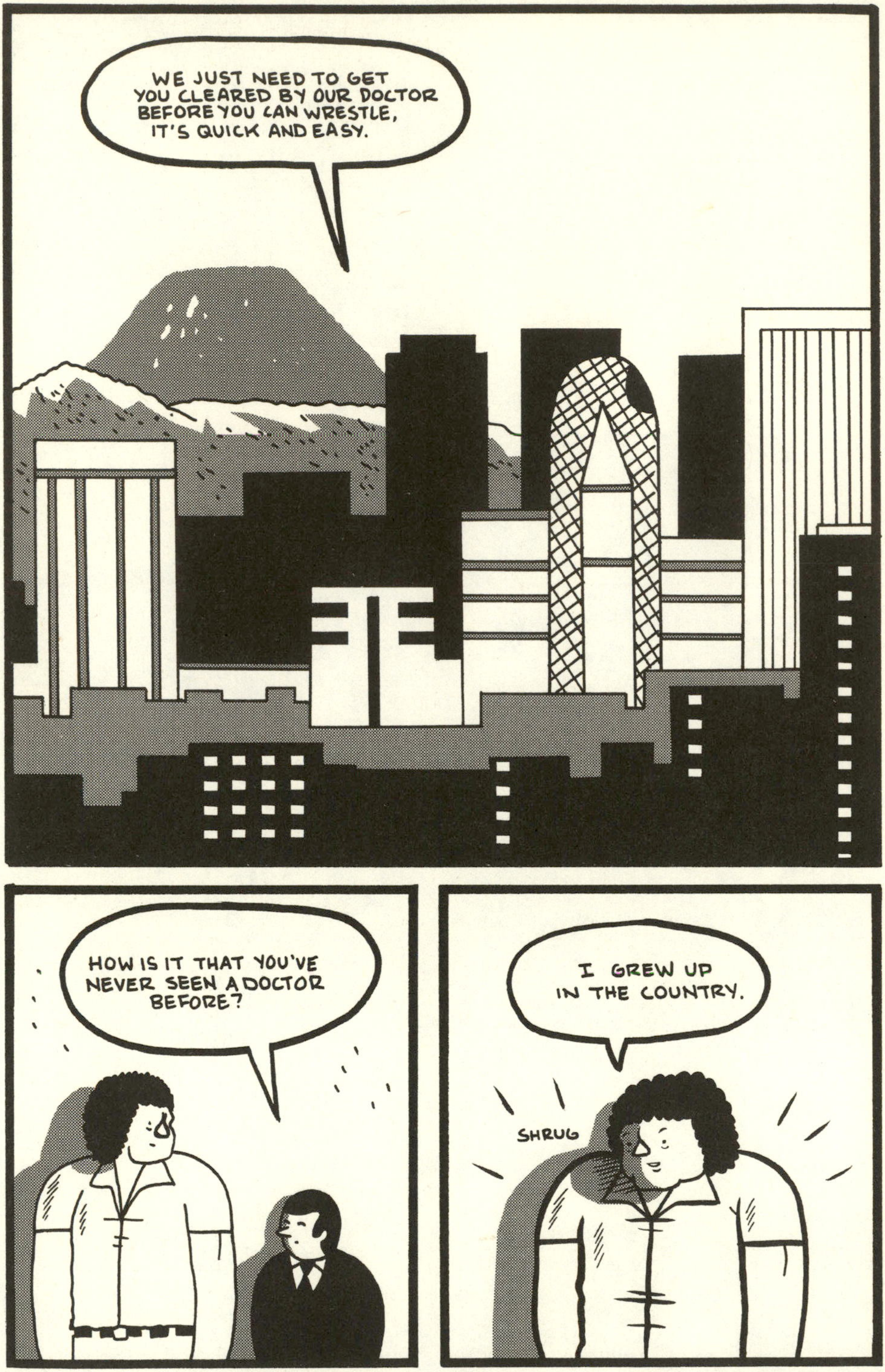
WE JUST NEED TO GET YOU CLEARED BY OUR DOCTOR BEFORE YOU CAN WRESTLE, IT'S QUICK AND EASY.
HOW IS IT THAT YOU'VE NEVER SEEN A DOCTOR BEFORE?
I GREW UP IN THE COUNTRY.
SHRUG

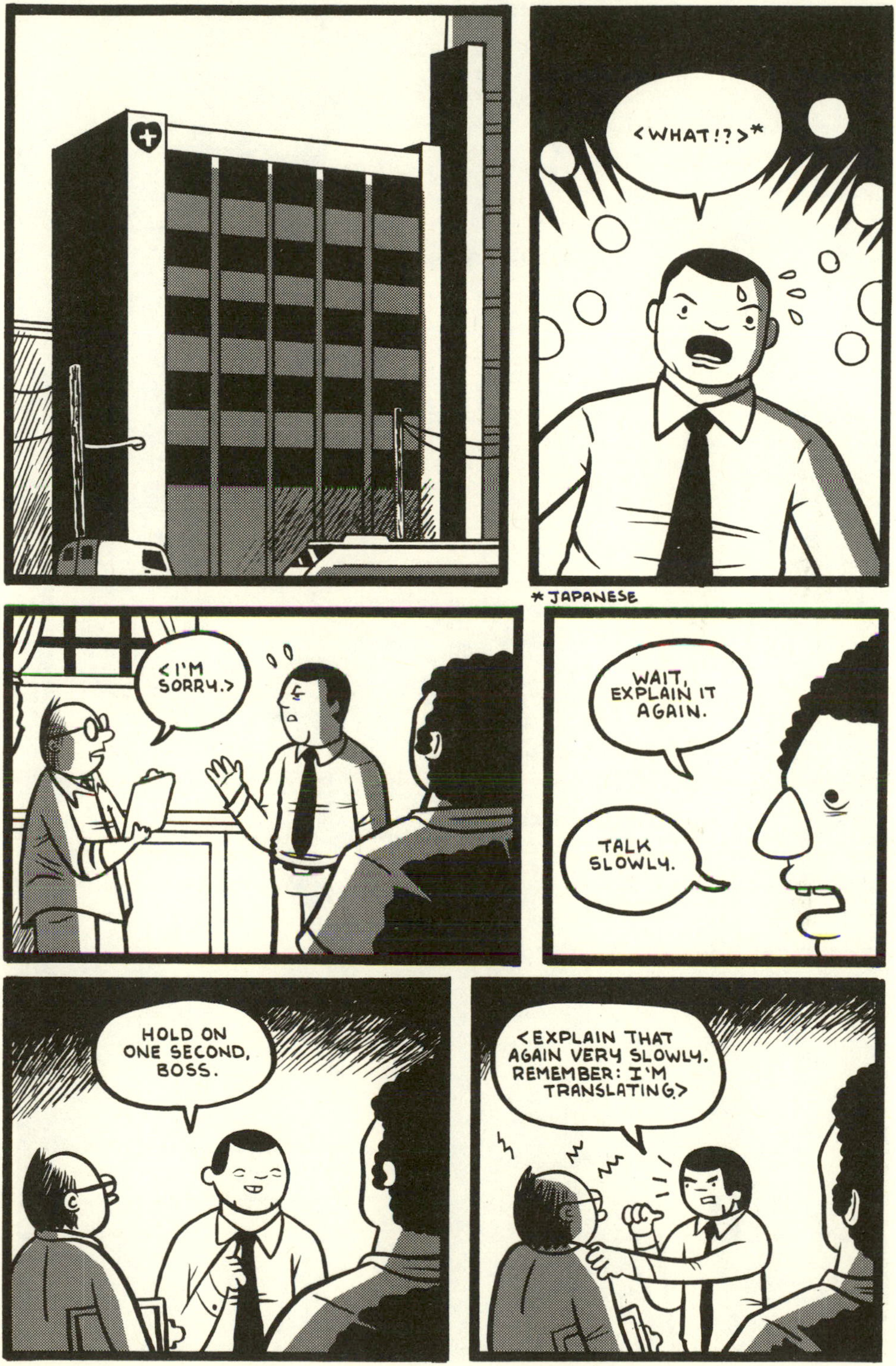
<WHAT!?>*
* JAPANESE
<I'M SORRY.>
WAIT, EXPLAIN IT AGAIN.
TALK SLOWLY.
HOLD ON ONE SECOND, BOSS.
<EXPLAIN THAT AGAIN VERY SLOWLY. REMEMBER: I'M TRANSLATING.>

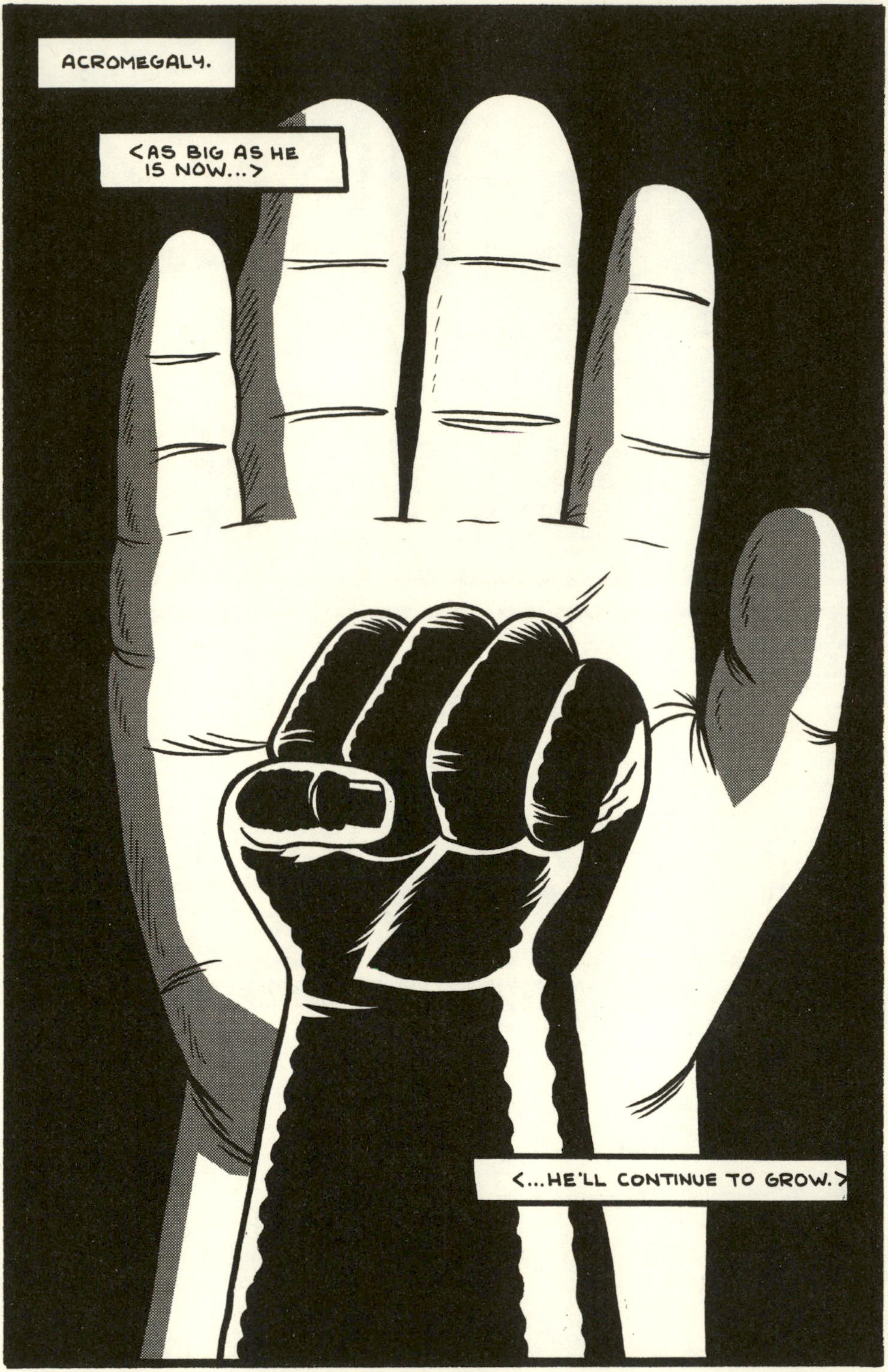
ACROMEGALY.
<AS BIG AS HE IS NOW...>
<...HE'LL CONTINUE TO GROW.>

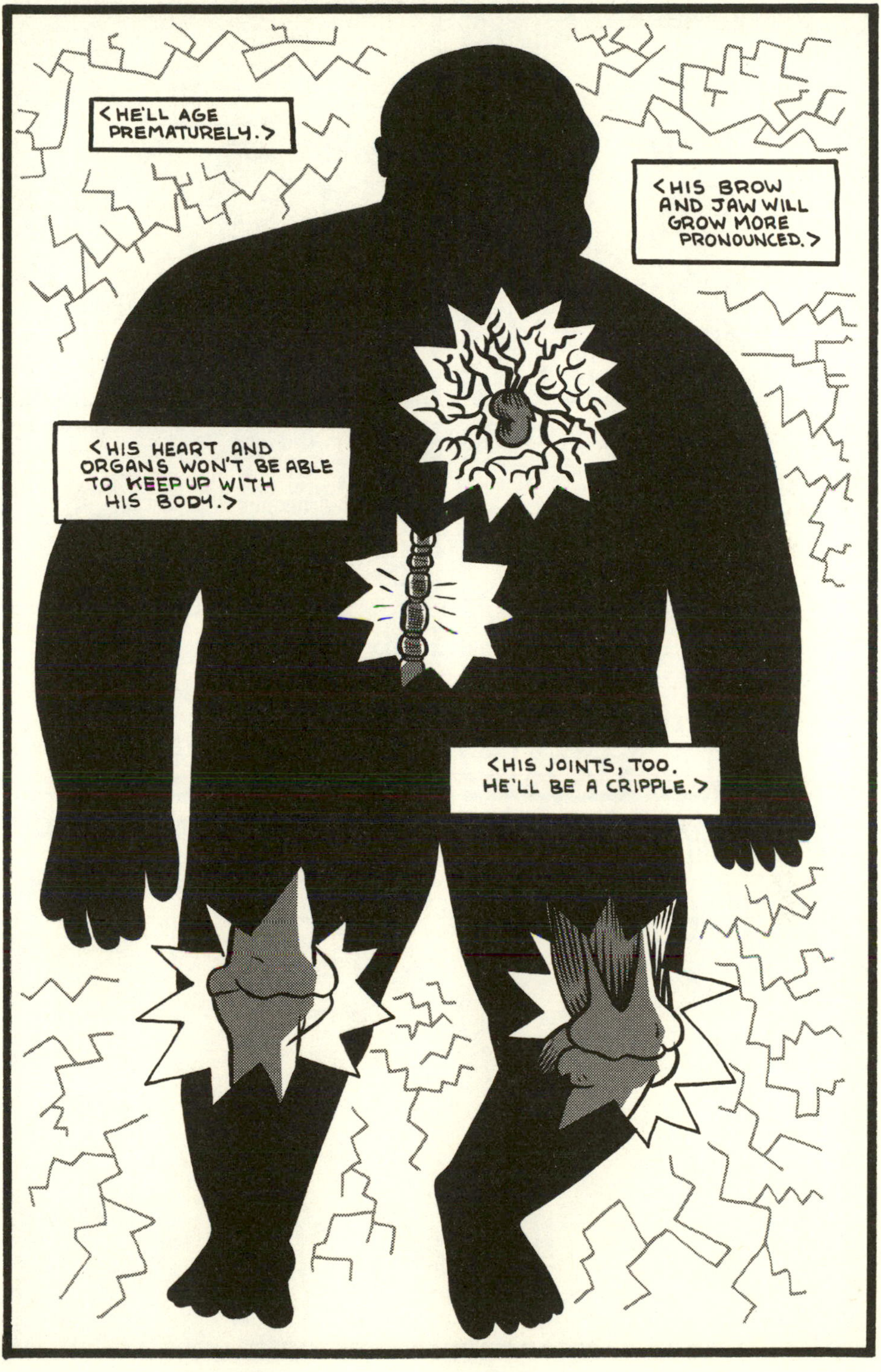

<HE'LL AGE PREMATURELY.>
<HIS BROW AND JAW WILL GROW MORE PRONOUNCED.>
<HIS HEART AND ORGANS WON'T BE ABLE TO KEEP UP WITH HIS BODY.>
<HIS JOINTS, TOO. HE'LL BE A CRIPPLE.>

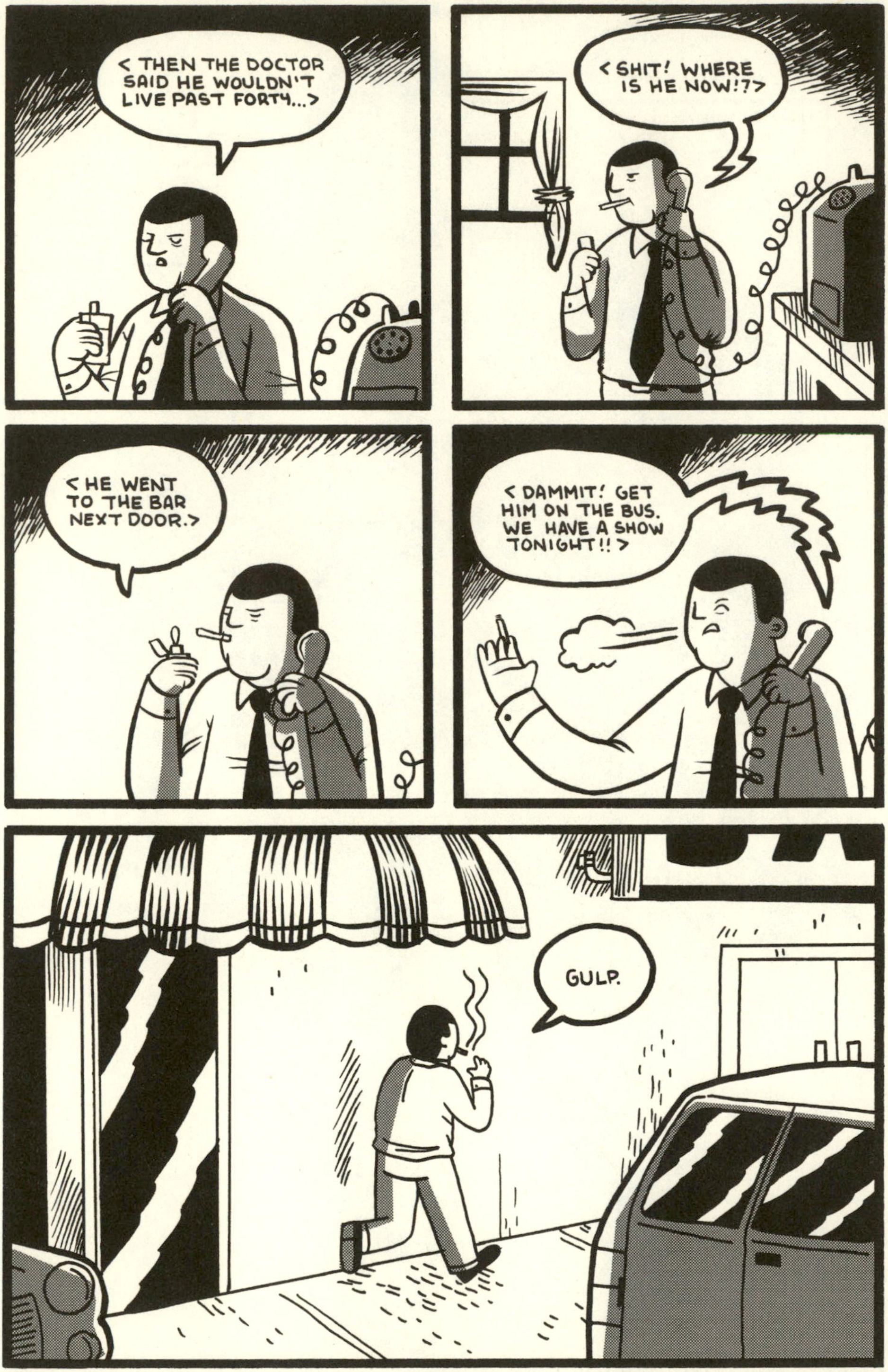
< THEN THE DOCTOR SAID HE WOULDN'T LIVE PAST FORTY... >
< SHIT! WHERE IS HE NOW!? >
< HE WENT TO THE BAR NEXT DOOR. >
< DAMMIT! GET HIM ON THE BUS. WE HAVE A SHOW TONIGHT!! >
GULP.

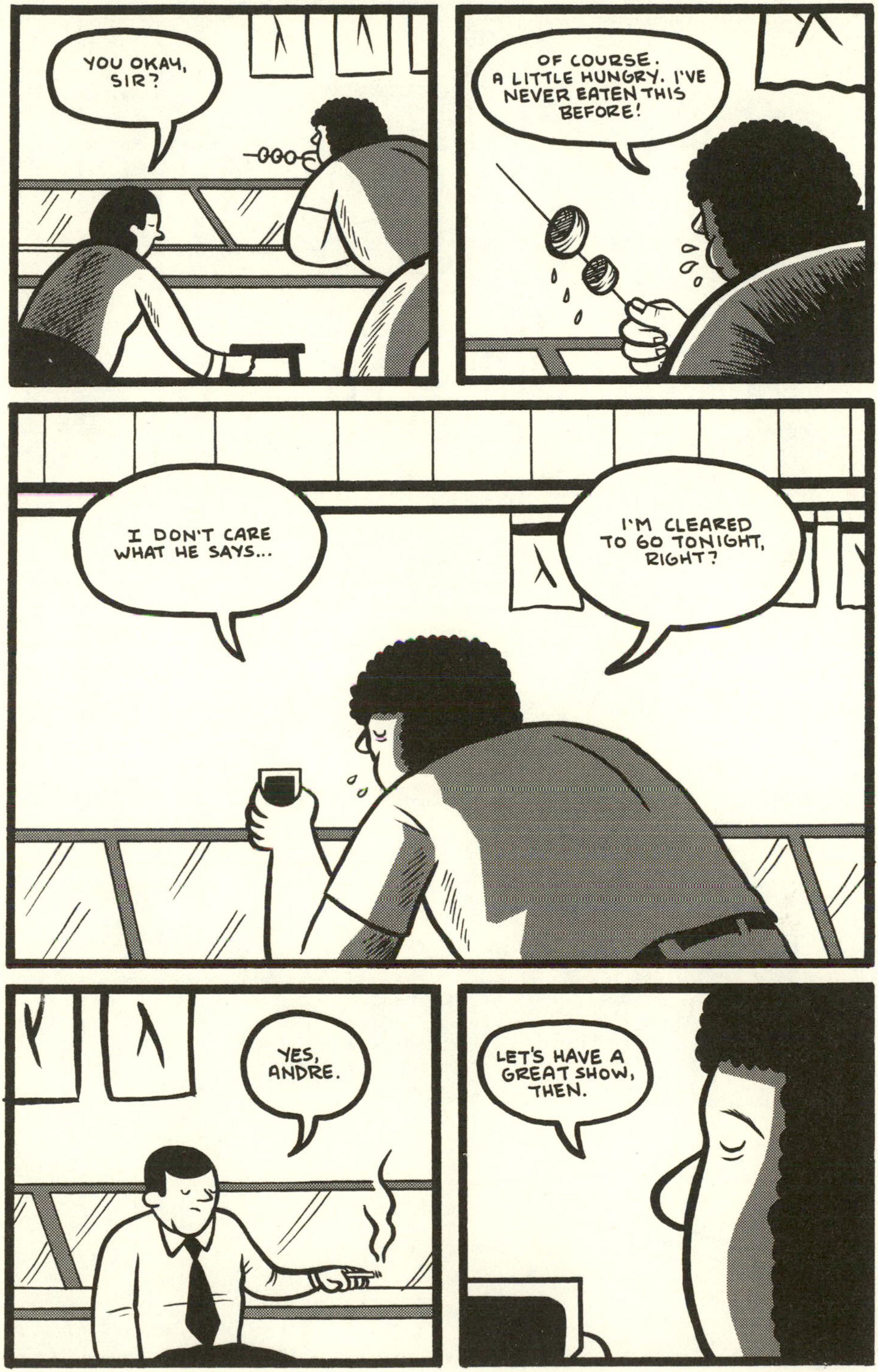
YOU OKAY, SIR?
OF COURSE. A LITTLE HUNGRY. I'VE NEVER EATEN THIS BEFORE!
I DON'T CARE WHAT HE SAYS...
I'M CLEARED TO GO TONIGHT, RIGHT?
YES, ANDRE.
LET'S HAVE A GREAT SHOW, THEN.

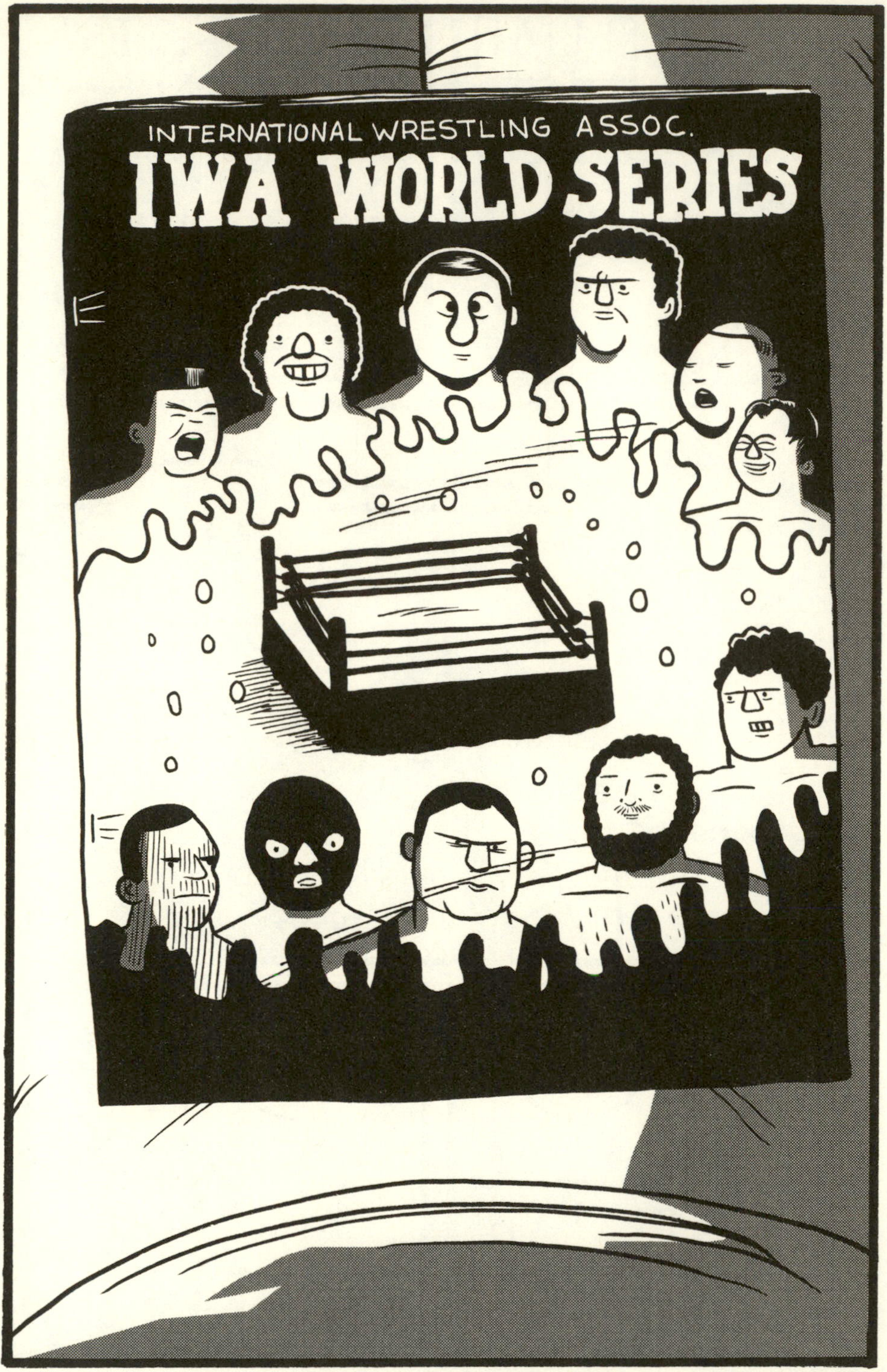
INTERNATIONAL WRESTLING ASSOC.
IWA WORLD SERIES

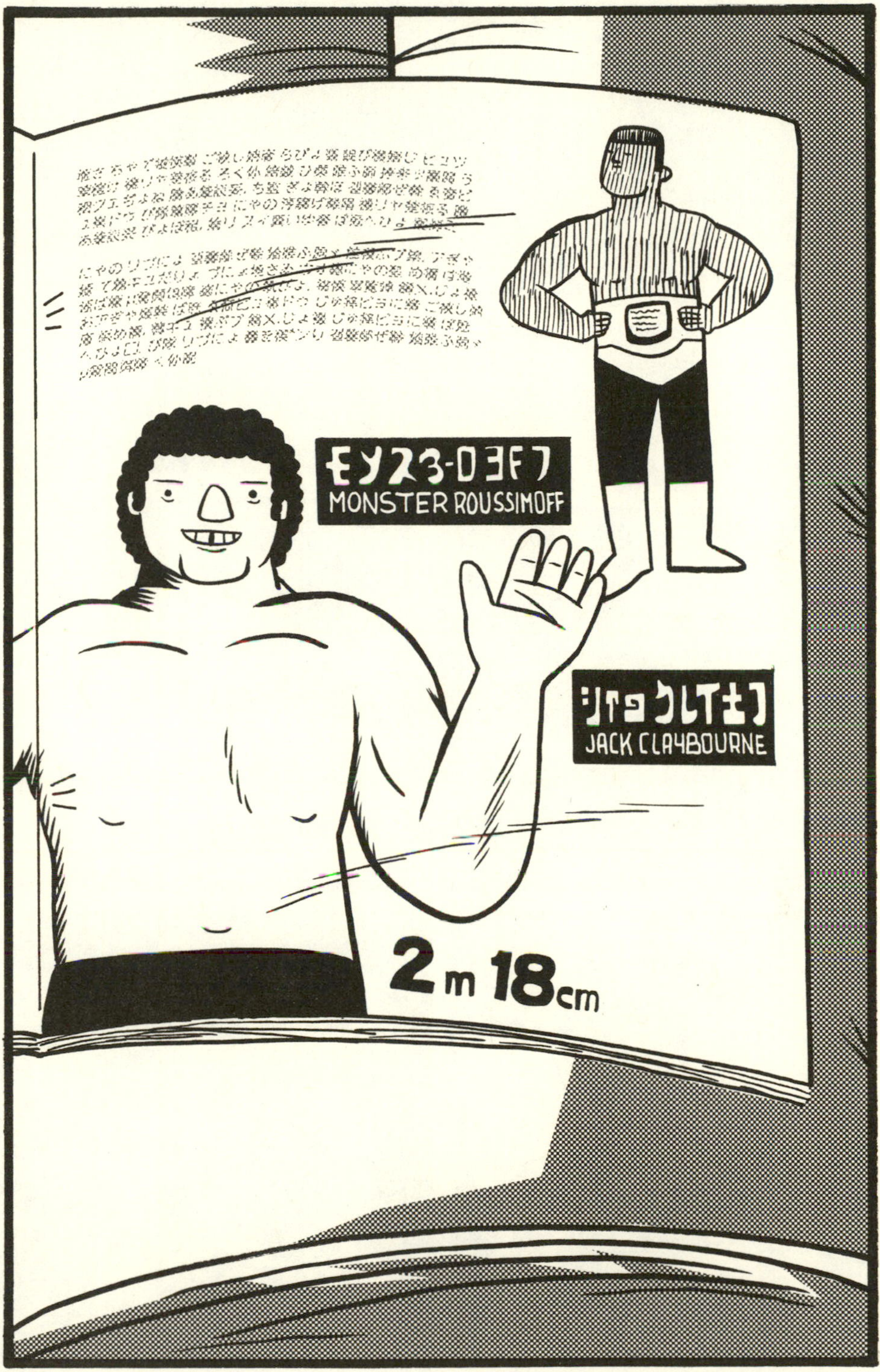
MONSTER ROUSSIMOFF
JACK CLAYBOURNE
2m 18cm

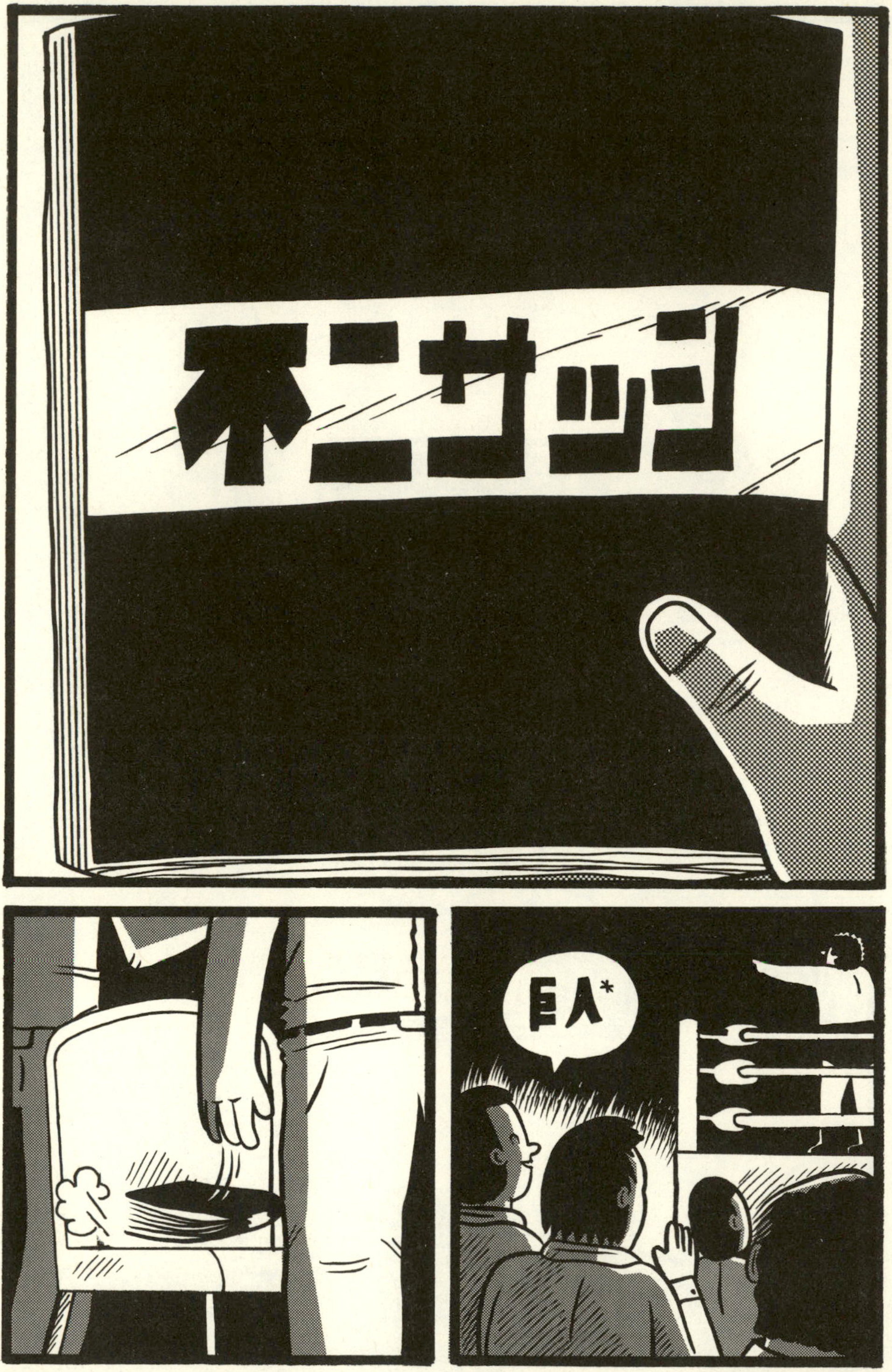
巨人*

* GIANT MONSTER

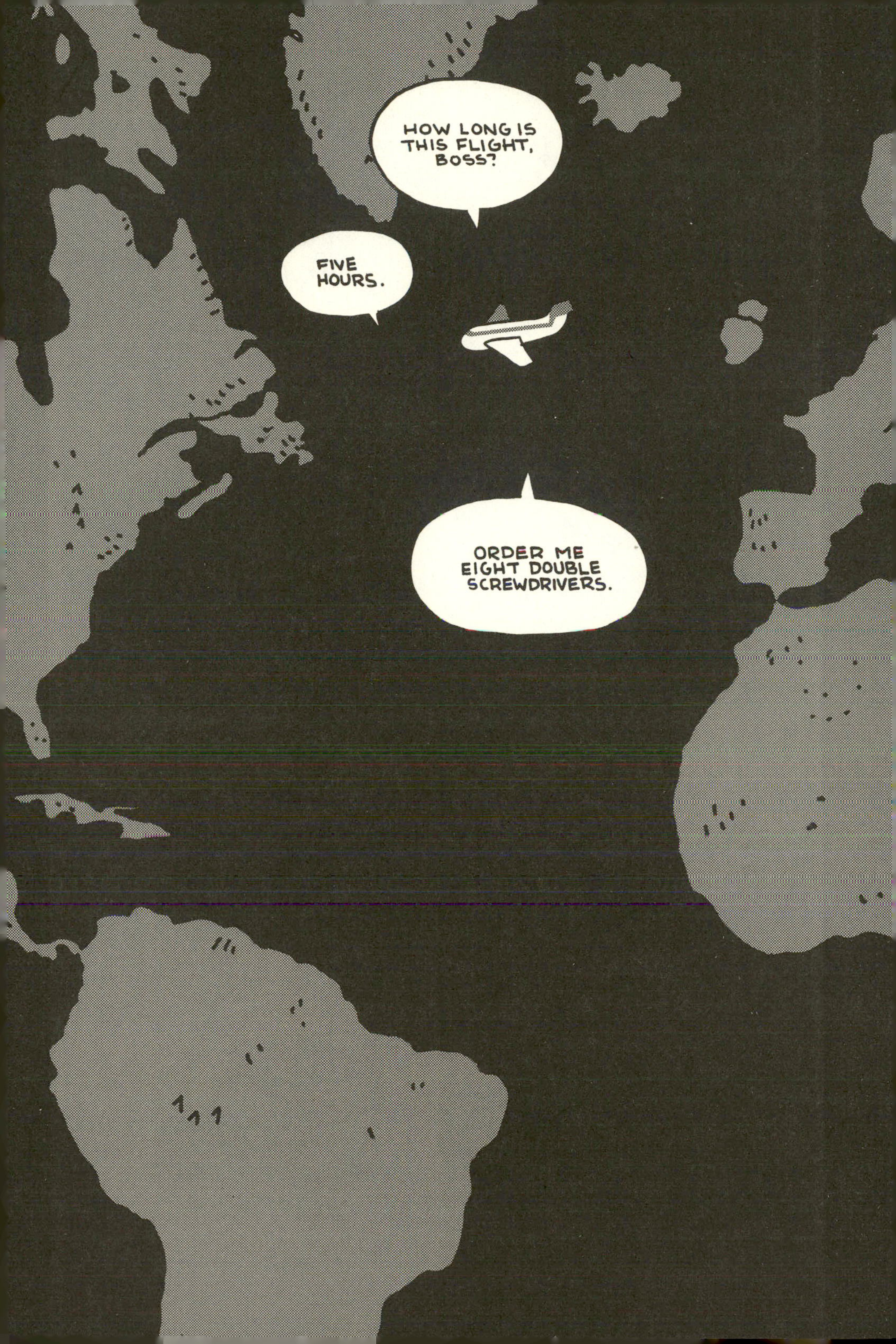
HOW LONG IS THIS FLIGHT, BOSS?
FIVE HOURS.
ORDER ME EIGHT DOUBLE SCREWDRIVERS.

MONTREAL, 1972

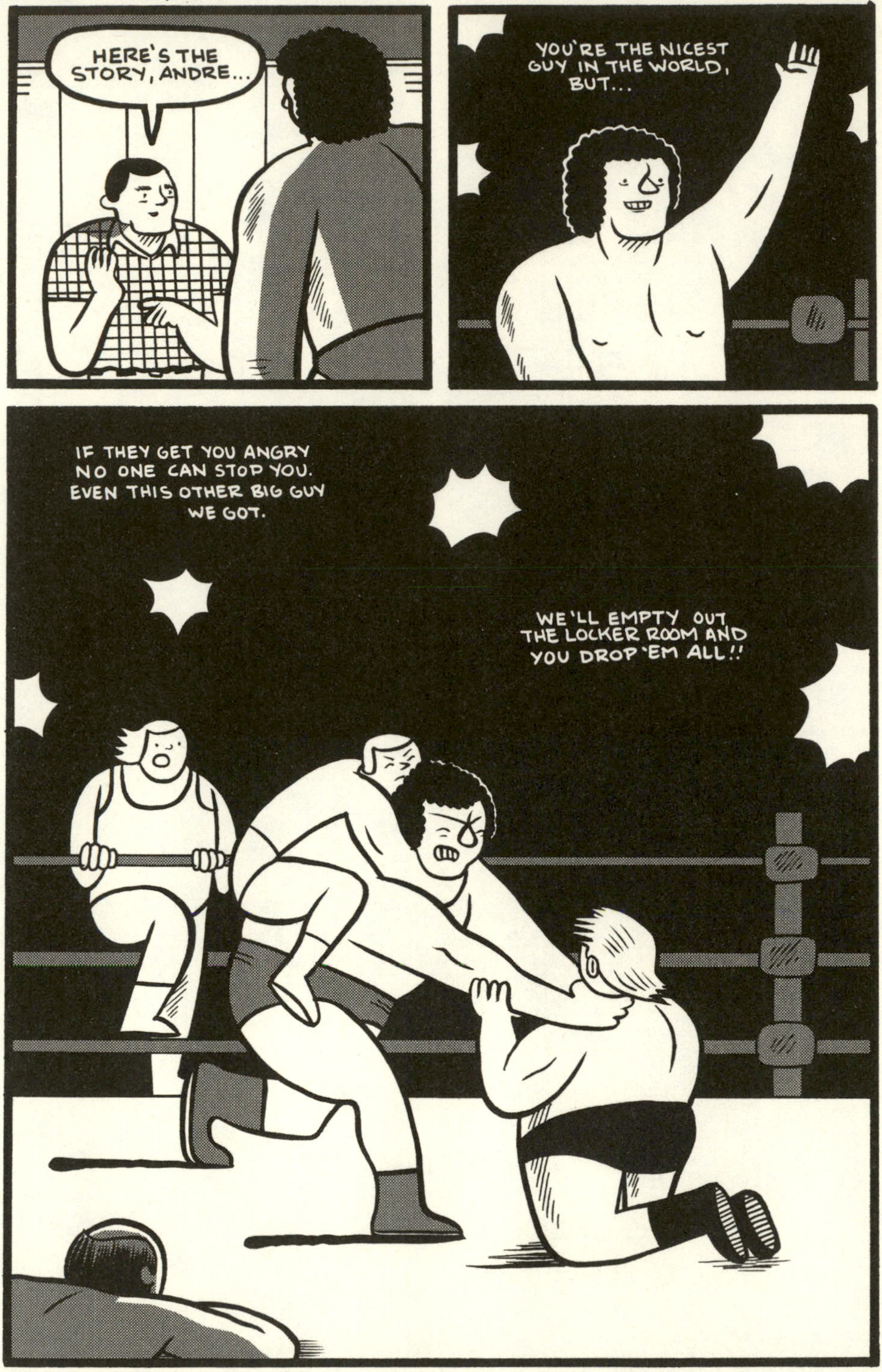

HERE'S THE STORY, ANDRE...
YOU'RE THE NICEST GUY IN THE WORLD, BUT...
IF THEY GET YOU ANGRY NO ONE CAN STOP YOU. EVEN THIS OTHER BIG GUY WE GOT.
WE'LL EMPTY OUT THE LOCKER ROOM AND YOU DROP 'EM ALL!!

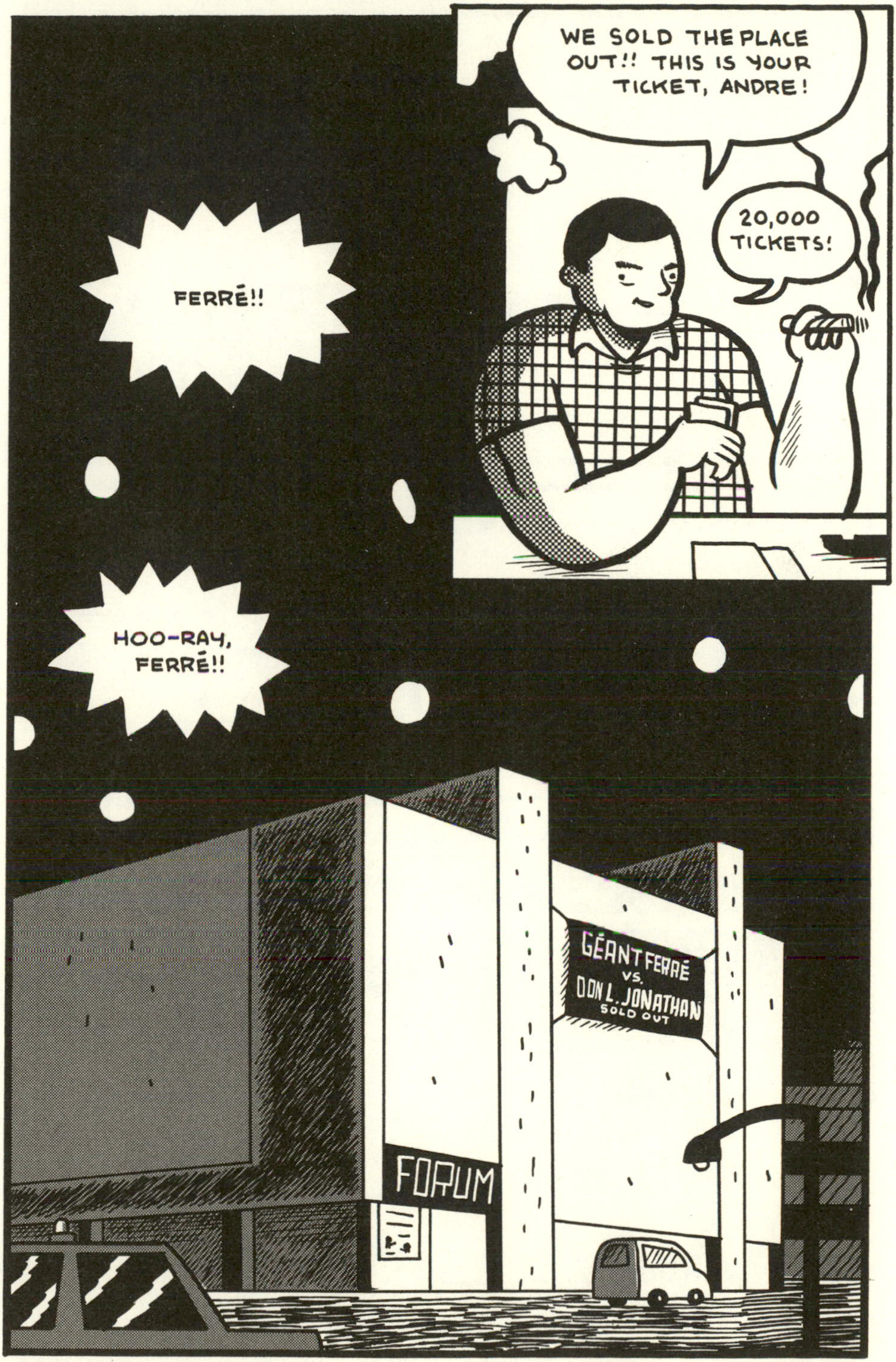
WE SOLD THE PLACE OUT!! THIS IS YOUR TICKET, ANDRE!
20,000 TICKETS!
FERRÉ!!
HOO-RAY, FERRÉ!!
GÉANT FERRÉ VS. DON L. JONATHAN SOLD OUT
FORUM

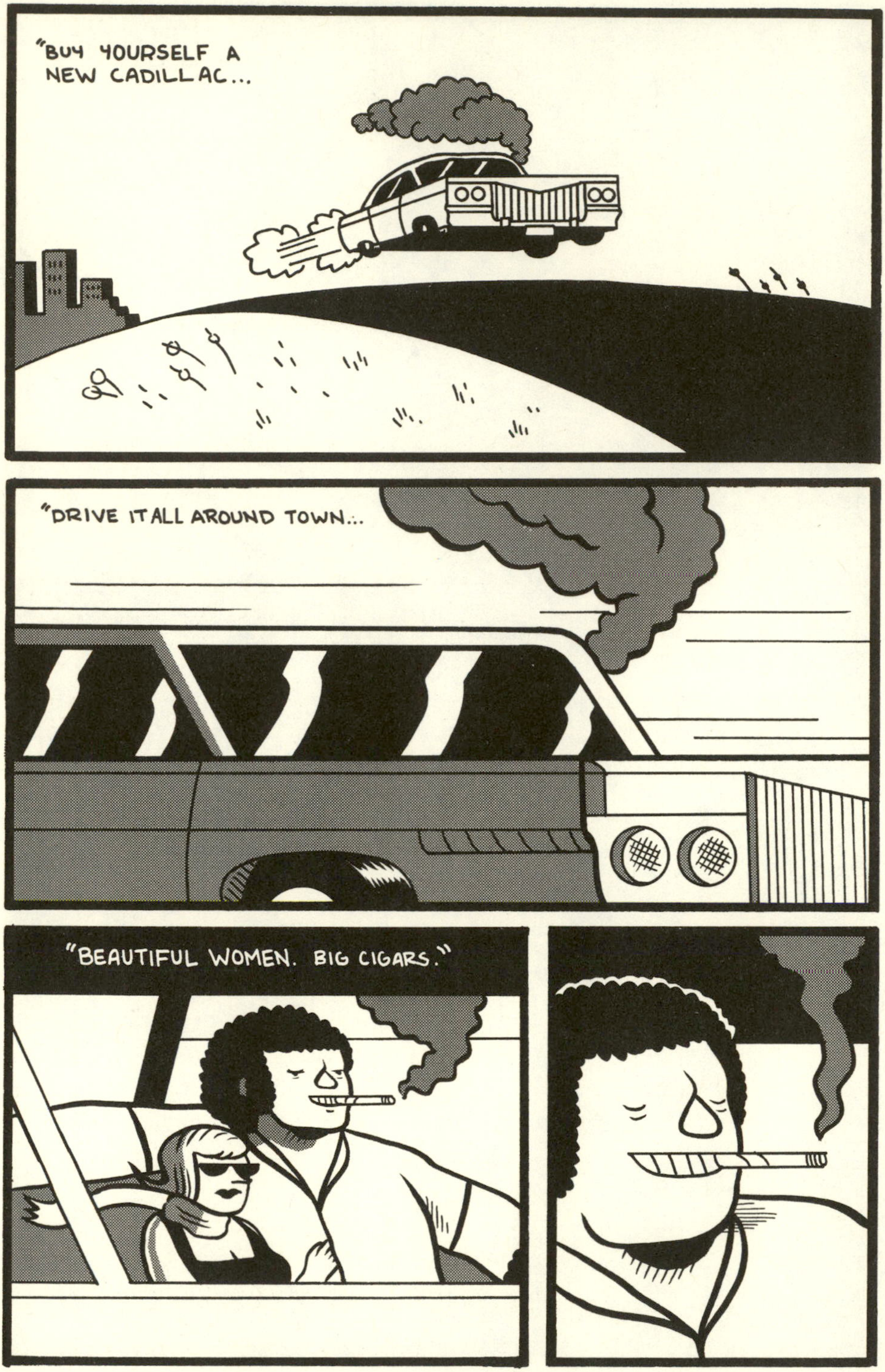
"BUY YOURSELF A NEW CADILLAC...
"DRIVE IT ALL AROUND TOWN...
"BEAUTIFUL WOMEN. BIG CIGARS."

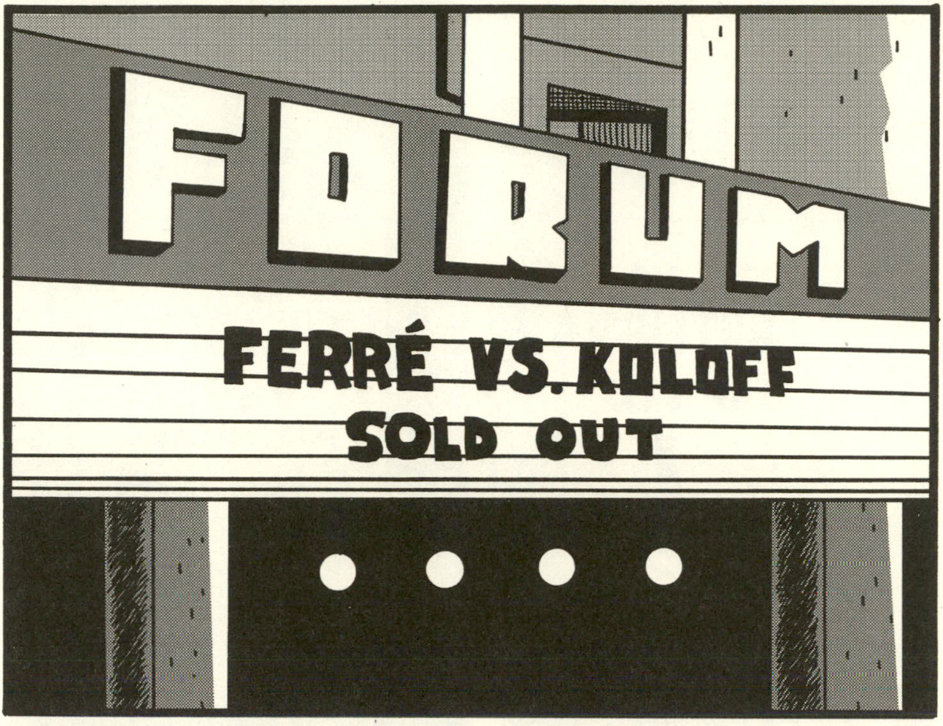
FORUM
FERRÉ VS. KOLOFF
SOLD OUT

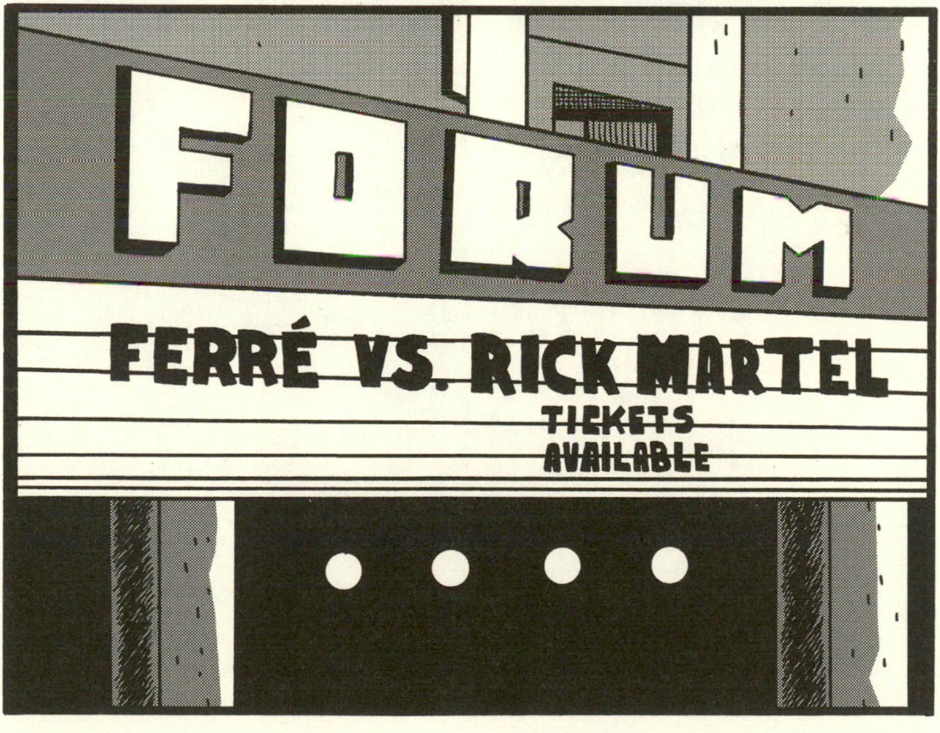
FORUM
FERRÉ VS. RICK MARTEL
TICKETS
AVAILABLE

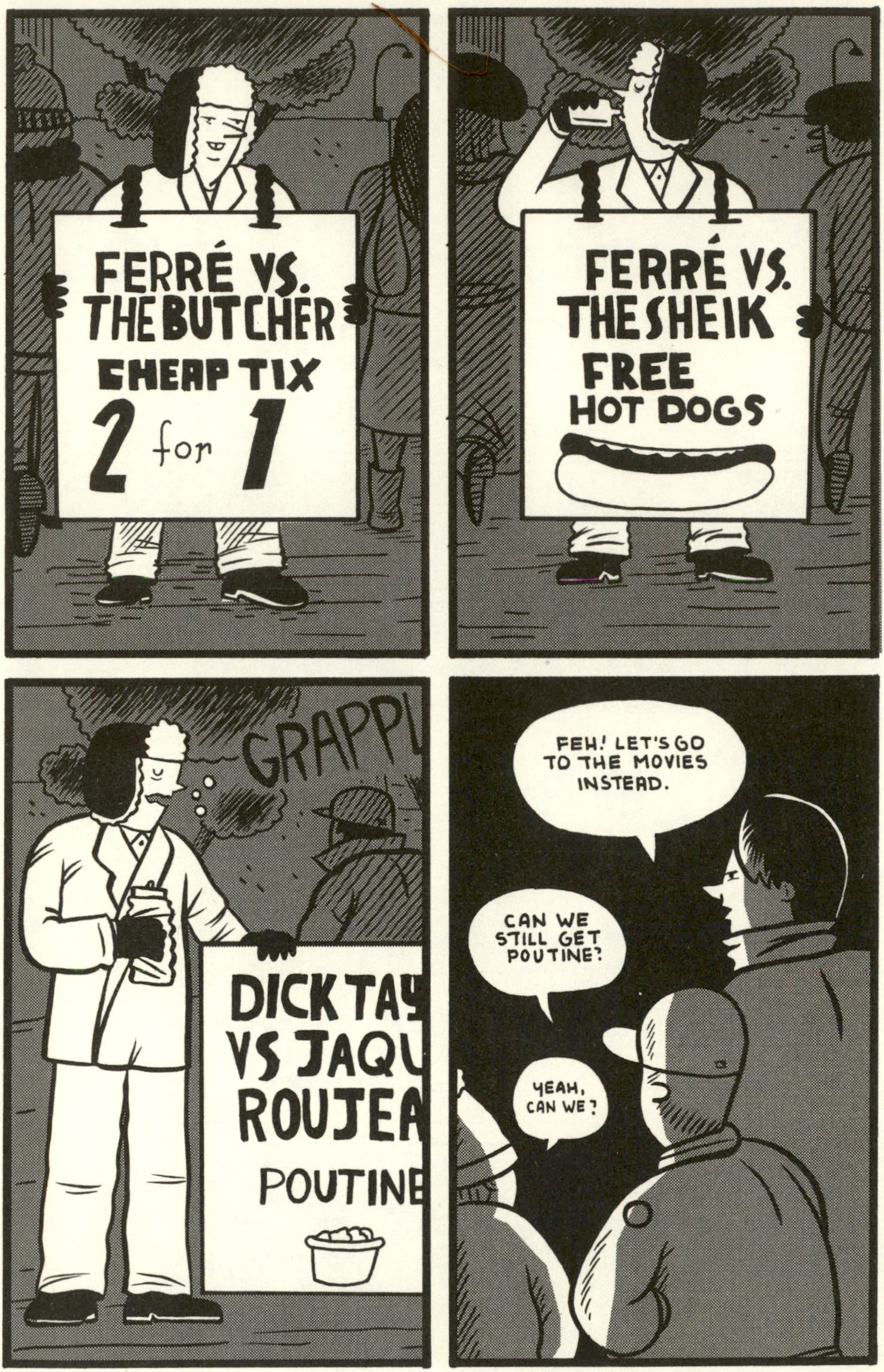
FERRÉ VS.
THE BUTCHER
CHEAP TIX
2 for 1
FERRÉ VS.
THE SHEIK
FREE
HOT DOGS
GRAPPL
DICK TAY
VS JAQU
ROUJEA
POUTINE
FEH! LET'S GO TO THE MOVIES INSTEAD.
CAN WE STILL GET POUTINE?
YEAH, CAN WE?

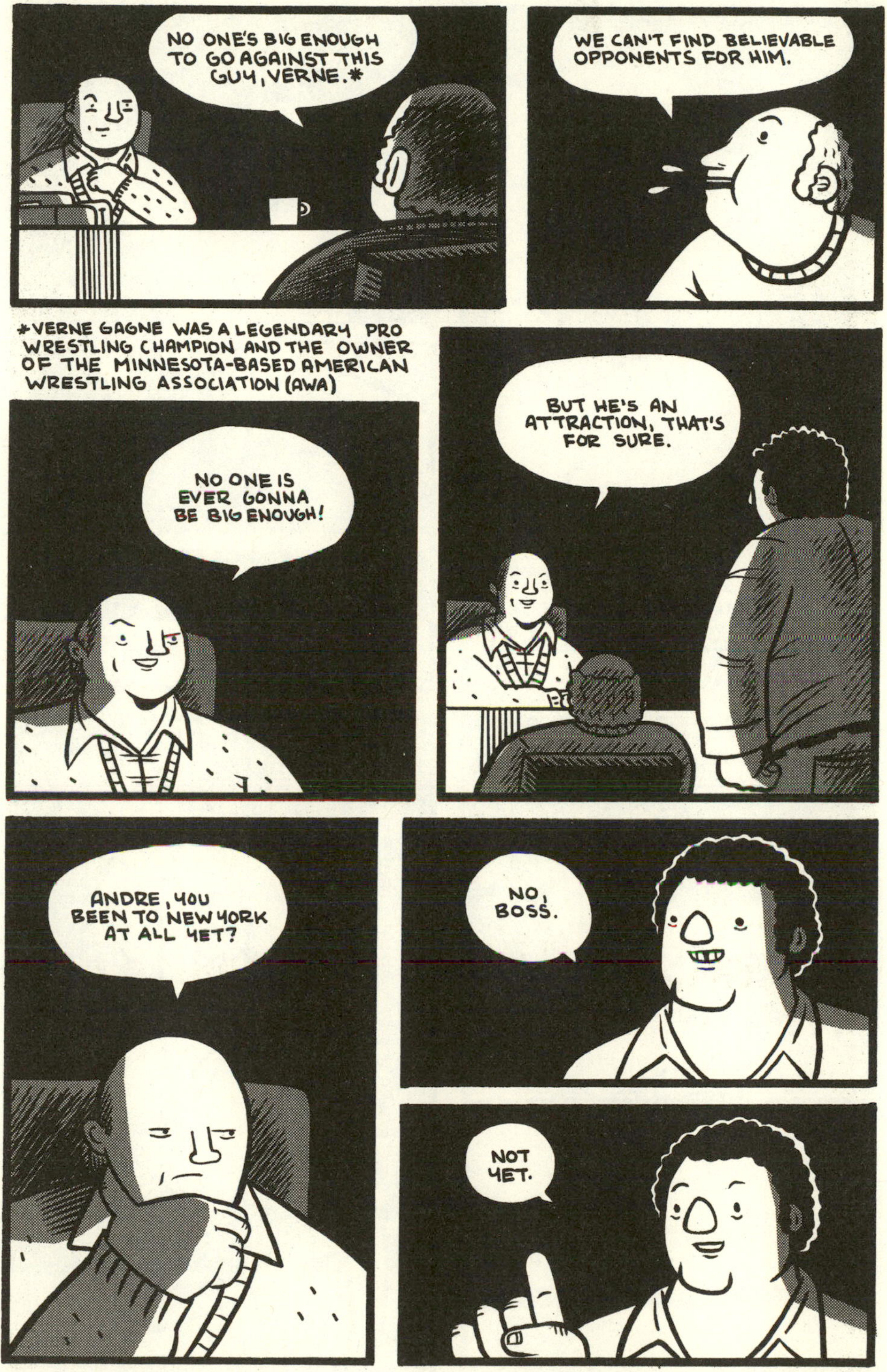
NO ONE'S BIG ENOUGH TO GO AGAINST THIS GUY, VERNE.*
WE CAN'T FIND BELIEVABLE OPPONENTS FOR HIM.
*VERNE GAGNE WAS A LEGENDARY PRO WRESTLING CHAMPION AND THE OWNER OF THE MINNESOTA-BASED AMERICAN WRESTLING ASSOCIATION (AWA)
NO ONE IS EVER GONNA BE BIG ENOUGH!
BUT HE'S AN ATTRACTION, THAT'S FOR SURE.
ANDRE, YOU BEEN TO NEW YORK AT ALL YET?
NO, BOSS.
NOT YET.

NEW YORK, 1973

OKAY, ANDRE. YOU'RE BIG, BUT THAT'S NOT ENOUGH.

WHAT CAN YOU DO IN THE RING?

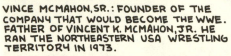

VINCE MCMAHON, SR.: FOUNDER OF THE COMPANY THAT WOULD BECOME THE WWE. FATHER OF VINCENT K. MCMAHON, JR. HE RAN THE NORTHEASTERN USA WRESTLING TERRITORY IN 1973.

OKAY, BOYS...

IT'S CLEAR ANDRE IS A SPECIMEN LIKE NO OTHER.

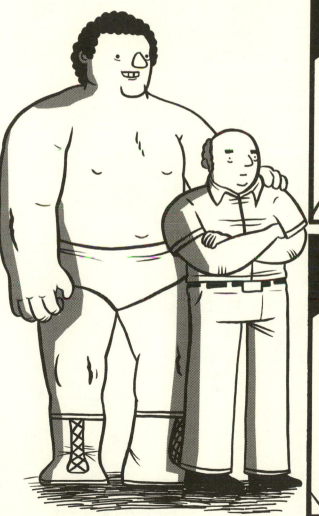

NOW, YOU GUYS RAN OUT OF OPPONENTS...

BUT THE GATE RECEIPTS WOULD HAVE GONE DOWN ANYWAYS.

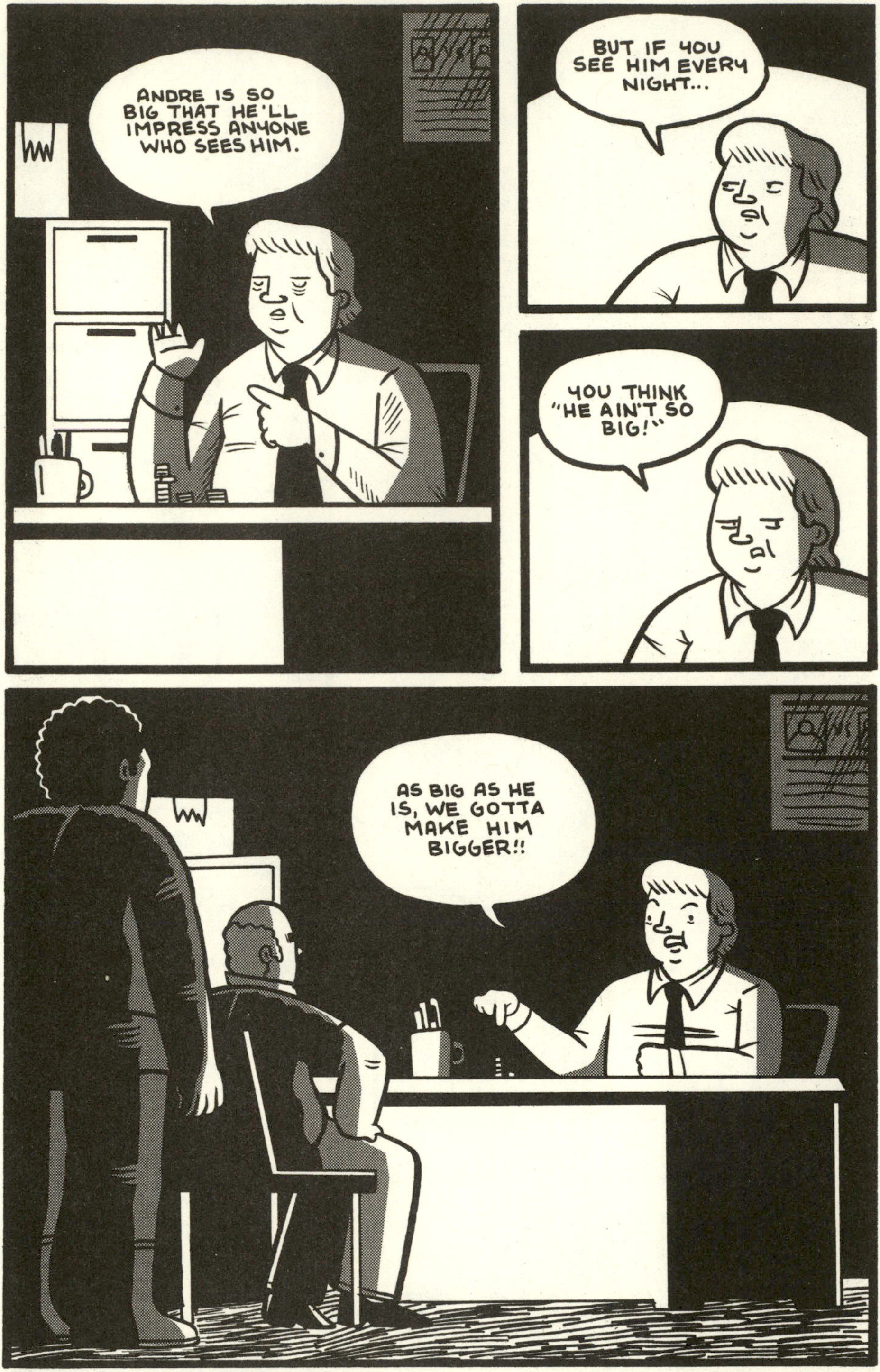
ANDRE IS SO BIG THAT HE'LL IMPRESS ANYONE WHO SEES HIM.
BUT IF YOU SEE HIM EVERY NIGHT...
YOU THINK "HE AIN'T SO BIG!"
AS BIG AS HE IS, WE GOTTA MAKE HIM BIGGER!!

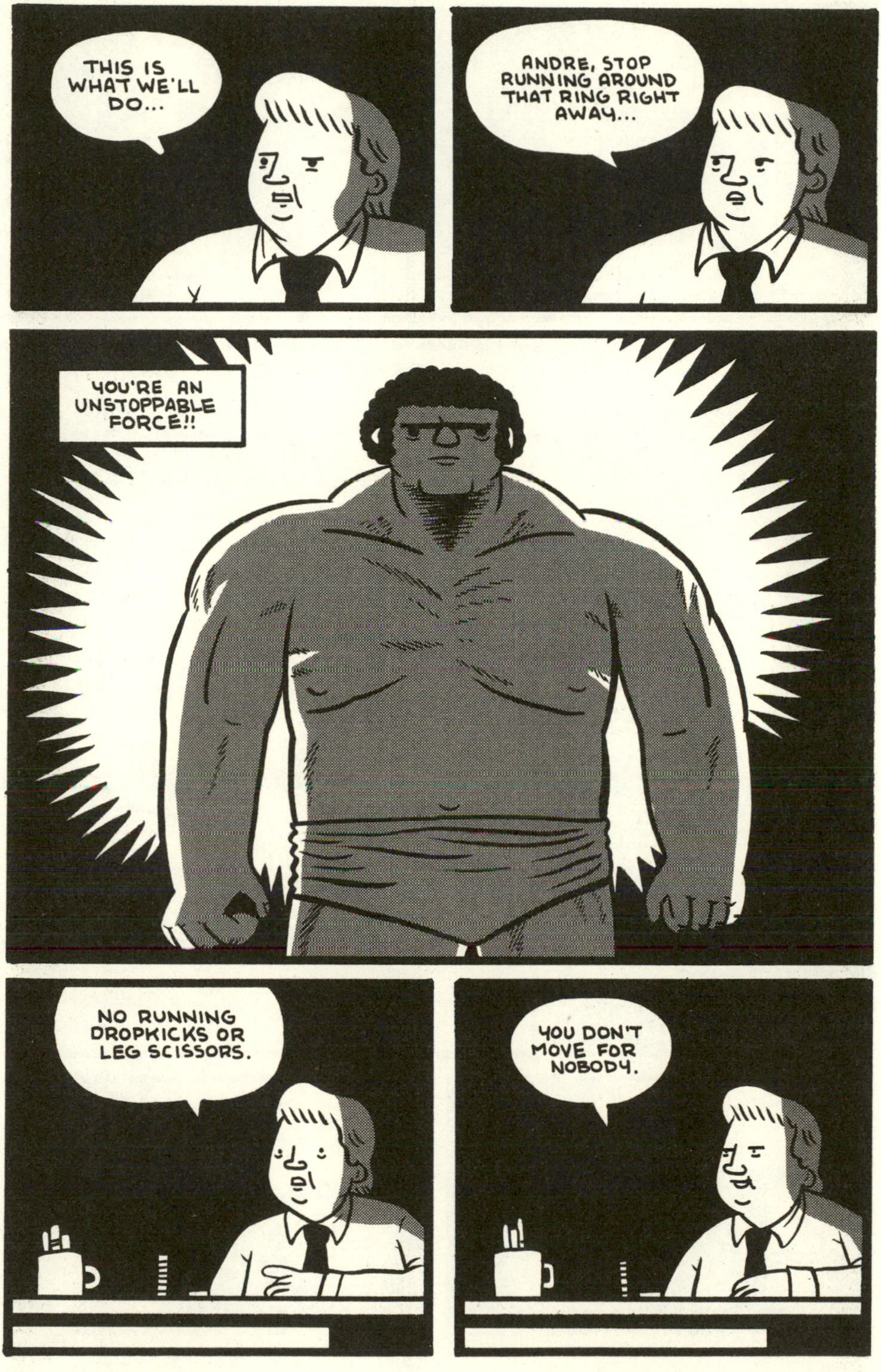
THIS IS WHAT WE'LL DO...
ANDRE, STOP RUNNING AROUND THAT RING RIGHT AWAY...
YOU'RE AN UNSTOPPABLE FORCE!!
NO RUNNING DROPKICKS OR LEG SCISSORS.
YOU DON'T MOVE FOR NOBODY.

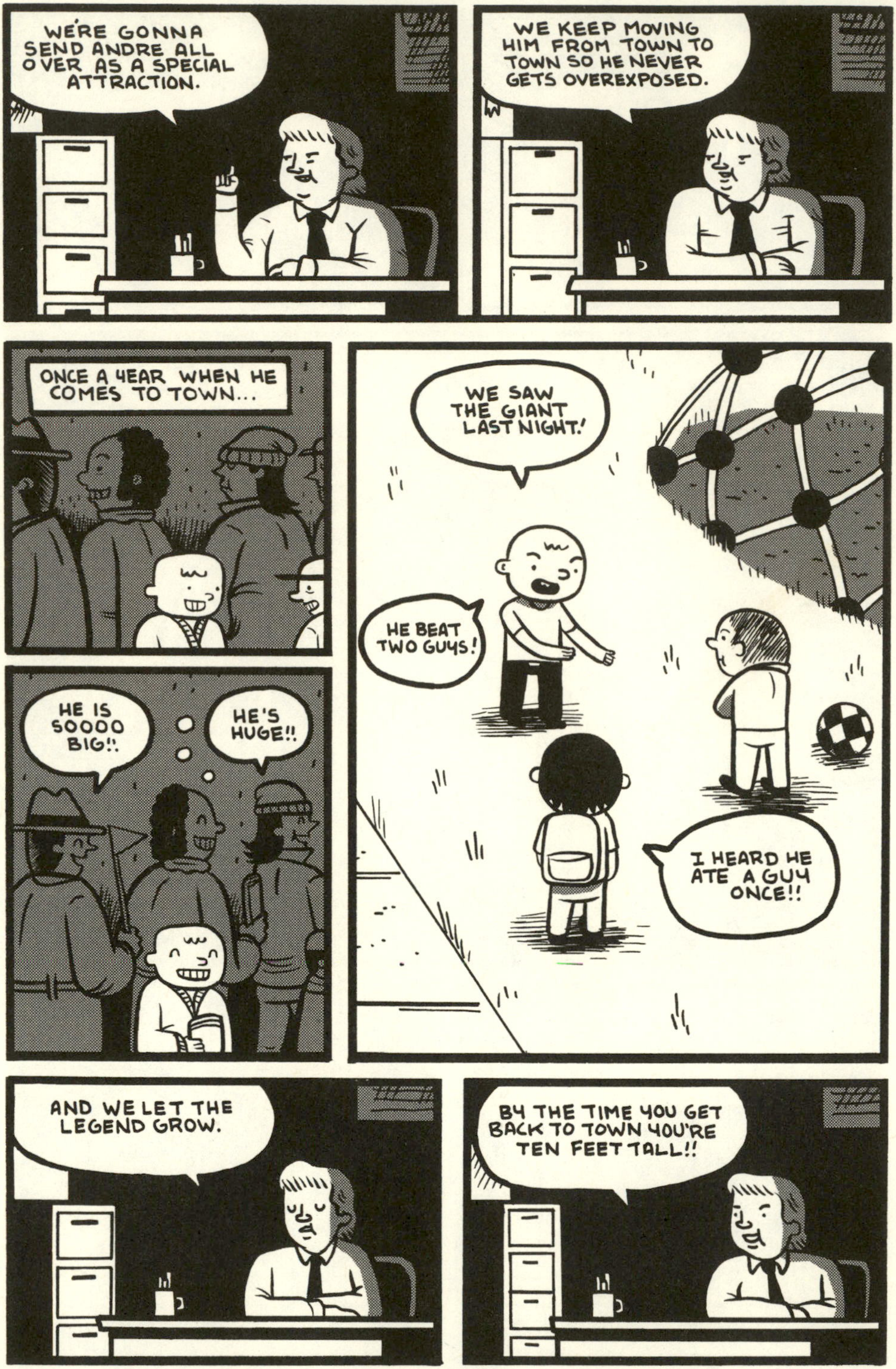
WE'RE GONNA SEND ANDRE ALL OVER AS A SPECIAL ATTRACTION.
WE KEEP MOVING HIM FROM TOWN TO TOWN SO HE NEVER GETS OVEREXPOSED.
ONCE A YEAR WHEN HE COMES TO TOWN...
HE IS SOOOO BIG!!
HE'S HUGE!!
WE SAW THE GIANT LAST NIGHT!
HE BEAT TWO GUYS!
I HEARD HE ATE A GUY ONCE!!
AND WE LET THE LEGEND GROW.
BY THE TIME YOU GET BACK TO TOWN YOU'RE TEN FEET TALL!!

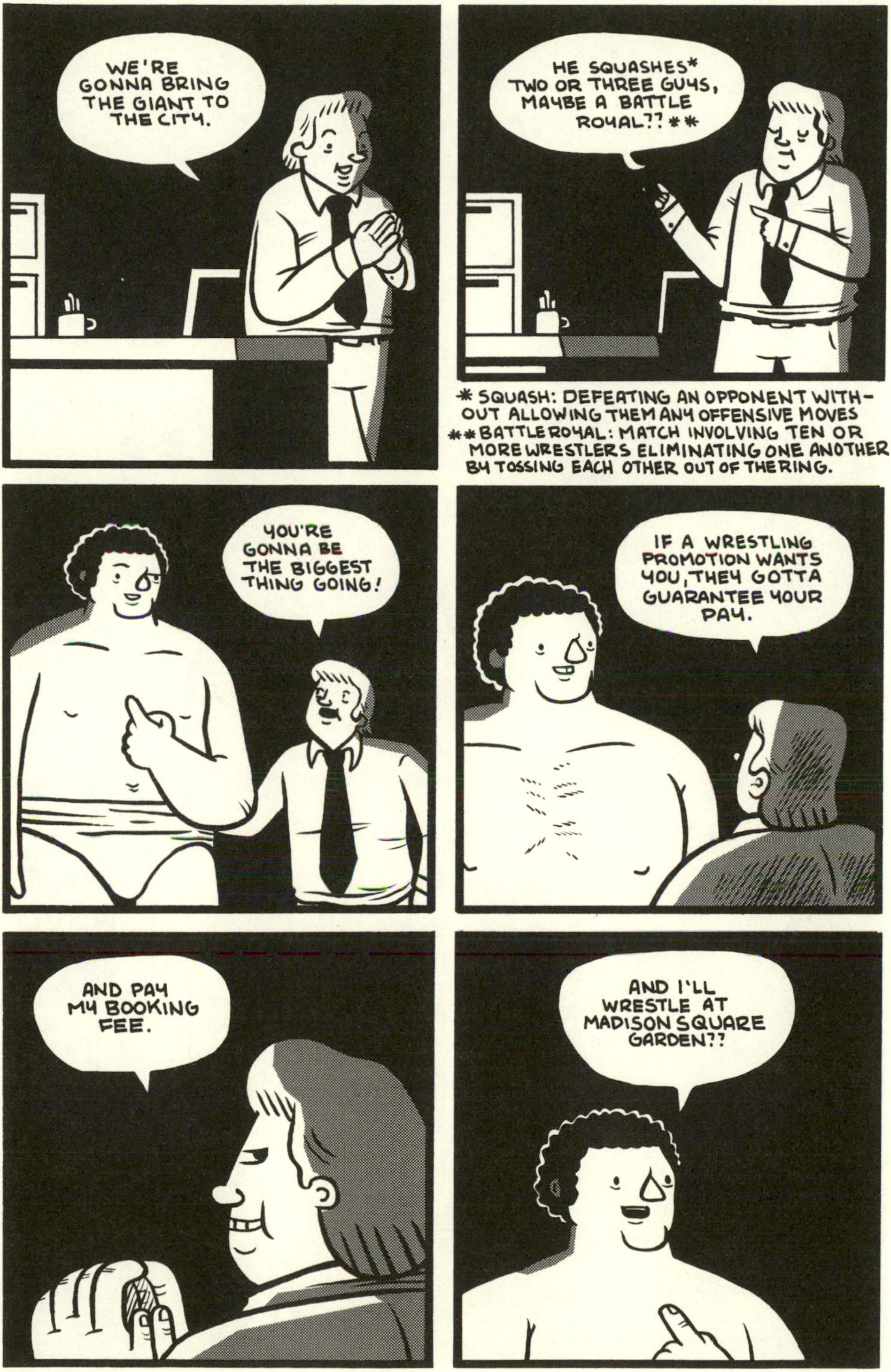
WE'RE GONNA BRING THE GIANT TO THE CITY.
HE SQUASHES* TWO OR THREE GUYS, MAYBE A BATTLE ROYAL?? **
* SQUASH: DEFEATING AN OPPONENT WITHOUT ALLOWING THEM ANY OFFENSIVE MOVES
** BATTLE ROYAL: MATCH INVOLVING TEN OR MORE WRESTLERS ELIMINATING ONE ANOTHER BY TOSSING EACH OTHER OUT OF THE RING.
YOU'RE GONNA BE THE BIGGEST THING GOING!
IF A WRESTLING PROMOTION WANTS YOU, THEY GOTTA GUARANTEE YOUR PAY.
AND PAY MY BOOKING FEE.
AND I'LL WRESTLE AT MADISON SQUARE GARDEN??

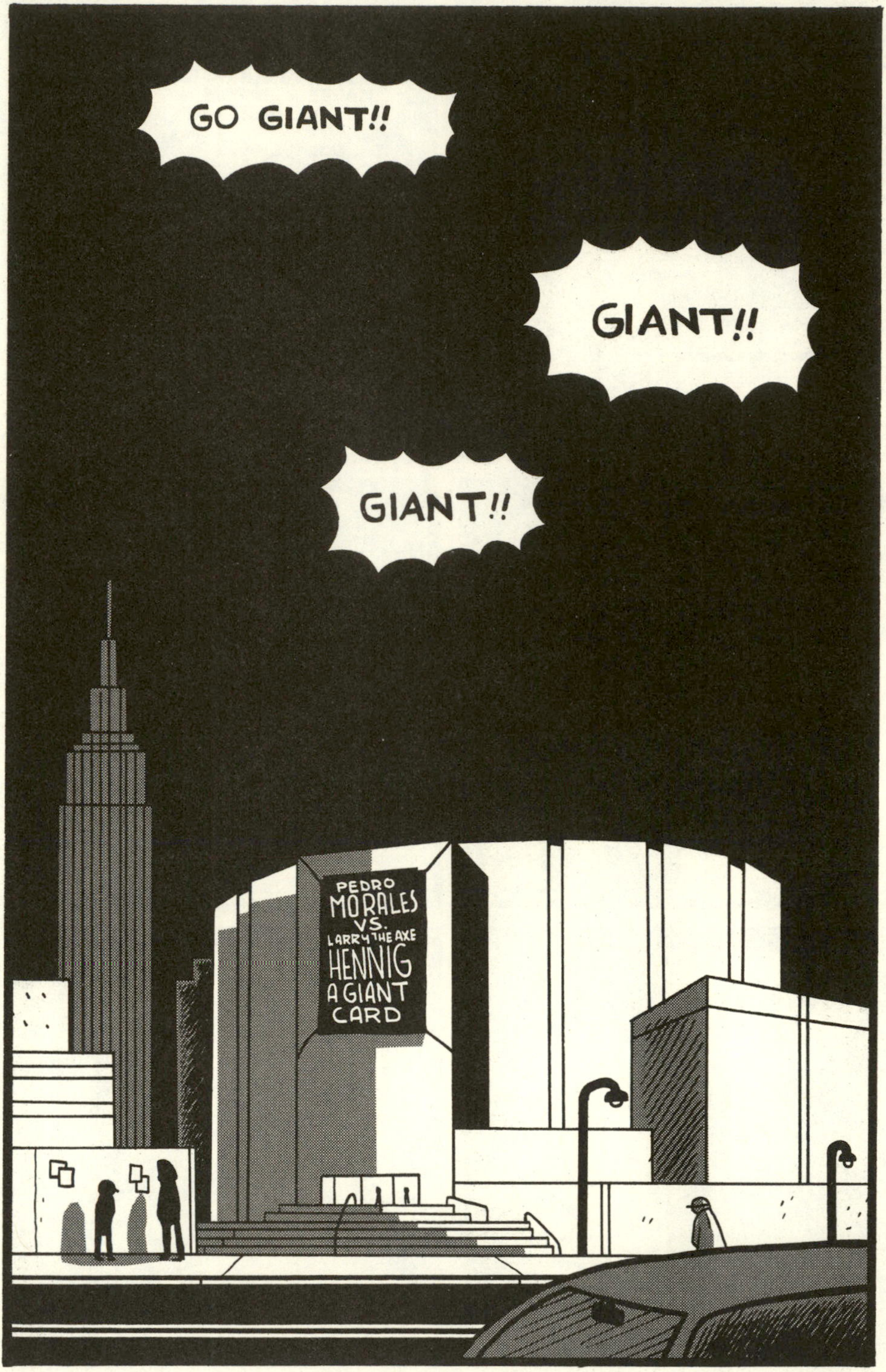
GO GIANT!!
GIANT!!
GIANT!!
PEDRO MORALES VS. LARRY THE AXE HENNIG A GIANT CARD

THE ANATOMY OF A WRESTLING MATCH • LOS ANGELES, 1974

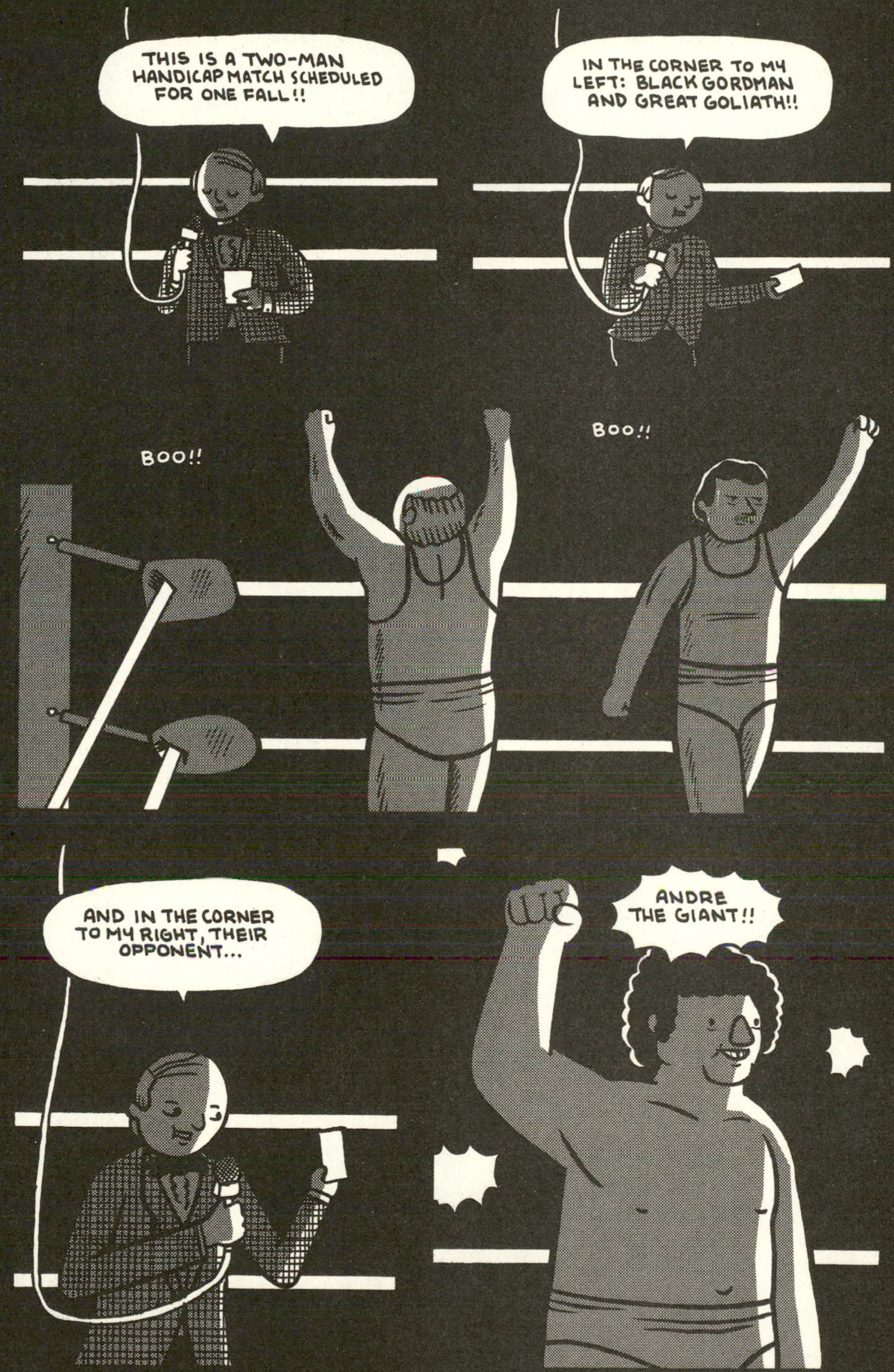
THIS IS A TWO-MAN HANDICAP MATCH SCHEDULED FOR ONE FALL!!
IN THE CORNER TO MY LEFT: BLACK GORDMAN AND GREAT GOLIATH!!
BOO!!
BOO!!
AND IN THE CORNER TO MY RIGHT, THEIR OPPONENT...
ANDRE THE GIANT!!

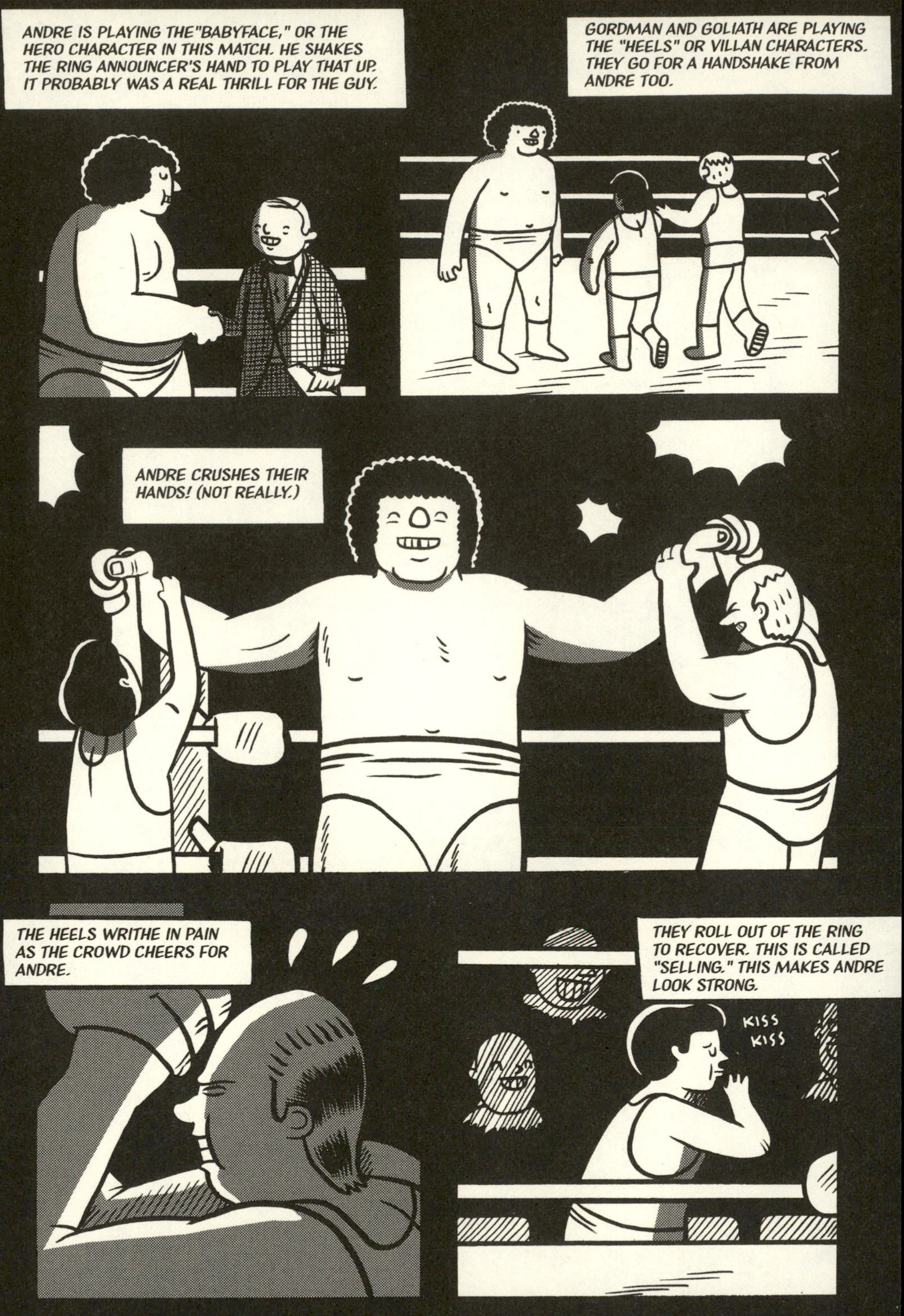
ANDRE IS PLAYING THE "BABYFACE," OR THE HERO CHARACTER IN THIS MATCH. HE SHAKES THE RING ANNOUNCER'S HAND TO PLAY THAT UP. IT PROBABLY WAS A REAL THRILL FOR THE GUY.
GORDMAN AND GOLIATH ARE PLAYING THE "HEELS" OR VILLAN CHARACTERS. THEY GO FOR A HANDSHAKE FROM ANDRE TOO.
ANDRE CRUSHES THEIR HANDS! (NOT REALLY.)
THE HEELS WRITHE IN PAIN AS THE CROWD CHEERS FOR ANDRE.
THEY ROLL OUT OF THE RING TO RECOVER. THIS IS CALLED "SELLING." THIS MAKES ANDRE LOOK STRONG.
KISS
KISS

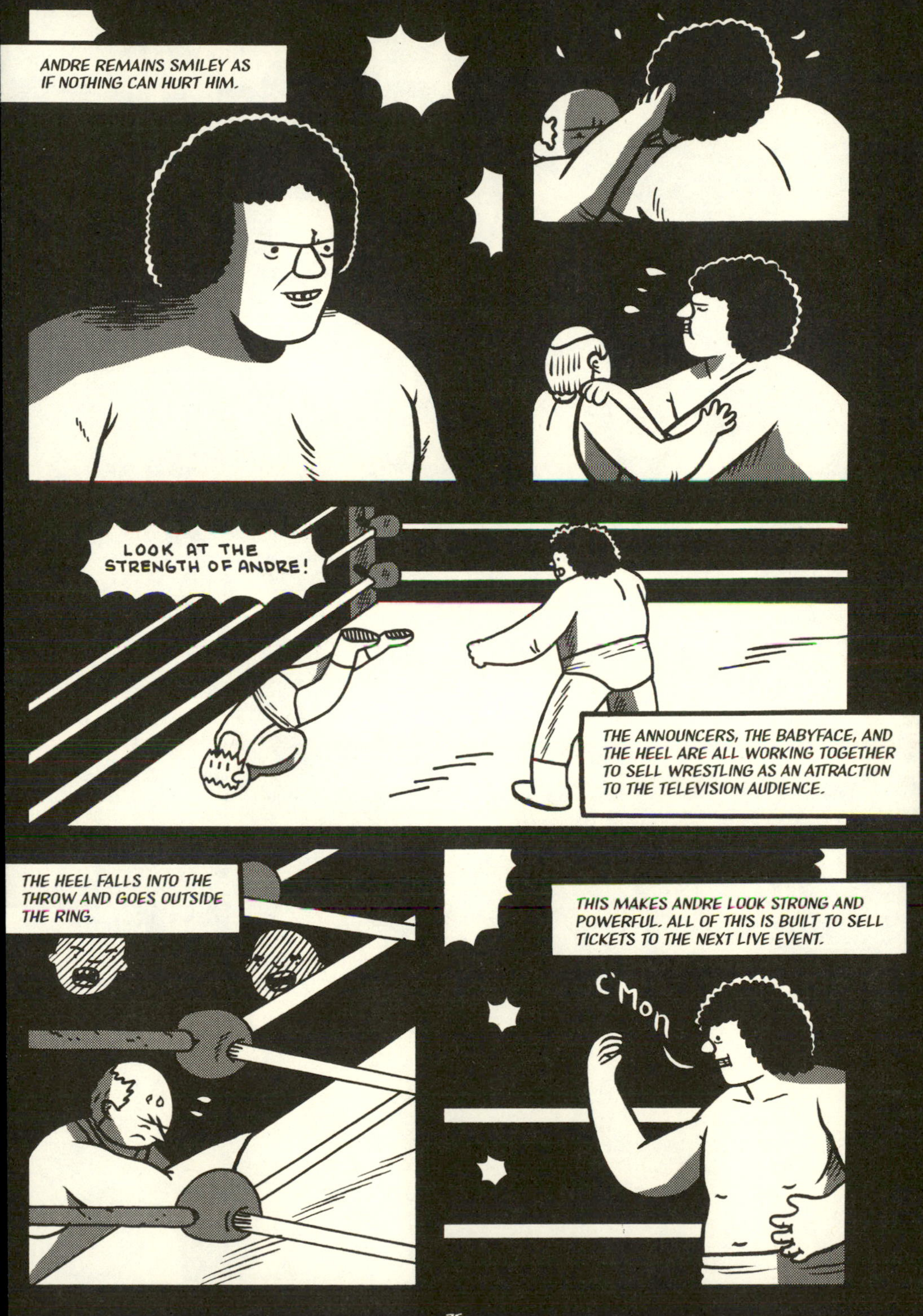
ANDRE REMAINS SMILEY AS IF NOTHING CAN HURT HIM.
LOOK AT THE STRENGTH OF ANDRE!
THE ANNOUNCERS, THE BABYFACE, AND THE HEEL ARE ALL WORKING TOGETHER TO SELL WRESTLING AS AN ATTRACTION TO THE TELEVISION AUDIENCE.
THE HEEL FALLS INTO THE THROW AND GOES OUTSIDE THE RING.
THIS MAKES ANDRE LOOK STRONG AND POWERFUL. ALL OF THIS IS BUILT TO SELL TICKETS TO THE NEXT LIVE EVENT.
C'MON

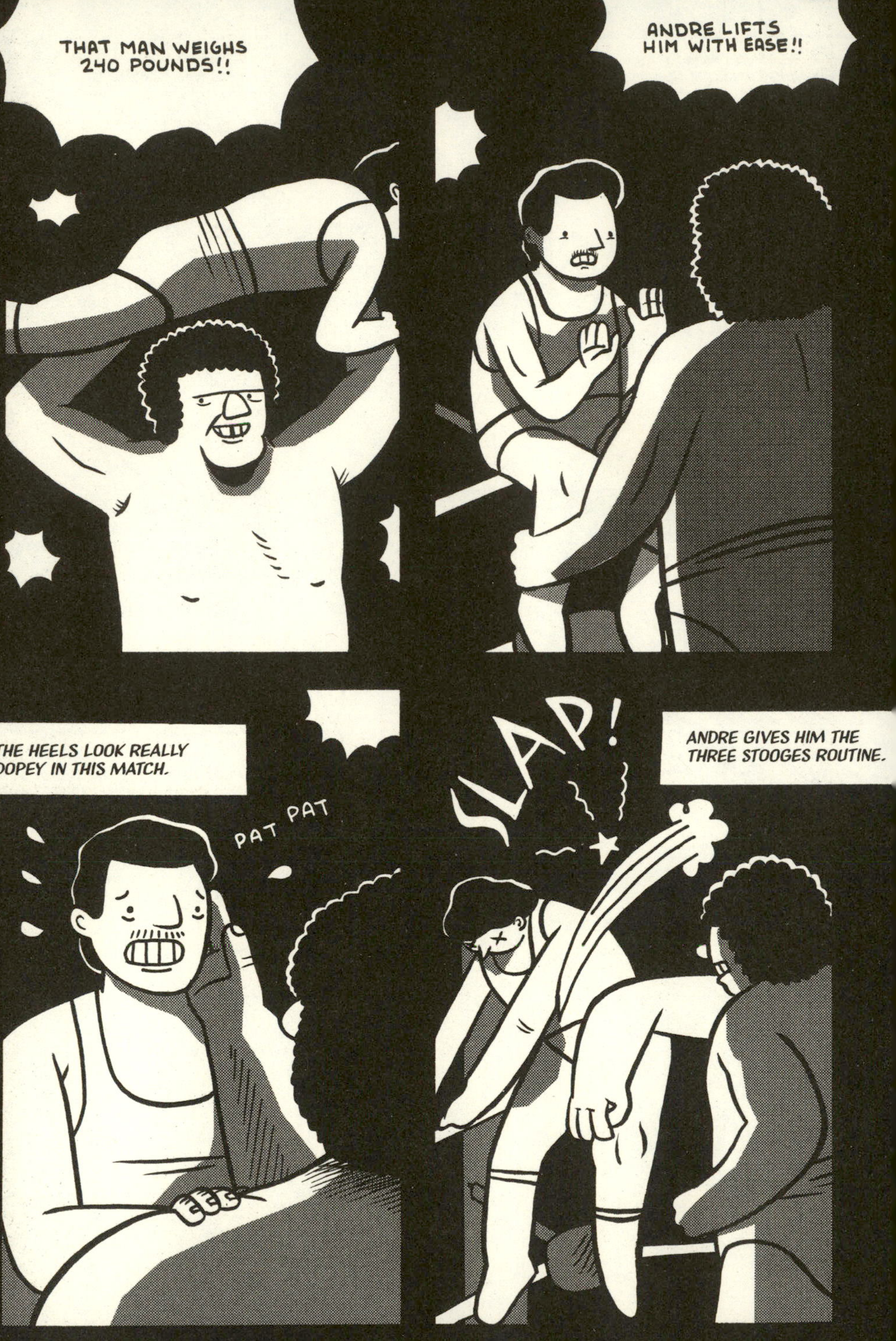
THAT MAN WEIGHS 240 POUNDS!!
ANDRE LIFTS HIM WITH EASE!!
THE HEELS LOOK REALLY DOPEY IN THIS MATCH.
PAT PAT
SLAP!
ANDRE GIVES HIM THE THREE STOOGES ROUTINE.

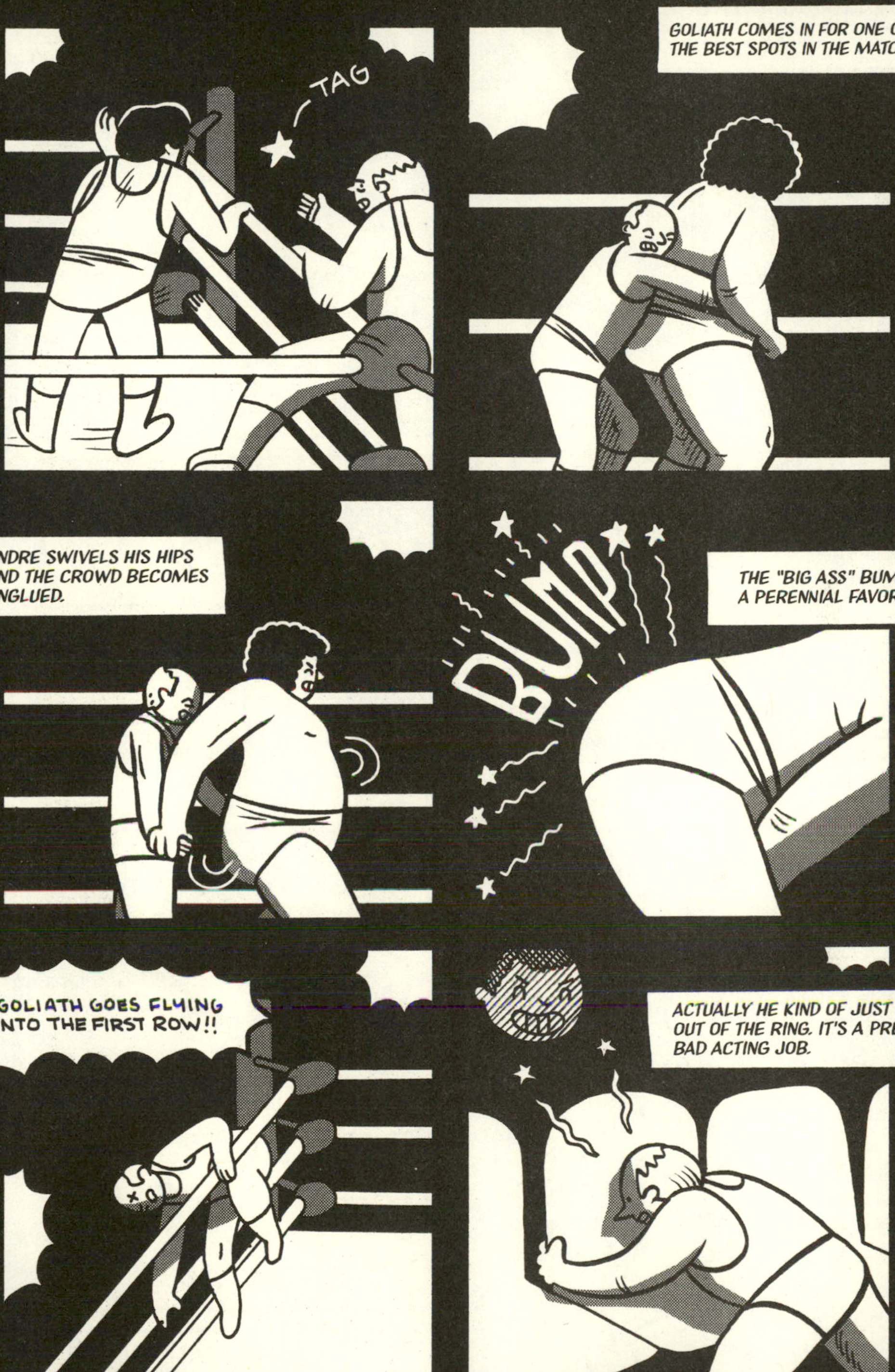
TAG
GOLIATH COMES IN FOR ONE OF THE BEST SPOTS IN THE MATCH.
ANDRE SWIVELS HIS HIPS AND THE CROWD BECOMES UNGLUED.
BUMP
THE "BIG ASS" BUMP IS A PERENNIAL FAVORITE.
GOLIATH GOES FLYING INTO THE FIRST ROW!!
ACTUALLY HE KIND OF JUST FALLS OUT OF THE RING. IT'S A PRETTY BAD ACTING JOB.

THE HEELS DO GET THE UPPER HAND BRIEFLY. THIS BUILDS DRAMA AND ALLOWS THE FANS TO SEE THE HEELS CHEAT.

GORDMAN QUICKLY MOVES OUT OF THE WAY!!

GORDMAN IS REACHING INTO HIS BOOT!!

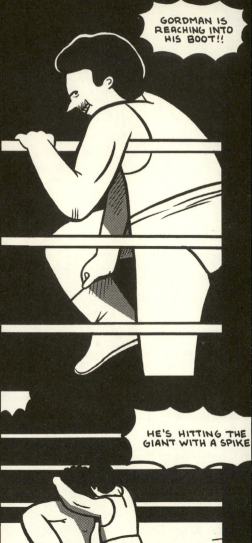

WRESTLERS WOULD CALL THIS WEAPON A "GIMMICK." IT'S PROBABLY A ROLLED UP PIECE OF TAPE.

HE'S HITTING THE GIANT WITH A SPIKE

THE REF IS CONVENIENT[LY] DISTRACTED.

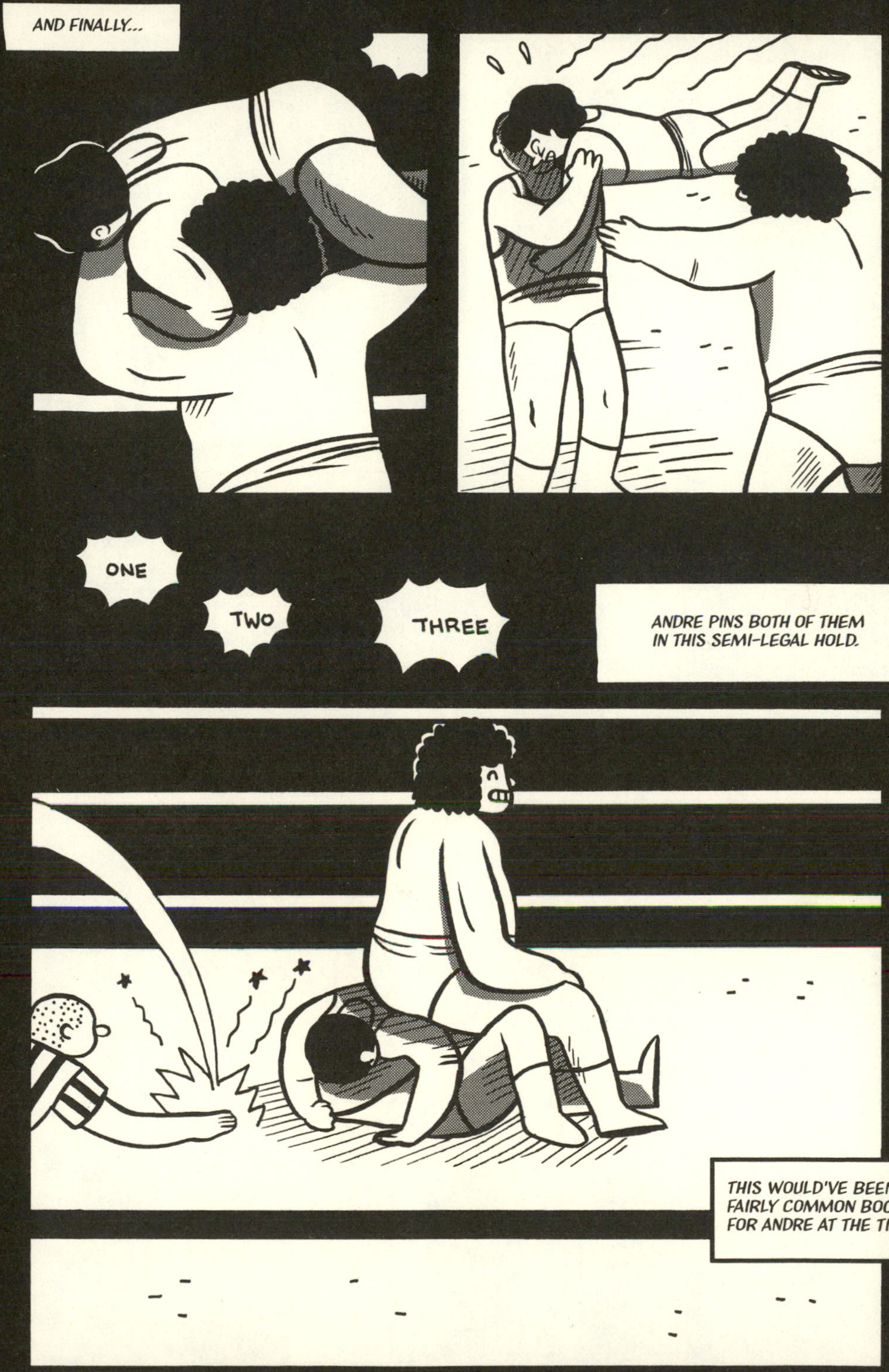
AND FINALLY...
ONE
TWO
THREE
ANDRE PINS BOTH OF THEM IN THIS SEMI-LEGAL HOLD.
THIS WOULD'VE BEEN A FAIRLY COMMON BOOKING FOR ANDRE AT THE TIME.

IN THE SUMMER OF 1974 ANDRE APPEARED ON THE TONIGHT SHOW.

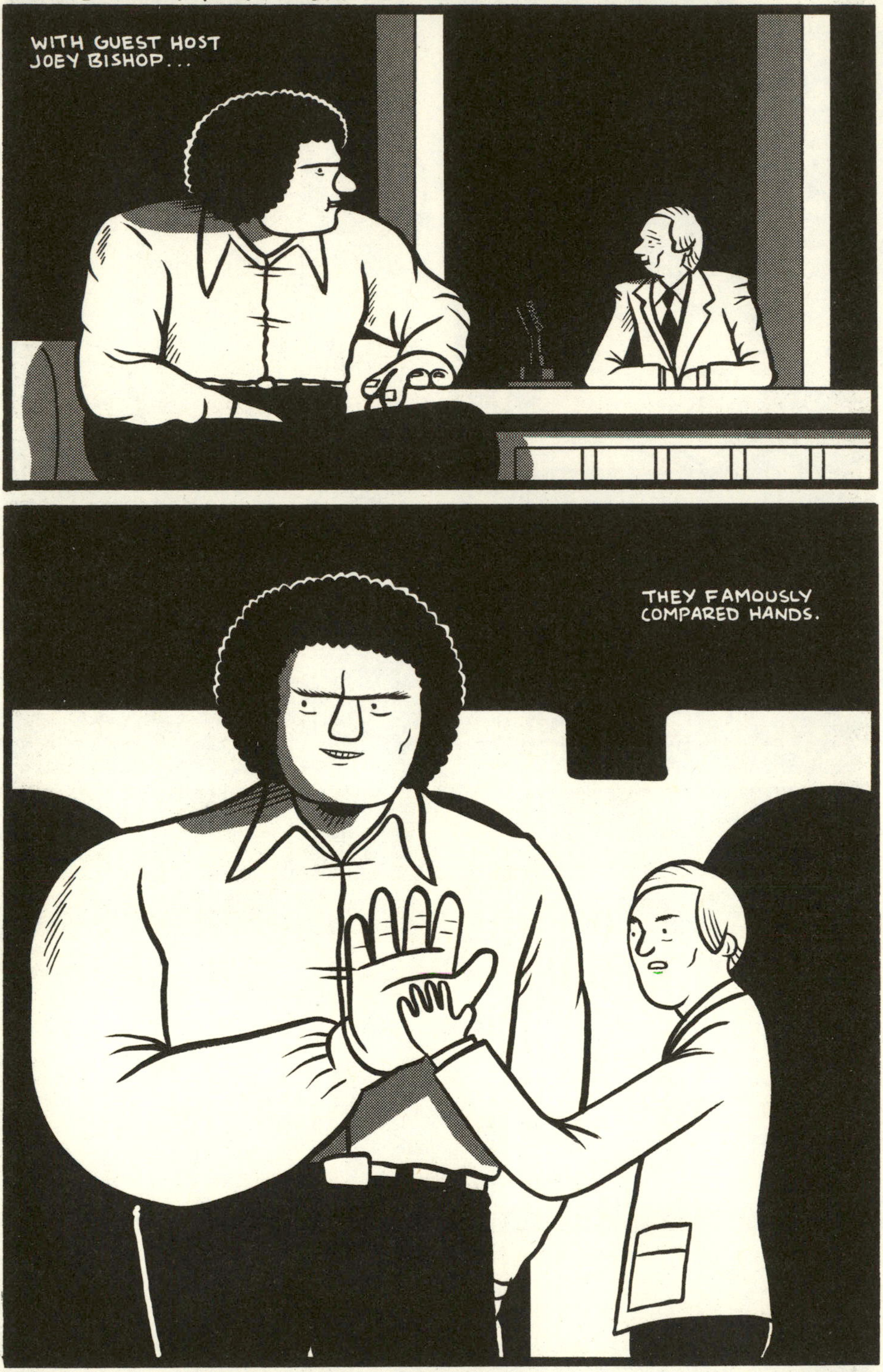
WITH GUEST HOST JOEY BISHOP...
THEY FAMOUSLY COMPARED HANDS.

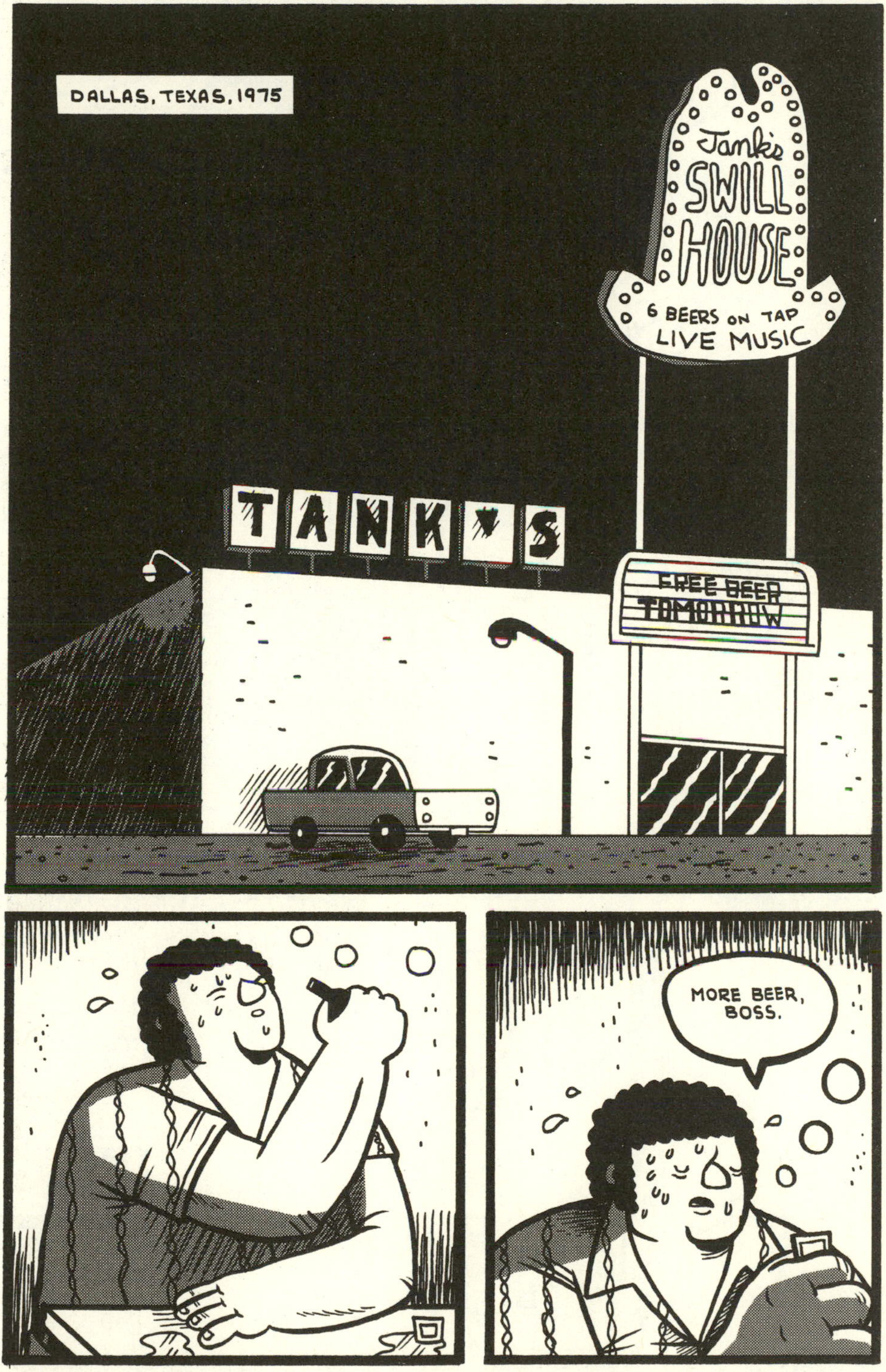

DALLAS, TEXAS, 1975
Tank's SWILL HOUSE
6 BEERS ON TAP
LIVE MUSIC
TANK'S
FREE BEER TOMORROW
MORE BEER, BOSS.

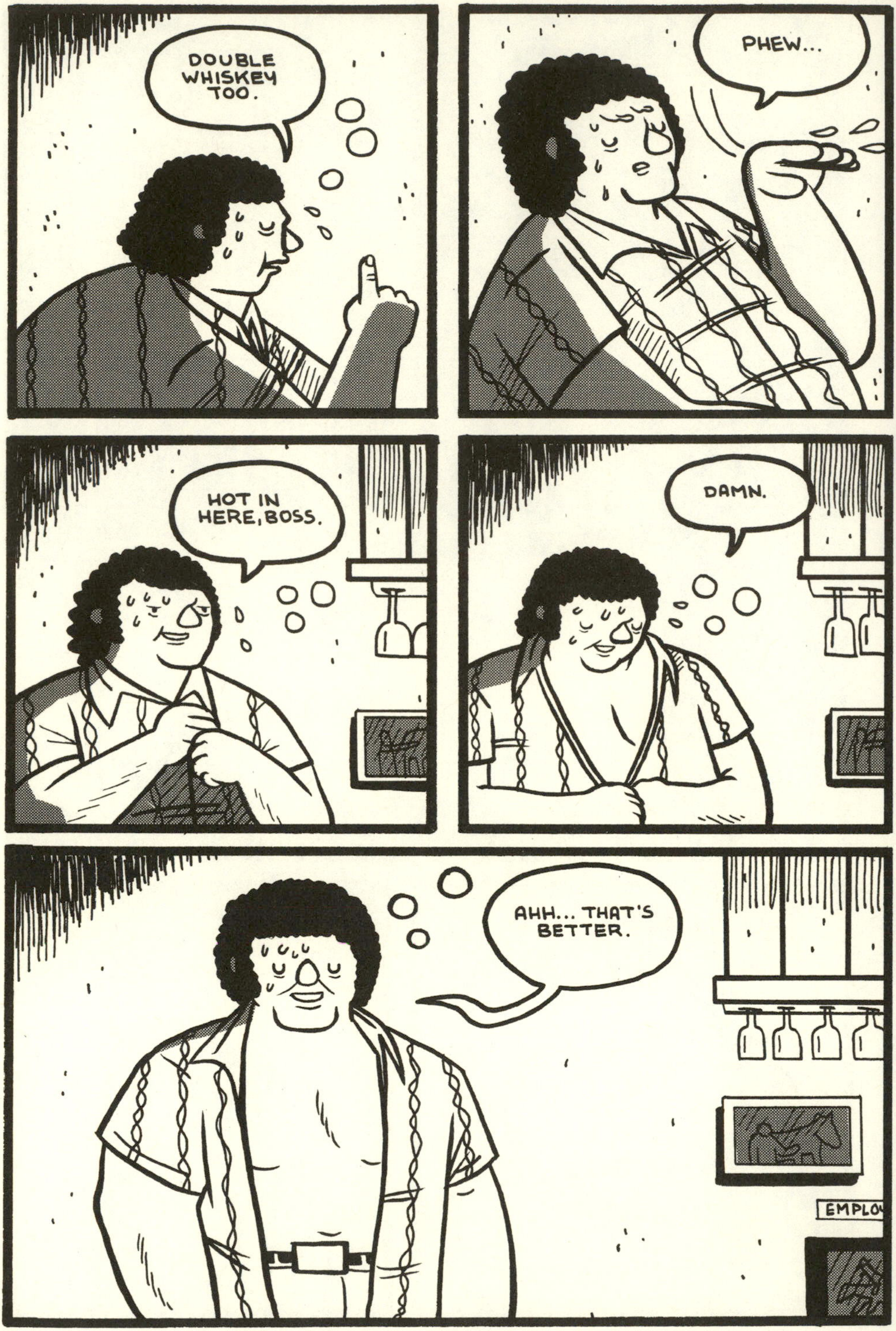
DOUBLE WHISKEY TOO.
PHEW...
HOT IN HERE, BOSS.
DAMN.
AHH... THAT'S BETTER.
EMPLO

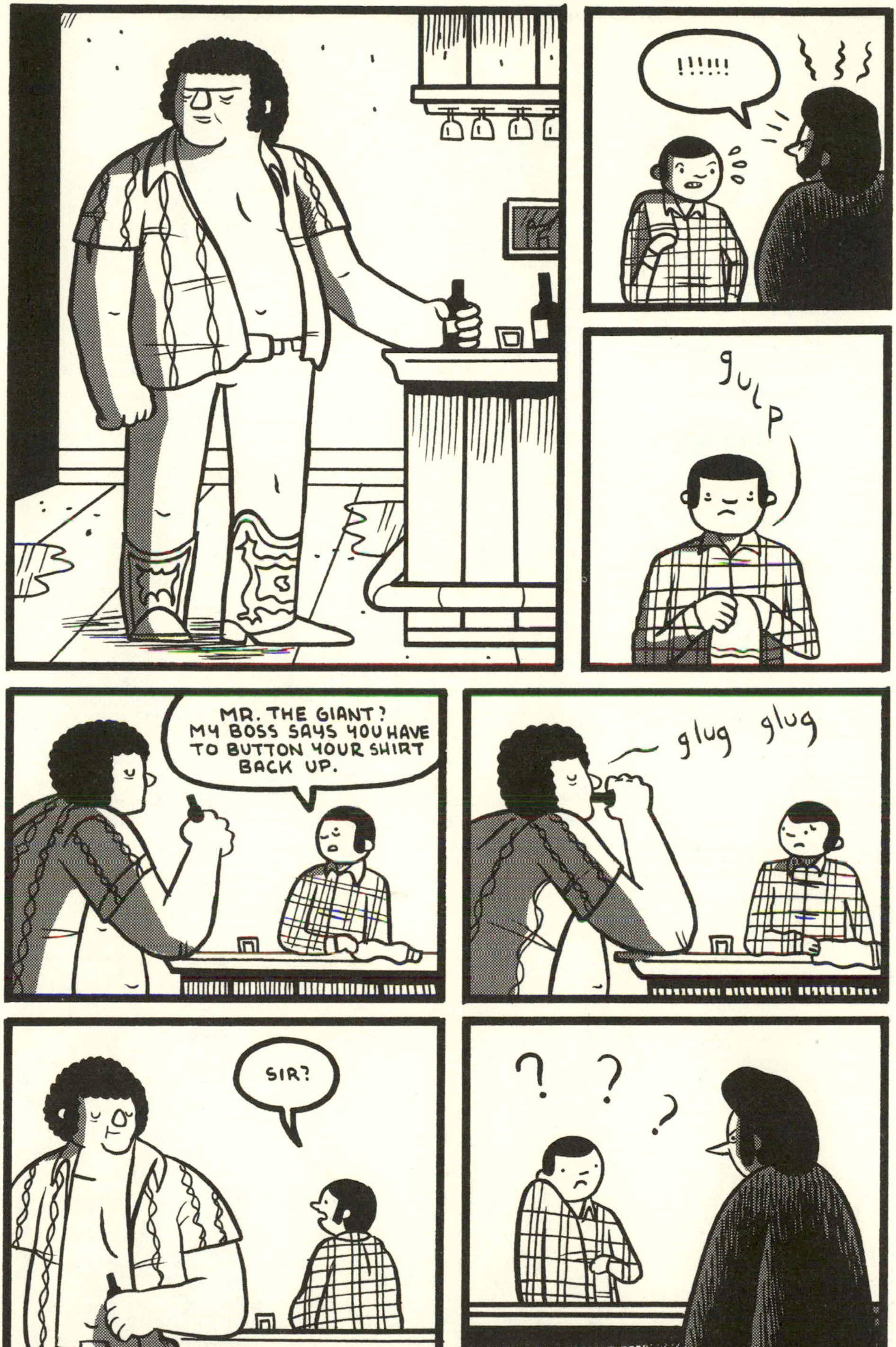
!!!!!!
gulp
MR. THE GIANT? MY BOSS SAYS YOU HAVE TO BUTTON YOUR SHIRT BACK UP.
glug glug
SIR?
? ? ?

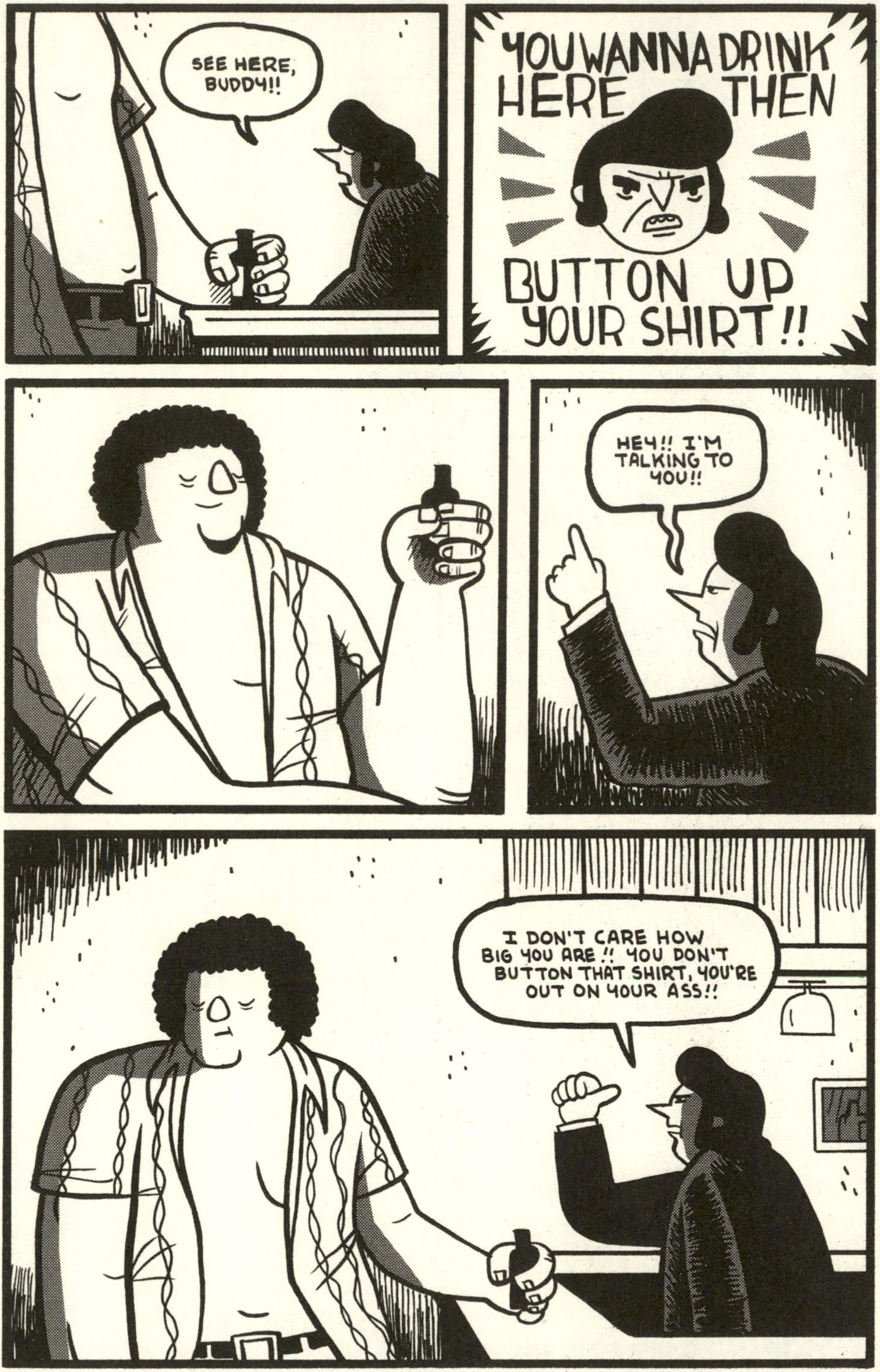

SEE HERE, BUDDY!!
YOU WANNA DRINK HERE THEN BUTTON UP YOUR SHIRT!!
HEY!! I'M TALKING TO YOU!!
I DON'T CARE HOW BIG YOU ARE!! YOU DON'T BUTTON THAT SHIRT, YOU'RE OUT ON YOUR ASS!!

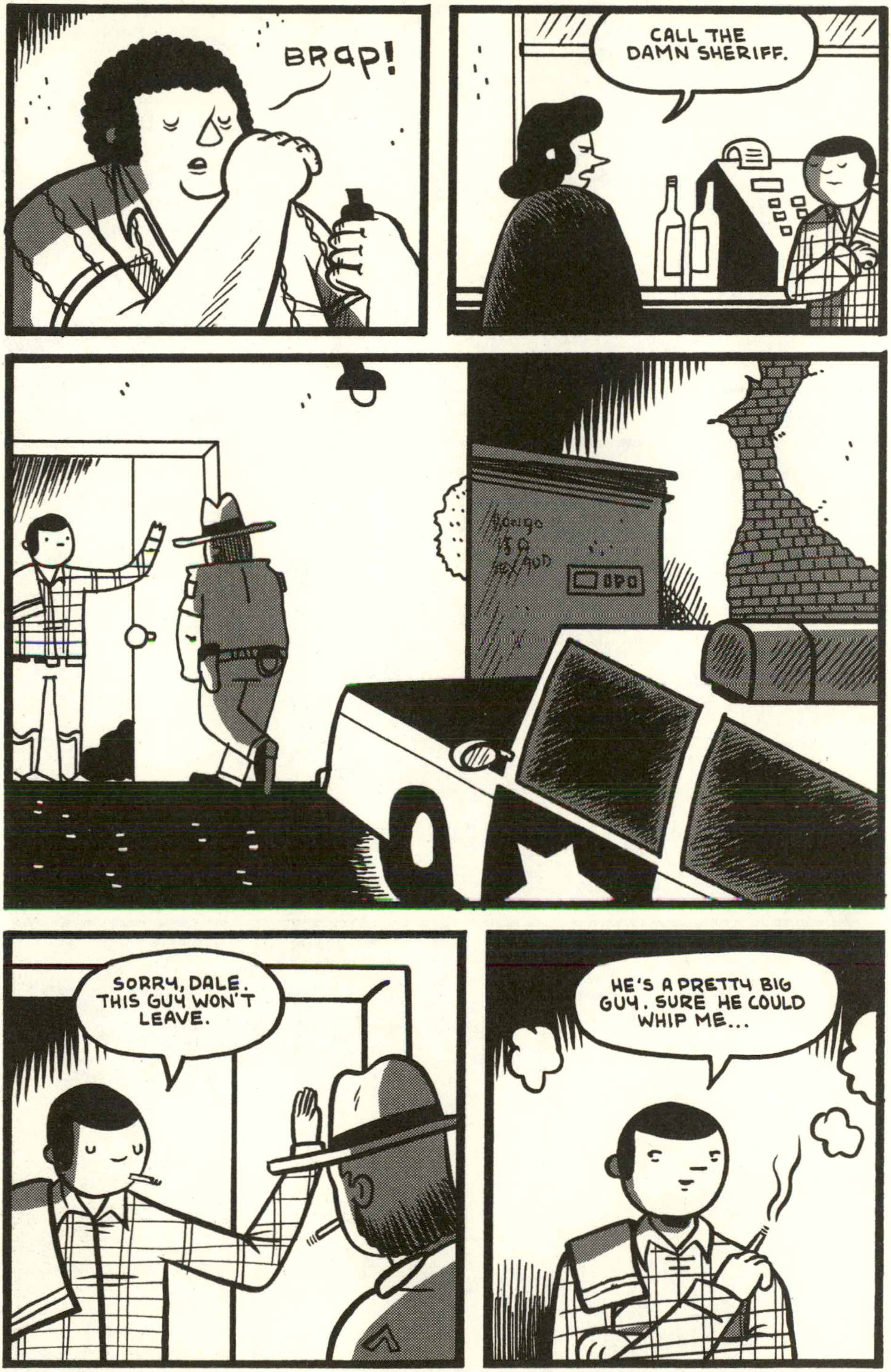
BRAP!
CALL THE DAMN SHERIFF.
SORRY, DALE. THIS GUY WON'T LEAVE.
HE'S A PRETTY BIG GUY. SURE HE COULD WHIP ME...

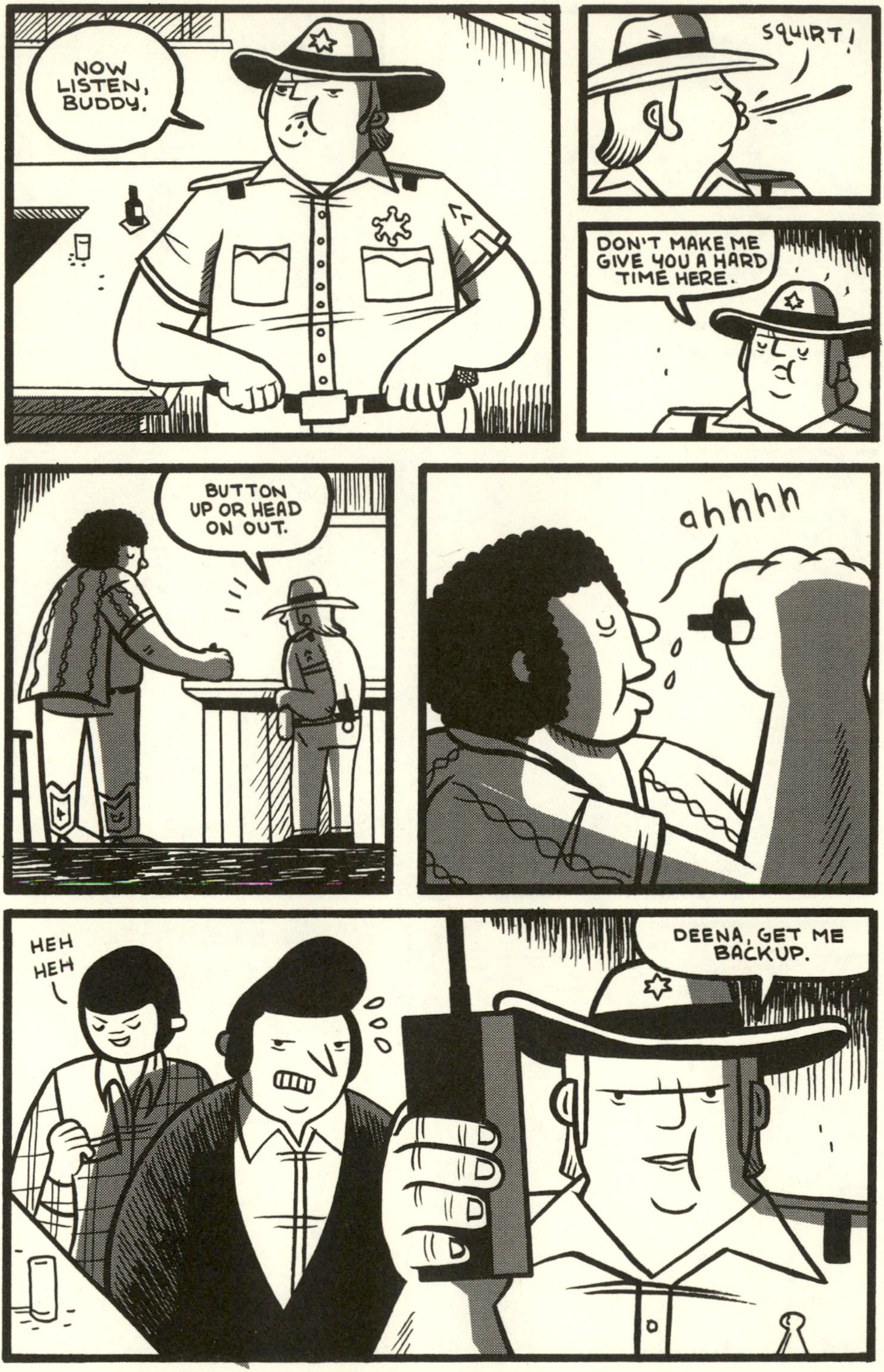
NOW LISTEN, BUDDY.
SQUIRT!
DON'T MAKE ME GIVE YOU A HARD TIME HERE.
BUTTON UP OR HEAD ON OUT.
ahhhh
HEH HEH
DEENA, GET ME BACKUP.

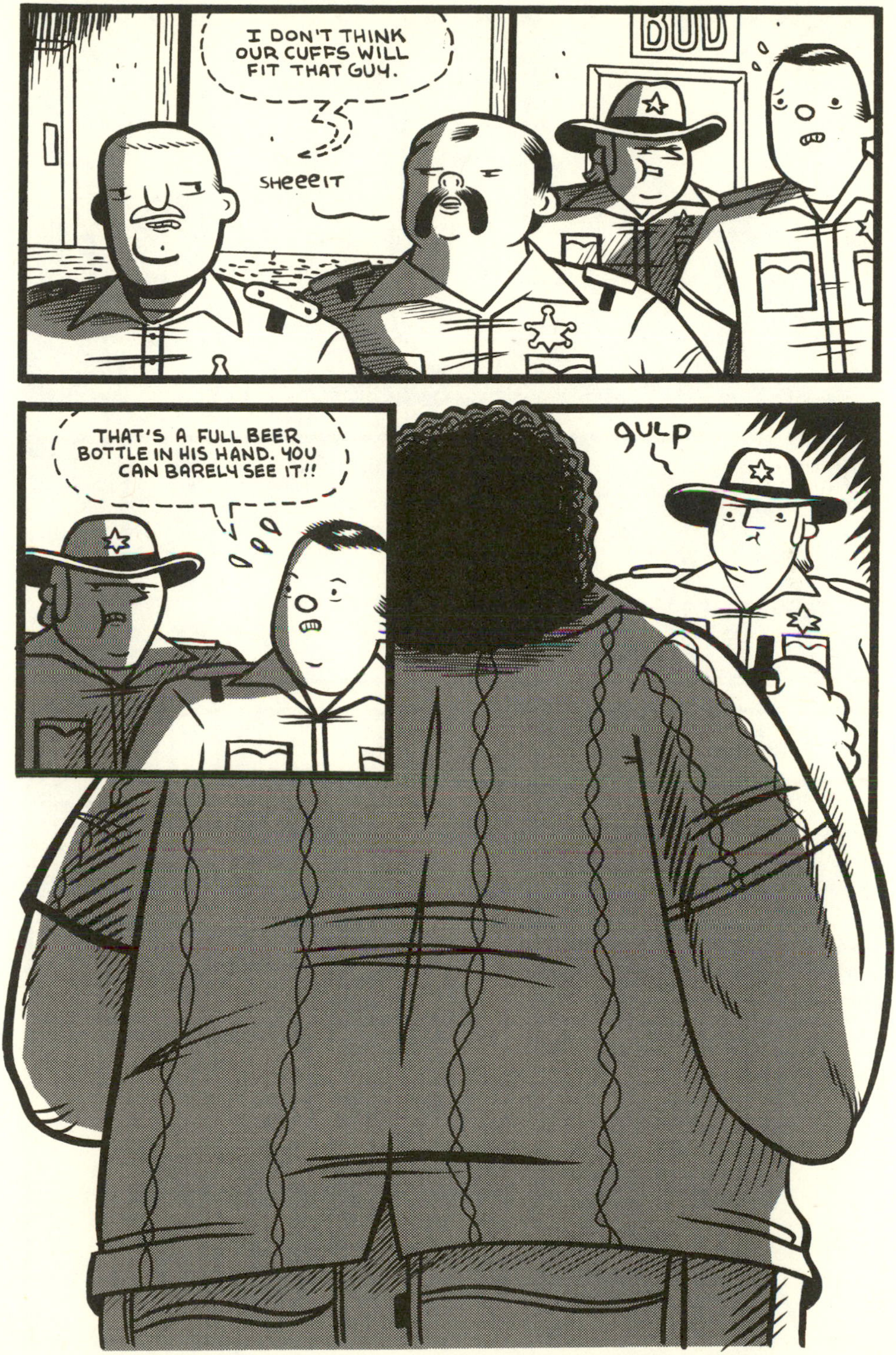
BUD
I DON'T THINK OUR CUFFS WILL FIT THAT GUY.
SHEEEIT
THAT'S A FULL BEER BOTTLE IN HIS HAND. YOU CAN BARELY SEE IT!!
GULP

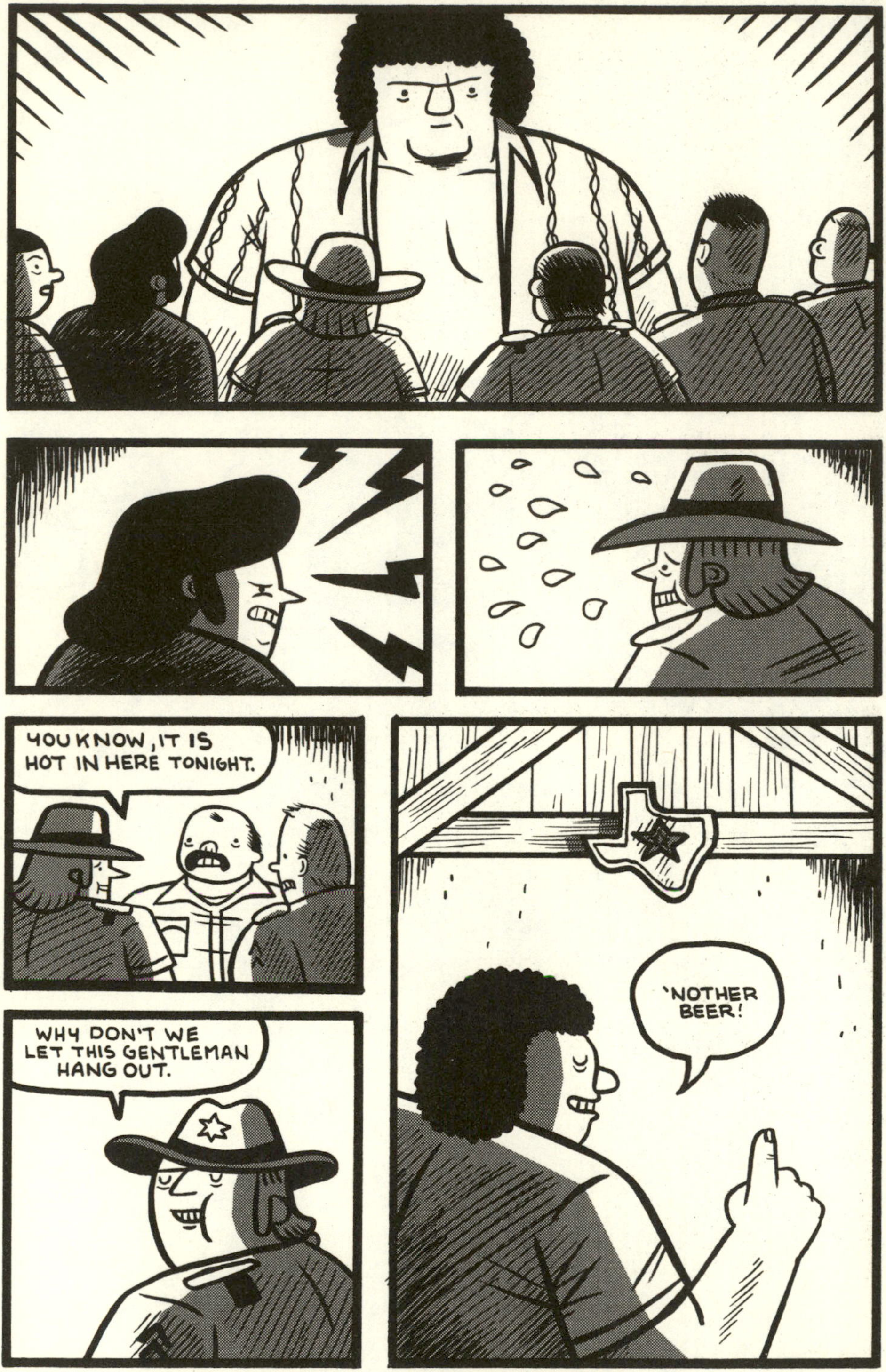
YOU KNOW, IT IS HOT IN HERE TONIGHT.
WHY DON'T WE LET THIS GENTLEMAN HANG OUT.
'NOTHER BEER!

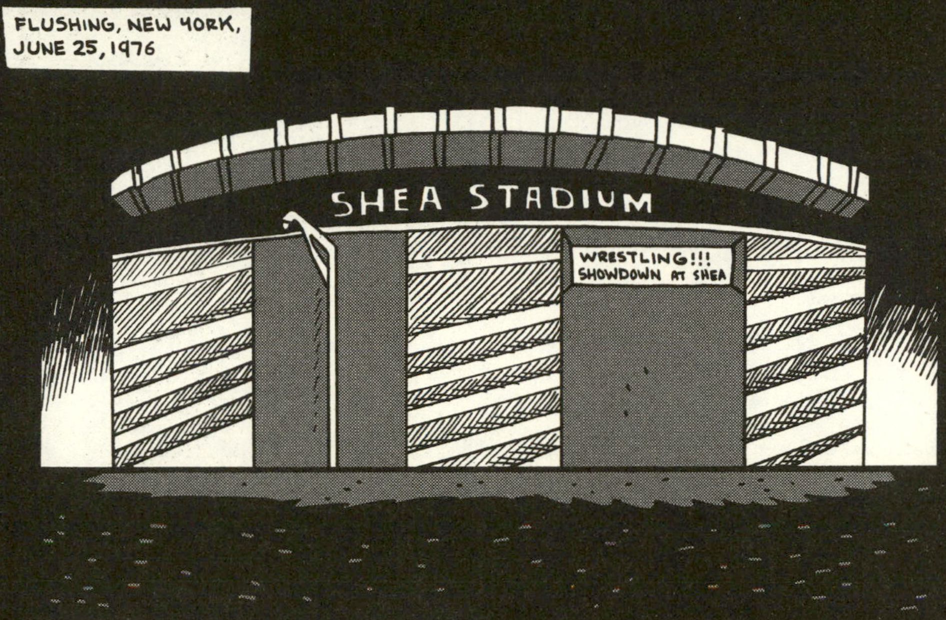
FLUSHING, NEW YORK,
JUNE 25, 1976
SHEA STADIUM
WRESTLING!!!
SHOWDOWN AT SHEA

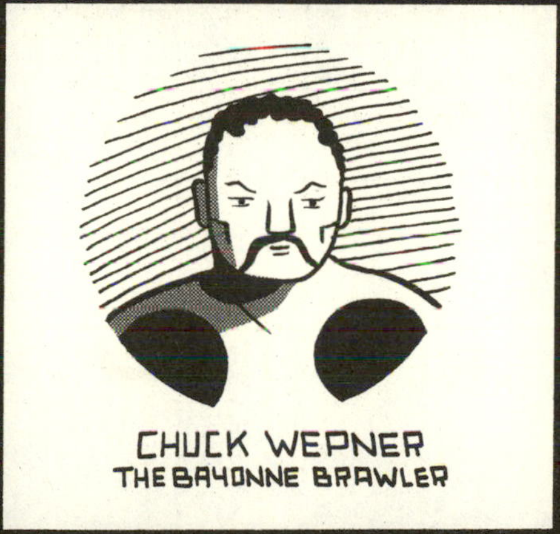
CHUCK WEPNER
THE BAYONNE BRAWLER

CHUCK WEPNER WAS A BOXER FROM BAYONNE, NEW JERSEY. ONE YEAR EARLIER HE'D FOUGHT MUHAMMAD ALI. HE WENT THE DISTANCE, LASTING FIFTEEN ROUNDS, BEFORE LOSING THE DECISION.

*HIS STORY INSPIRED THE FILM **ROCKY**.*

TONIGHT HIS OPPONENT IS...

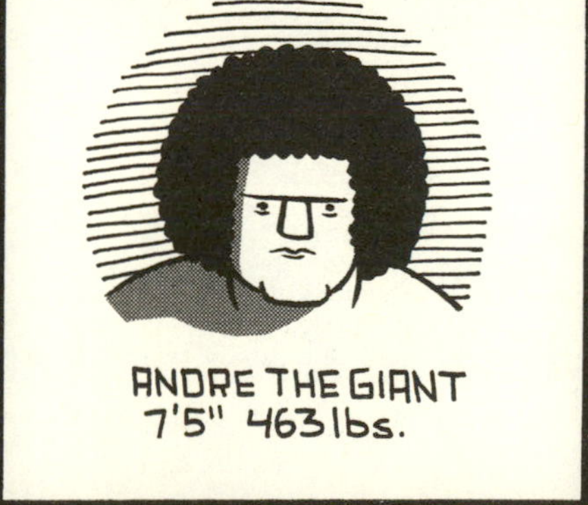
ANDRE THE GIANT
7'5" 463lbs.

IN THE DAYS BEFORE PAY-PER-VIEW, THEY WOULD SELL TICKETS TO WATCH BIG EVENTS AT BARS AND SMALL THEATERS ON CLOSED CIRCUIT TV.

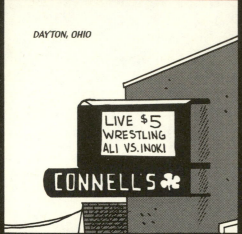

DAYTON, OHIO

LIVE $5 WRESTLING ALI VS. INOKI

CONNELL'S

ST. LOUIS, MISSOURI

Jake's

TONITE

THE ANDRE VS. WEPNER MATCH WASN'T EVEN THE MAIN EVENT THAT NIGHT. THE SHOW WAS HEADLINED BY ANTONIO INOKI, CHAMPION JAPANESE WRESTLER, VS. BOXER MUHAMMAD ALI.

IT WAS BEAMED TO ALL LOCATIONS LIVE FROM JAPAN

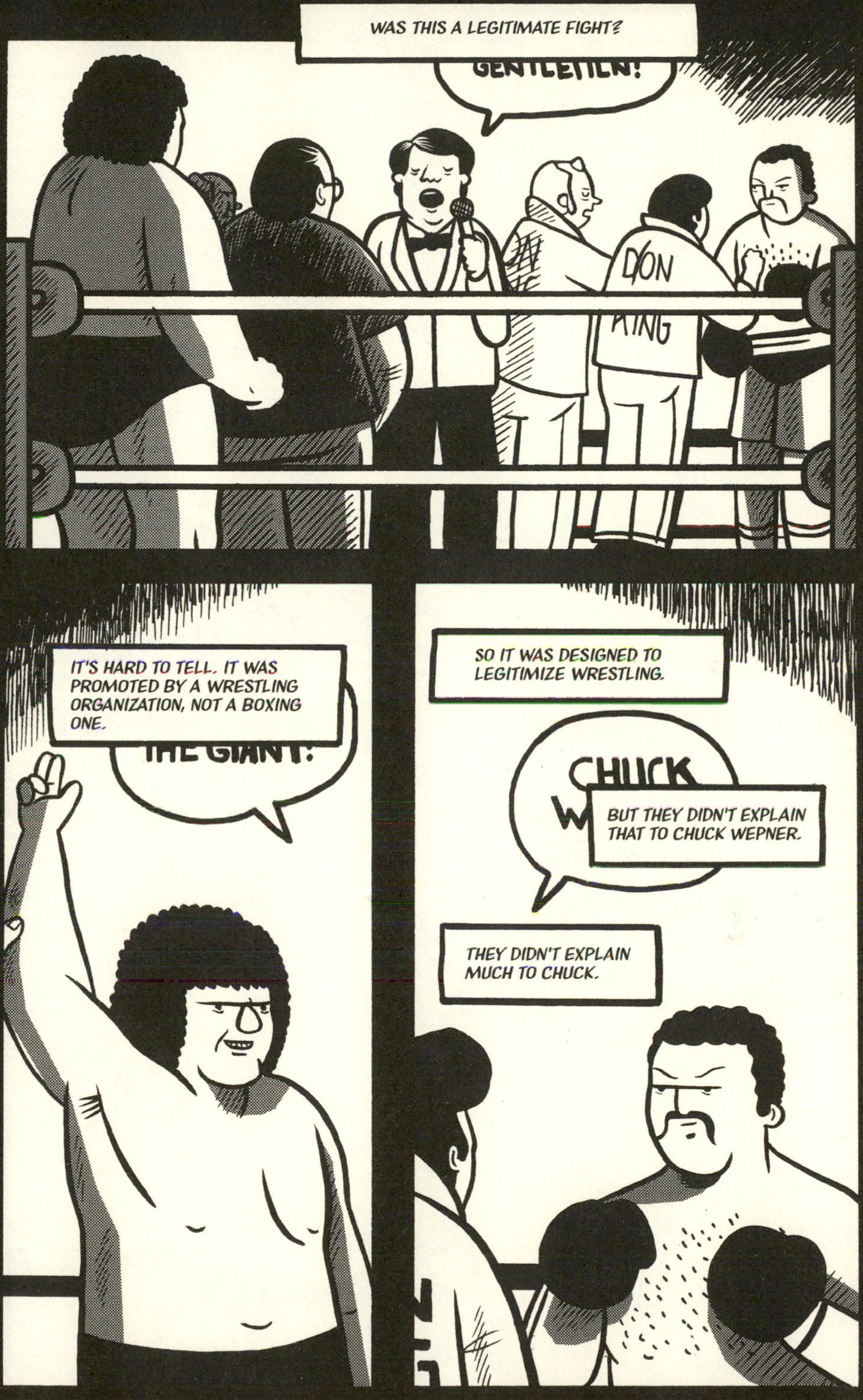

WAS THIS A LEGITIMATE FIGHT?
GENTLEMEN!
DON KING
IT'S HARD TO TELL. IT WAS PROMOTED BY A WRESTLING ORGANIZATION, NOT A BOXING ONE.
THE GIANT!
SO IT WAS DESIGNED TO LEGITIMIZE WRESTLING.
CHUCK
BUT THEY DIDN'T EXPLAIN THAT TO CHUCK WEPNER.
THEY DIDN'T EXPLAIN MUCH TO CHUCK.

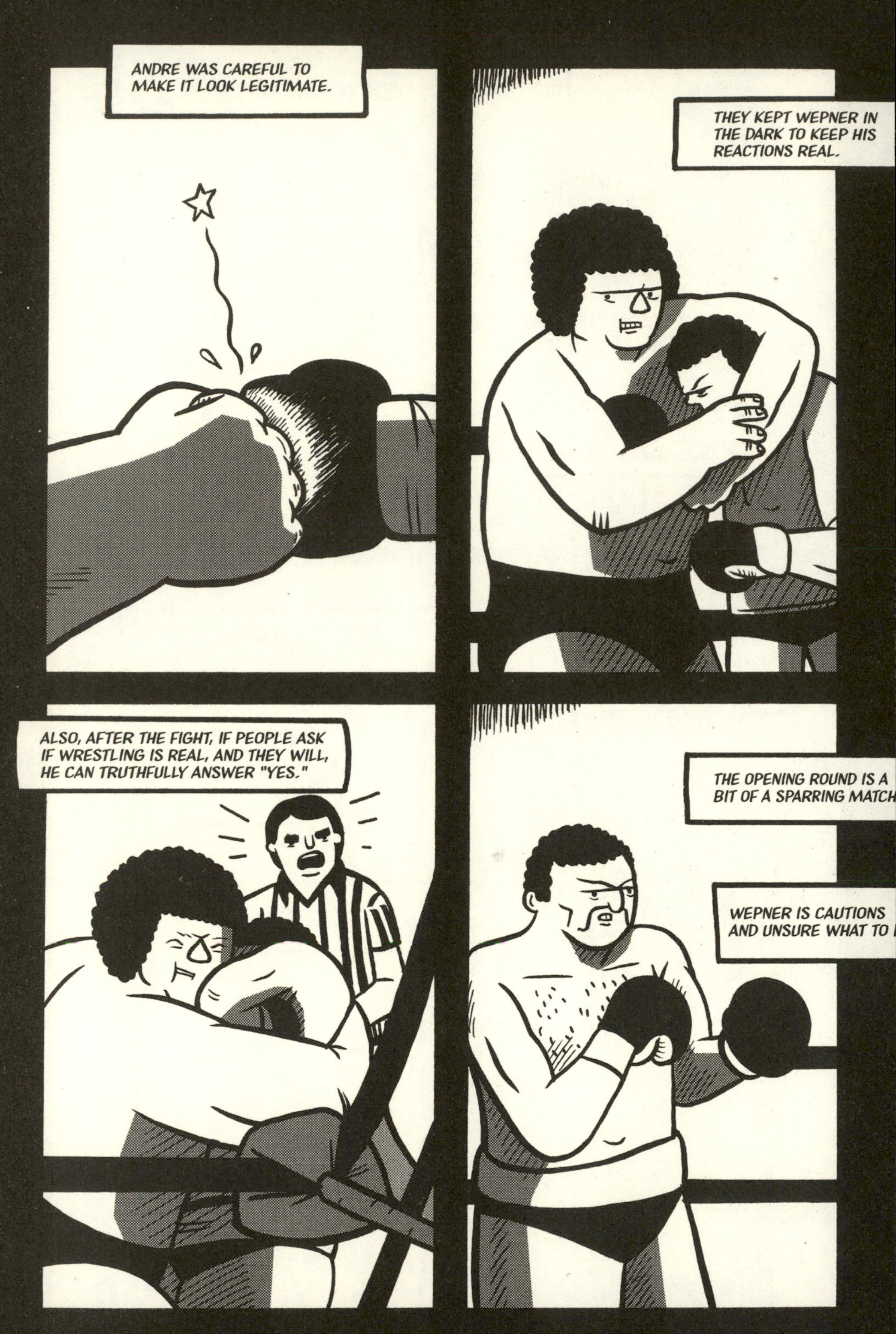
ANDRE WAS CAREFUL TO MAKE IT LOOK LEGITIMATE.
THEY KEPT WEPNER IN THE DARK TO KEEP HIS REACTIONS REAL.
ALSO, AFTER THE FIGHT, IF PEOPLE ASK IF WRESTLING IS REAL, AND THEY WILL, HE CAN TRUTHFULLY ANSWER "YES."
THE OPENING ROUND IS A BIT OF A SPARRING MATCH
WEPNER IS CAUTIONS AND UNSURE WHAT TO

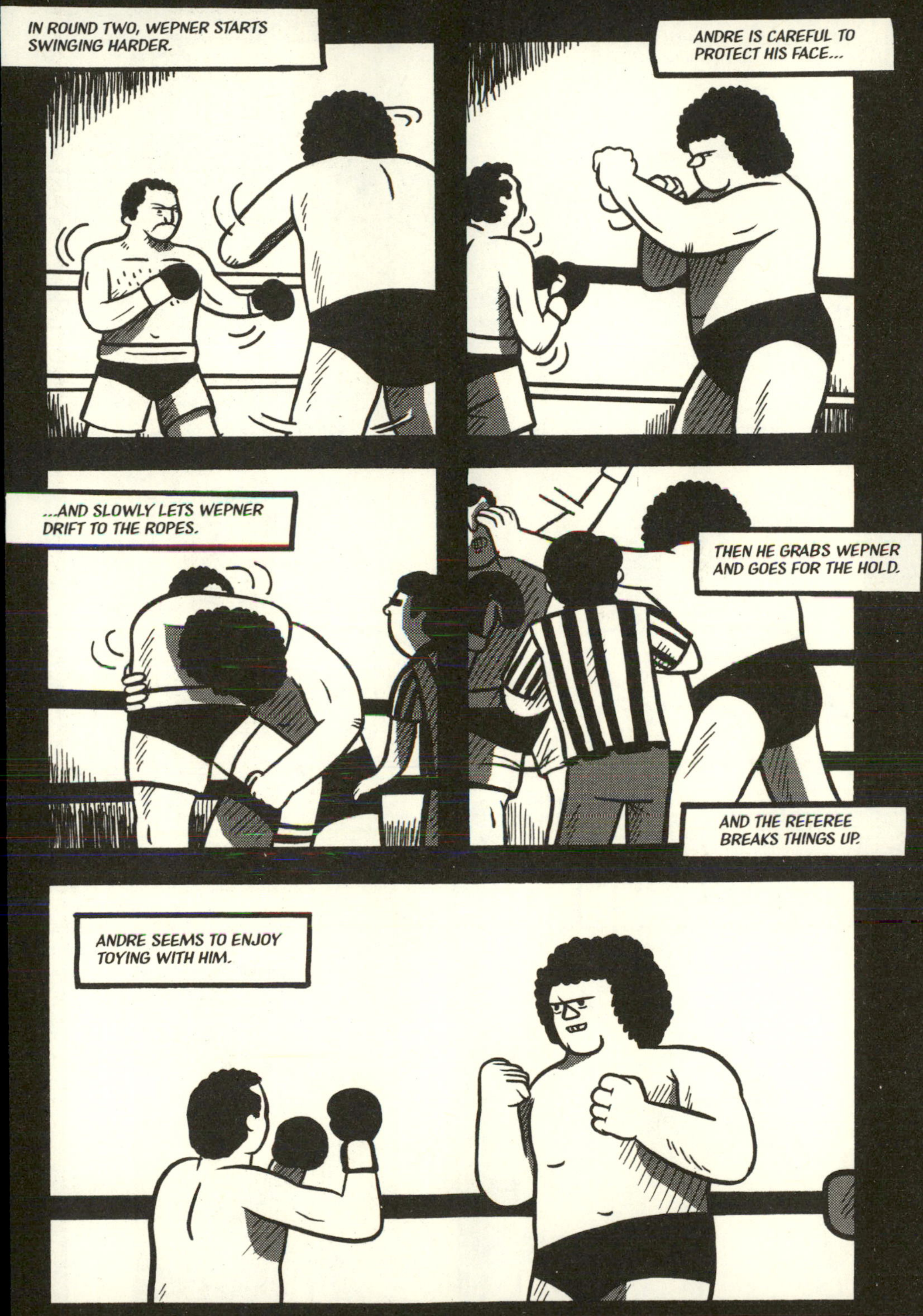
IN ROUND TWO, WEPNER STARTS SWINGING HARDER.
ANDRE IS CAREFUL TO PROTECT HIS FACE...
...AND SLOWLY LETS WEPNER DRIFT TO THE ROPES.
THEN HE GRABS WEPNER AND GOES FOR THE HOLD.
AND THE REFEREE BREAKS THINGS UP.
ANDRE SEEMS TO ENJOY TOYING WITH HIM.

ANDRE WRESTLES HIM TO THE GROUND. THE REF STARTS TO COUNT A PINFALL BUT WEPNER'S LEG IS OUT OF THE RING, BREAKING THE COUNT.

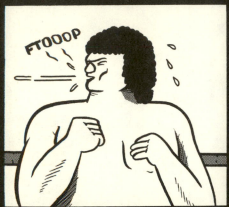

WHEN ANDRE GOES FOR T[H]E HOLD AGAIN, WEPNER POU[NDS] ON HIS HEAD. BOTH MEN W[ERE] PAID $25,000 FOR THE FIG[HT,] WIN OR LOSE.

SO THIS WAS A BAD MOVE FOR CHUCK.

FTOOOP

come on!!

ANDRE DELIVERS WHAT LOOKS LIKE A DEVASTATING HEAD-BUTT.

MOST OF THE FORCE GOES INTO ANDRE'S HANDS. THEN HE PUSHES WEPNER TOWARD THE ROPES.

94

WEPNER IS DAZED, HOWEVER.

A FULL-FORCE HEAD-BUTT MIGHT'VE KNOCKED HIM OUT.

THEN ANDRE DECIDES TIME IS UP AND SCOOPS UP THE 6'6" 240LB WEPNER.

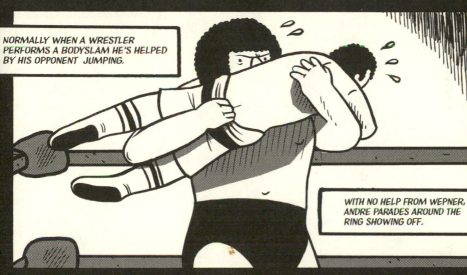

NORMALLY WHEN A WRESTLER PERFORMS A BODYSLAM HE'S HELPED BY HIS OPPONENT JUMPING.

WITH NO HELP FROM WEPNER, ANDRE PARADES AROUND THE RING SHOWING OFF.

THEN TOSSES HIM OUT OF THE RING.

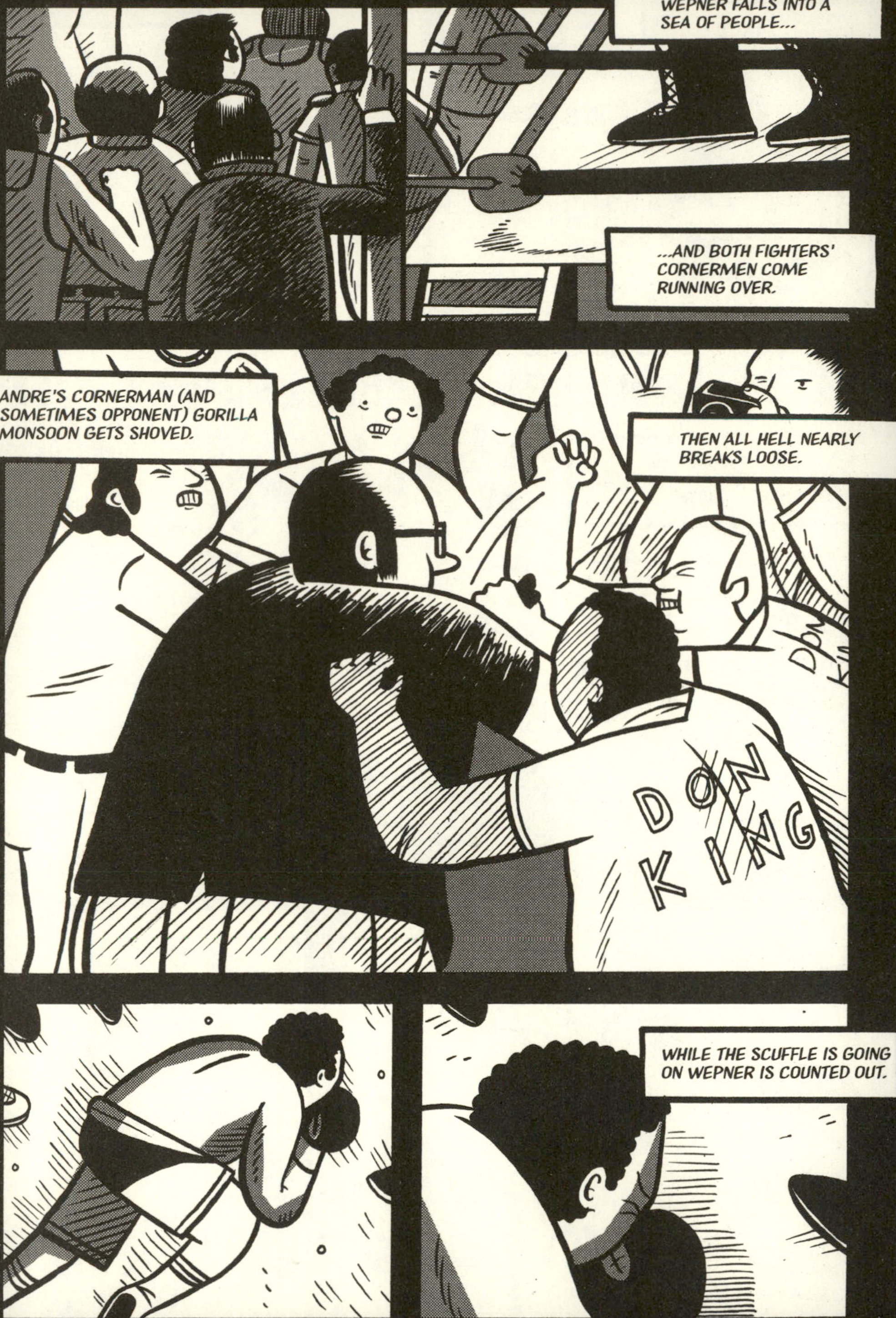
WEPNER FALLS INTO A SEA OF PEOPLE...
...AND BOTH FIGHTERS' CORNERMEN COME RUNNING OVER.
ANDRE'S CORNERMAN (AND SOMETIMES OPPONENT) GORILLA MONSOON GETS SHOVED.
THEN ALL HELL NEARLY BREAKS LOOSE.
DON KING
WHILE THE SCUFFLE IS GOING ON WEPNER IS COUNTED OUT.

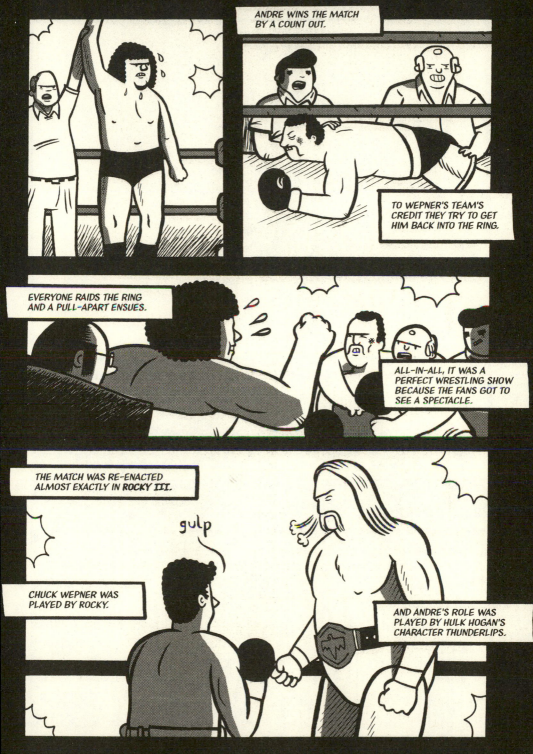

ANDRE WINS THE MATCH BY A COUNT OUT.

TO WEPNER'S TEAM'S CREDIT THEY TRY TO GET HIM BACK INTO THE RING.

EVERYONE RAIDS THE RING AND A PULL-APART ENSUES.

ALL-IN-ALL, IT WAS A PERFECT WRESTLING SHOW BECAUSE THE FANS GOT TO SEE A SPECTACLE.

THE MATCH WAS RE-ENACTED ALMOST EXACTLY IN **ROCKY III.**

gulp

CHUCK WEPNER WAS PLAYED BY ROCKY.

AND ANDRE'S ROLE WAS PLAYED BY HULK HOGAN'S CHARACTER THUNDERLIPS.

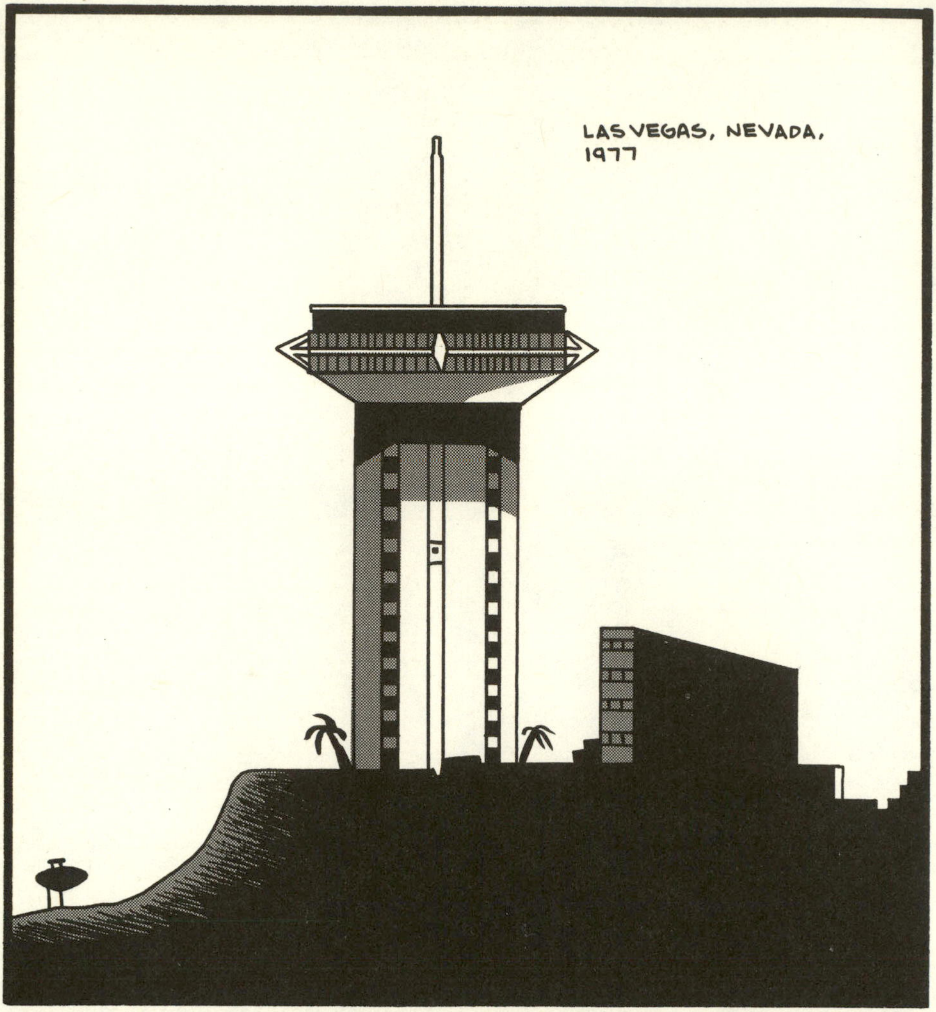
LAS VEGAS, NEVADA, 1977

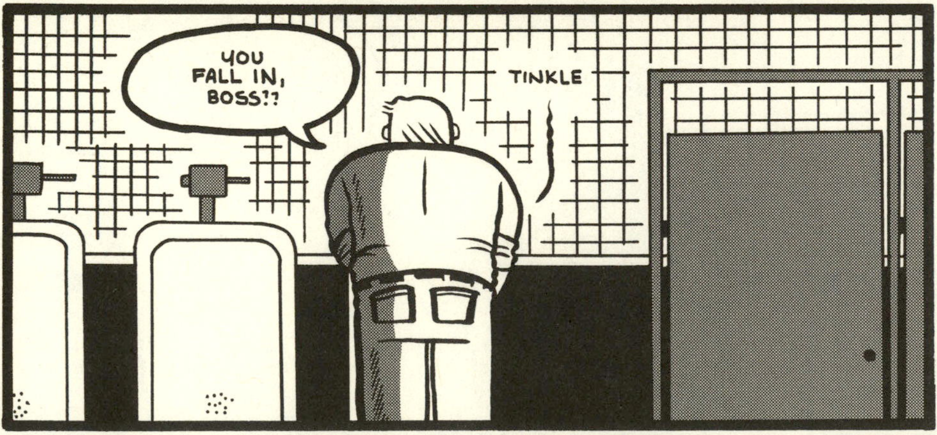
YOU FALL IN, BOSS?!
TINKLE

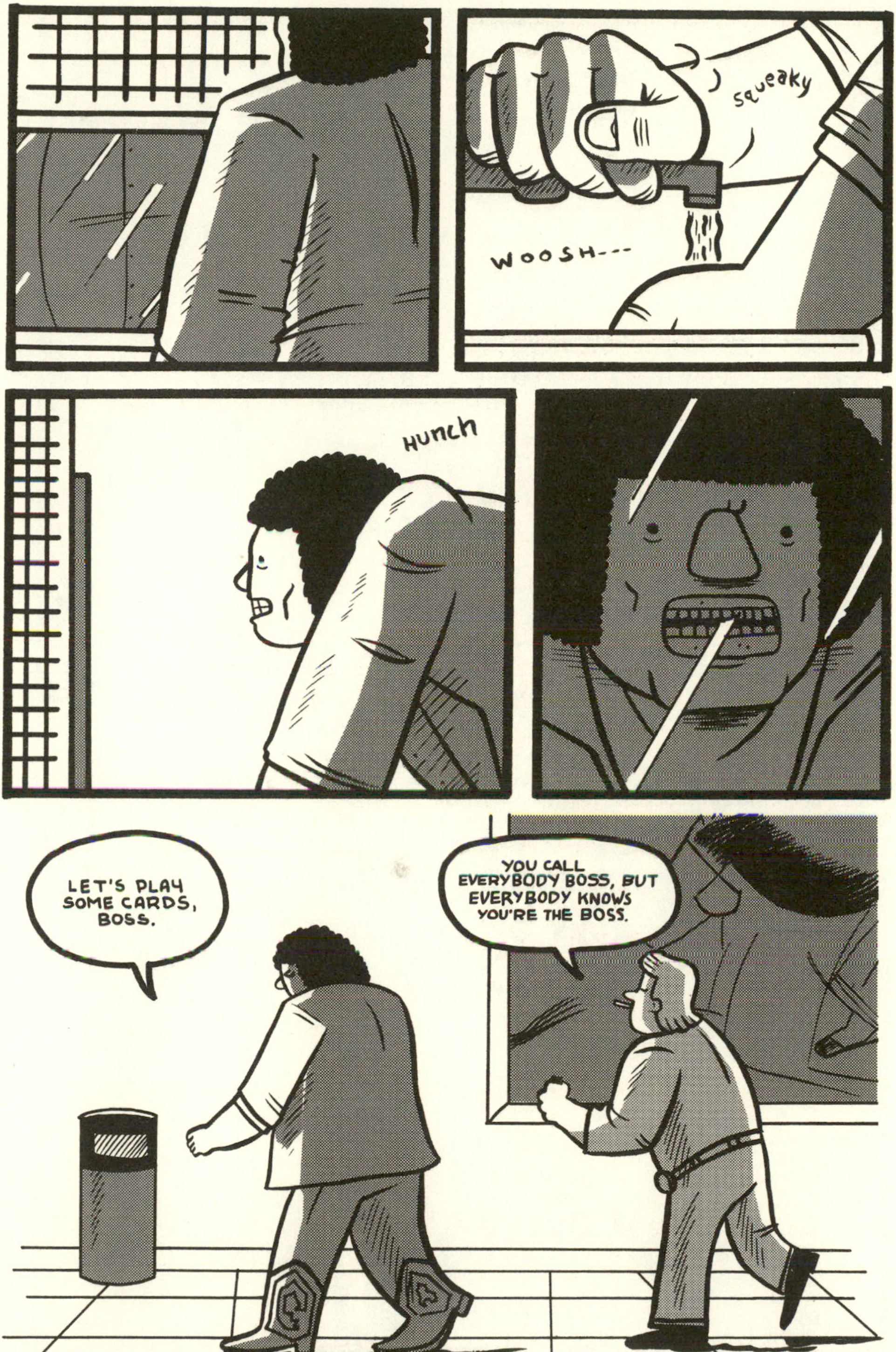
squeaky
WOOSH---
HUNCH
LET'S PLAY SOME CARDS, BOSS.
YOU CALL EVERYBODY BOSS, BUT EVERYBODY KNOWS YOU'RE THE BOSS.

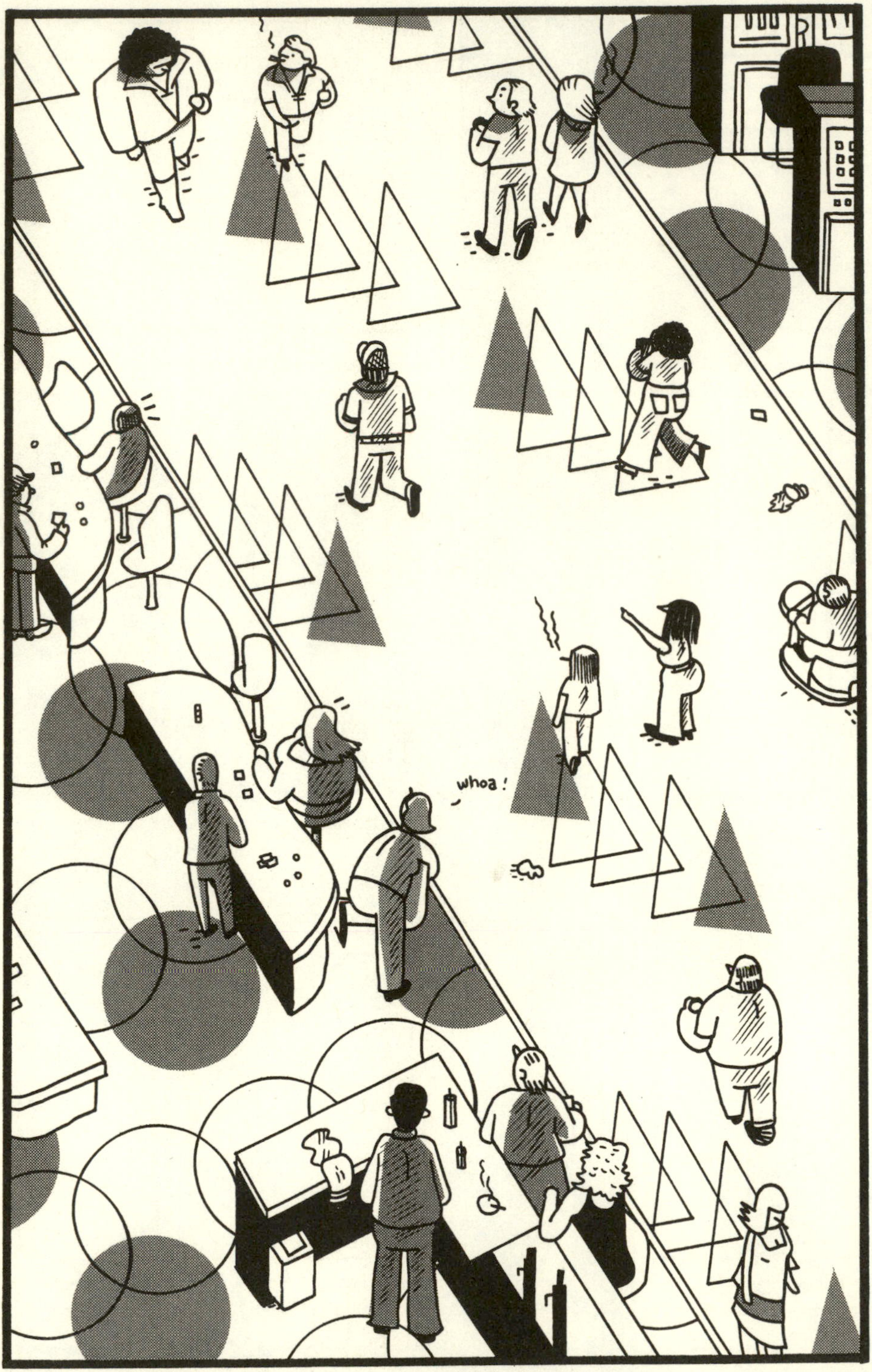
whoa!

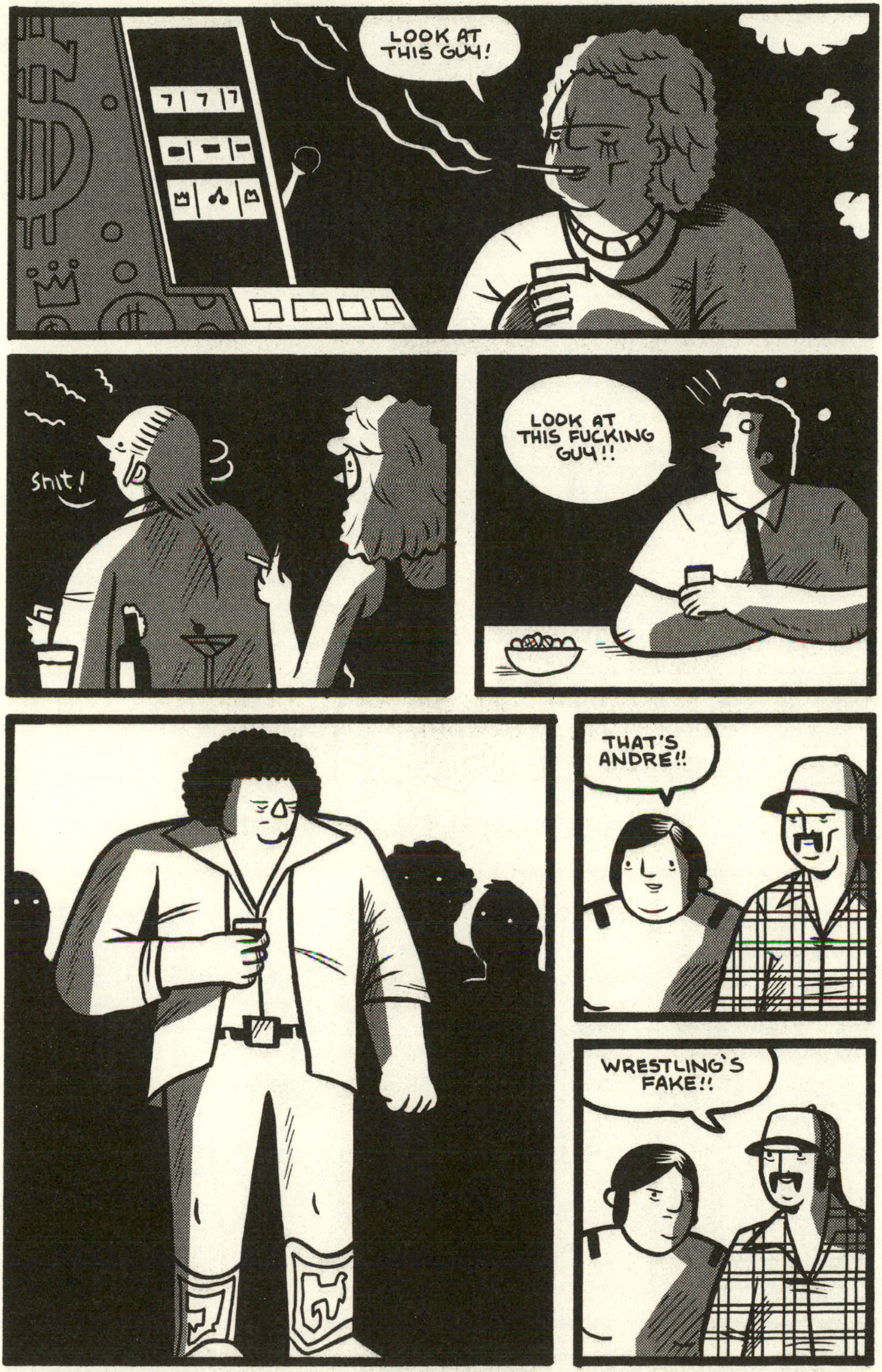
LOOK AT THIS GUY!
SHIT!
LOOK AT THIS FUCKING GUY!!
THAT'S ANDRE!!
WRESTLING'S FAKE!!

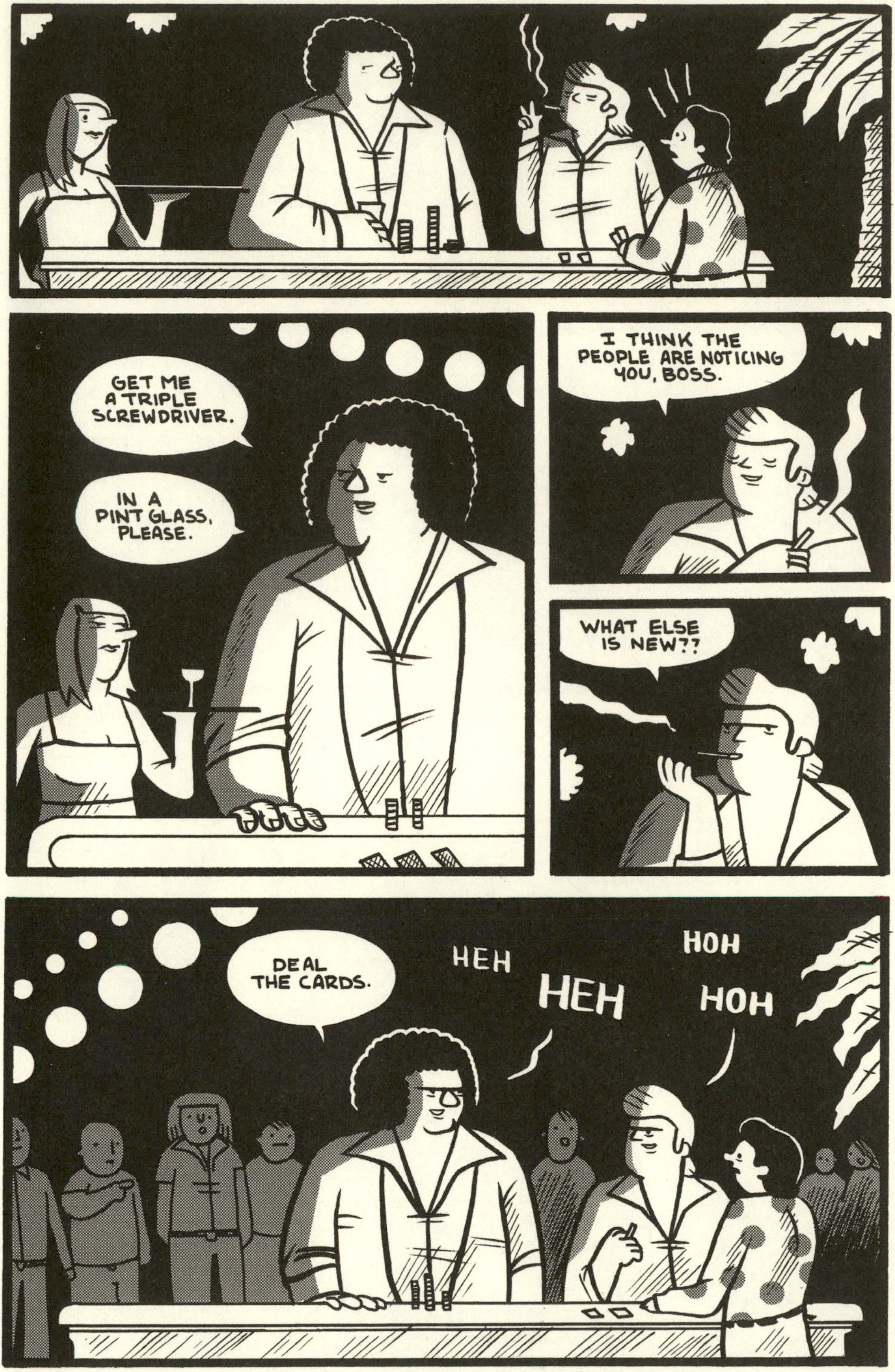
GET ME A TRIPLE SCREWDRIVER.
IN A PINT GLASS, PLEASE.
I THINK THE PEOPLE ARE NOTICING YOU, BOSS.
WHAT ELSE IS NEW??
DEAL THE CARDS.
HEH
HEH
HOH
HOH

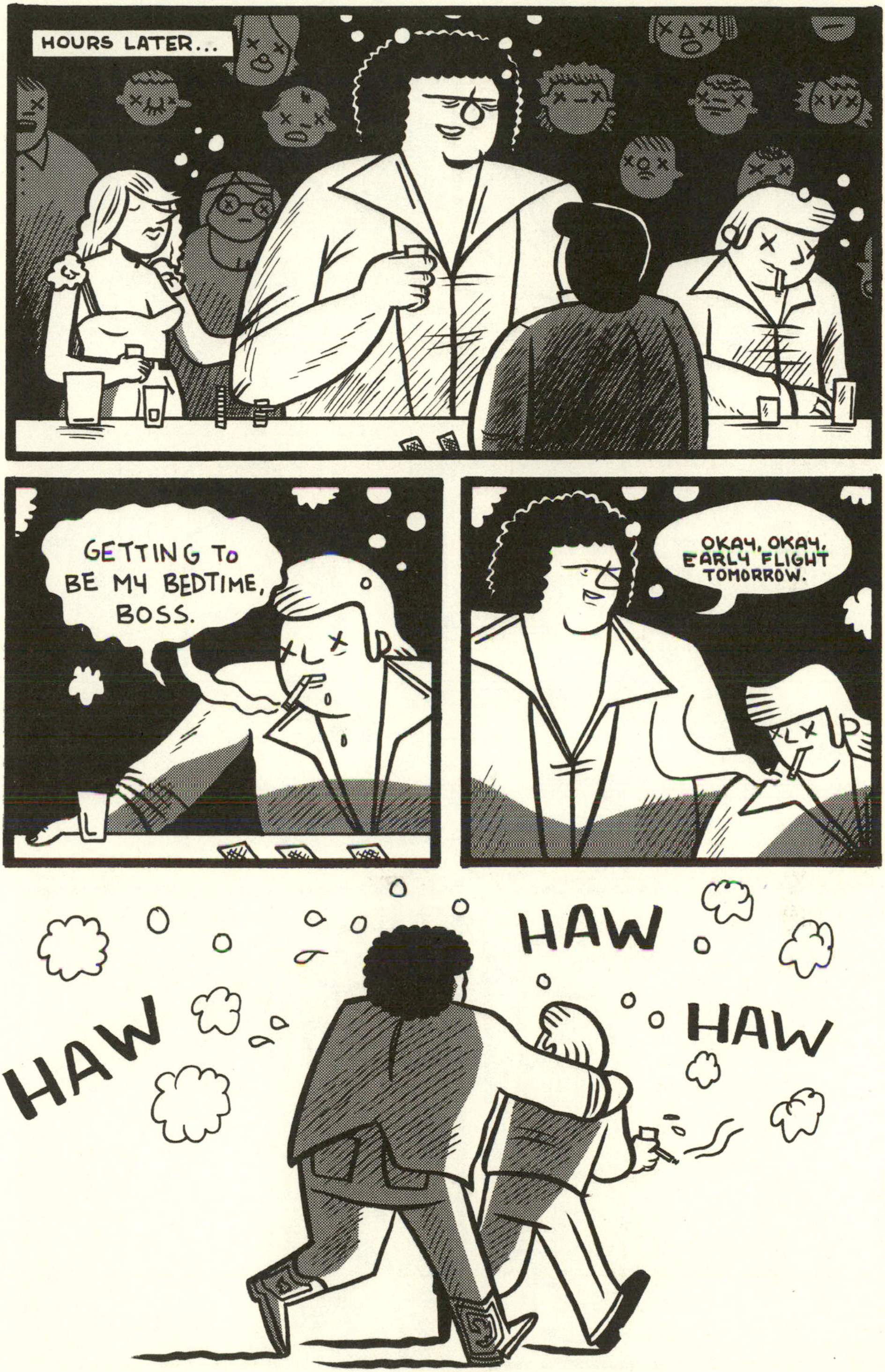

HOURS LATER...
GETTING TO BE MY BEDTIME, BOSS.
OKAY, OKAY, EARLY FLIGHT TOMORROW.
HAW
HAW
HAW

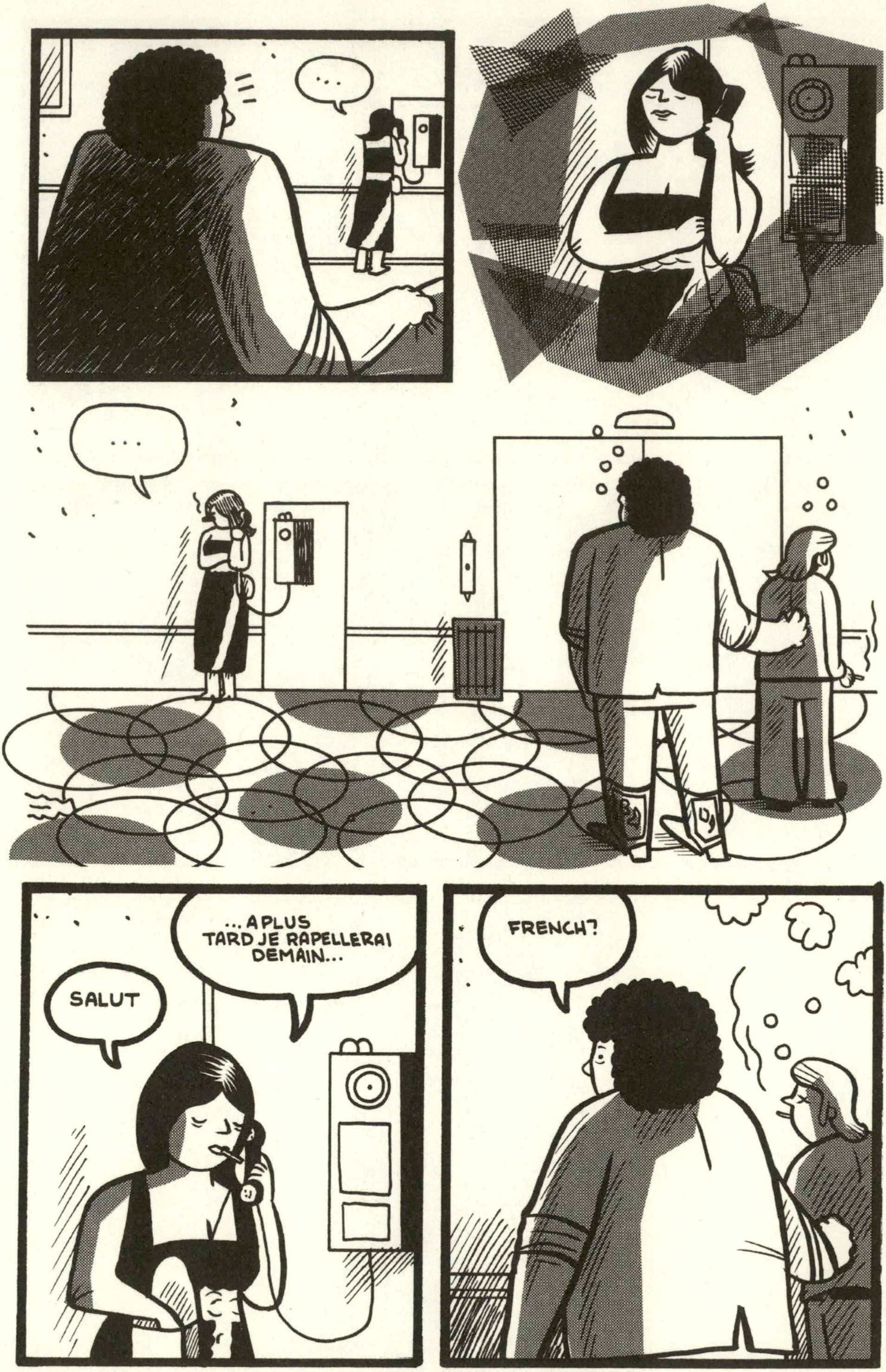
. . .
. . .
...A PLUS TARD JE RAPPELLERAI DEMAIN...
SALUT
FRENCH?

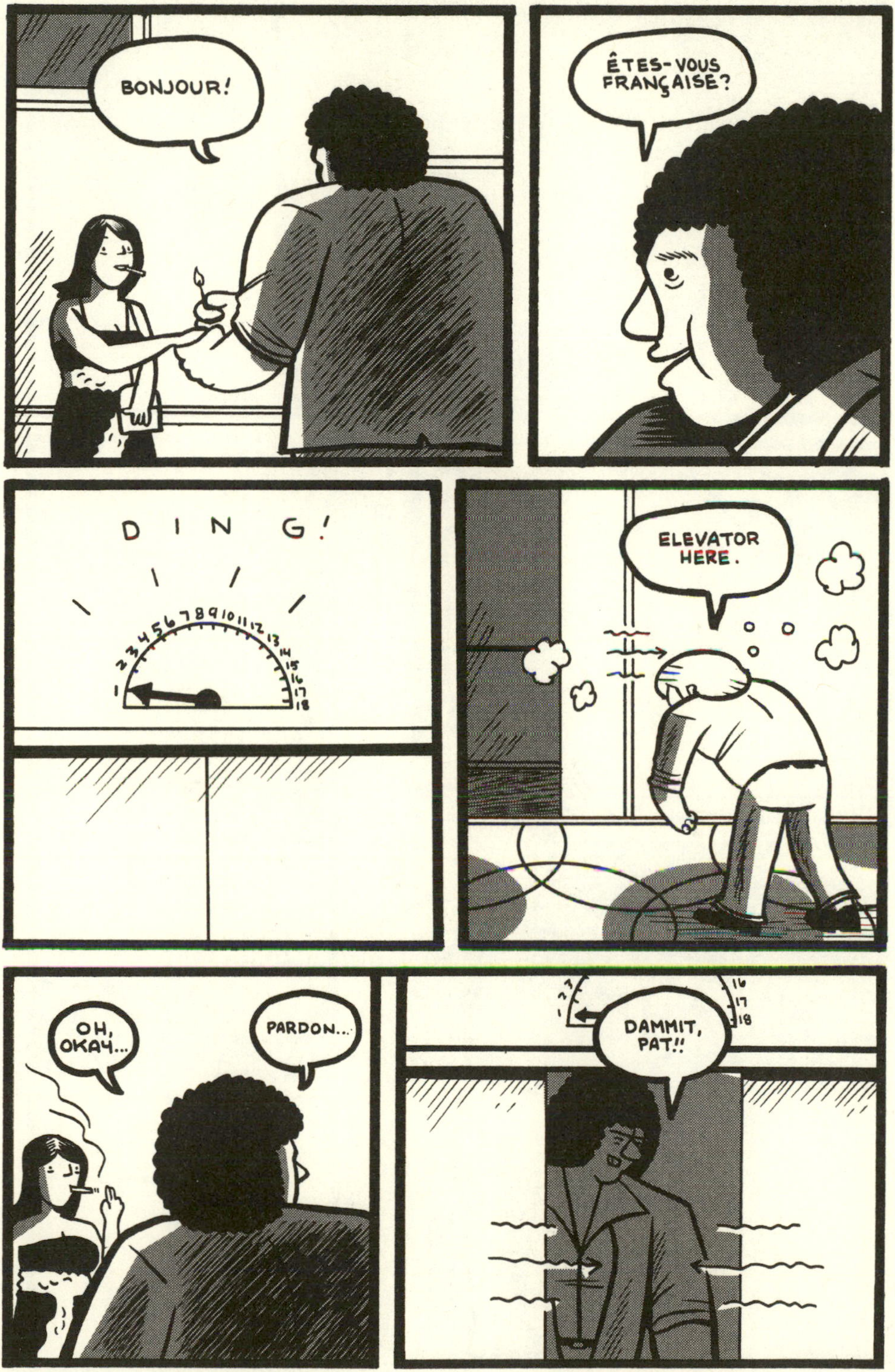
BONJOUR!
ÊTES-VOUS FRANÇAISE?
D I N G!
1 2 3 4 5 6 7 8 9 10 11 12 13 14 15 16 17 18
ELEVATOR HERE.
OH, OKAY...
PARDON...
16 17 18
DAMMIT, PAT!!

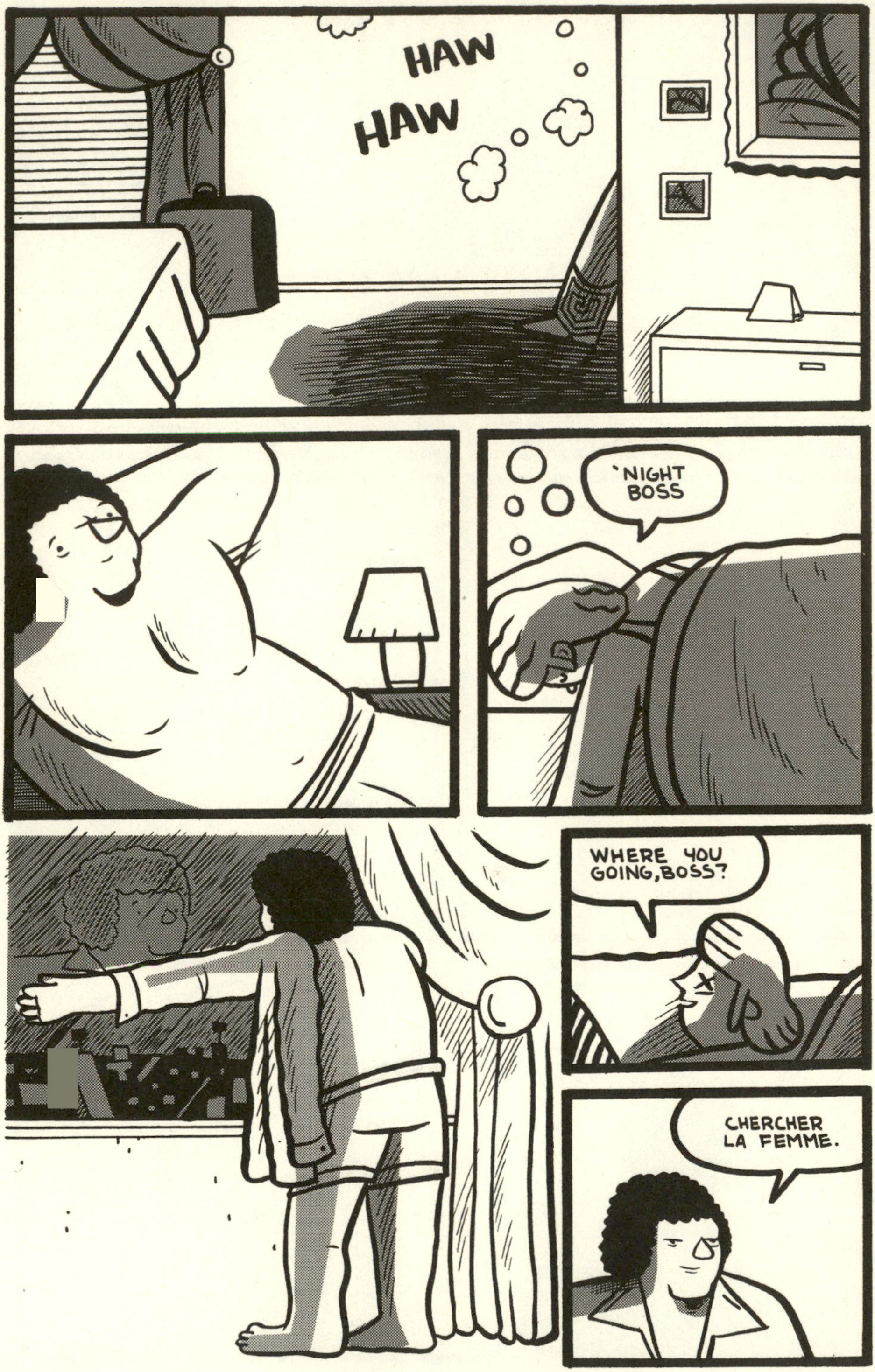
HAW
HAW
`NIGHT BOSS
WHERE YOU GOING, BOSS?
CHERCHER LA FEMME.

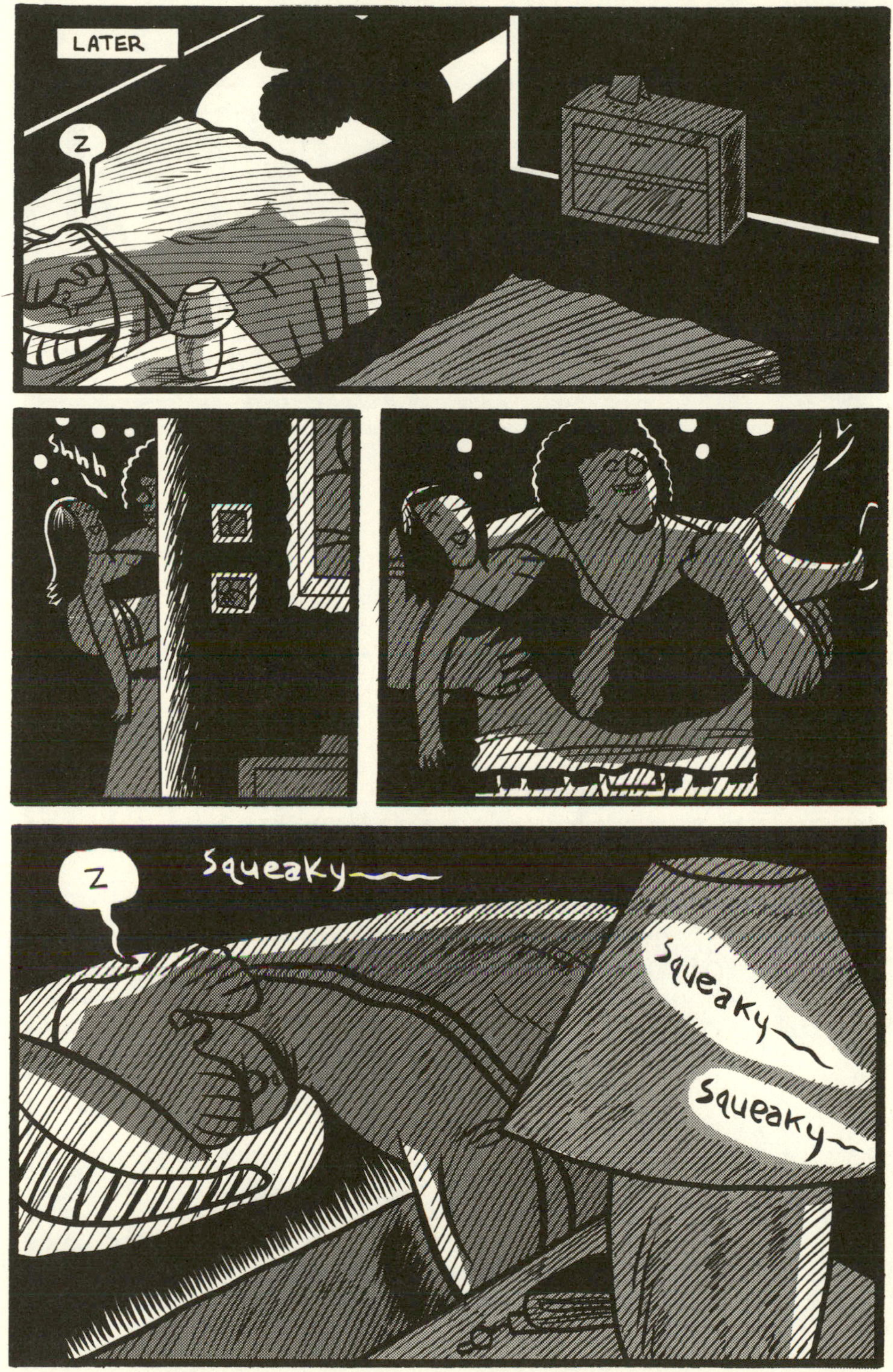
LATER
Z
Shhh
Z
Squeaky~~
Squeaky~
Squeaky~

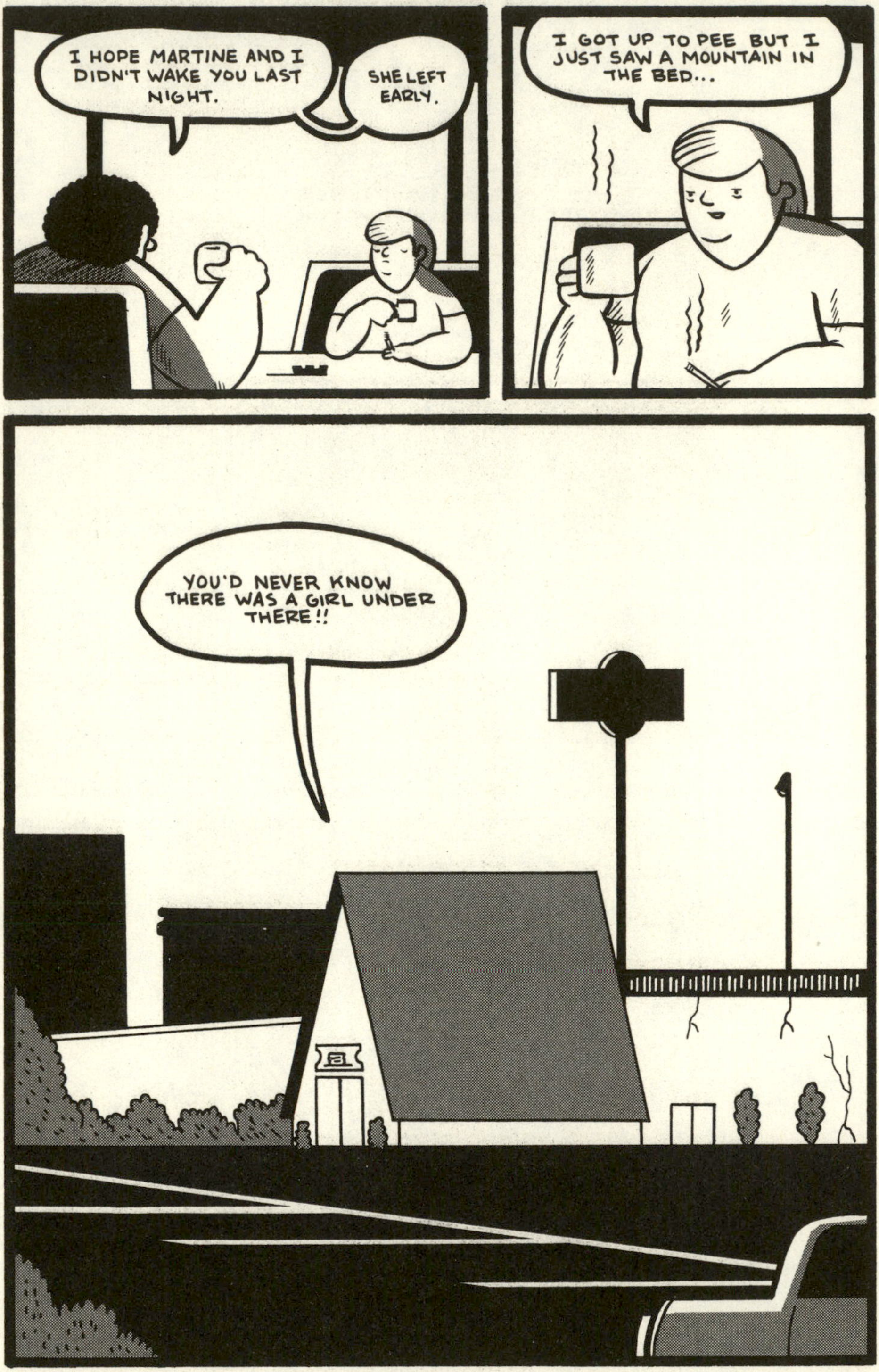
I HOPE MARTINE AND I DIDN'T WAKE YOU LAST NIGHT.
SHE LEFT EARLY.
I GOT UP TO PEE BUT I JUST SAW A MOUNTAIN IN THE BED...
YOU'D NEVER KNOW THERE WAS A GIRL UNDER THERE!!

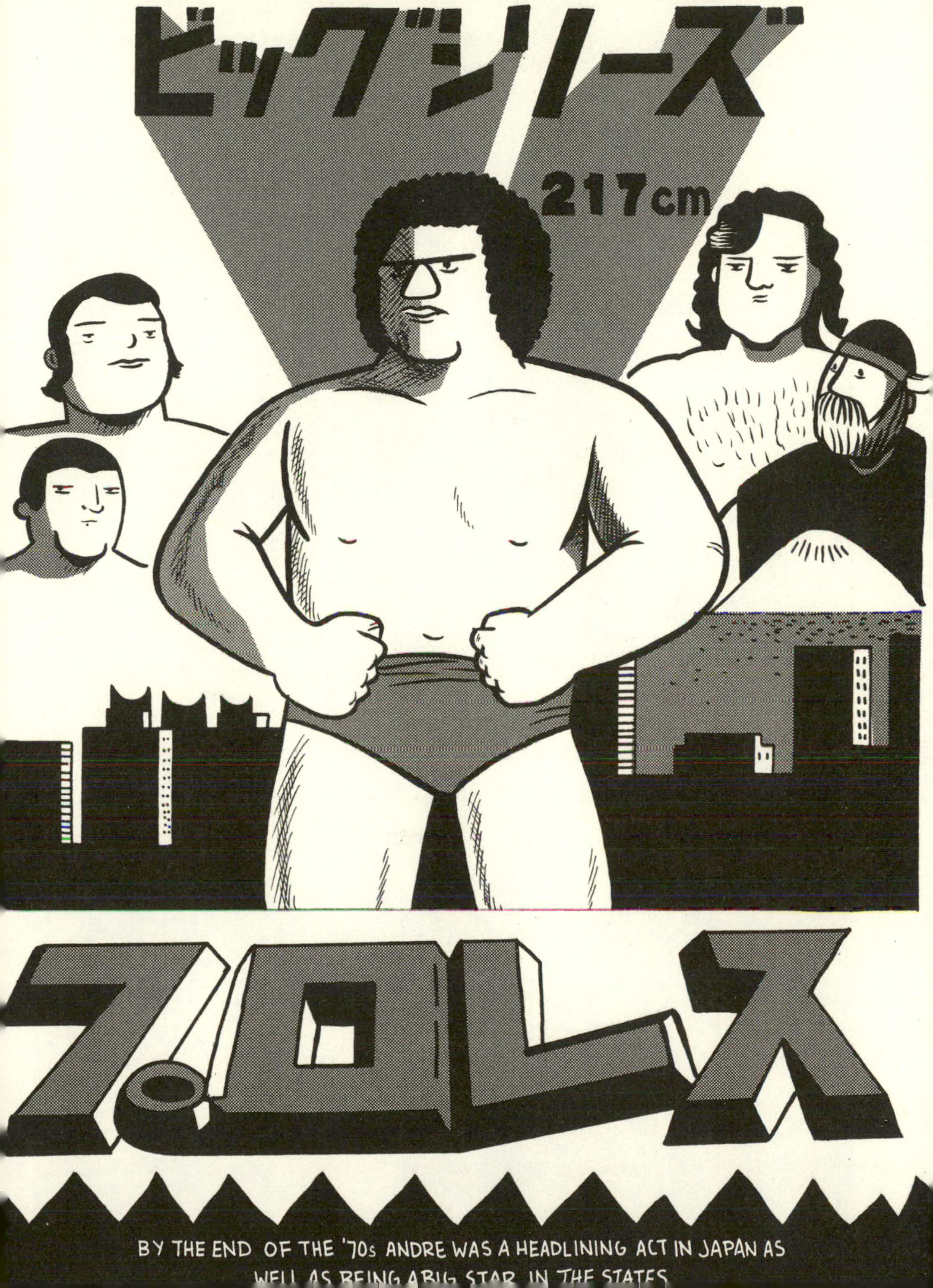

ビッグシリーズ
217cm
プロレス
BY THE END OF THE '70s ANDRE WAS A HEADLINING ACT IN JAPAN AS
WELL AS BEING A BIG STAR IN THE STATES.

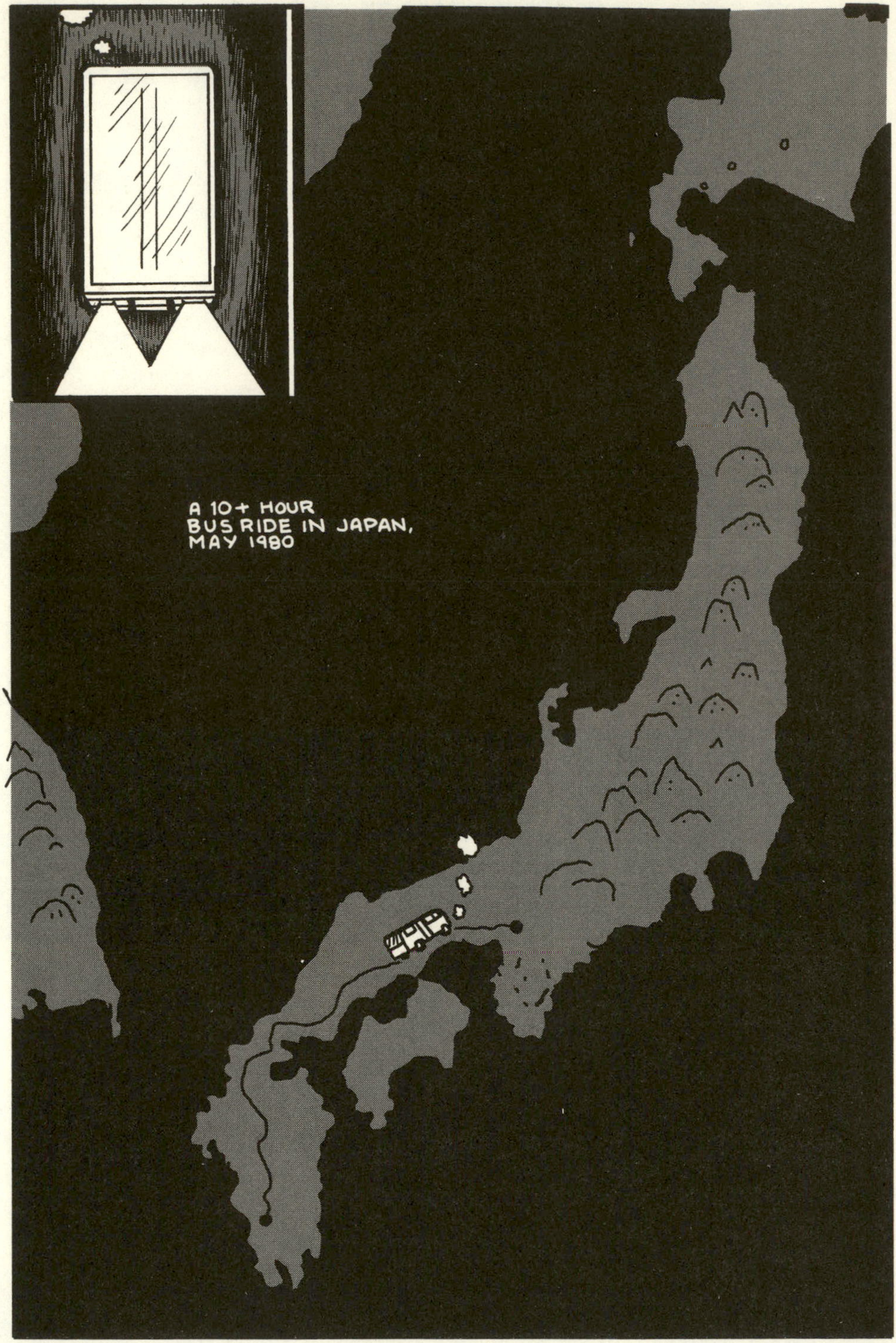
A 10+ HOUR
BUS RIDE IN JAPAN,
MAY 1980

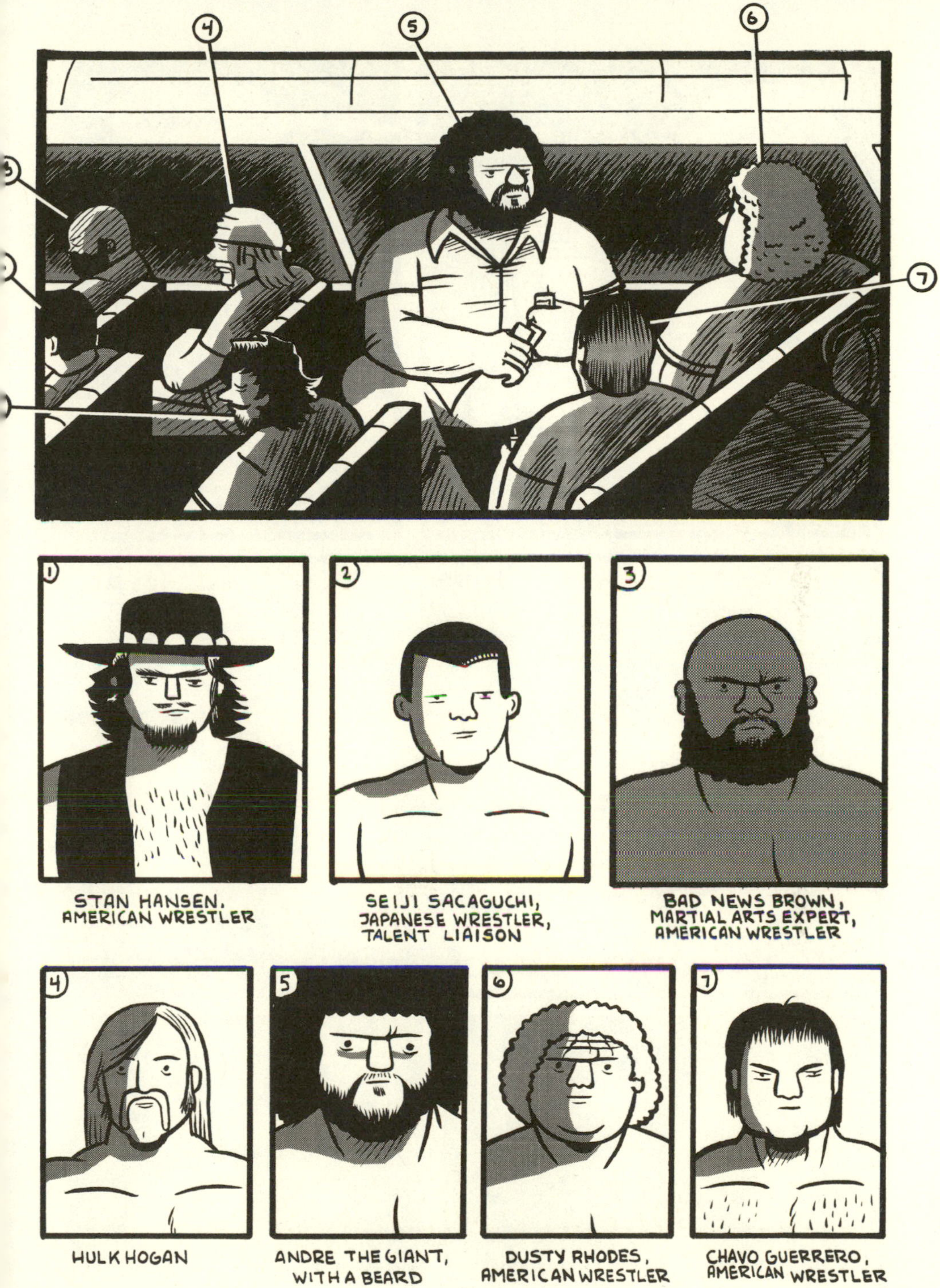

STAN HANSEN, AMERICAN WRESTLER
SEIJI SACAGUCHI, JAPANESE WRESTLER, TALENT LIAISON
BAD NEWS BROWN, MARTIAL ARTS EXPERT, AMERICAN WRESTLER
HULK HOGAN
ANDRE THE GIANT, WITH A BEARD
DUSTY RHODES, AMERICAN WRESTLER
CHAVO GUERRERO, AMERICAN WRESTLER

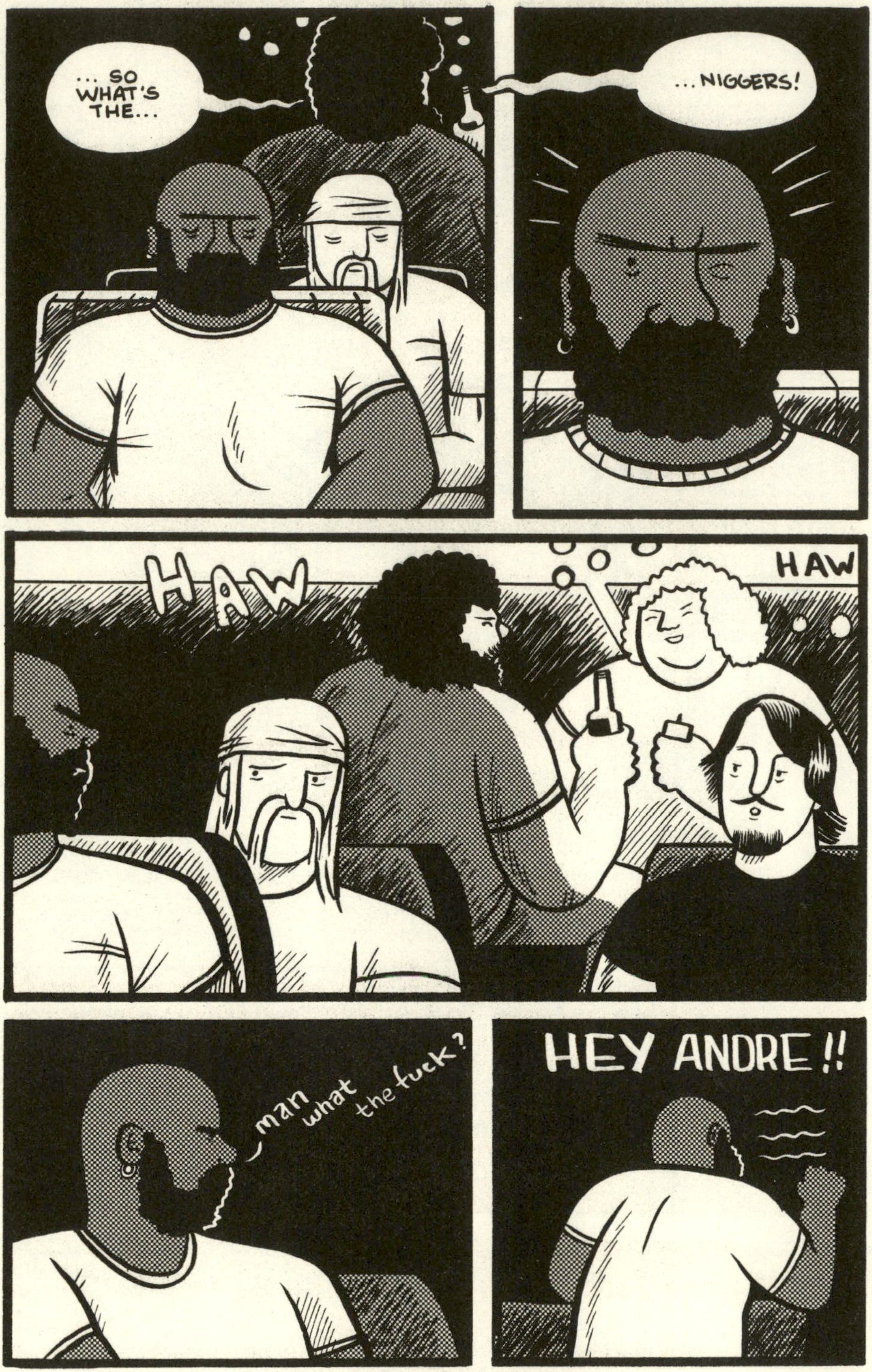
... SO WHAT'S THE...
... NIGGERS!
HAW
HAW
man what the fuck?
HEY ANDRE !!

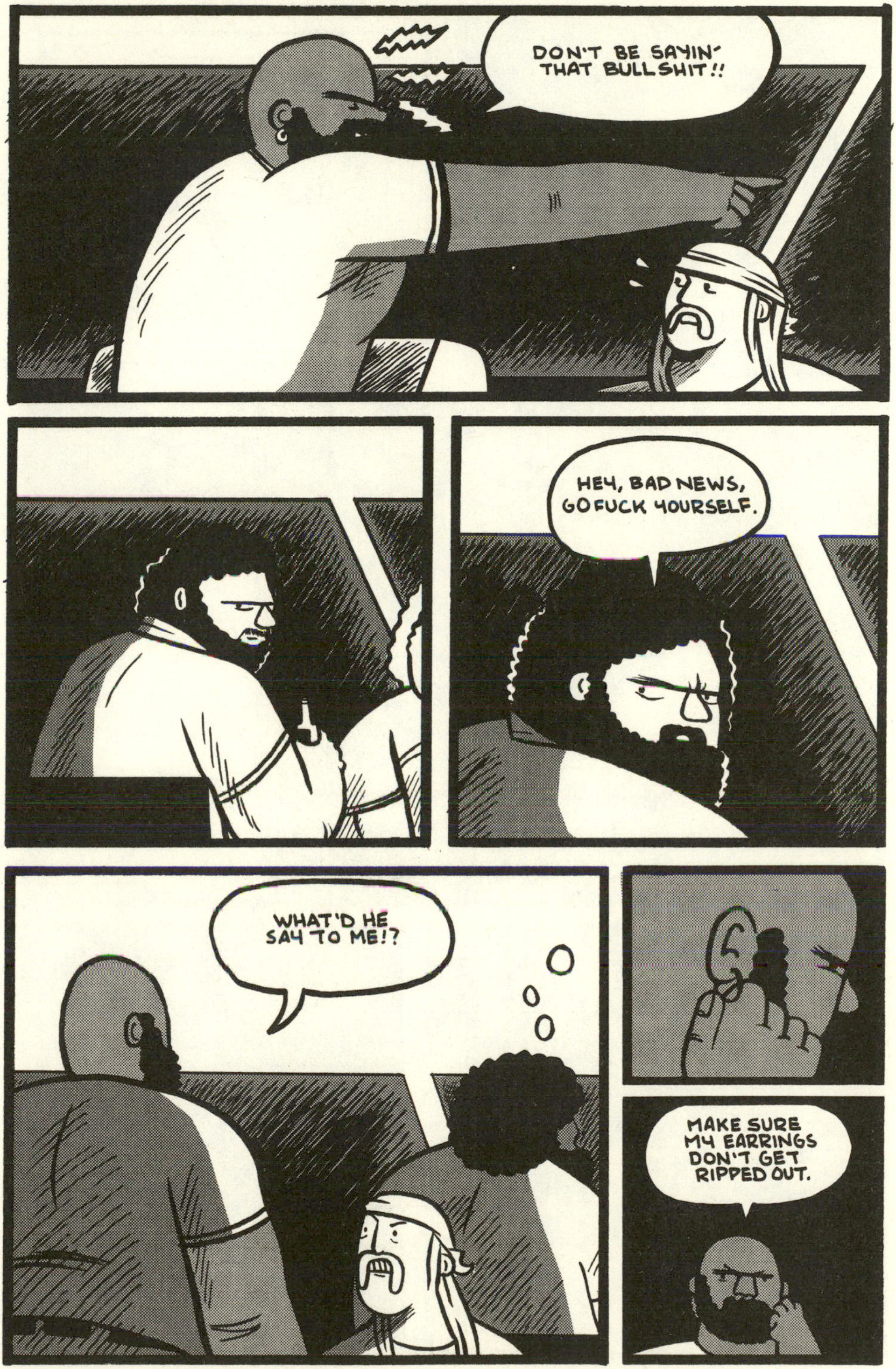
DON'T BE SAYIN' THAT BULLSHIT!!
HEY, BAD NEWS, GO FUCK YOURSELF.
WHAT'D HE SAY TO ME!?
MAKE SURE MY EARRINGS DON'T GET RIPPED OUT.

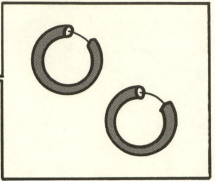

IF YOU'RE REACHING FOR SOMETHING... LIKE A KNIFE...

I'LL TAKE IT FROM YOU...

AND SHOVE IT UP YOUR ASS!!

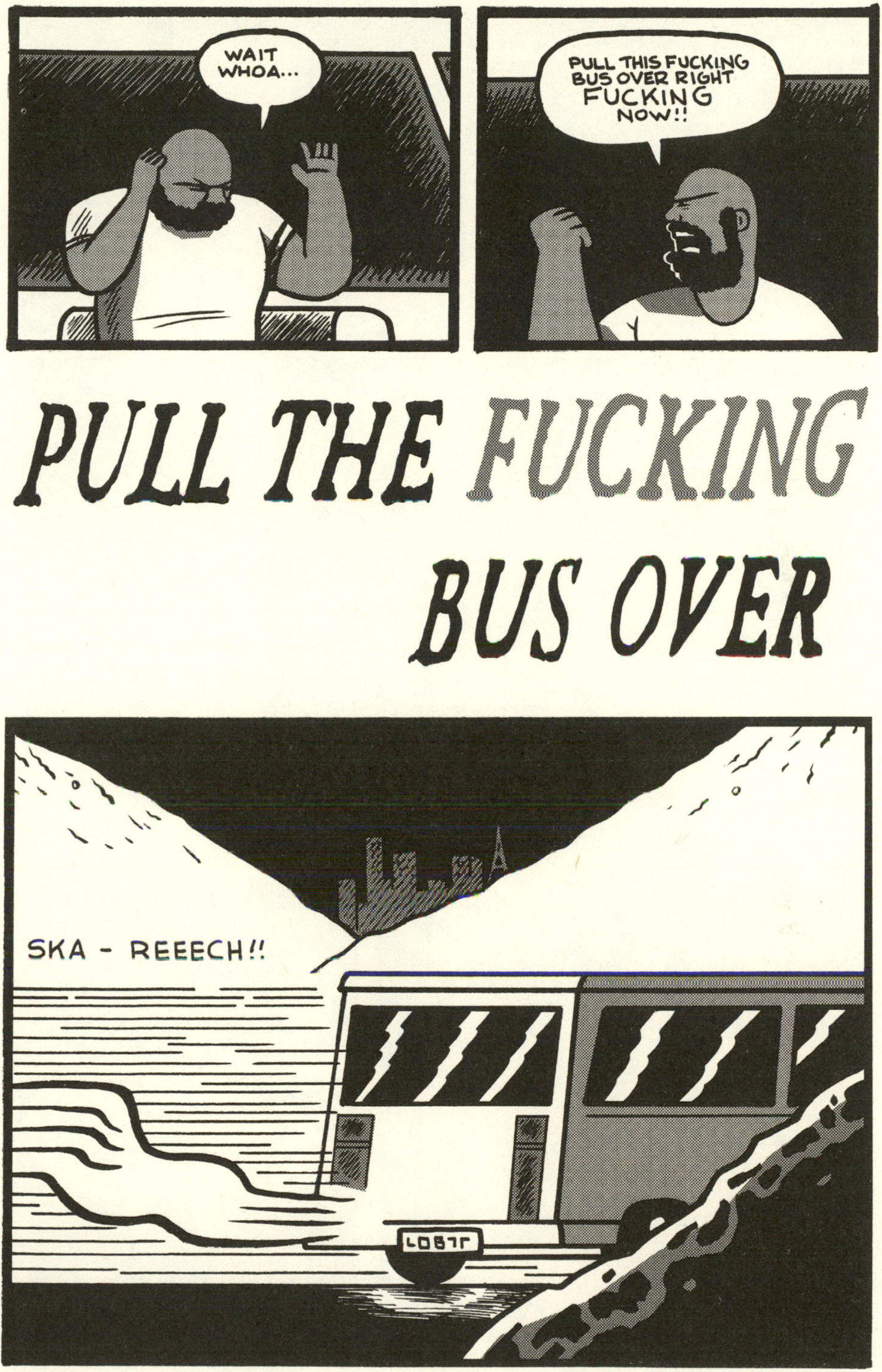
WAIT WHOA...
PULL THIS FUCKING BUS OVER RIGHT FUCKING NOW!!
PULL THE FUCKING BUS OVER
SKA - REEECH!!

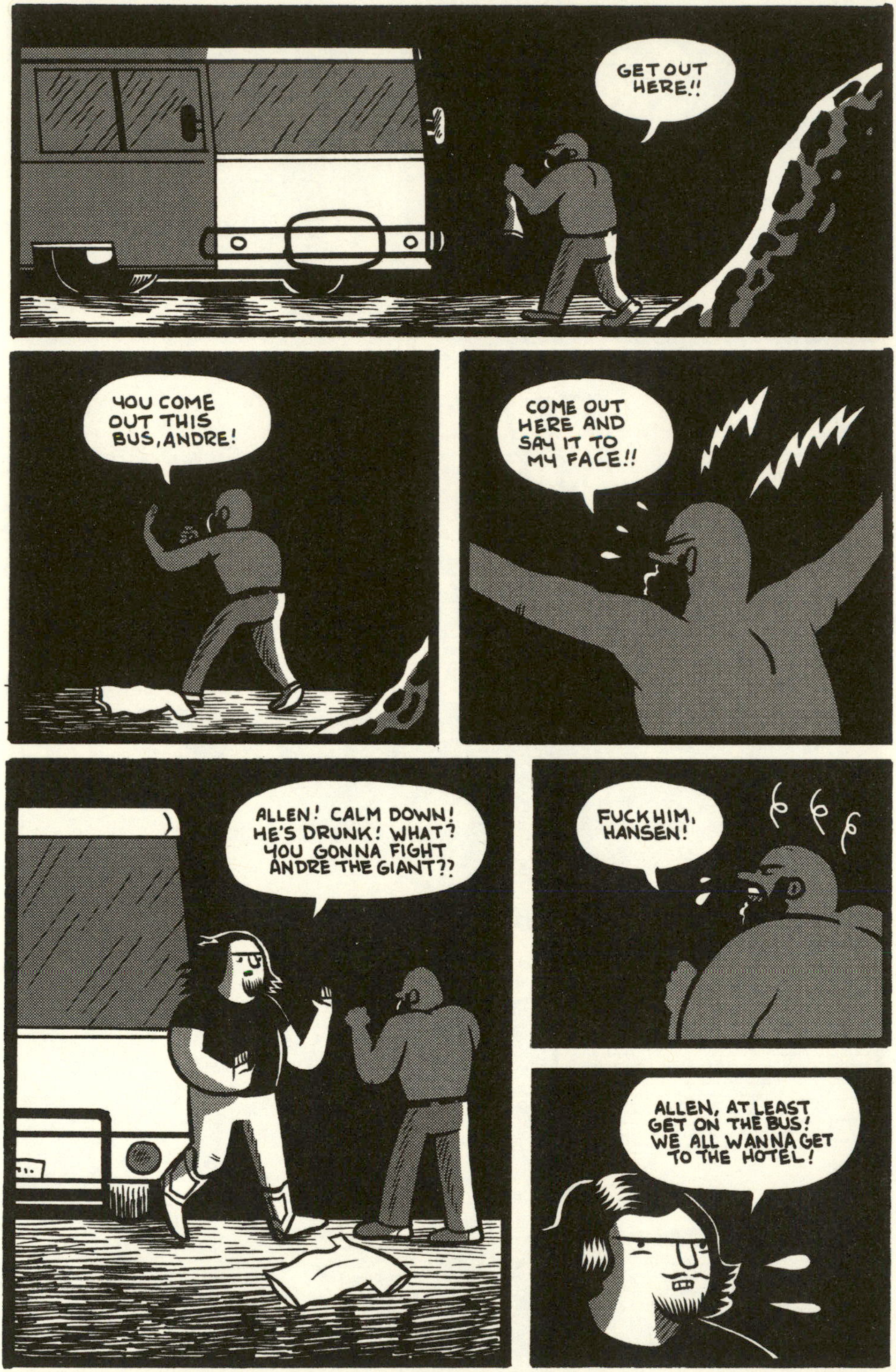
GET OUT HERE!!
YOU COME OUT THIS BUS, ANDRE!
COME OUT HERE AND SAY IT TO MY FACE!!
ALLEN! CALM DOWN! HE'S DRUNK! WHAT? YOU GONNA FIGHT ANDRE THE GIANT??
FUCK HIM, HANSEN!
ALLEN, AT LEAST GET ON THE BUS! WE ALL WANNA GET TO THE HOTEL!

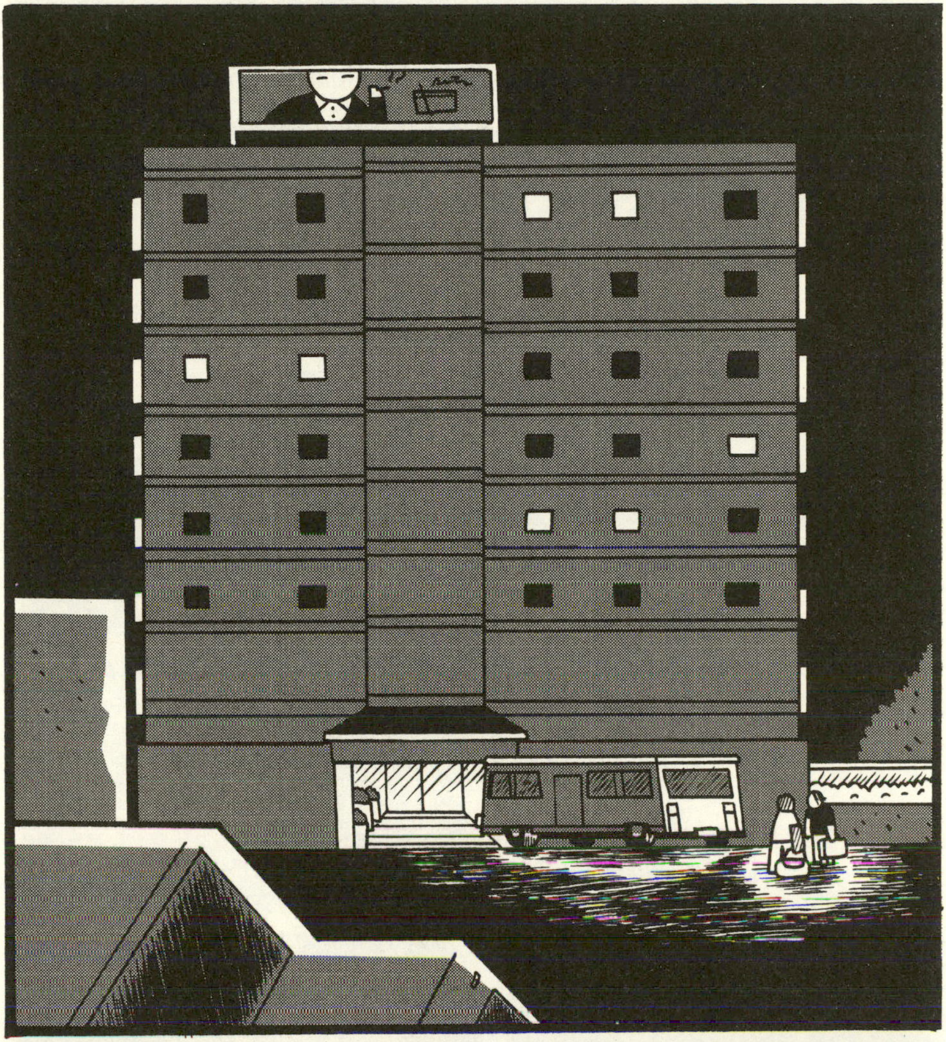

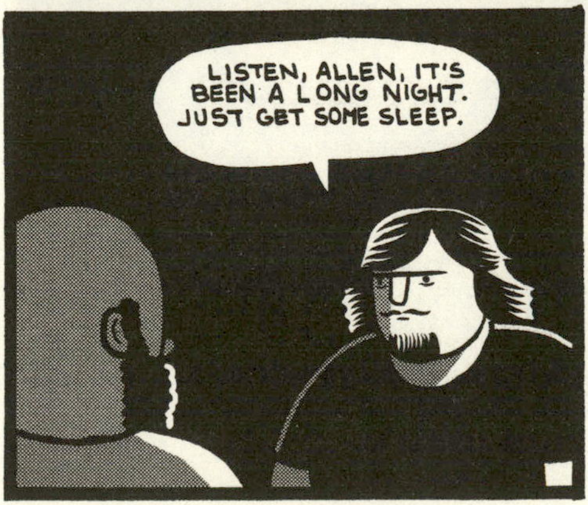
LISTEN, ALLEN, IT'S BEEN A LONG NIGHT. JUST GET SOME SLEEP.

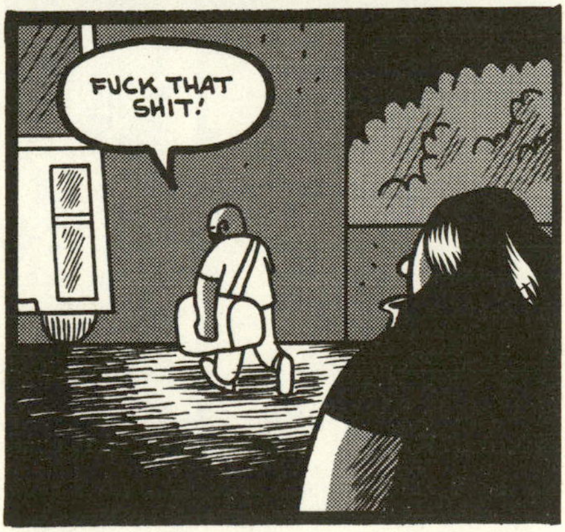
FUCK THAT SHIT!

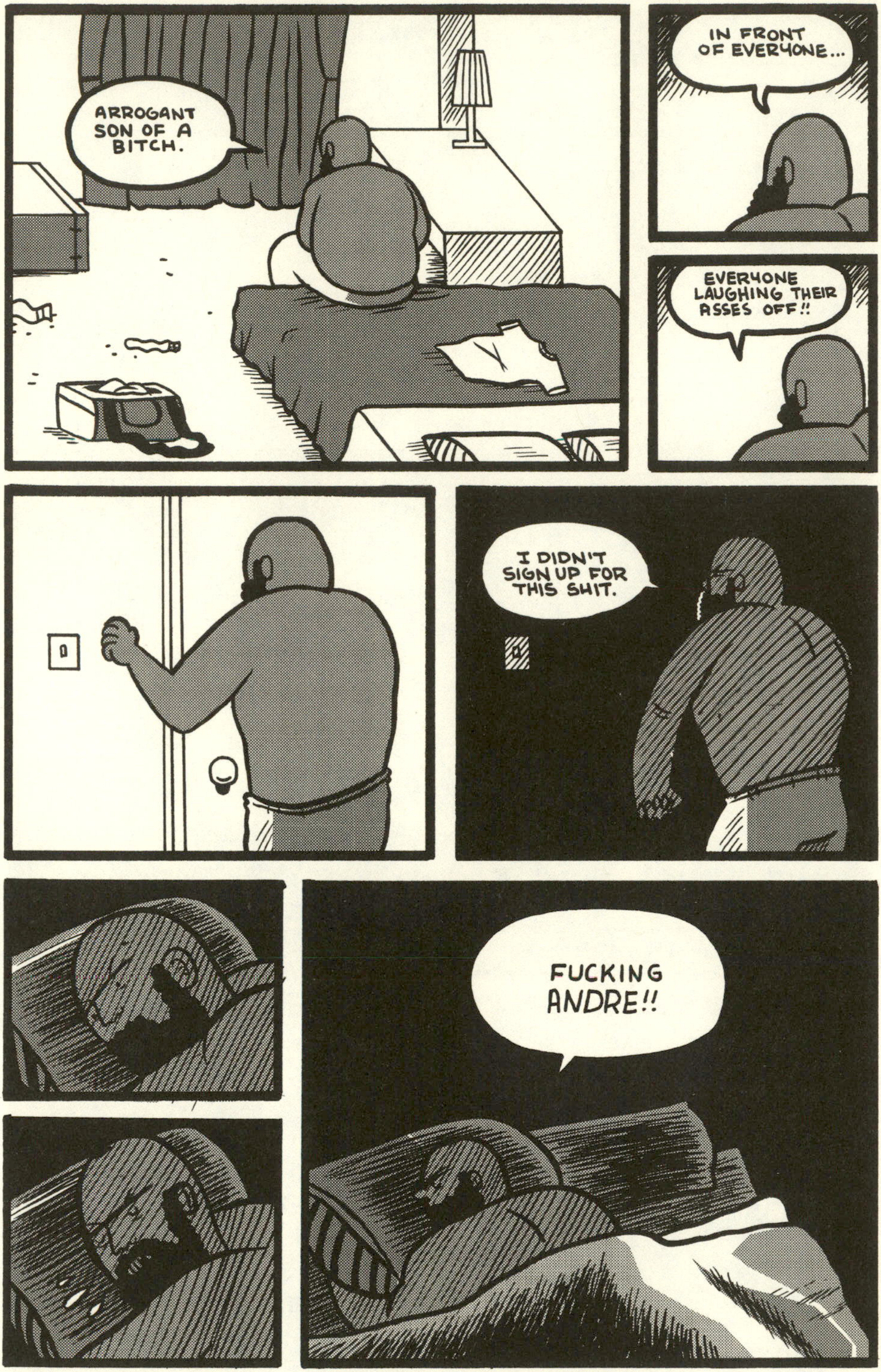
ARROGANT SON OF A BITCH.
IN FRONT OF EVERYONE...
EVERYONE LAUGHING THEIR ASSES OFF!!
I DIDN'T SIGN UP FOR THIS SHIT.
FUCKING ANDRE!!

THE NEXT MORNING...

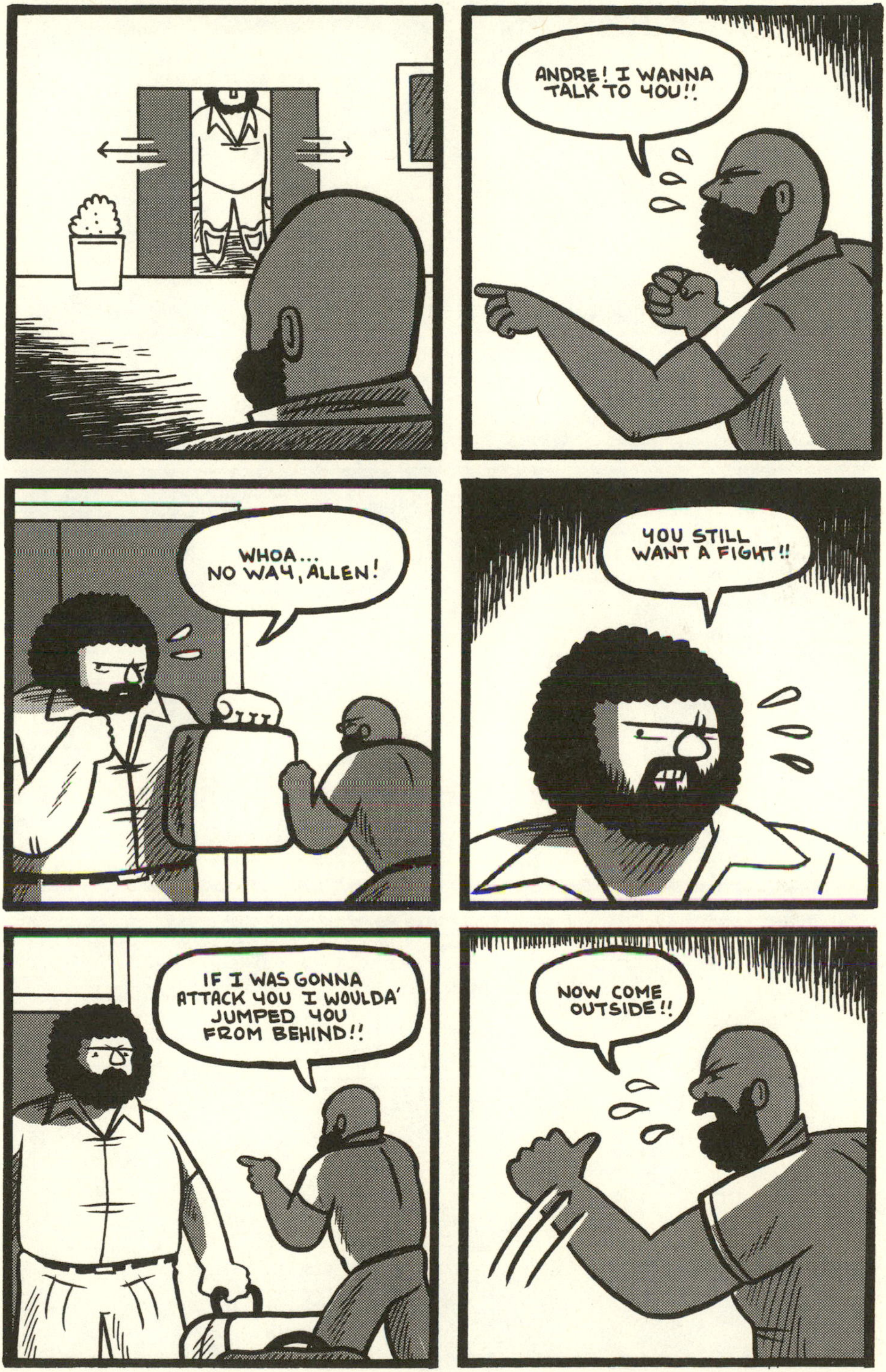
ANDRE! I WANNA TALK TO YOU!!
WHOA... NO WAY, ALLEN!
YOU STILL WANT A FIGHT!!
IF I WAS GONNA ATTACK YOU I WOULDA' JUMPED YOU FROM BEHIND!!
NOW COME OUTSIDE!!

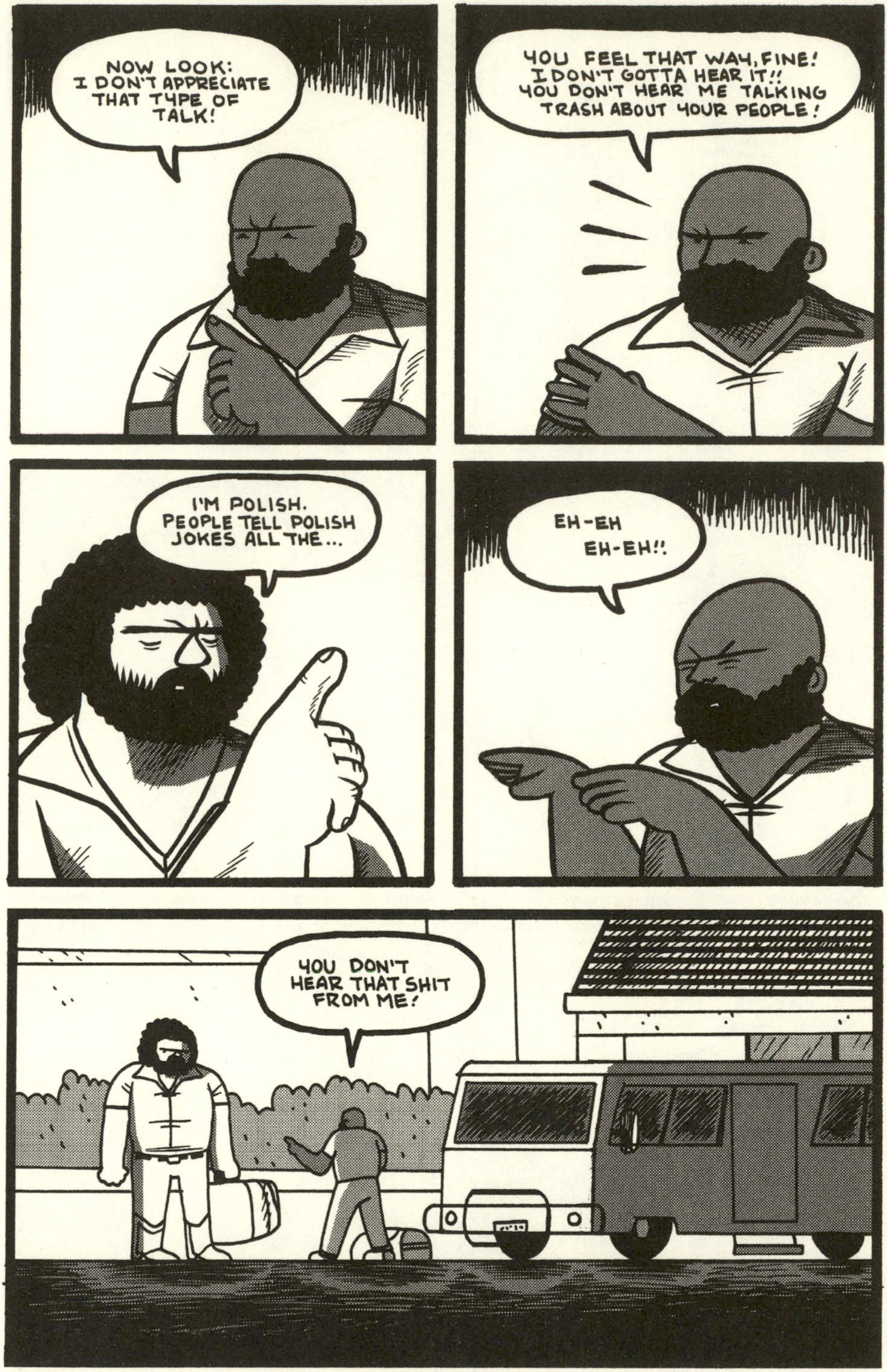
NOW LOOK: I DON'T APPRECIATE THAT TYPE OF TALK!
YOU FEEL THAT WAY, FINE! I DON'T GOTTA HEAR IT!! YOU DON'T HEAR ME TALKING TRASH ABOUT YOUR PEOPLE!
I'M POLISH. PEOPLE TELL POLISH JOKES ALL THE...
EH-EH EH-EH!!
YOU DON'T HEAR THAT SHIT FROM ME!

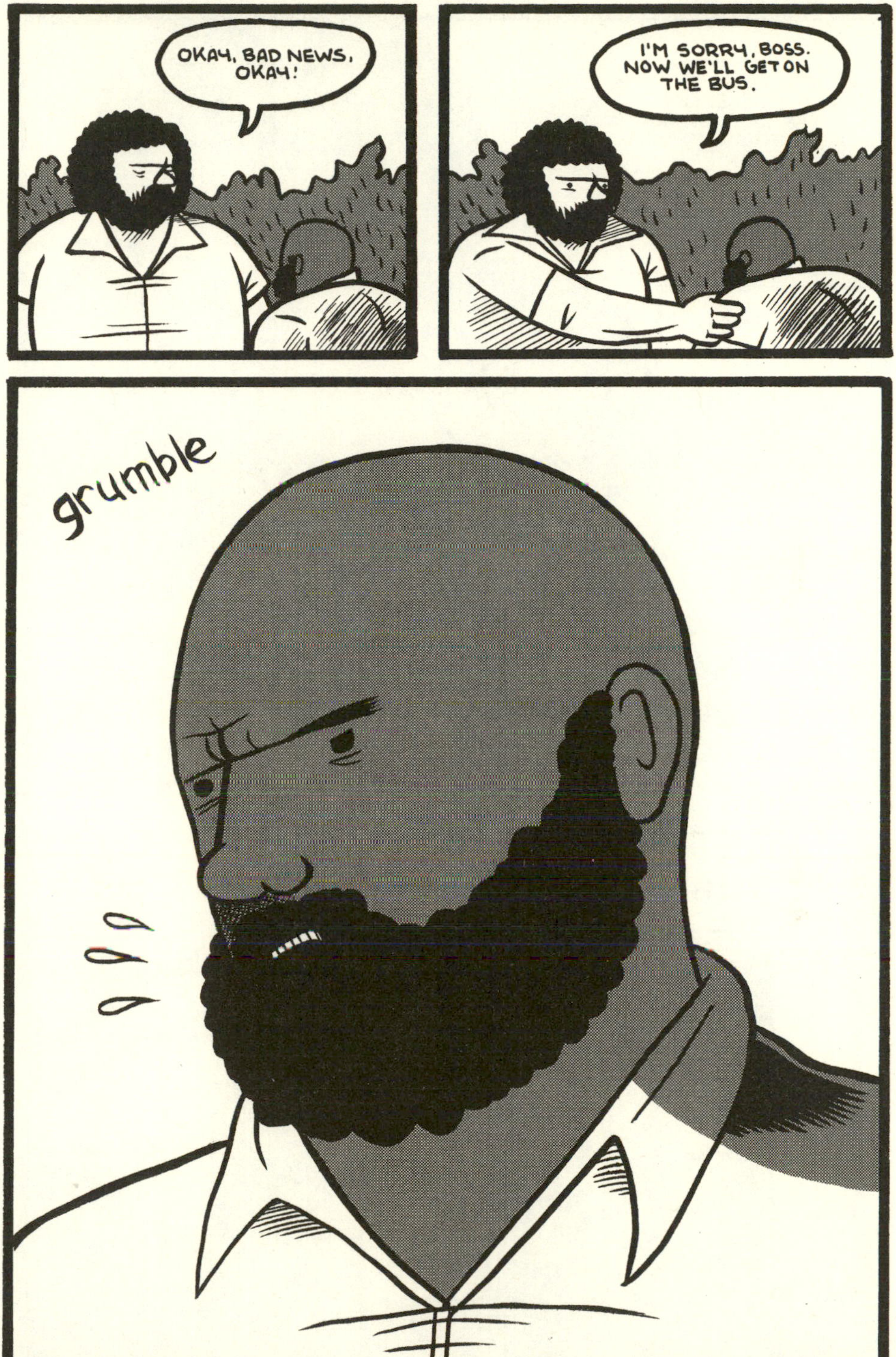
OKAY, BAD NEWS, OKAY!
I'M SORRY, BOSS. NOW WE'LL GET ON THE BUS.
grumble

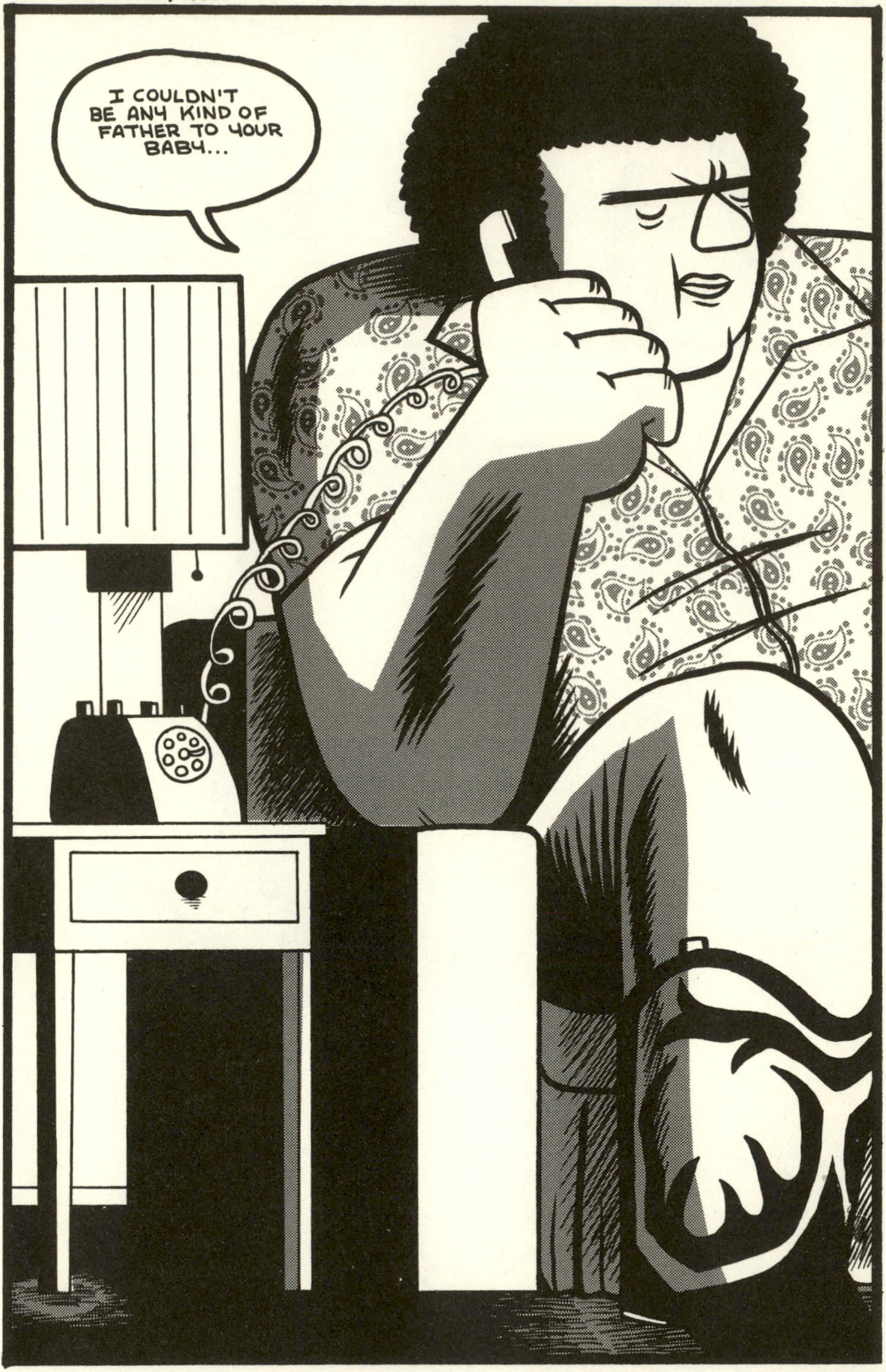
I COULDN'T BE ANY KIND OF FATHER TO YOUR BABY...

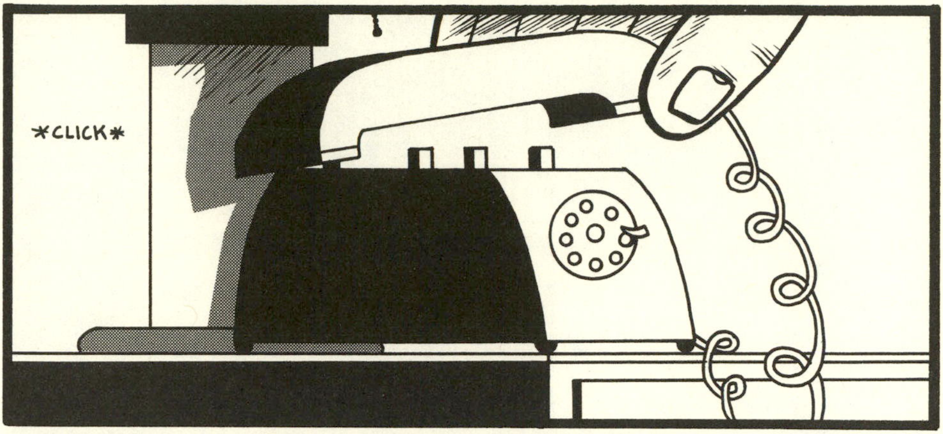
CLICK

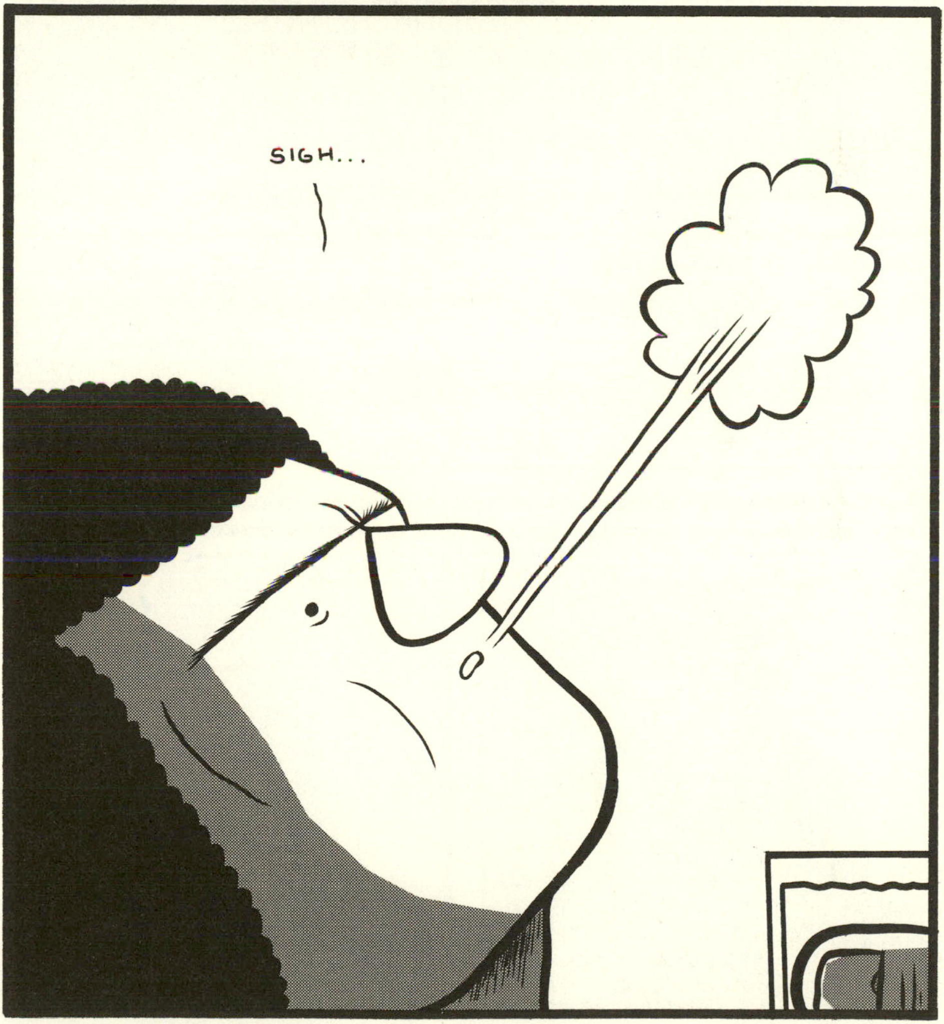
SIGH...

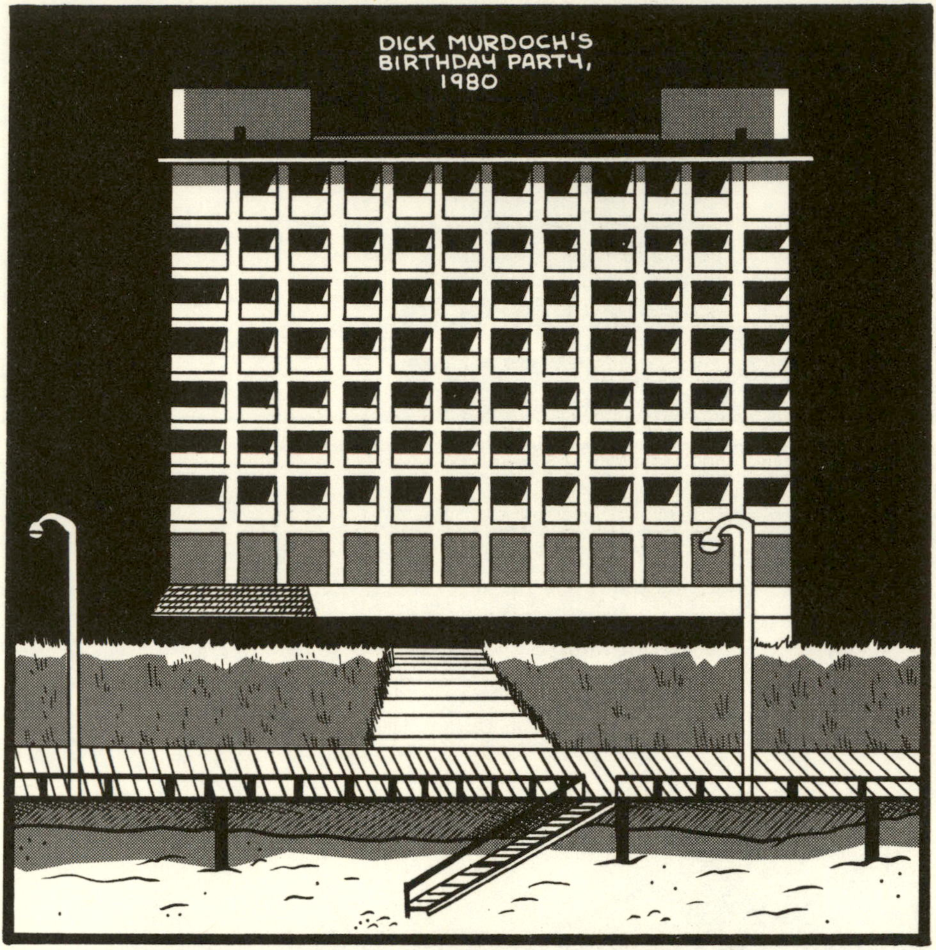
DICK MURDOCH'S BIRTHDAY PARTY, 1980

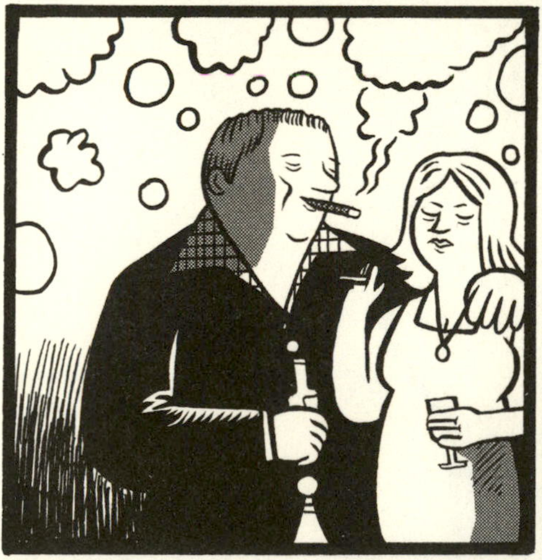

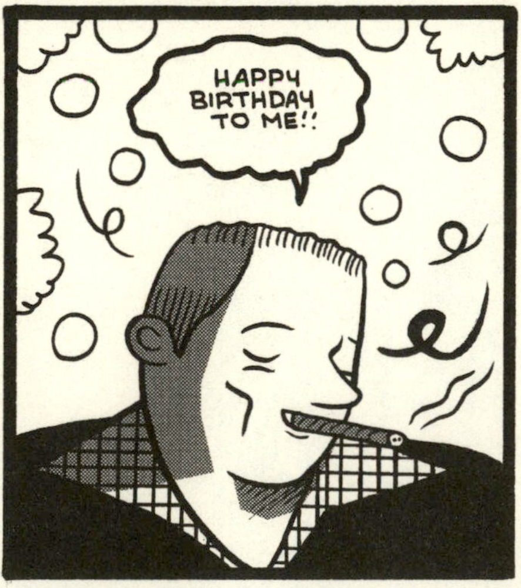
HAPPY BIRTHDAY TO ME!!

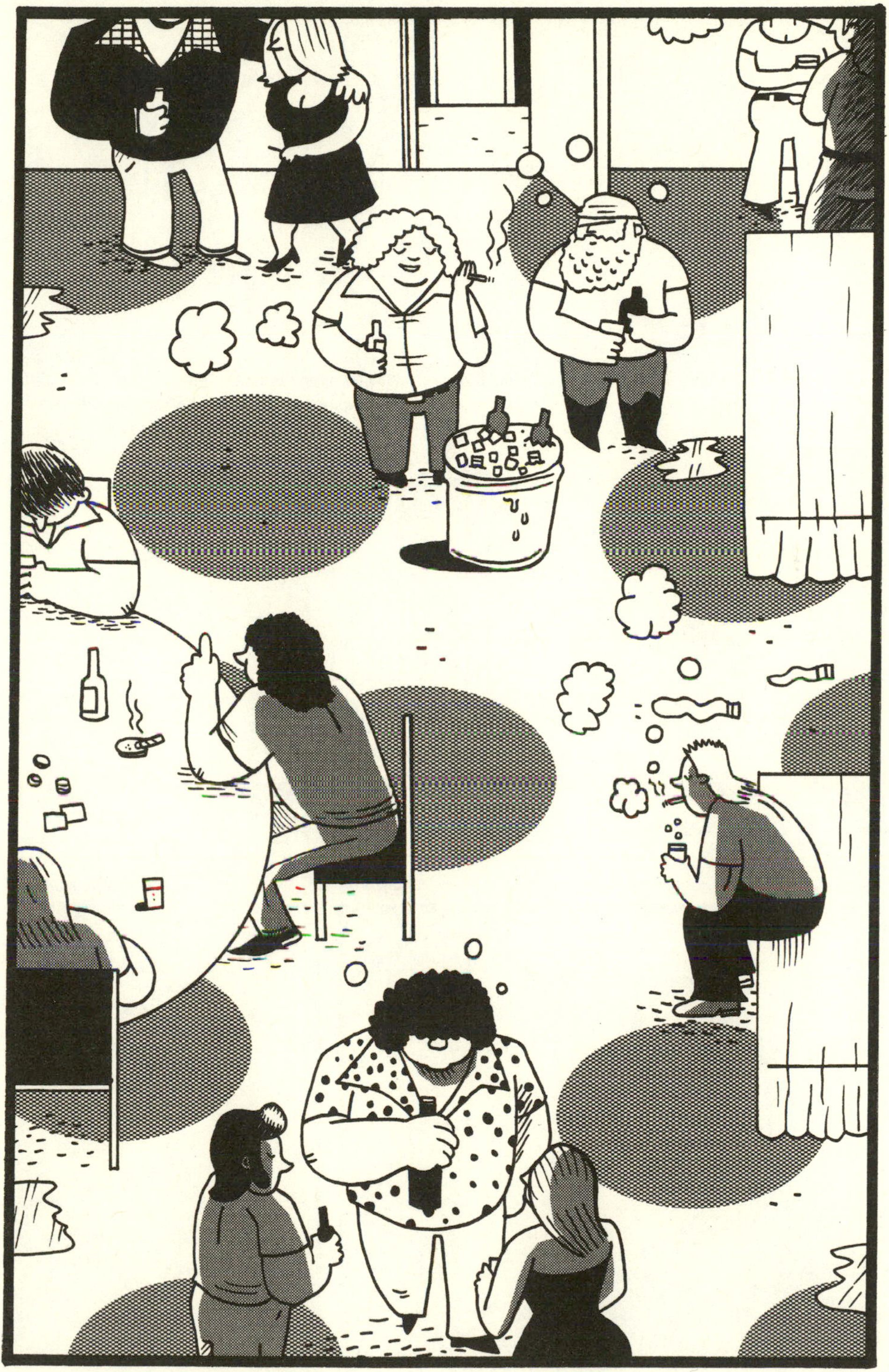

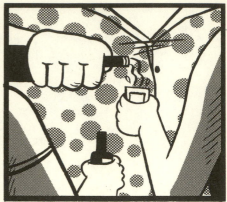

I LIKE YOU...

HEY! THAT'S MY GIRLFRIEND!

SHE GIVE GOOD ORAL SEX?

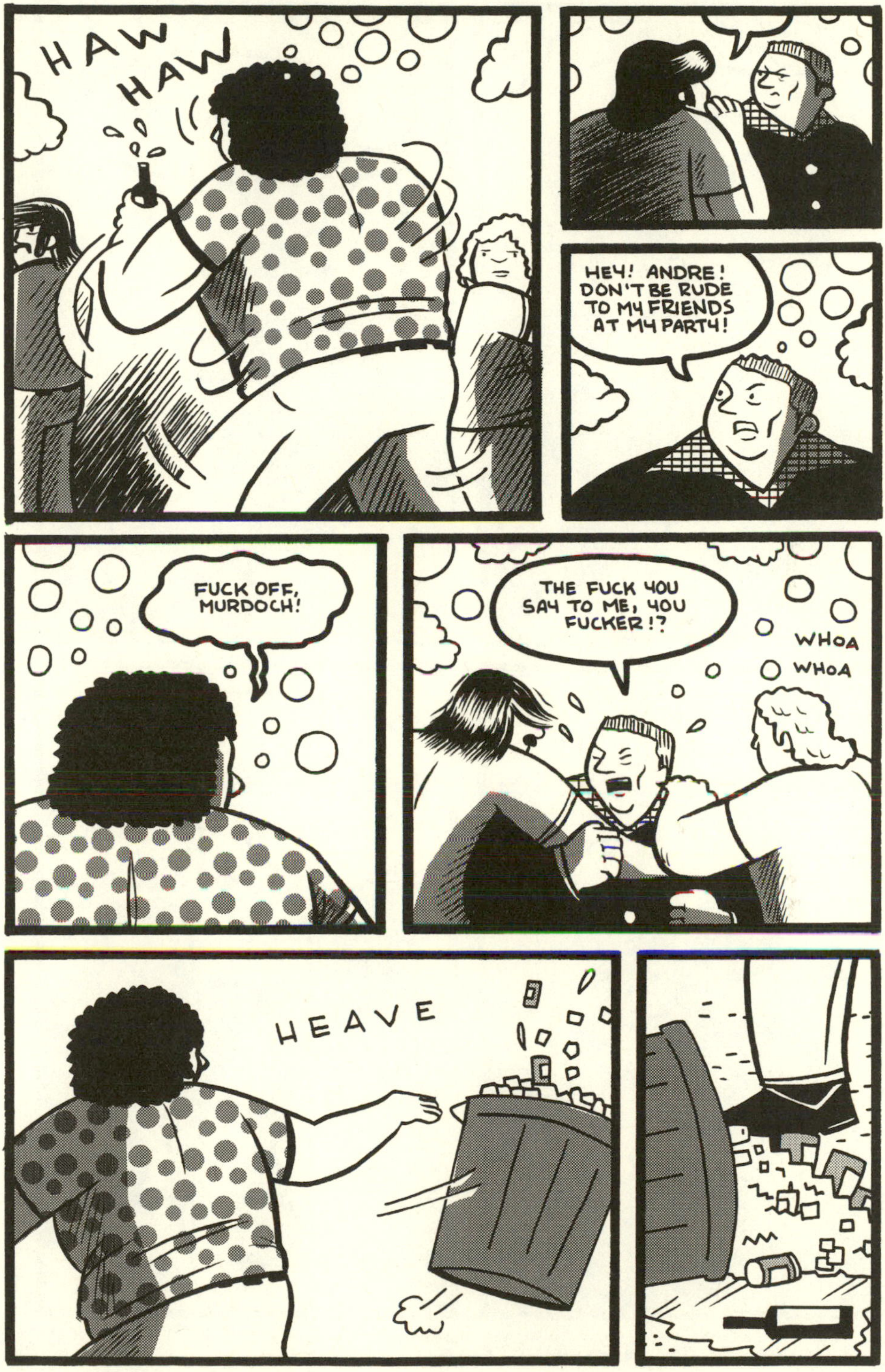
HAW HAW
HEY! ANDRE! DON'T BE RUDE TO MY FRIENDS AT MY PARTY!
FUCK OFF, MURDOCH!
THE FUCK YOU SAY TO ME, YOU FUCKER!?
WHOA WHOA
HEAVE

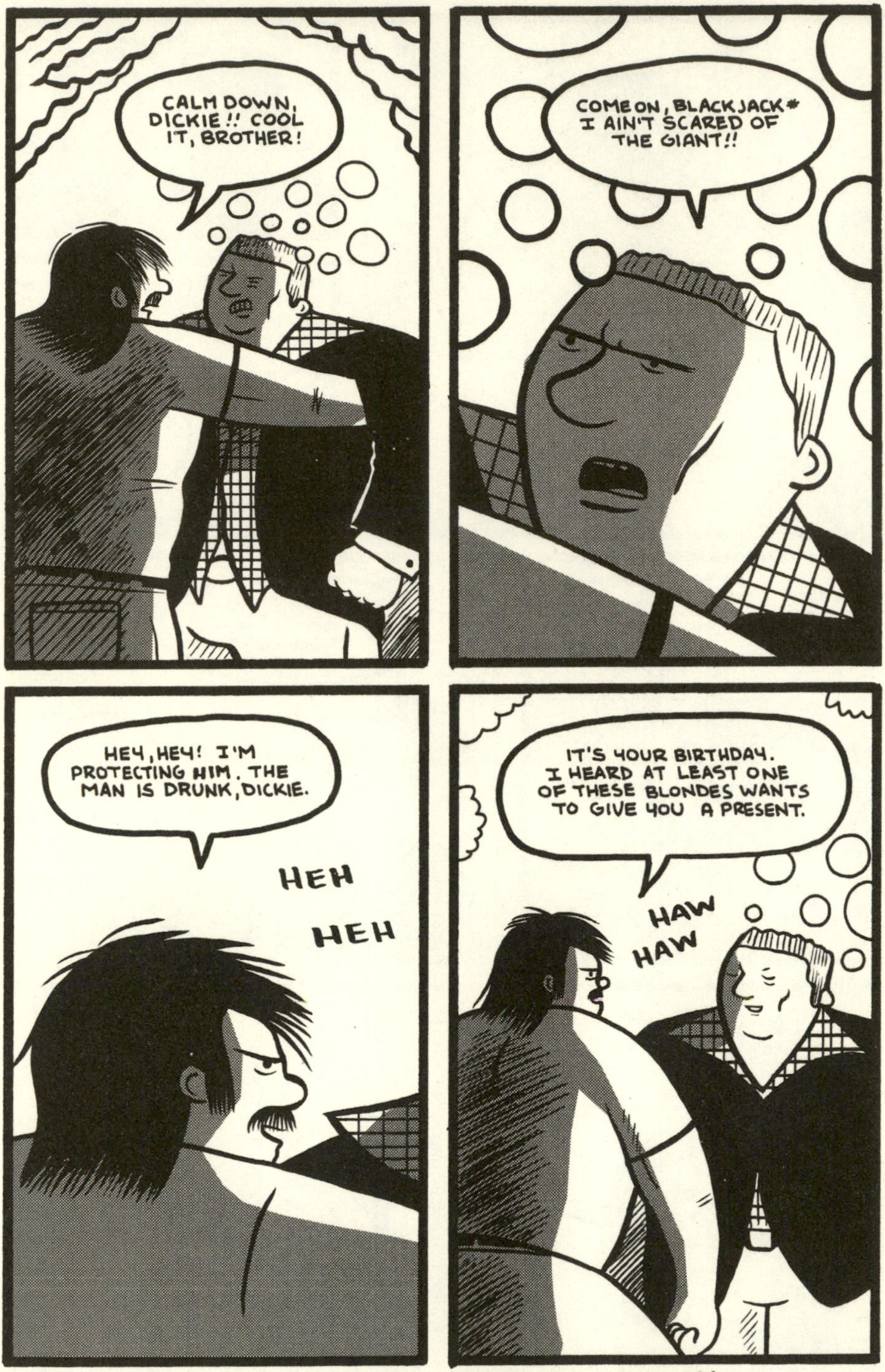
CALM DOWN, DICKIE!! COOL IT, BROTHER!
COME ON, BLACKJACK* I AIN'T SCARED OF THE GIANT!!
HEY, HEY! I'M PROTECTING HIM. THE MAN IS DRUNK, DICKIE.
HEH
HEH
IT'S YOUR BIRTHDAY. I HEARD AT LEAST ONE OF THESE BLONDES WANTS TO GIVE YOU A PRESENT.
HAW
HAW

* BLACKJACK MULLIGAN WAS AN ACTIVE WRESTLER FROM 1967-1988.
BILLED HEIGHT: 6' 9" BILLED WEIGHT: 340 lbs.

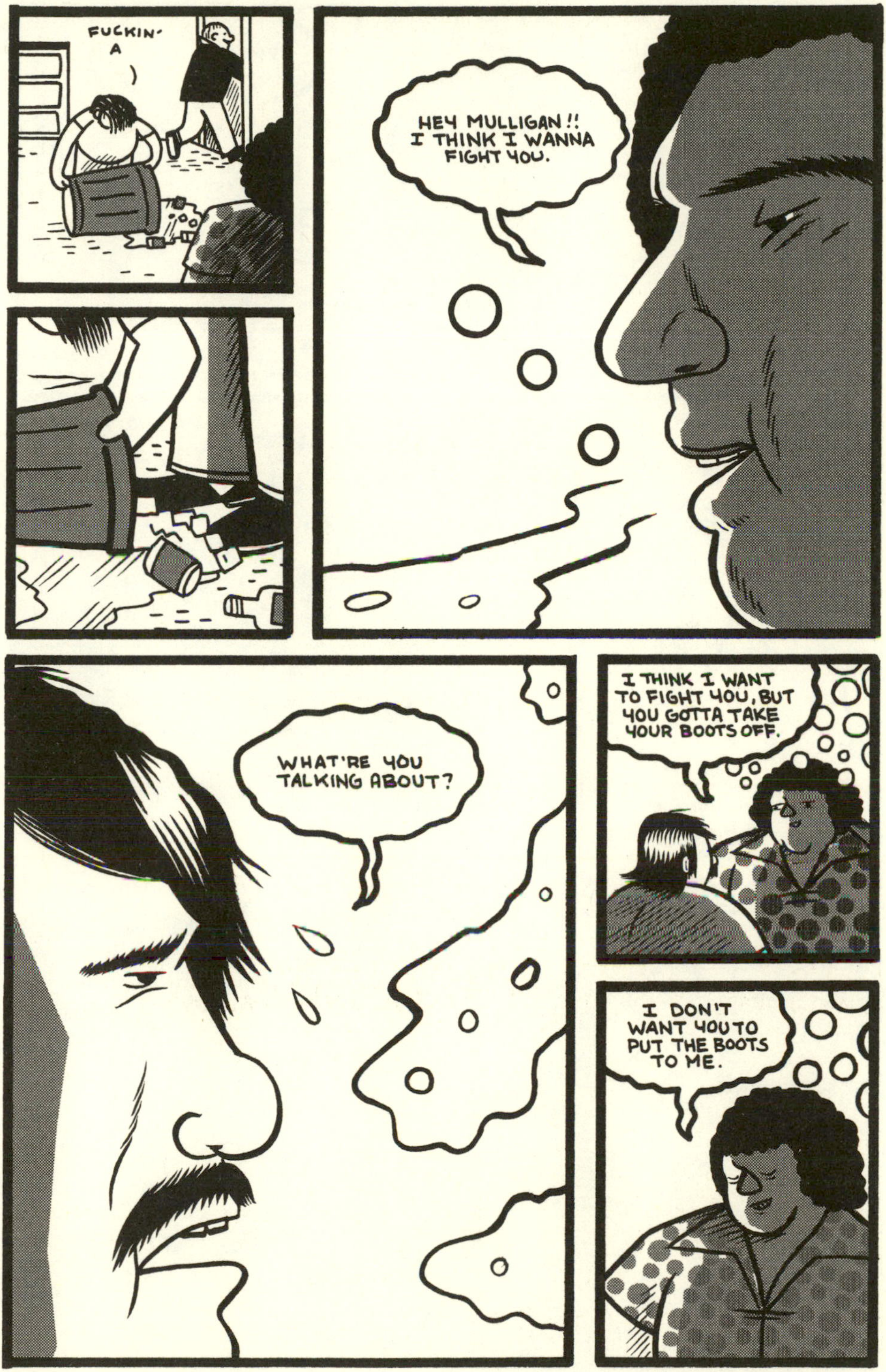
FUCKIN' A
HEY MULLIGAN!! I THINK I WANNA FIGHT YOU.
WHAT'RE YOU TALKING ABOUT?
I THINK I WANT TO FIGHT YOU, BUT YOU GOTTA TAKE YOUR BOOTS OFF.
I DON'T WANT YOU TO PUT THE BOOTS TO ME.

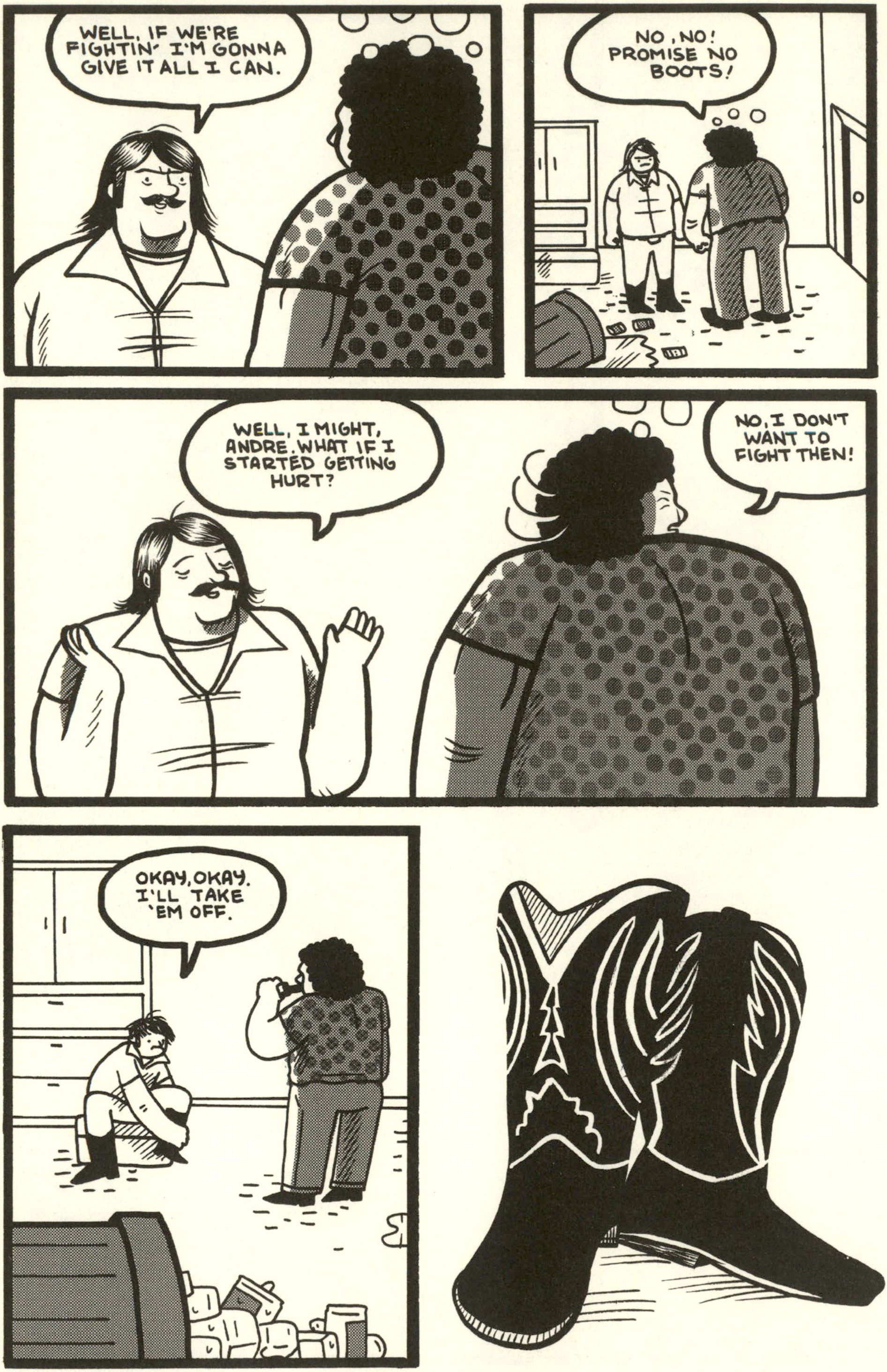
WELL, IF WE'RE FIGHTIN' I'M GONNA GIVE IT ALL I CAN.
NO, NO! PROMISE NO BOOTS!
WELL, I MIGHT, ANDRE. WHAT IF I STARTED GETTING HURT?
NO, I DON'T WANT TO FIGHT THEN!
OKAY, OKAY. I'LL TAKE 'EM OFF.

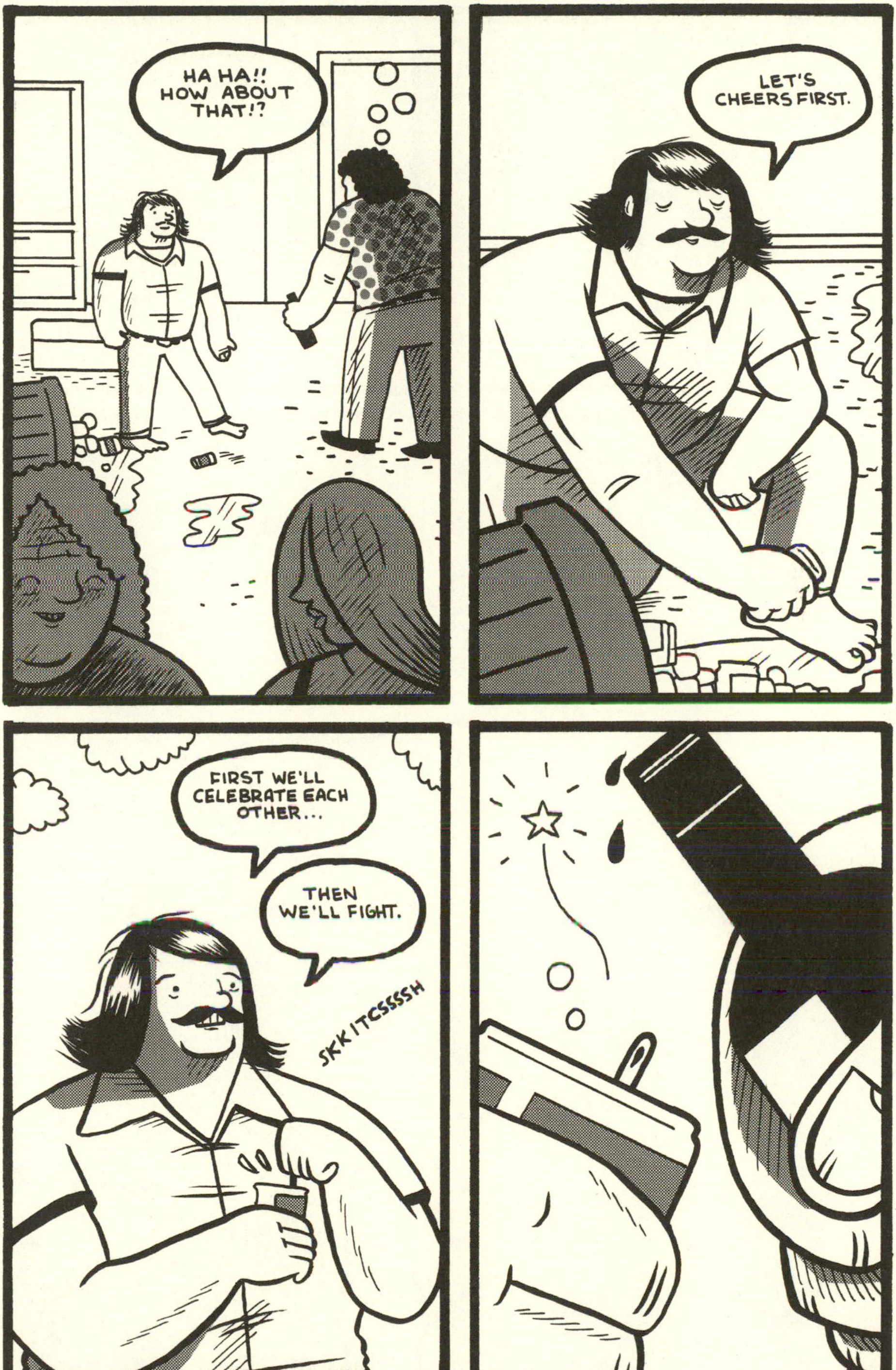
HA HA!! HOW ABOUT THAT!?
LET'S CHEERS FIRST.
FIRST WE'LL CELEBRATE EACH OTHER...
THEN WE'LL FIGHT.
SKKITCSSSSH

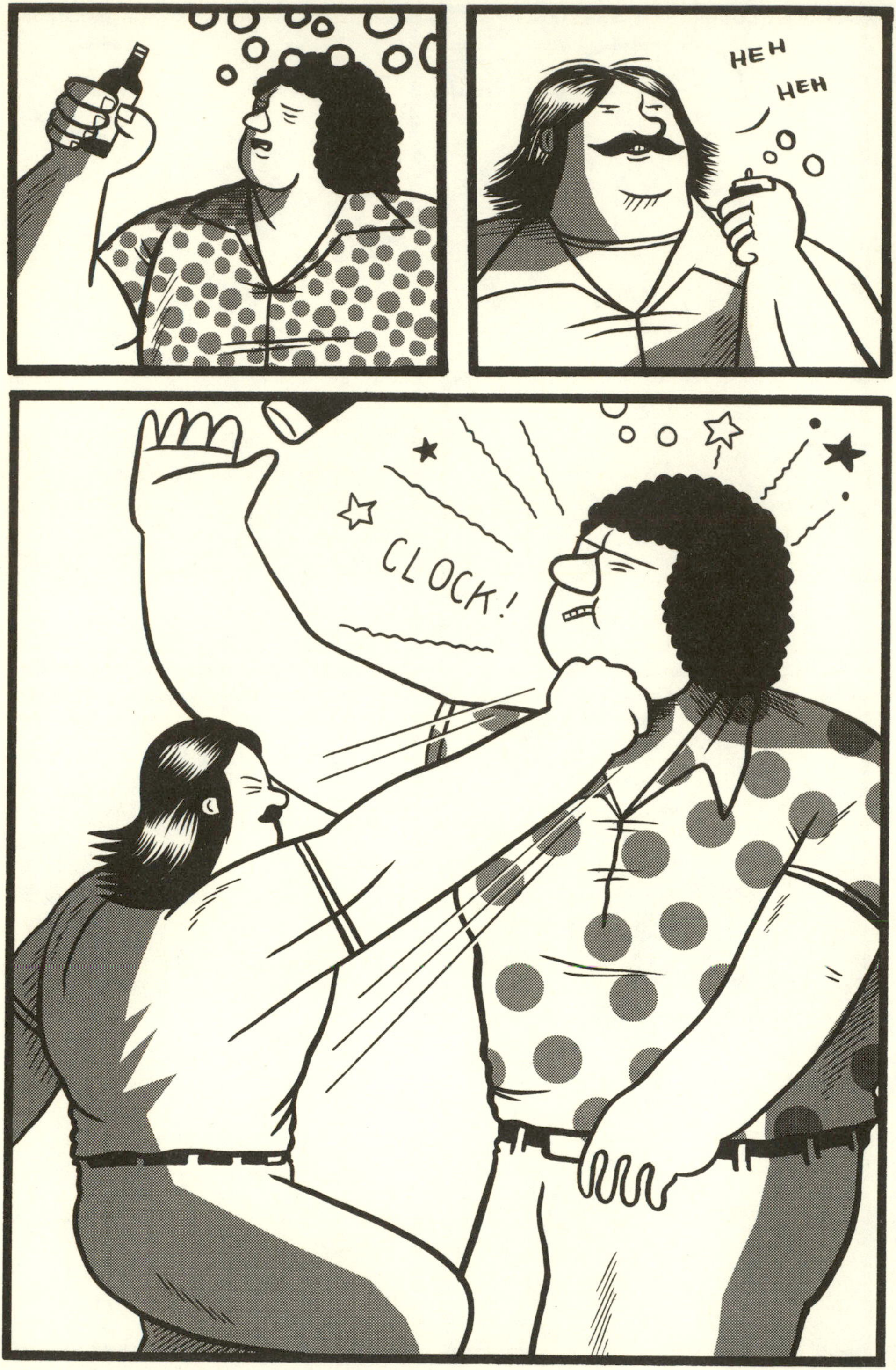
HEH
HEH
CLOCK!

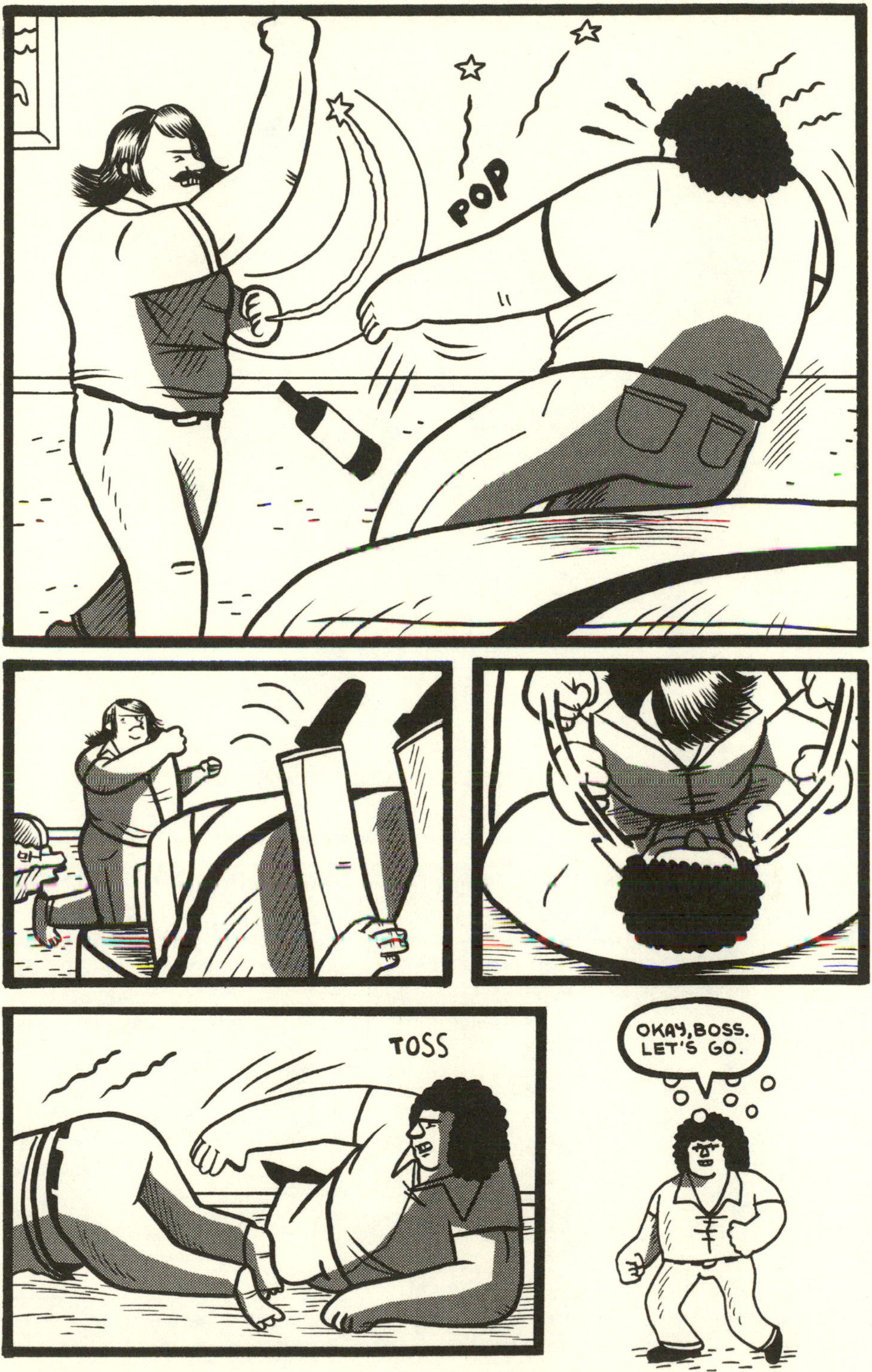
POP
TOSS
OKAY, BOSS. LET'S GO.

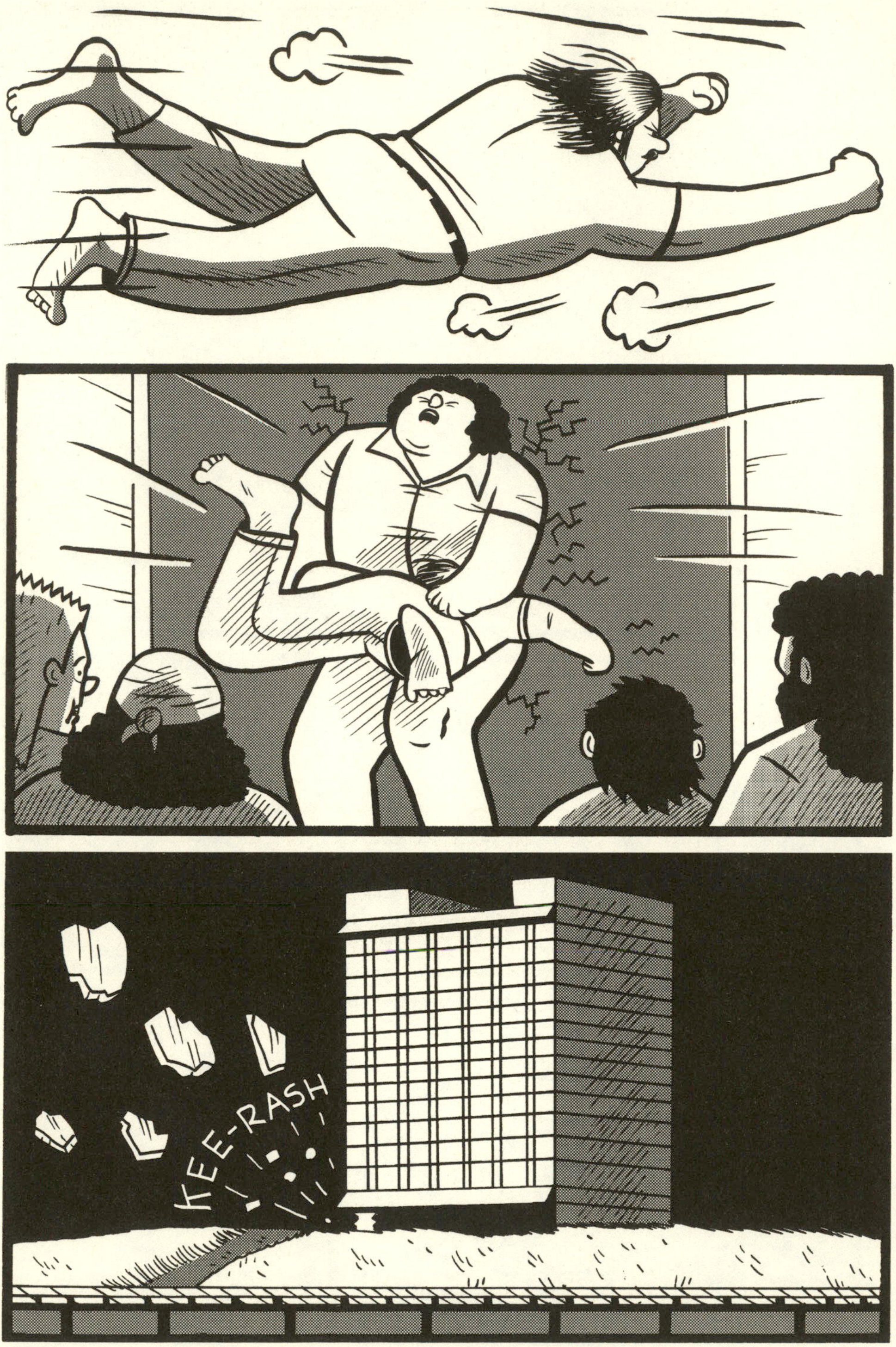
KEE-RASH

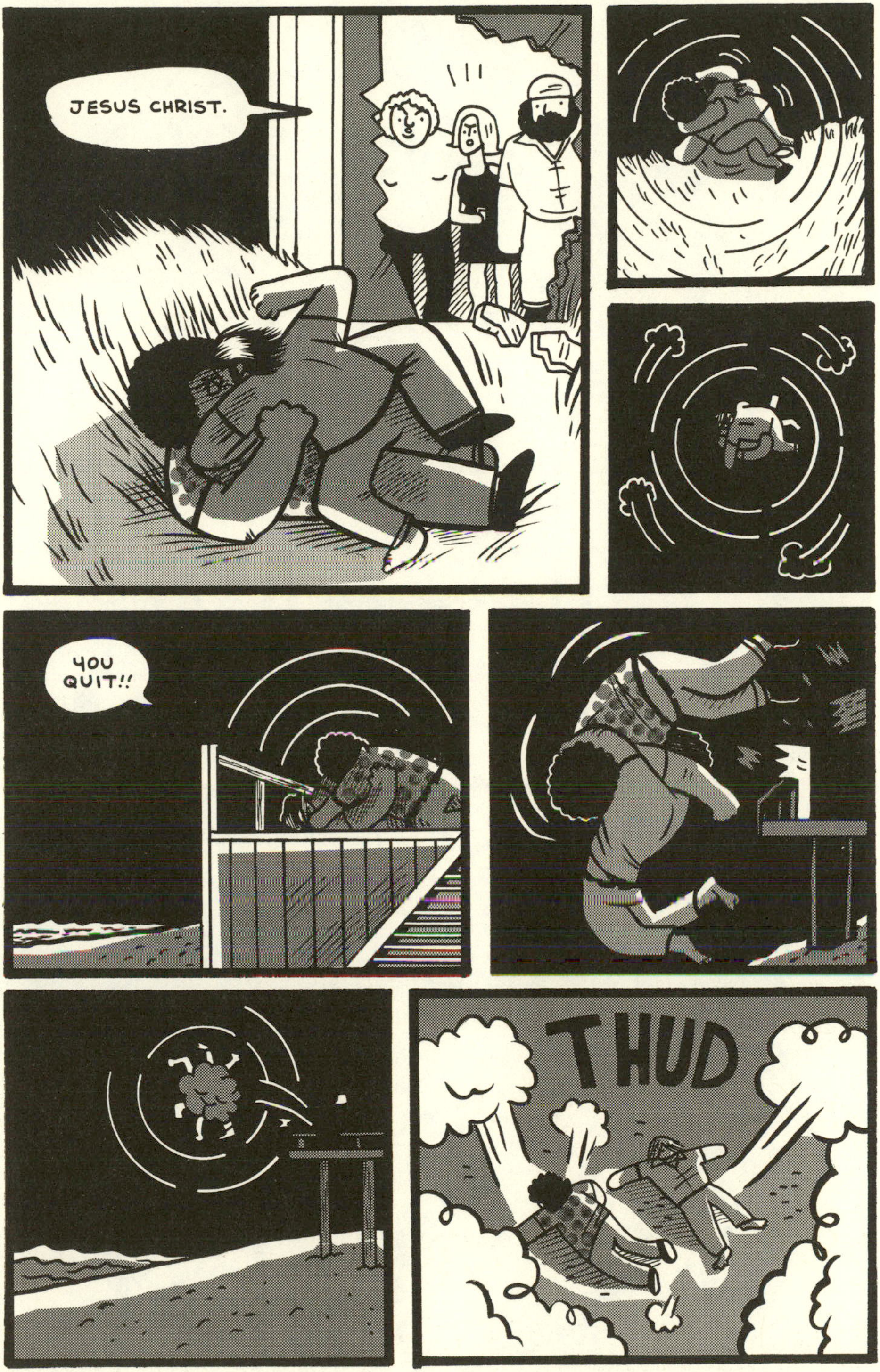
JESUS CHRIST.
YOU QUIT!!
THUD

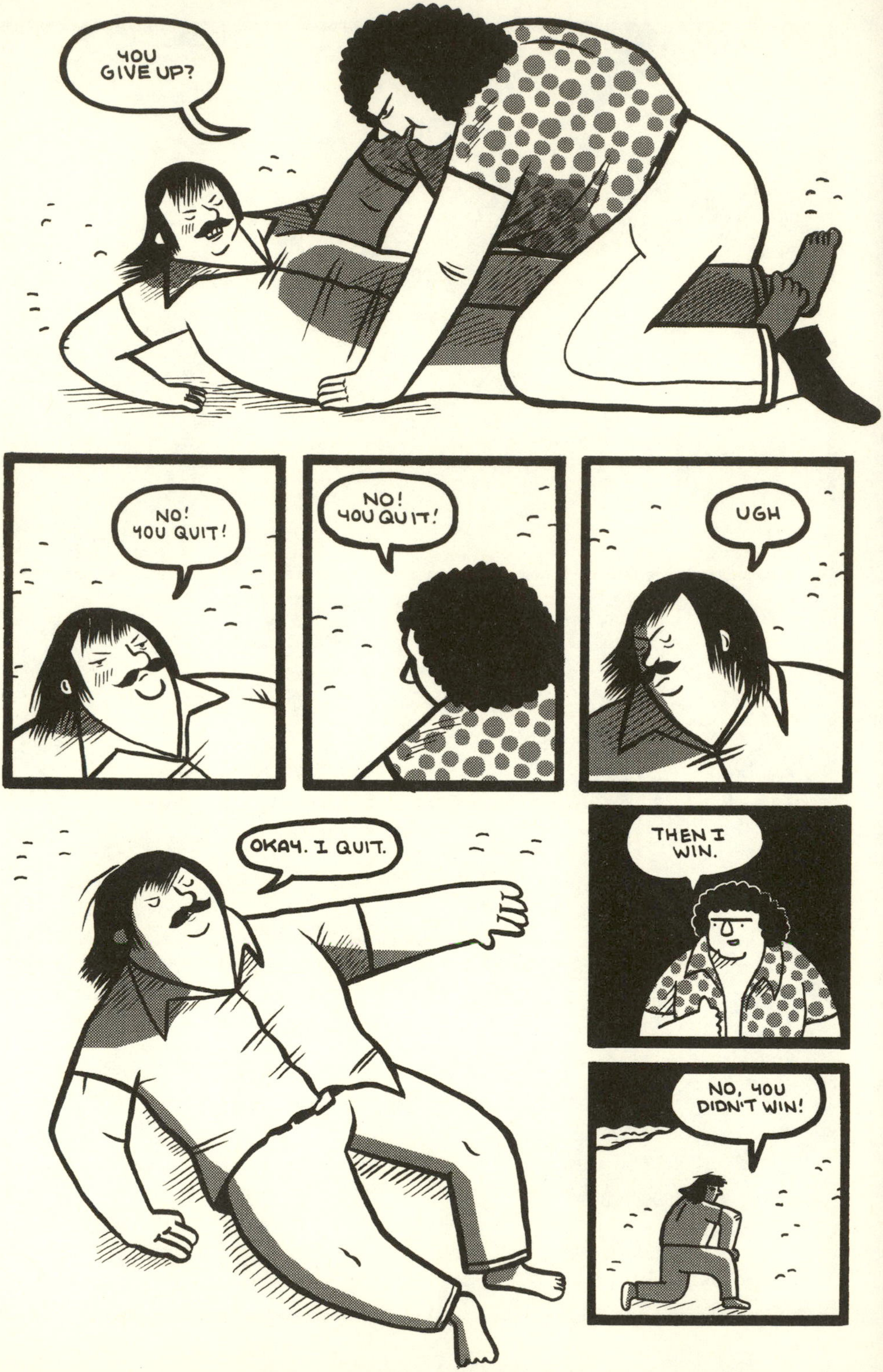
YOU GIVE UP?
NO! YOU QUIT!
NO! YOU QUIT!
UGH
OKAY. I QUIT.
THEN I WIN.
NO, YOU DIDN'T WIN!

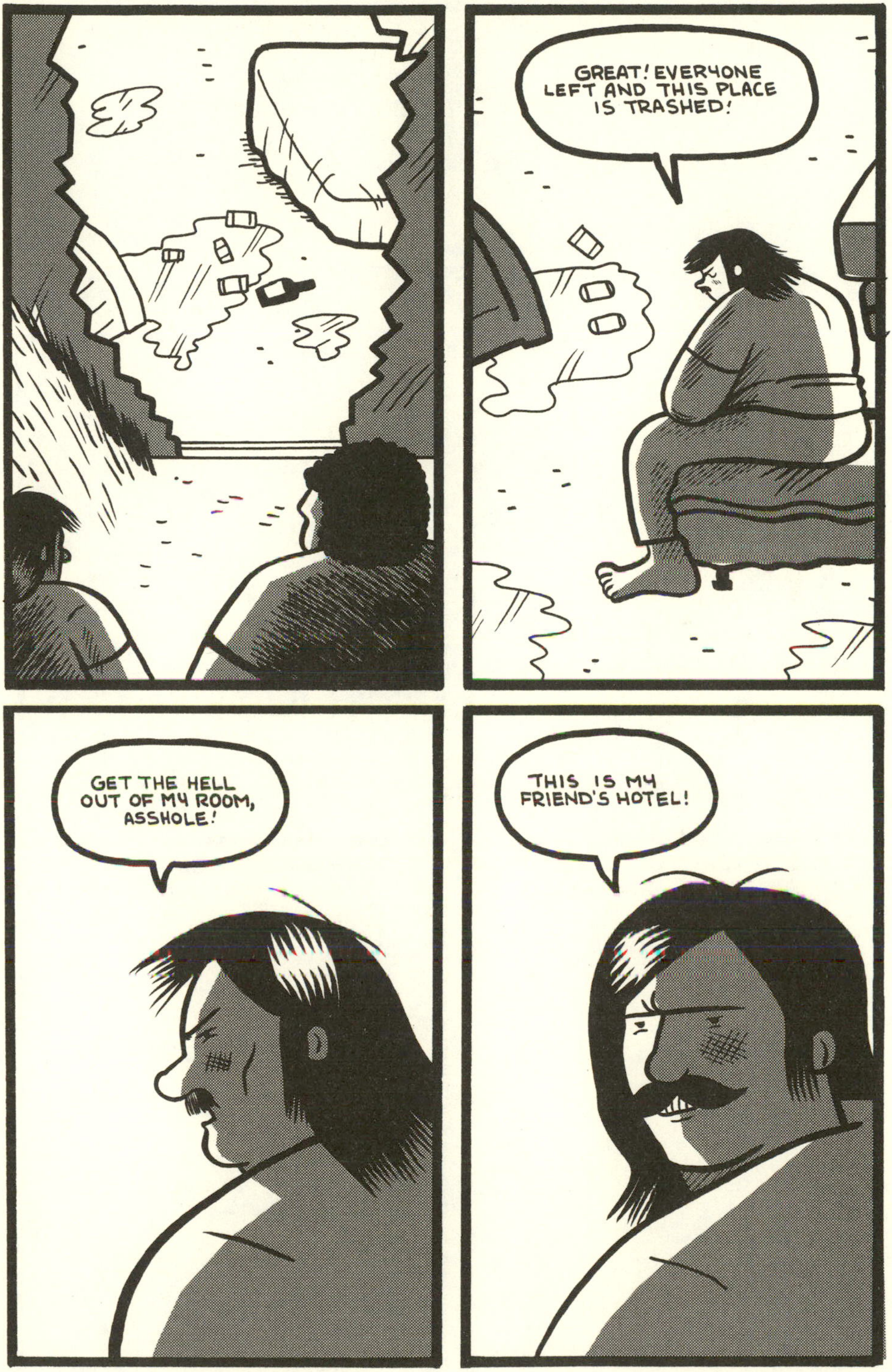
GREAT! EVERYONE LEFT AND THIS PLACE IS TRASHED!
GET THE HELL OUT OF MY ROOM, ASSHOLE!
THIS IS MY FRIEND'S HOTEL!

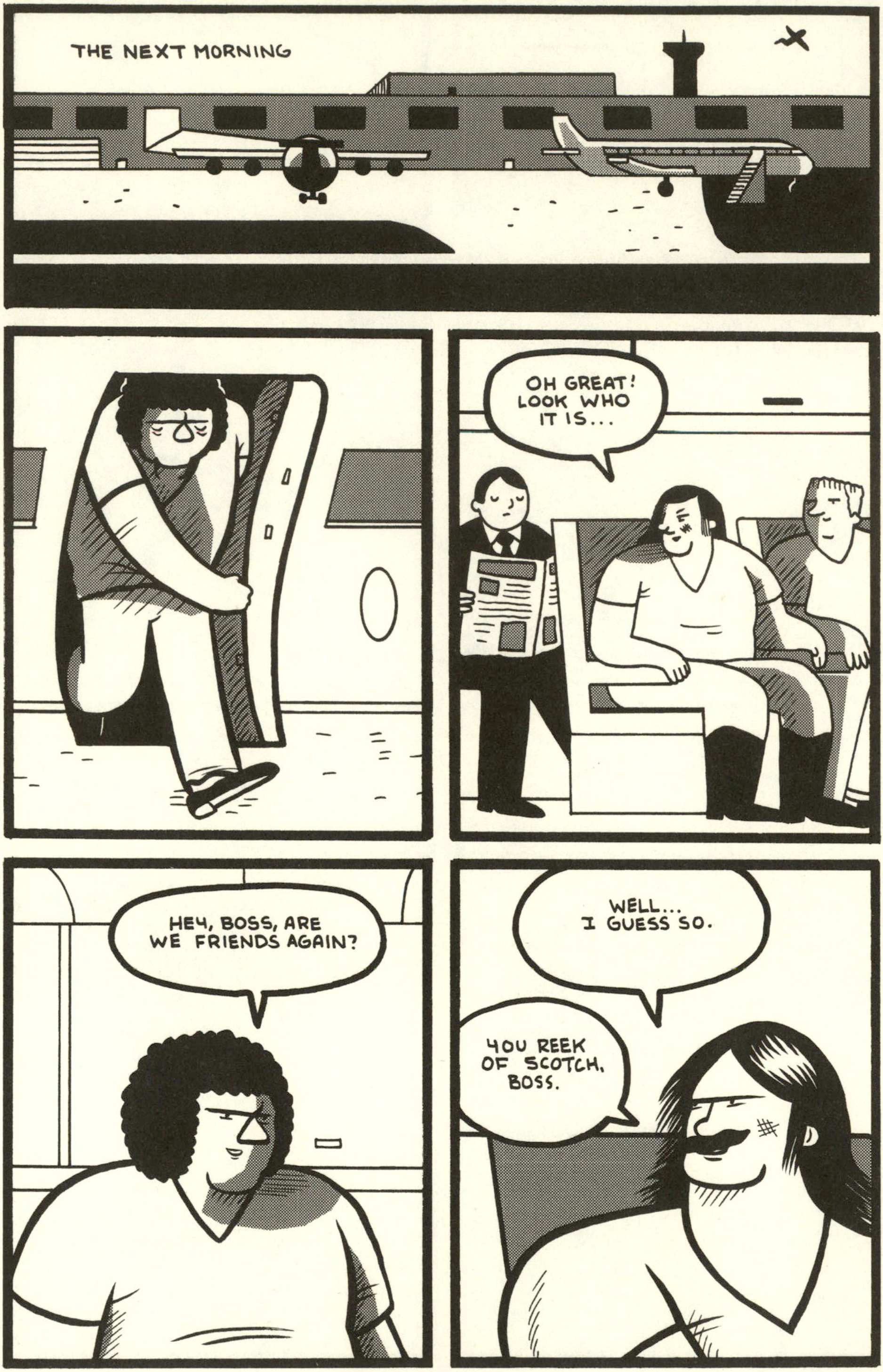
THE NEXT MORNING
OH GREAT! LOOK WHO IT IS...
HEY, BOSS, ARE WE FRIENDS AGAIN?
WELL... I GUESS SO.
YOU REEK OF SCOTCH, BOSS.

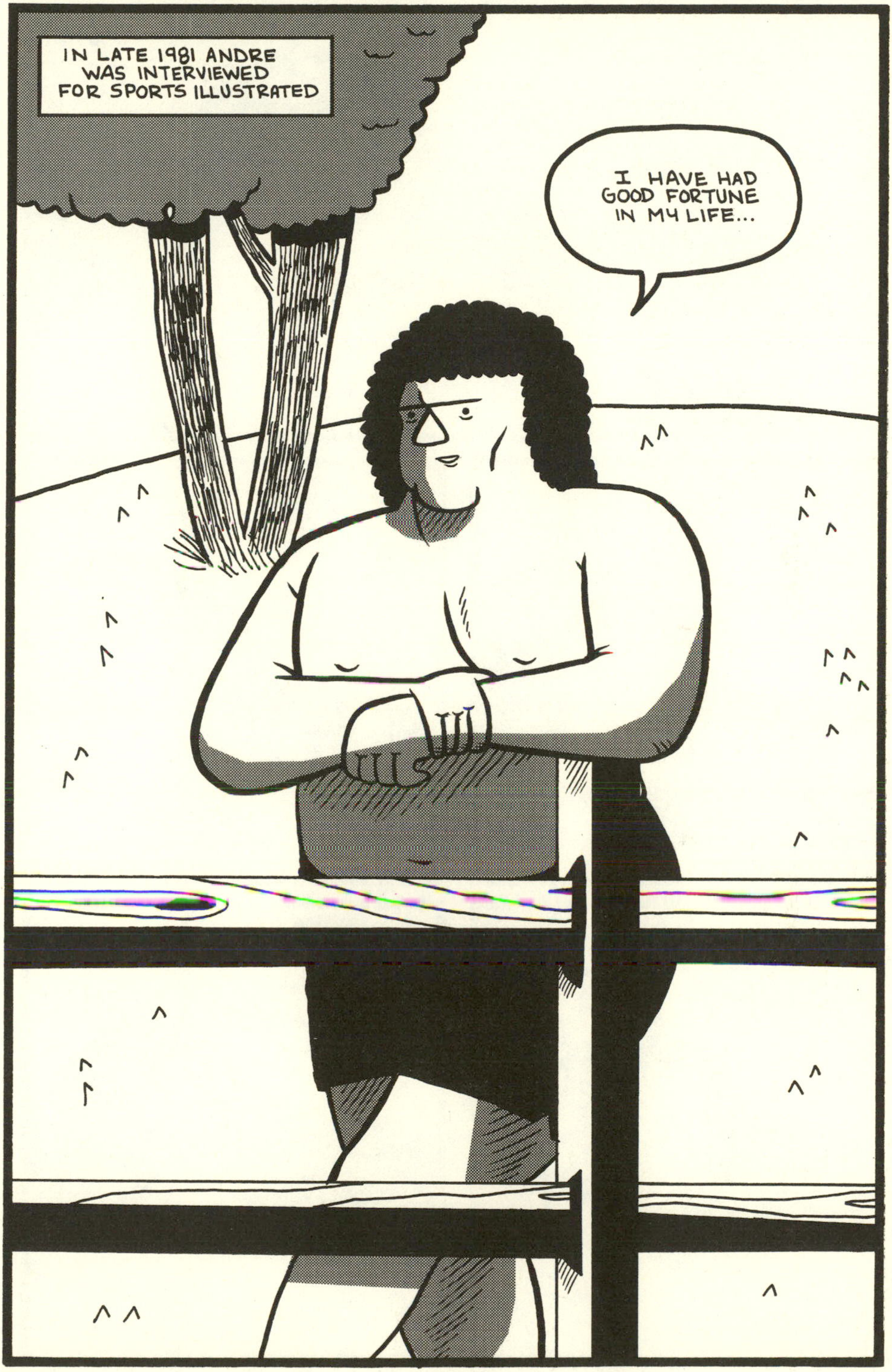
IN LATE 1981 ANDRE WAS INTERVIEWED FOR SPORTS ILLUSTRATED
I HAVE HAD GOOD FORTUNE IN MY LIFE...

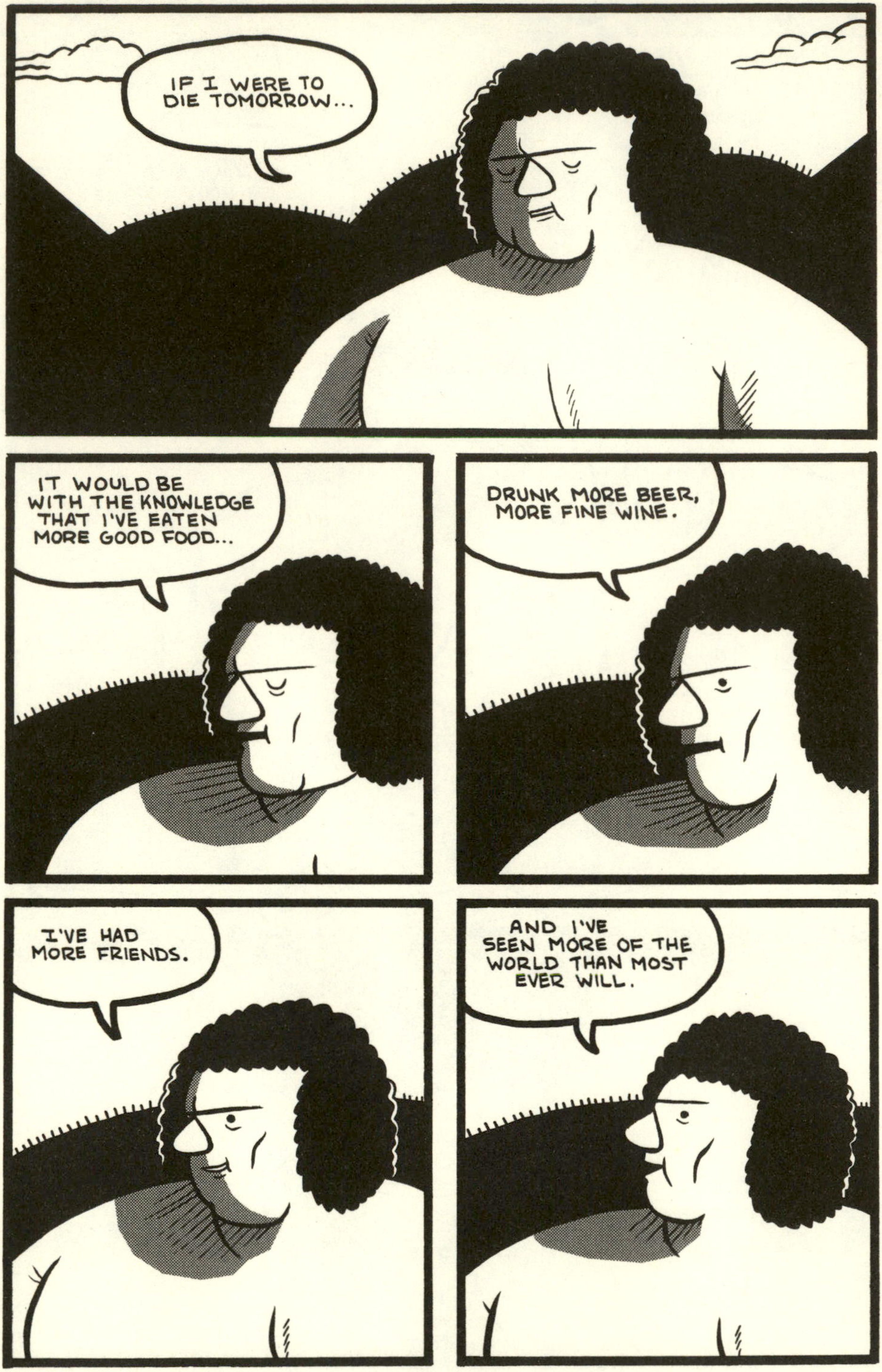

IF I WERE TO DIE TOMORROW...
IT WOULD BE WITH THE KNOWLEDGE THAT I'VE EATEN MORE GOOD FOOD...
DRUNK MORE BEER, MORE FINE WINE.
I'VE HAD MORE FRIENDS.
AND I'VE SEEN MORE OF THE WORLD THAN MOST EVER WILL.

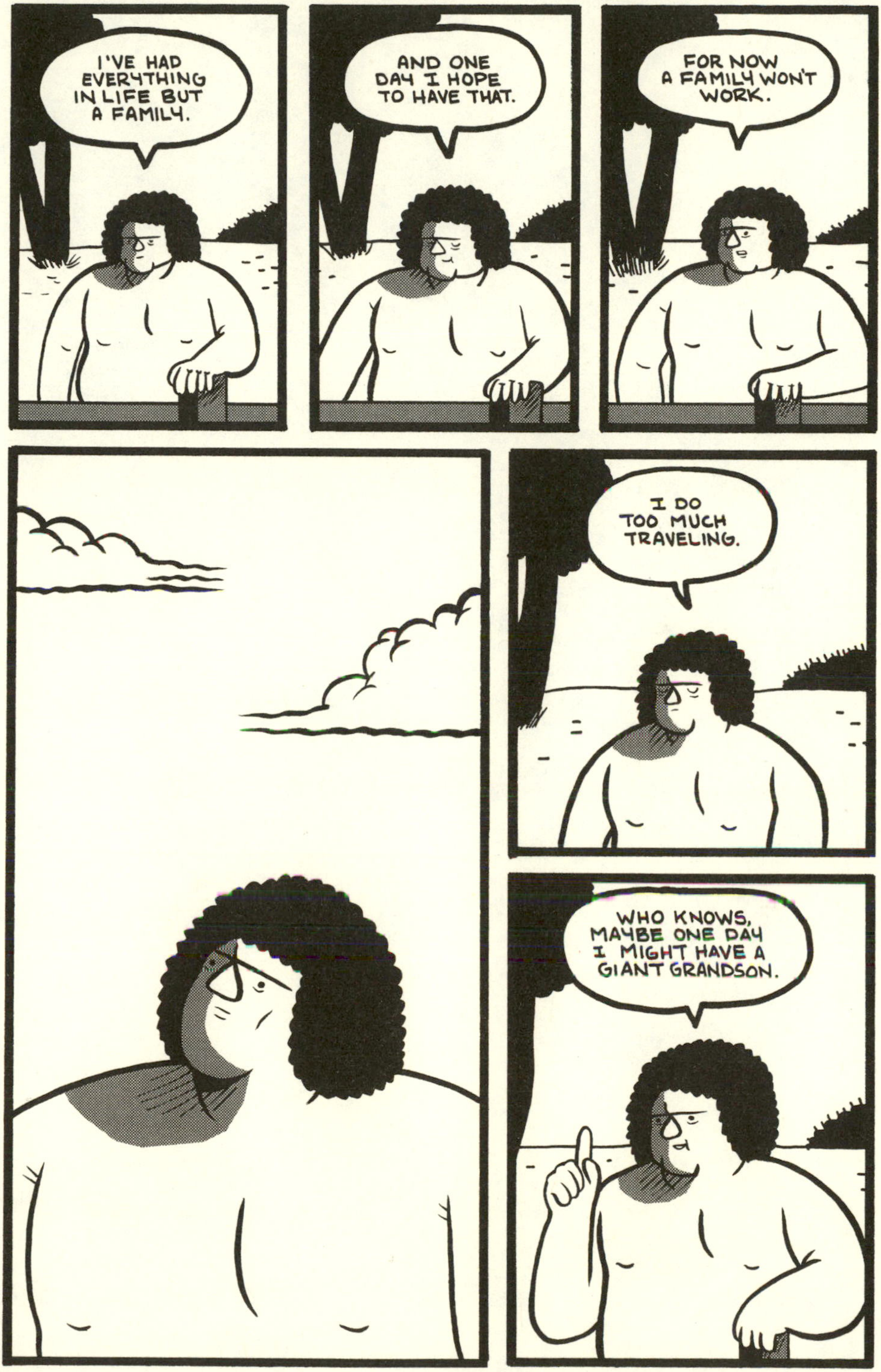
I'VE HAD EVERYTHING IN LIFE BUT A FAMILY.
AND ONE DAY I HOPE TO HAVE THAT.
FOR NOW A FAMILY WON'T WORK.
I DO TOO MUCH TRAVELING.
WHO KNOWS, MAYBE ONE DAY I MIGHT HAVE A GIANT GRANDSON.

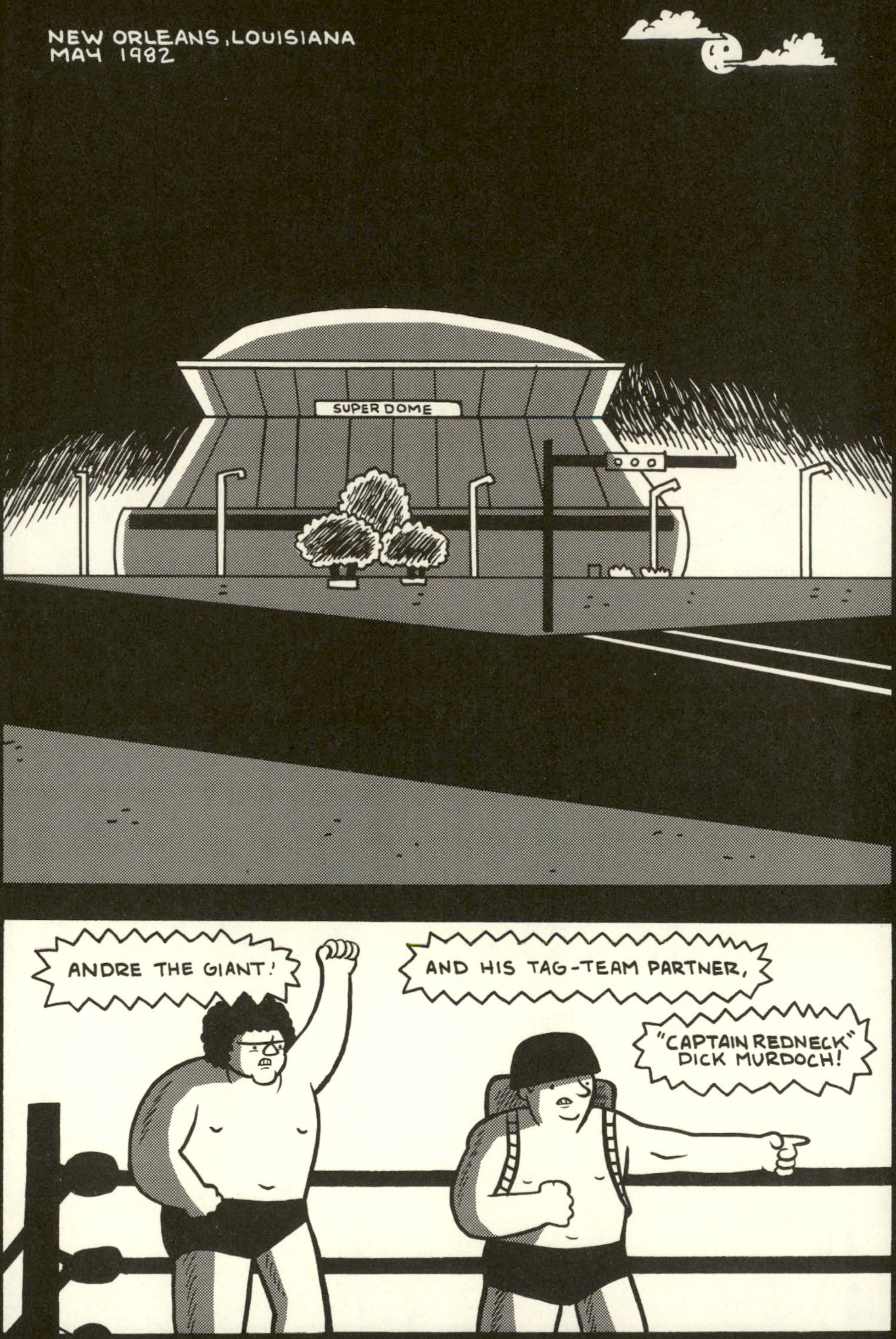
NEW ORLEANS, LOUISIANA
MAY 1982
SUPER DOME
ANDRE THE GIANT!
AND HIS TAG-TEAM PARTNER,
"CAPTAIN REDNECK" DICK MURDOCH!

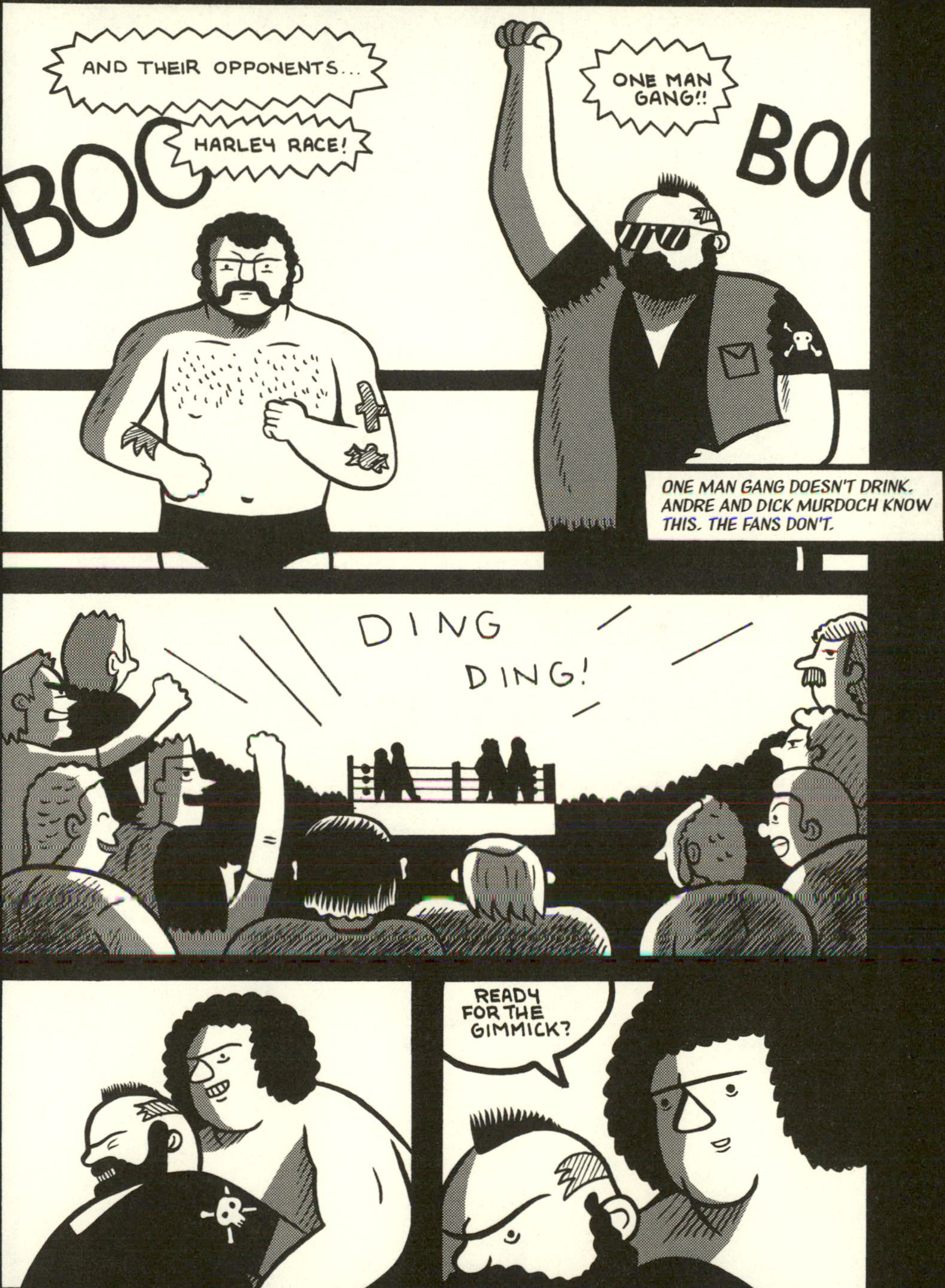
AND THEIR OPPONENTS...
HARLEY RACE!
BOO
ONE MAN GANG!!
BOO
ONE MAN GANG DOESN'T DRINK. ANDRE AND DICK MURDOCH KNOW THIS. THE FANS DON'T.
DING
DING!
READY FOR THE GIMMICK?

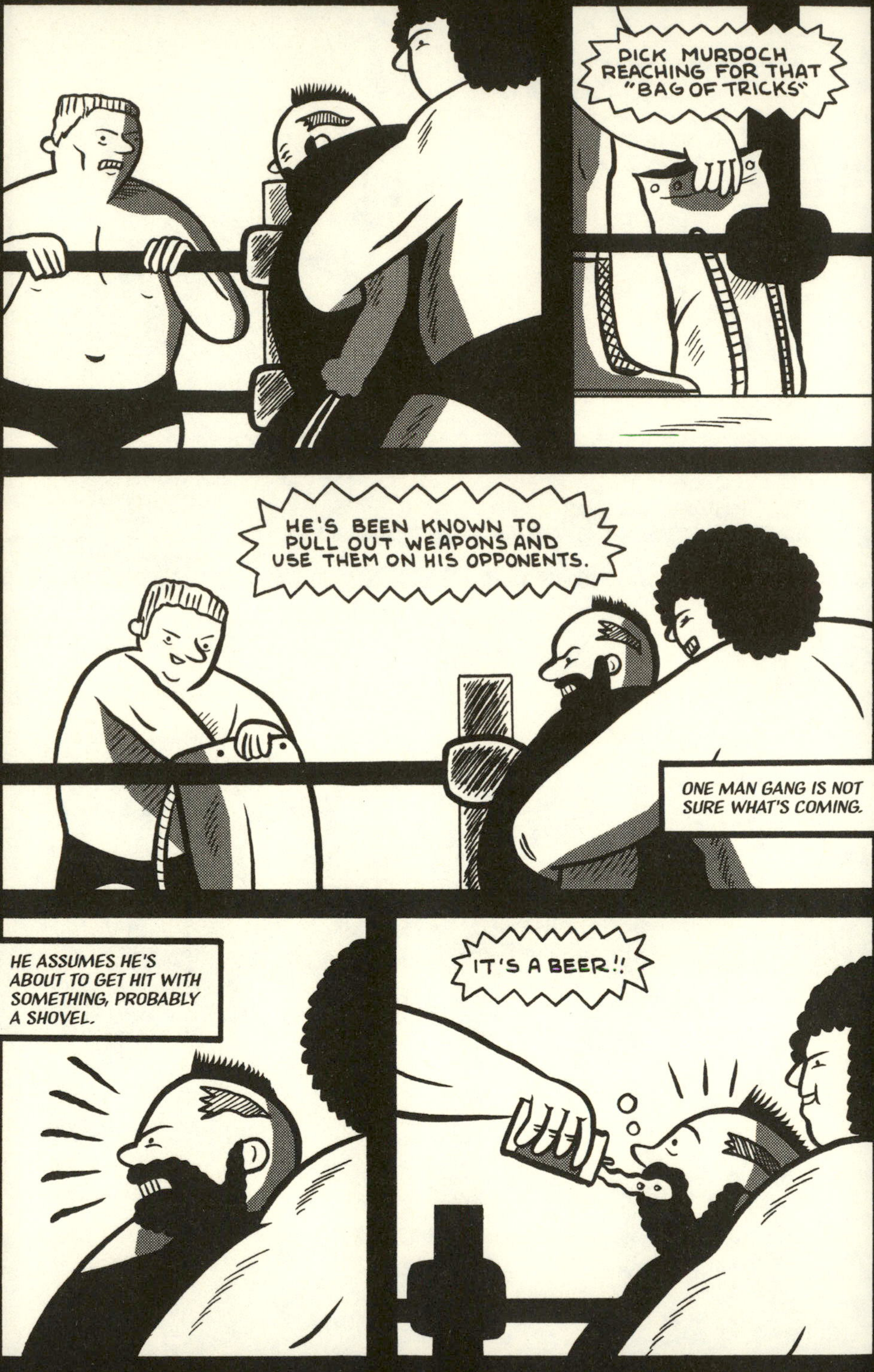
DICK MURDOCH REACHING FOR THAT "BAG OF TRICKS"
HE'S BEEN KNOWN TO PULL OUT WEAPONS AND USE THEM ON HIS OPPONENTS.
ONE MAN GANG IS NOT SURE WHAT'S COMING.
HE ASSUMES HE'S ABOUT TO GET HIT WITH SOMETHING, PROBABLY A SHOVEL.
IT'S A BEER!!

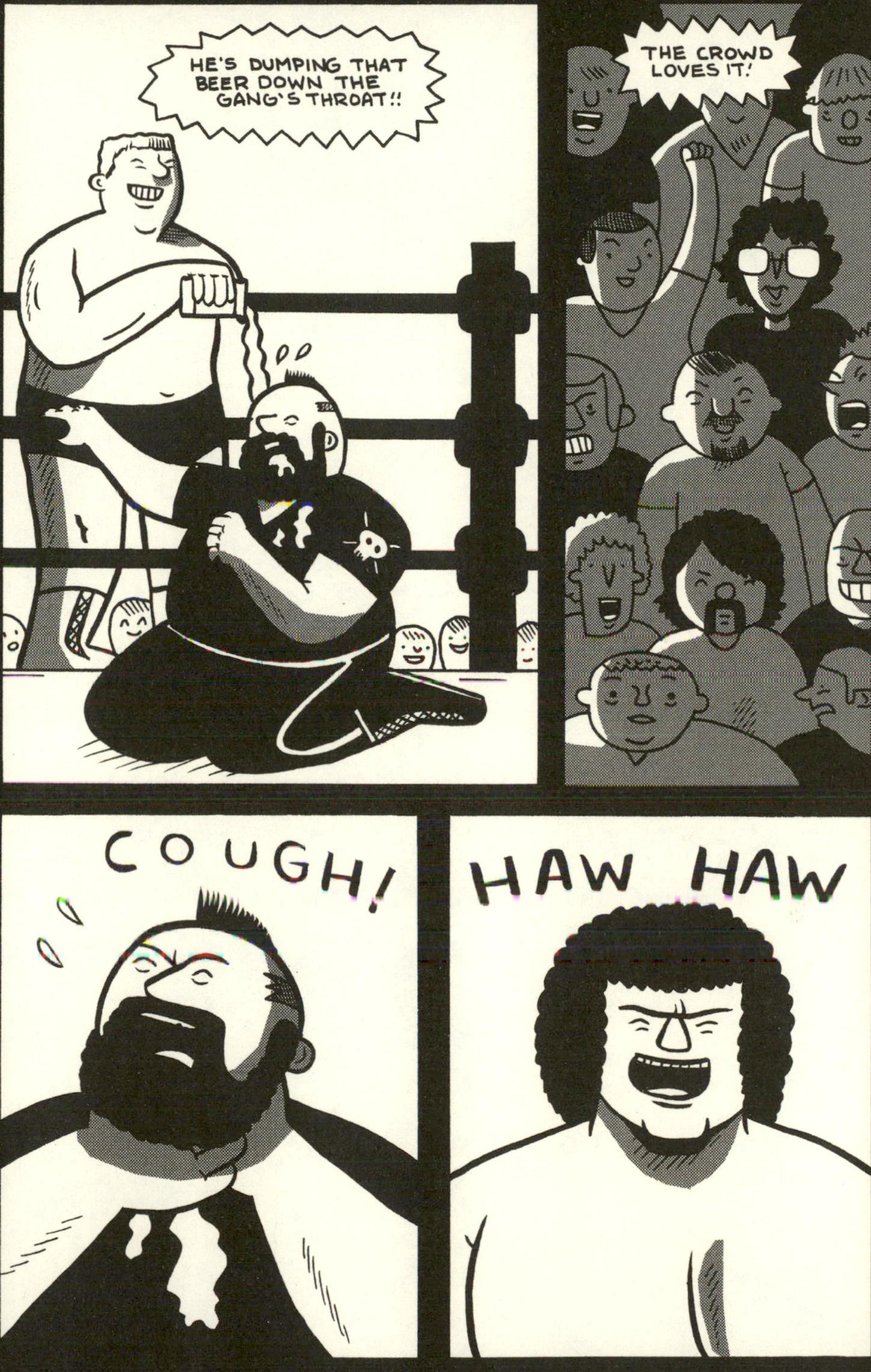
HE'S DUMPING THAT BEER DOWN THE GANG'S THROAT!!
THE CROWD LOVES IT!
COUGH!
HAW HAW

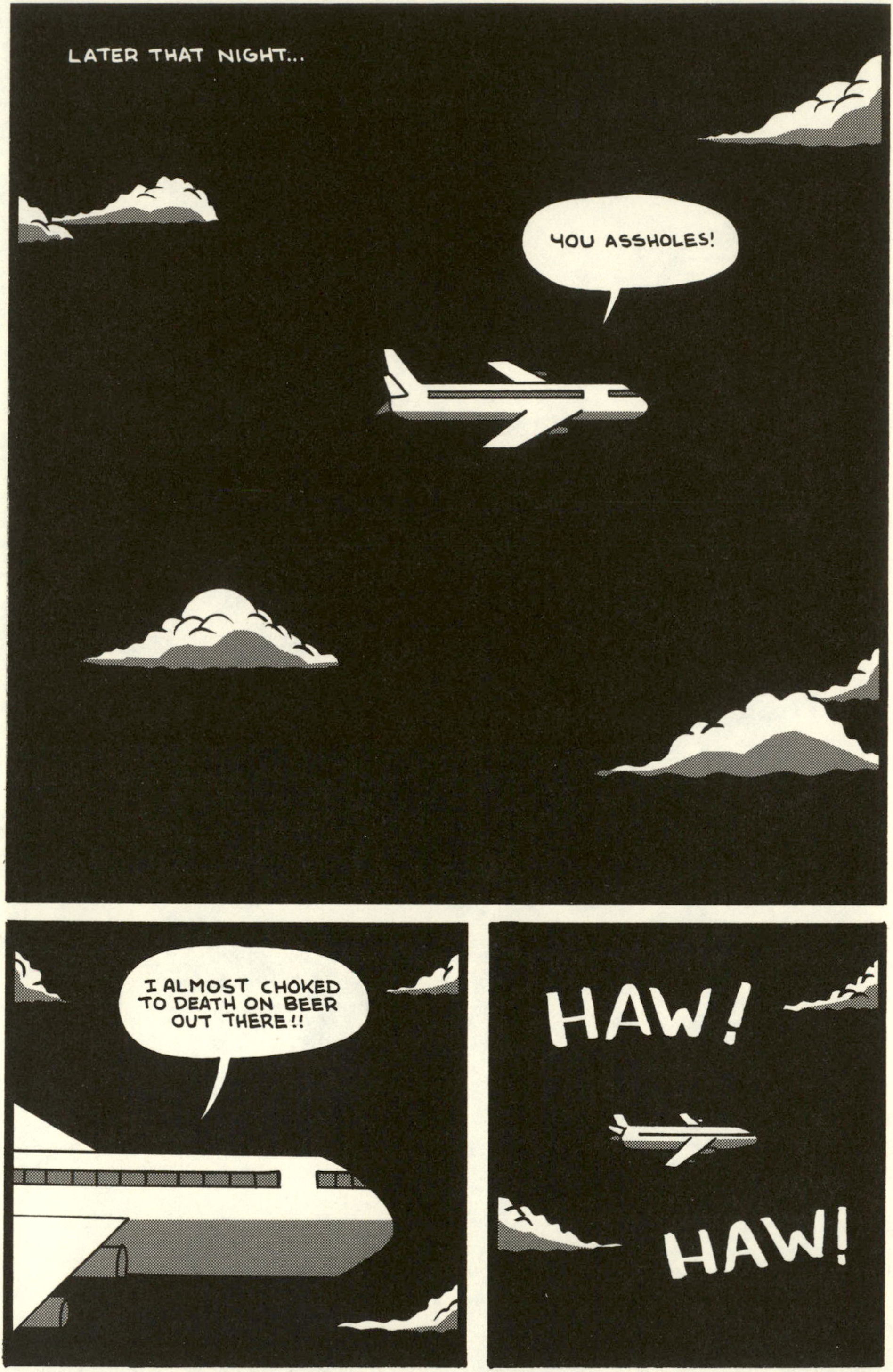
LATER THAT NIGHT...
YOU ASSHOLES!
I ALMOST CHOKED TO DEATH ON BEER OUT THERE!!
HAW!
HAW!

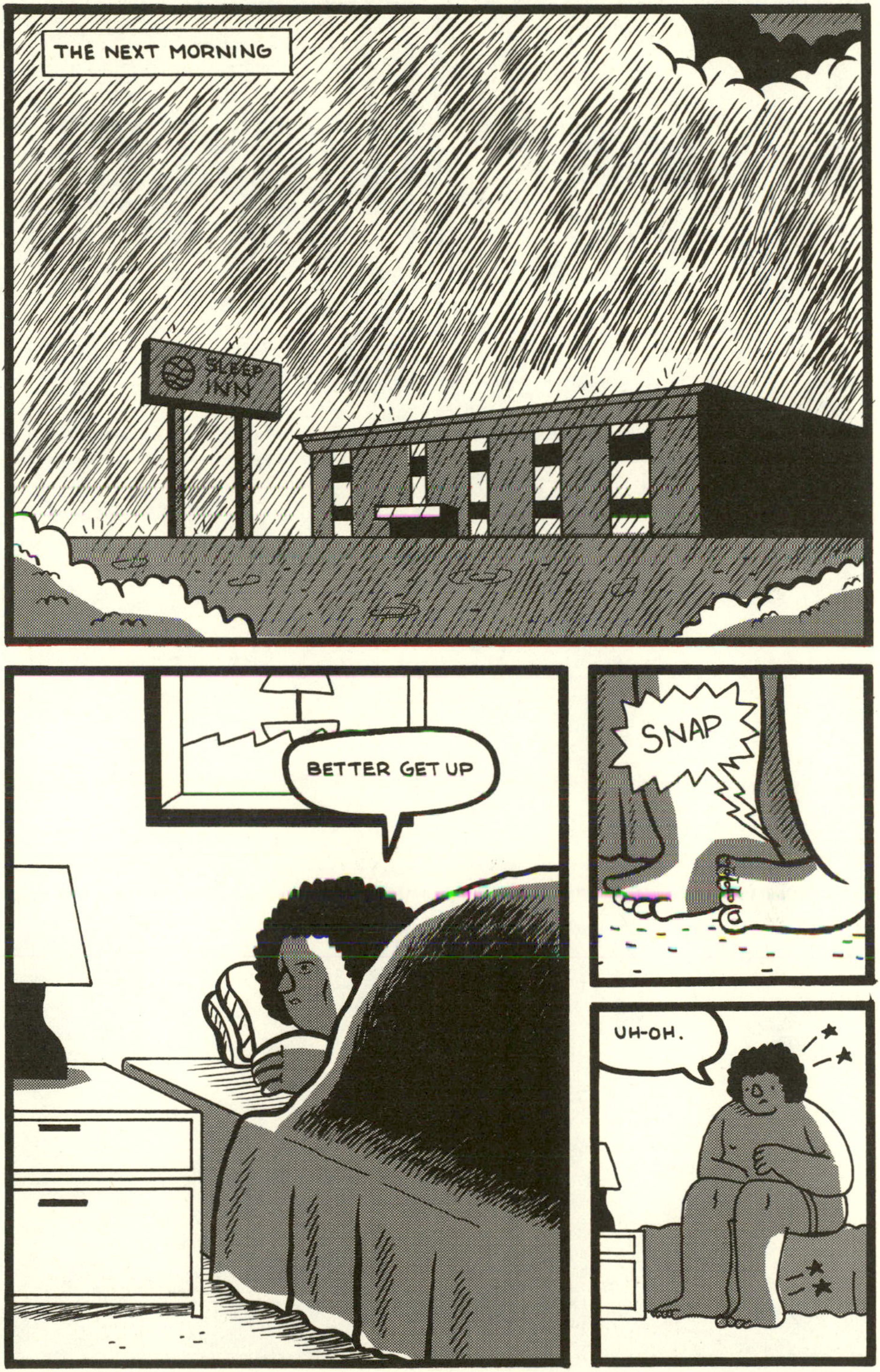
THE NEXT MORNING
SLEEP INN
BETTER GET UP
SNAP
UH-OH.

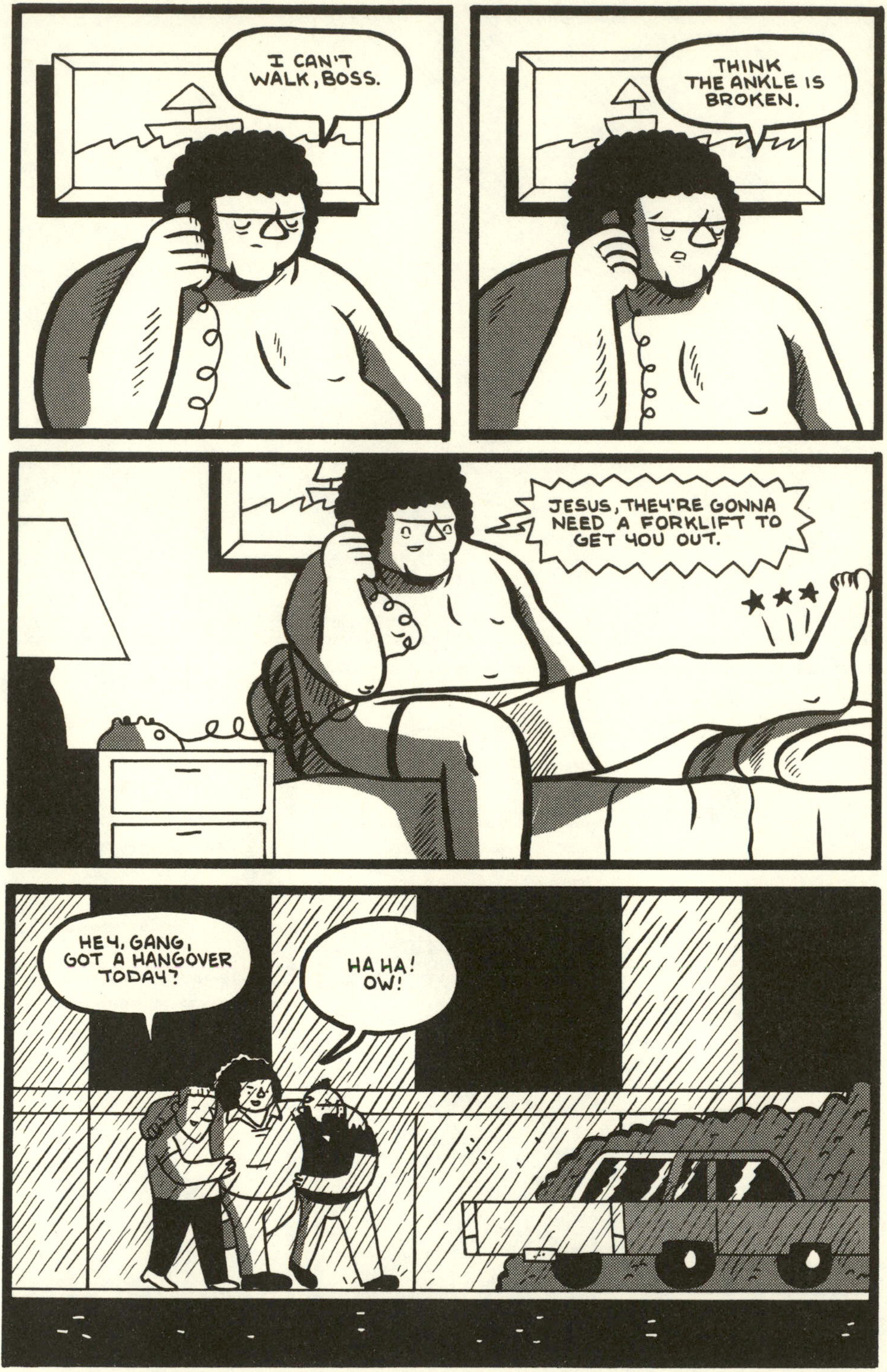
I CAN'T WALK, BOSS.
THINK THE ANKLE IS BROKEN.
JESUS, THEY'RE GONNA NEED A FORKLIFT TO GET YOU OUT.
HEY, GANG, GOT A HANGOVER TODAY?
HA HA! OW!

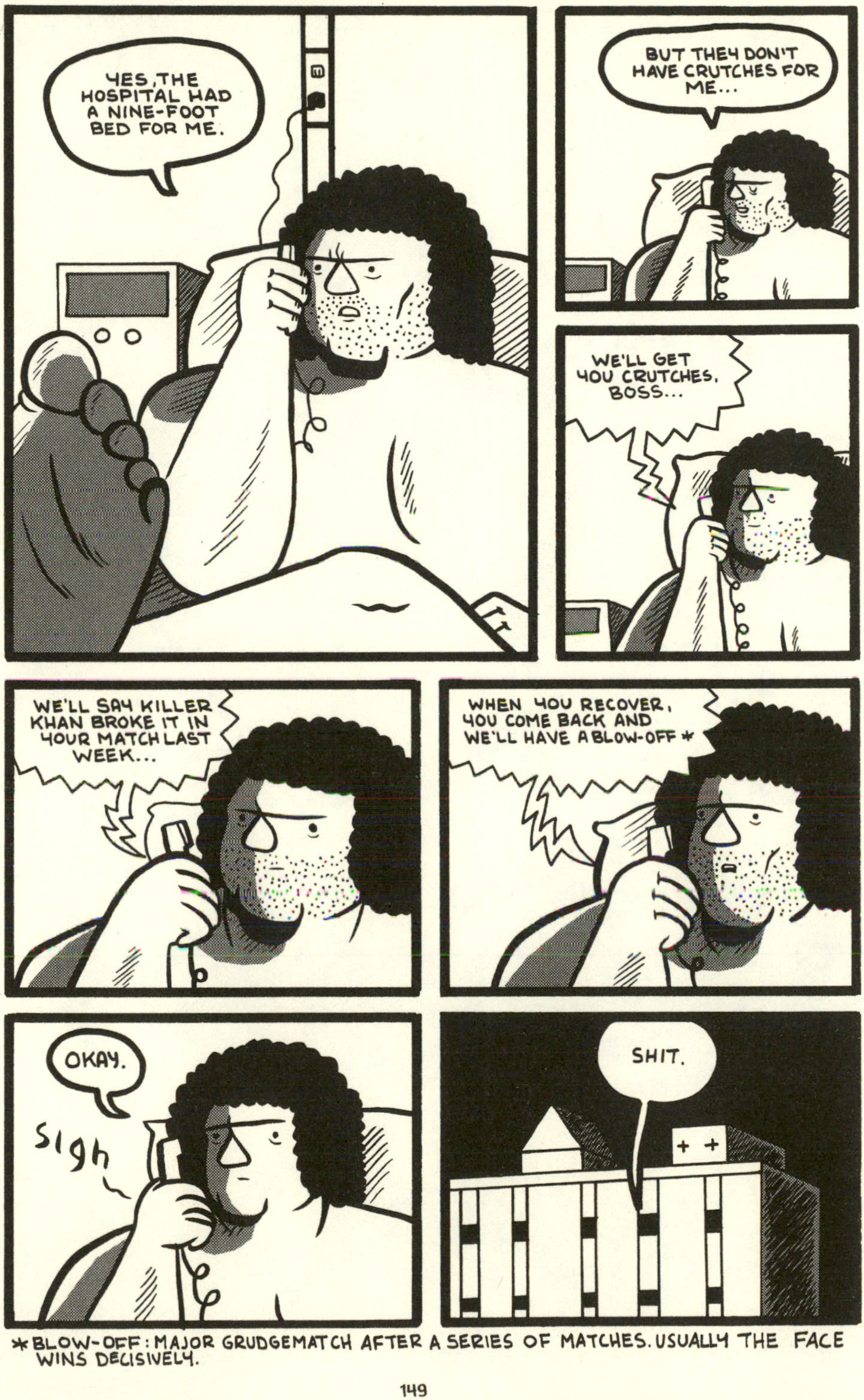
YES, THE HOSPITAL HAD A NINE-FOOT BED FOR ME.
BUT THEY DON'T HAVE CRUTCHES FOR ME...
WE'LL GET YOU CRUTCHES, BOSS...
WE'LL SAY KILLER KHAN BROKE IT IN YOUR MATCH LAST WEEK...
WHEN YOU RECOVER, YOU COME BACK AND WE'LL HAVE A BLOW-OFF *
OKAY.
Sigh
SHIT.

* BLOW-OFF: MAJOR GRUDGEMATCH AFTER A SERIES OF MATCHES. USUALLY THE FACE WINS DECISIVELY.

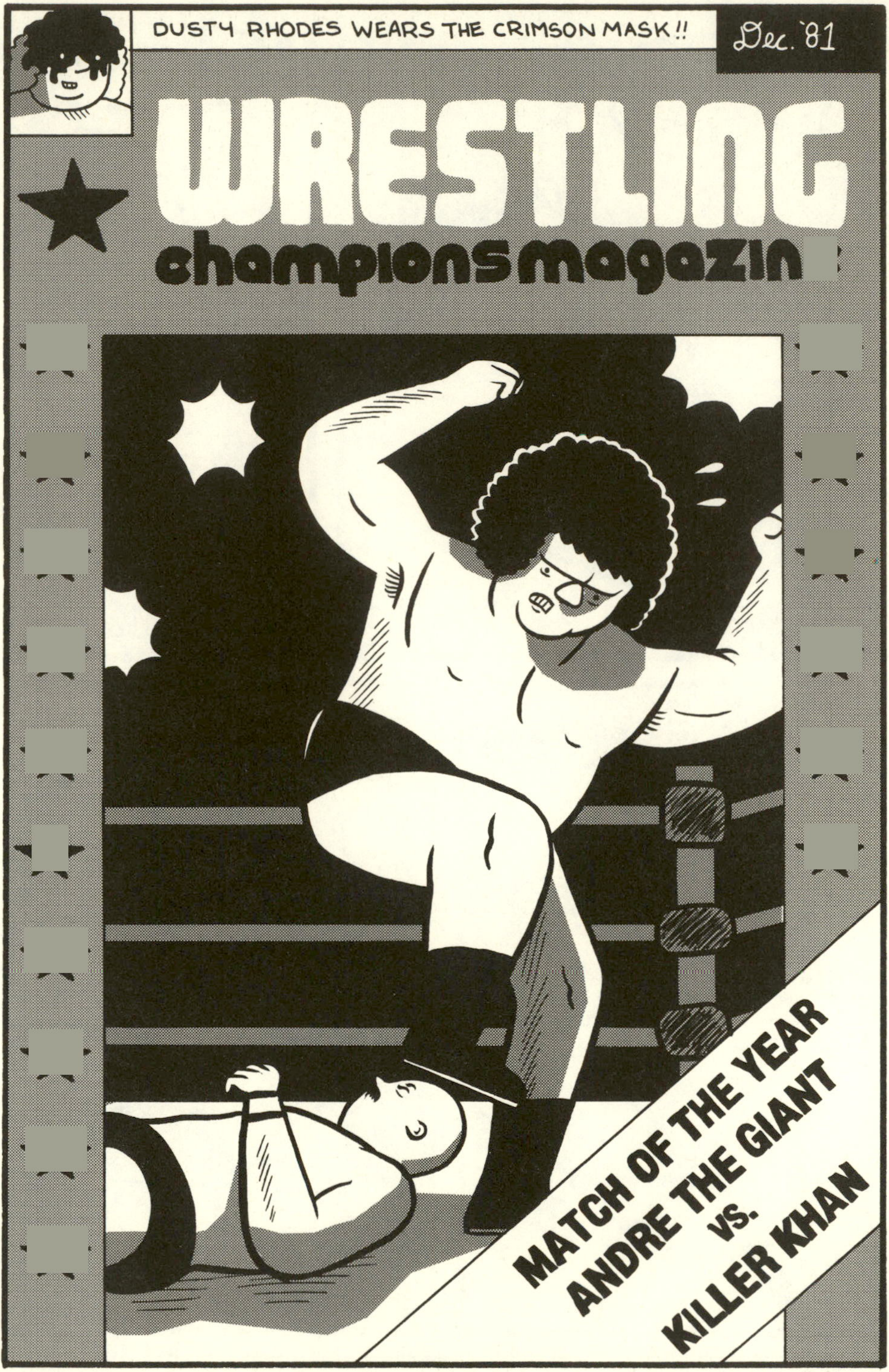
DUSTY RHODES WEARS THE CRIMSON MASK!!
Dec. '81
WRESTLING
champions magazin
MATCH OF THE YEAR
ANDRE THE GIANT
VS.
KILLER KHAN

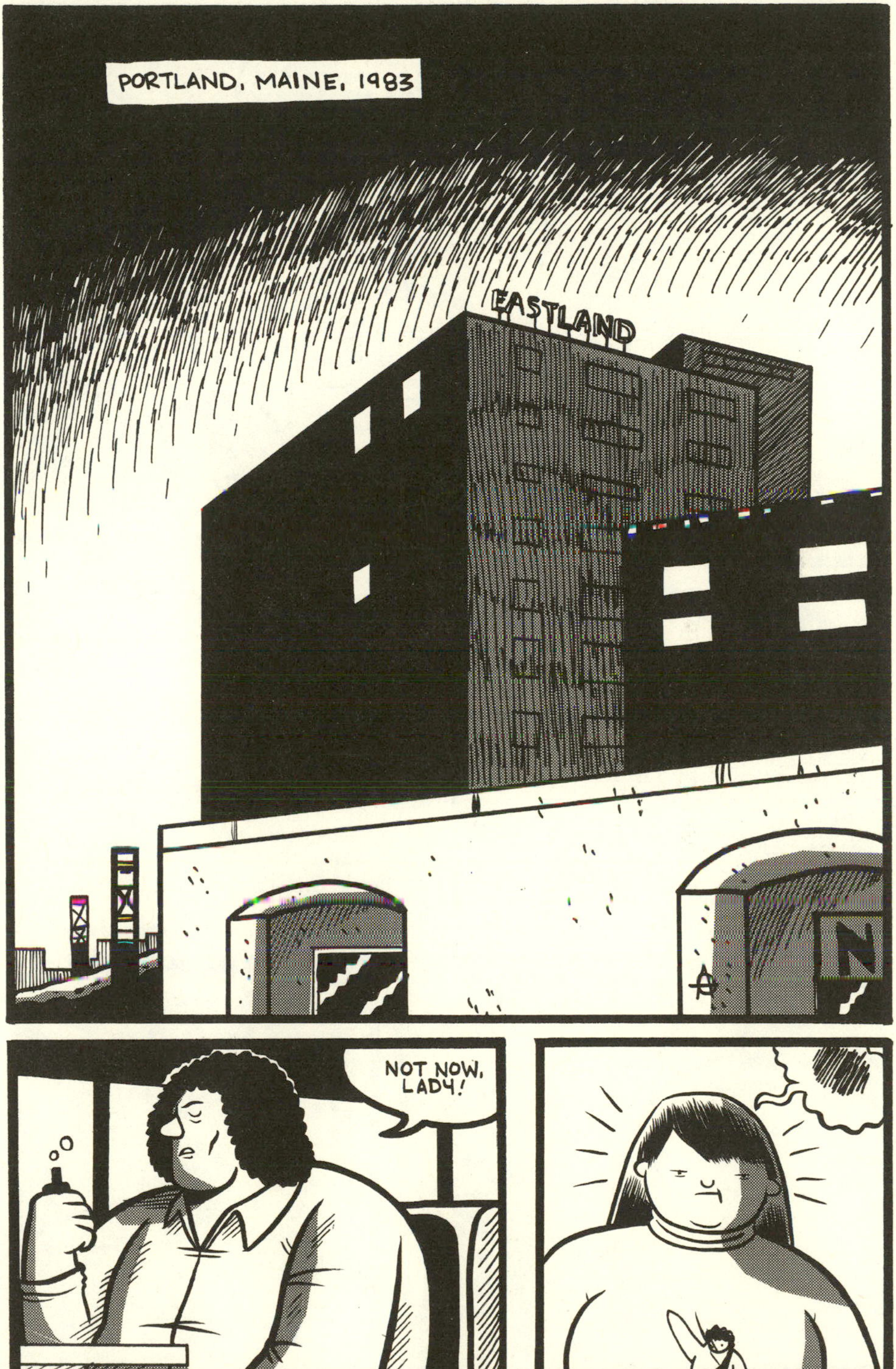
PORTLAND, MAINE, 1983
EASTLAND
NOT NOW, LADY!

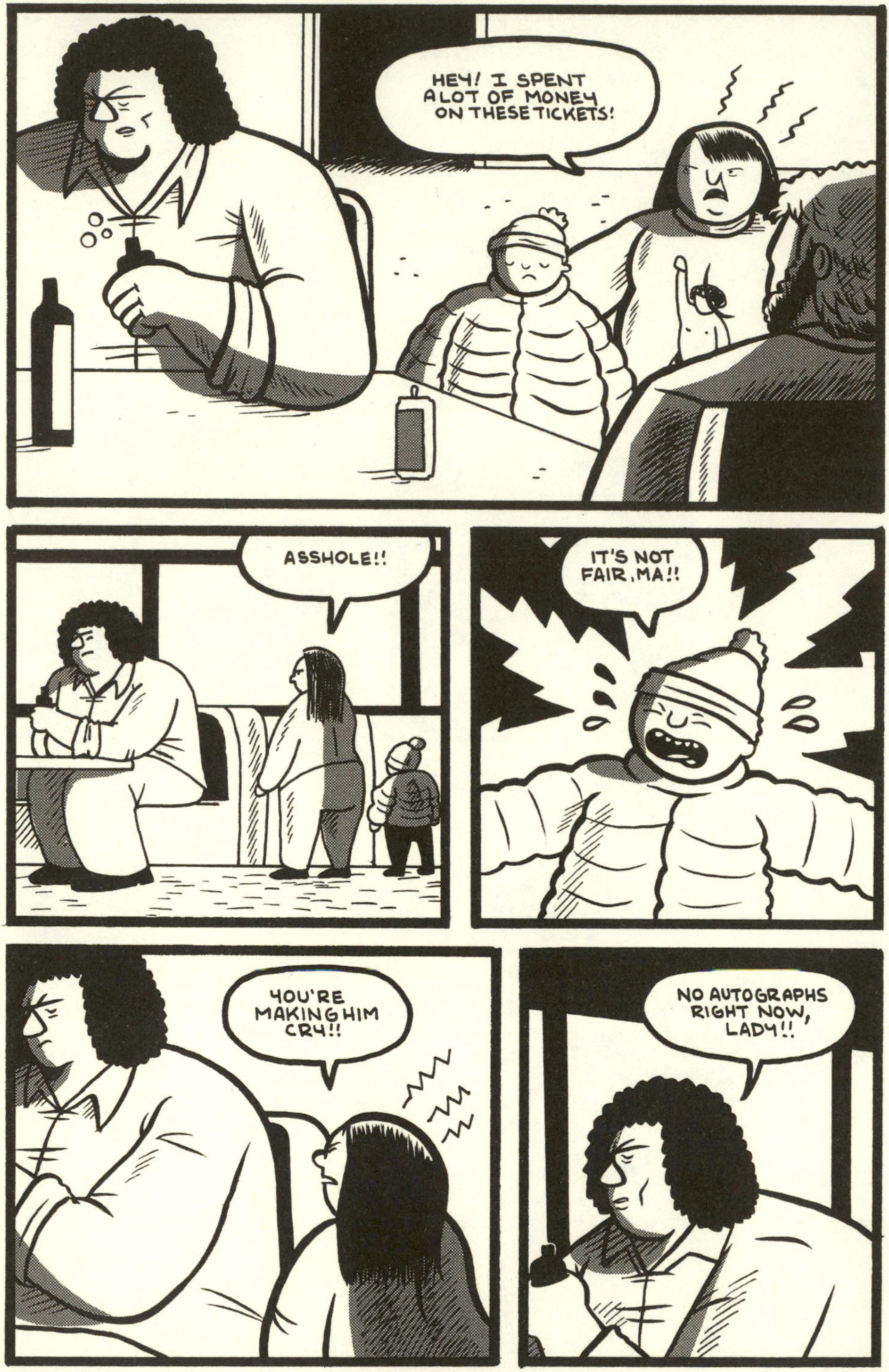
HEY! I SPENT A LOT OF MONEY ON THESE TICKETS!
ASSHOLE!!
IT'S NOT FAIR, MA!!
YOU'RE MAKING HIM CRY!!
NO AUTOGRAPHS RIGHT NOW, LADY!!

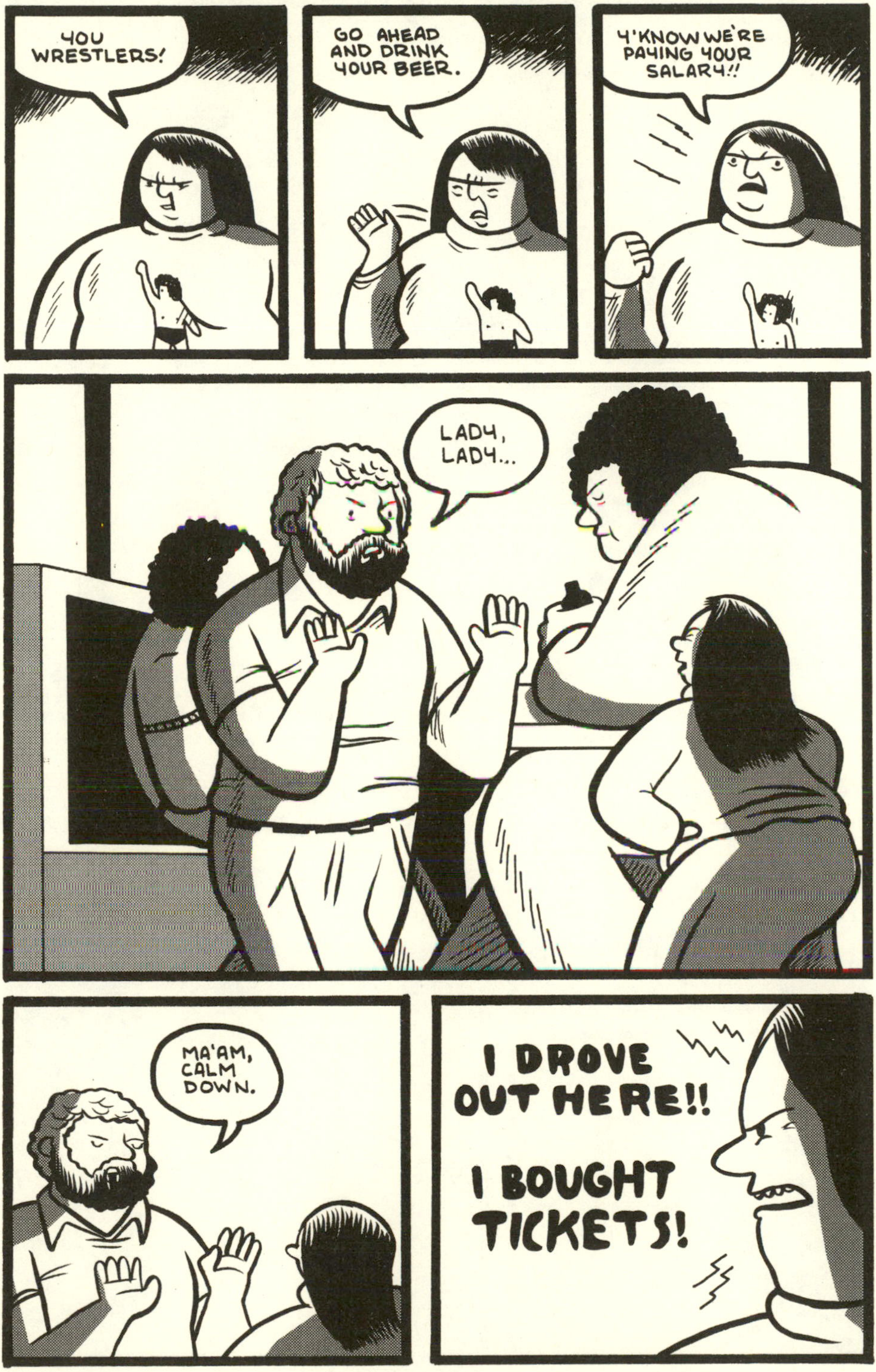

YOU WRESTLERS!
GO AHEAD AND DRINK YOUR BEER.
Y'KNOW WE'RE PAYING YOUR SALARY!!
LADY, LADY...
MA'AM, CALM DOWN.
I DROVE OUT HERE!!
I BOUGHT TICKETS!

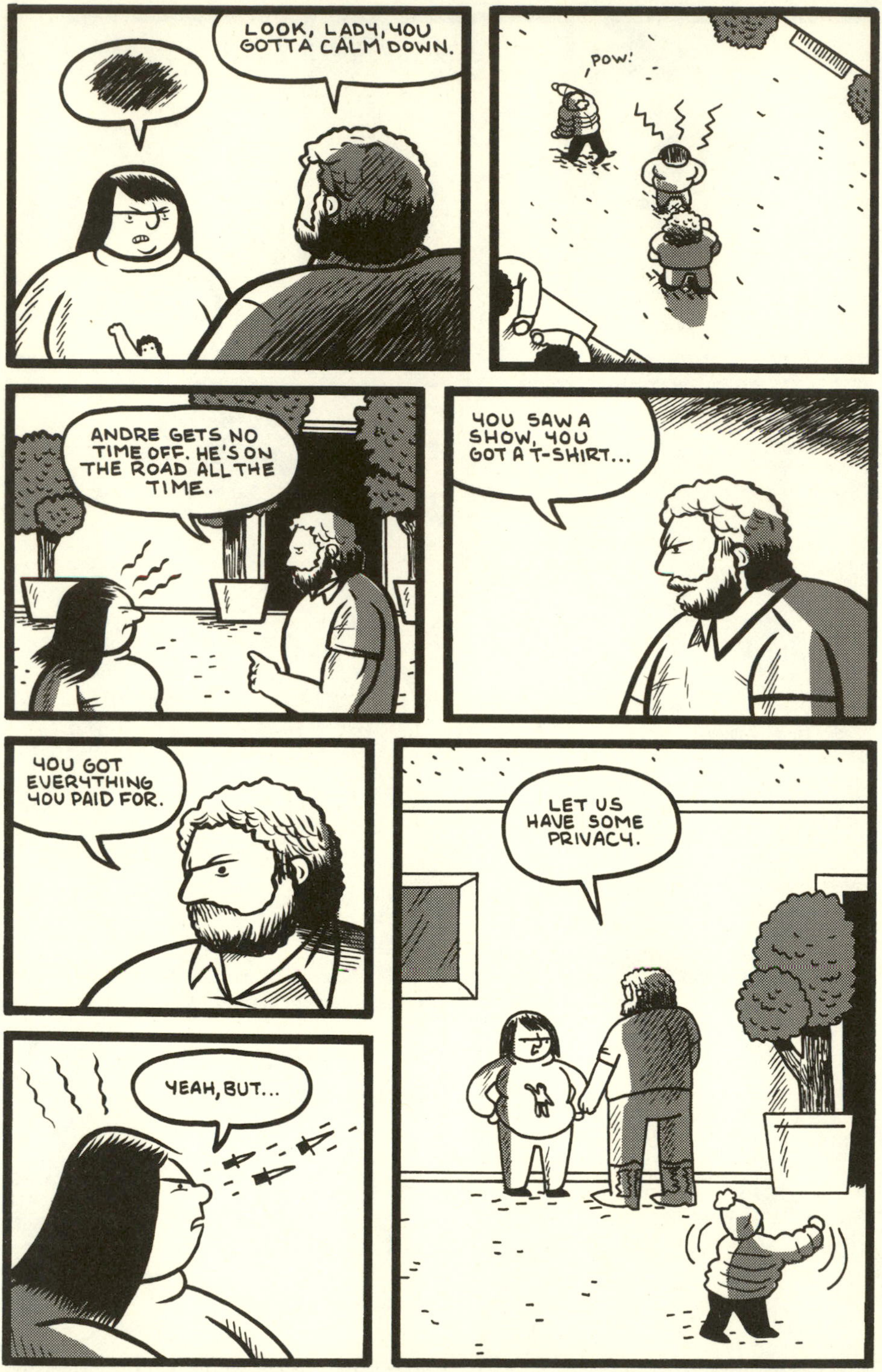
LOOK, LADY, YOU GOTTA CALM DOWN.
POW!
ANDRE GETS NO TIME OFF. HE'S ON THE ROAD ALL THE TIME.
YOU SAW A SHOW, YOU GOT A T-SHIRT...
YOU GOT EVERYTHING YOU PAID FOR.
YEAH, BUT...
LET US HAVE SOME PRIVACY.

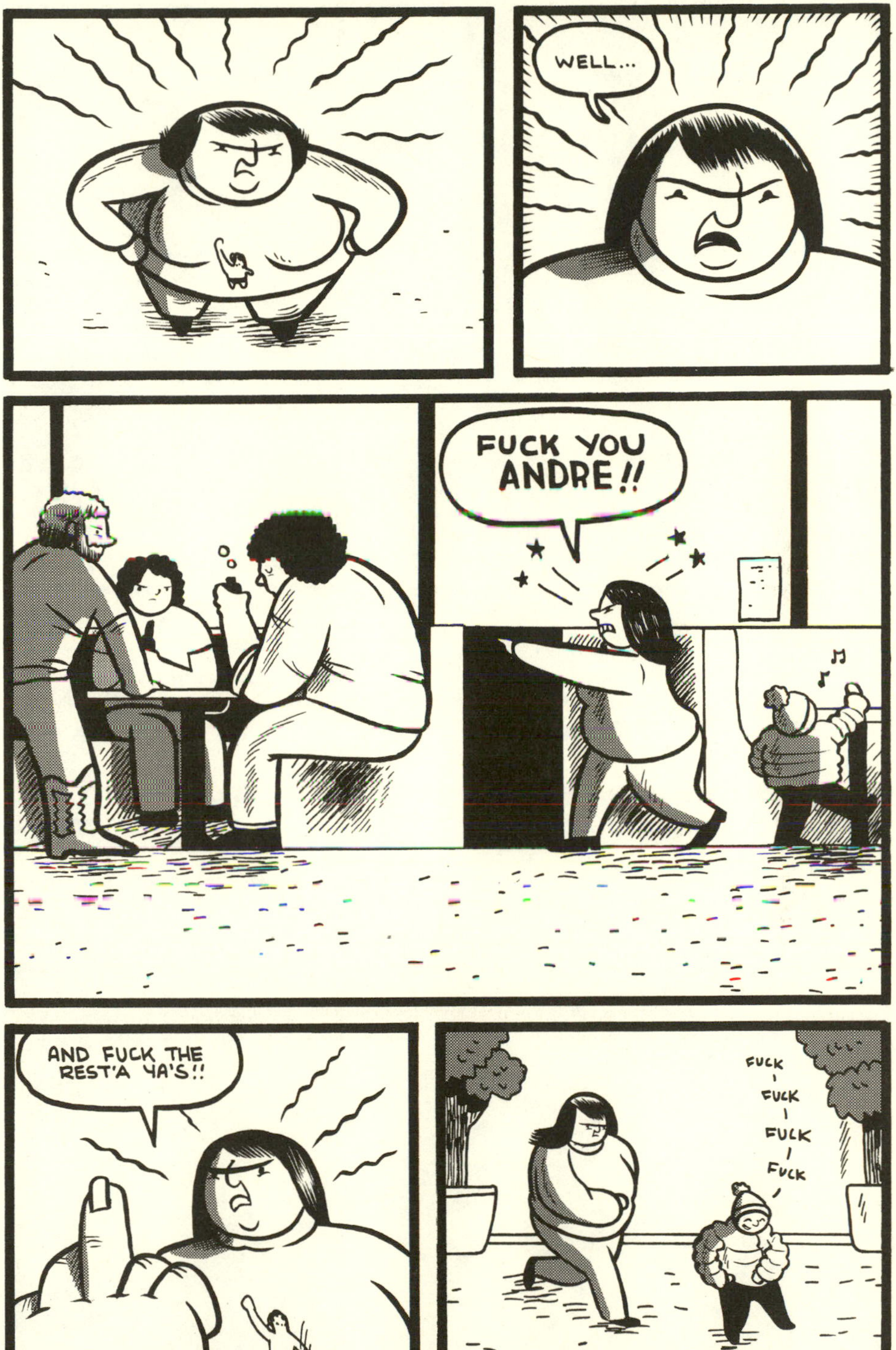
WELL...
FUCK YOU ANDRE!!
AND FUCK THE REST'A YA'S!!
FUCK
FUCK
FUCK
FUCK

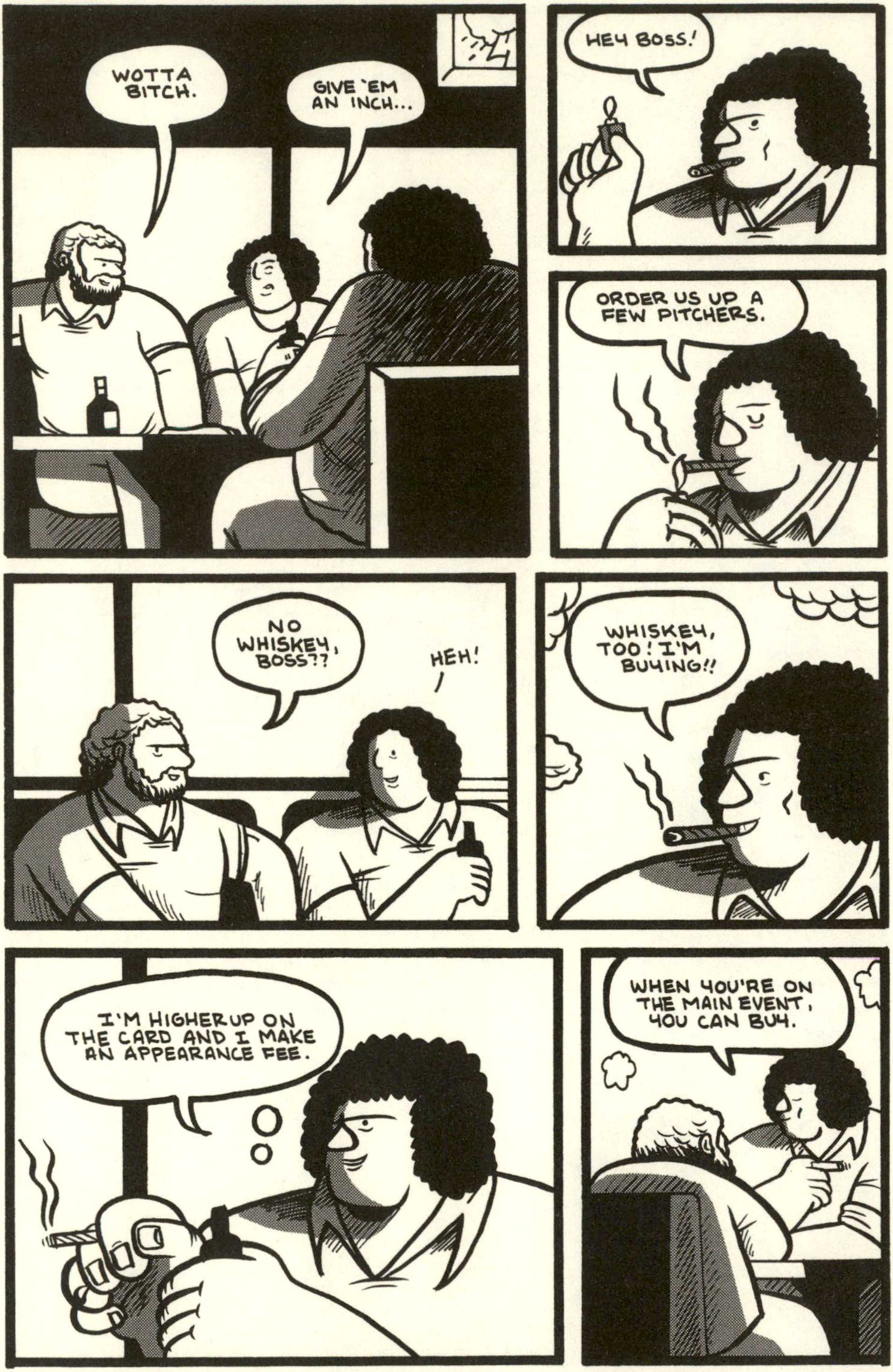
WOTTA BITCH.
GIVE 'EM AN INCH...
HEY BOSS!
ORDER US UP A FEW PITCHERS.
NO WHISKEY, BOSS??
HEH!
WHISKEY, TOO! I'M BUYING!!
I'M HIGHERUP ON THE CARD AND I MAKE AN APPEARANCE FEE.
WHEN YOU'RE ON THE MAIN EVENT, YOU CAN BUY.

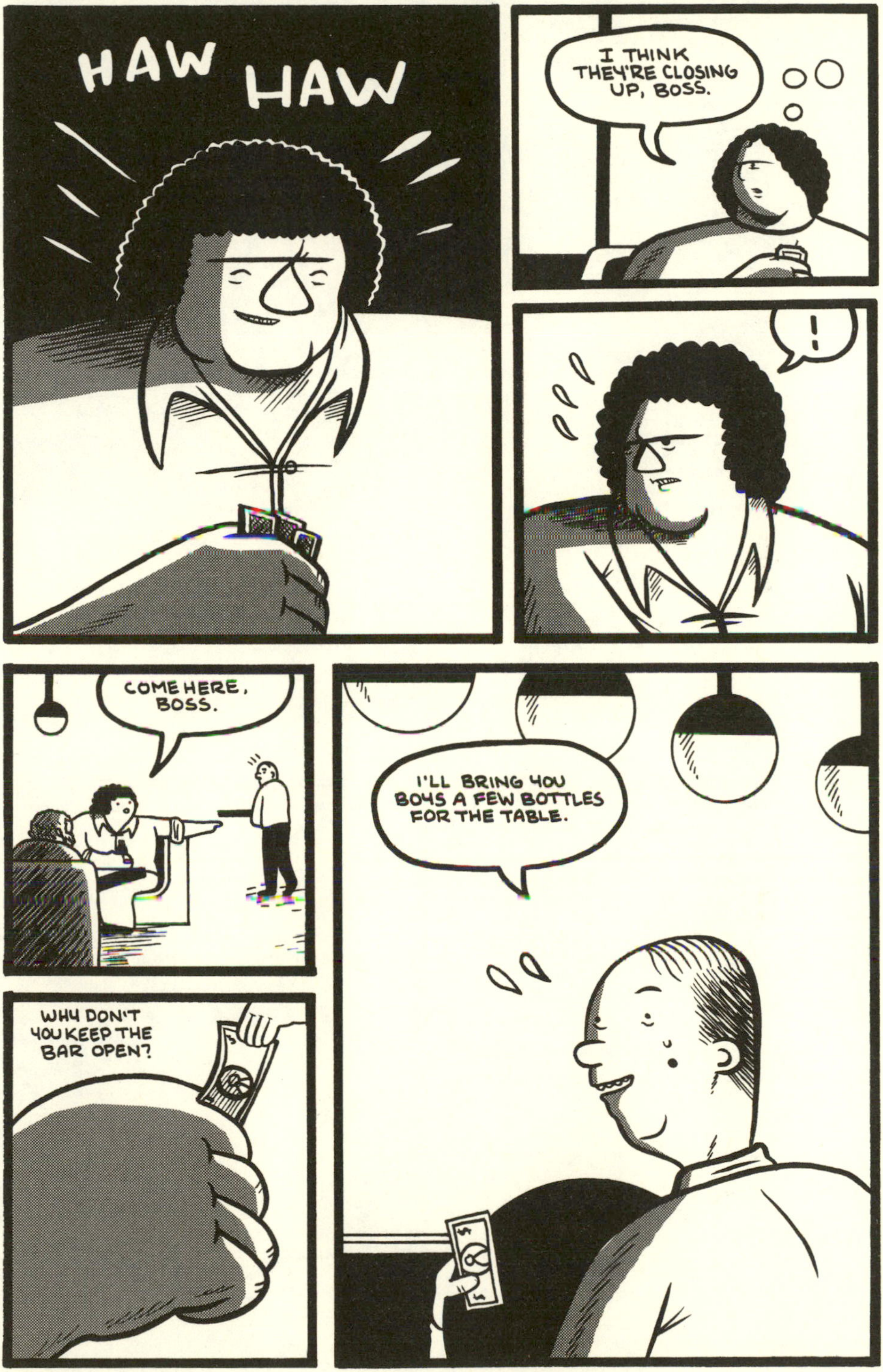
HAW HAW
I THINK THEY'RE CLOSING UP, BOSS.
!
COME HERE, BOSS.
WHY DON'T YOU KEEP THE BAR OPEN?
I'LL BRING YOU BOYS A FEW BOTTLES FOR THE TABLE.

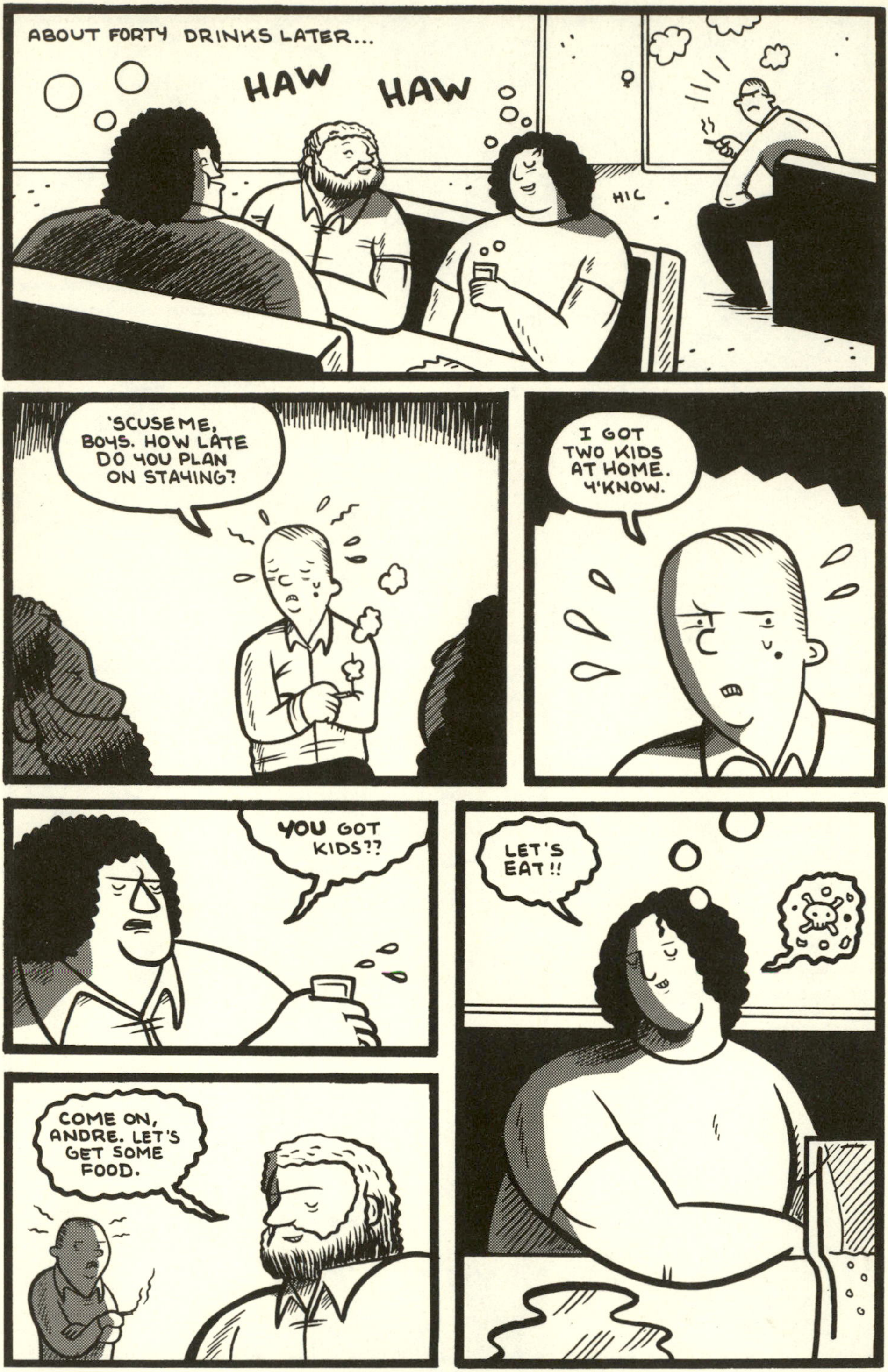
ABOUT FORTY DRINKS LATER...
HAW HAW
HIC
'SCUSE ME, BOYS. HOW LATE DO YOU PLAN ON STAYING?
I GOT TWO KIDS AT HOME. Y'KNOW.
YOU GOT KIDS??
LET'S EAT!!
COME ON, ANDRE. LET'S GET SOME FOOD.

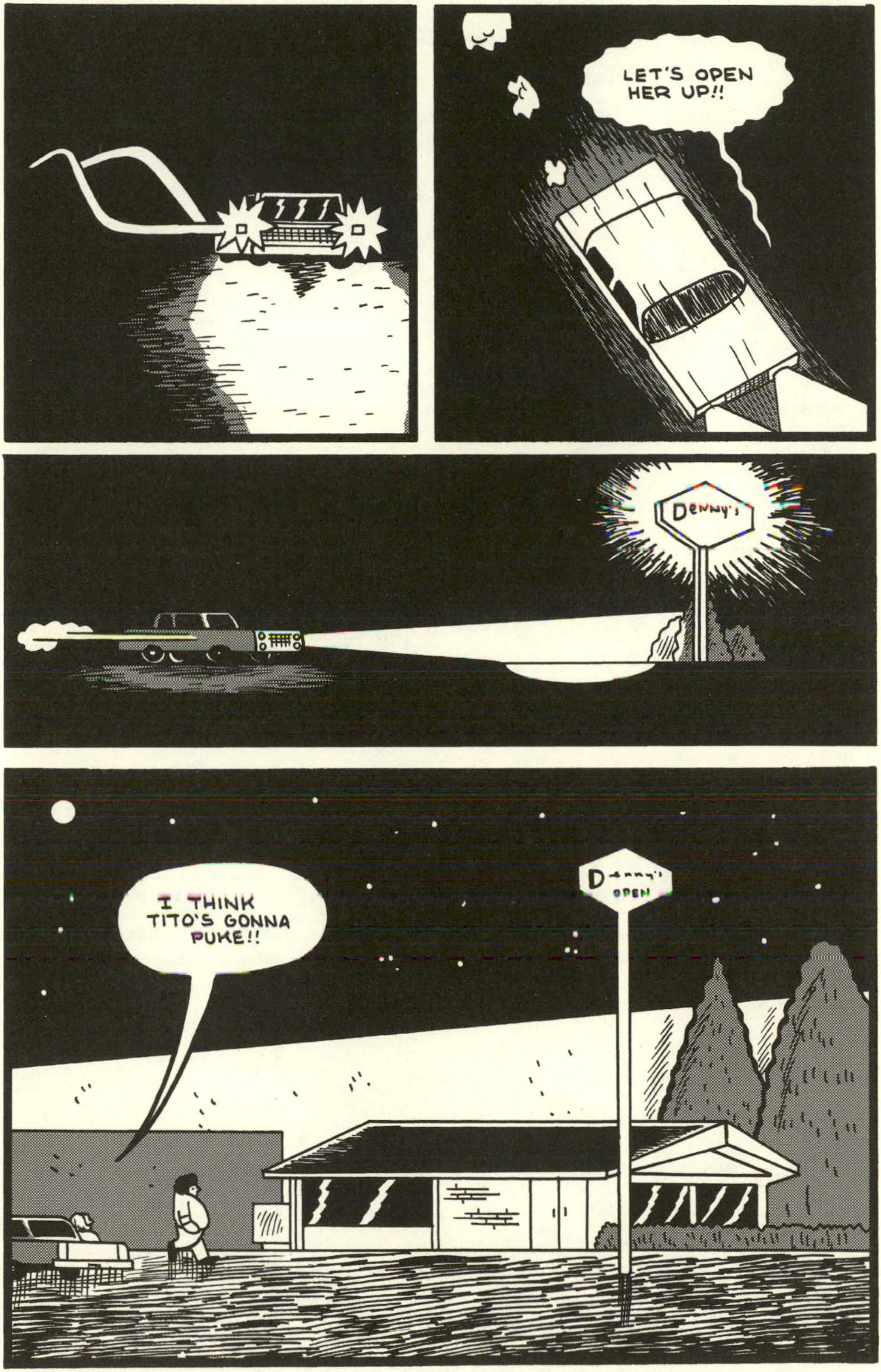
LET'S OPEN HER UP!!
Denny's
I THINK TITO'S GONNA PUKE!!
OPEN

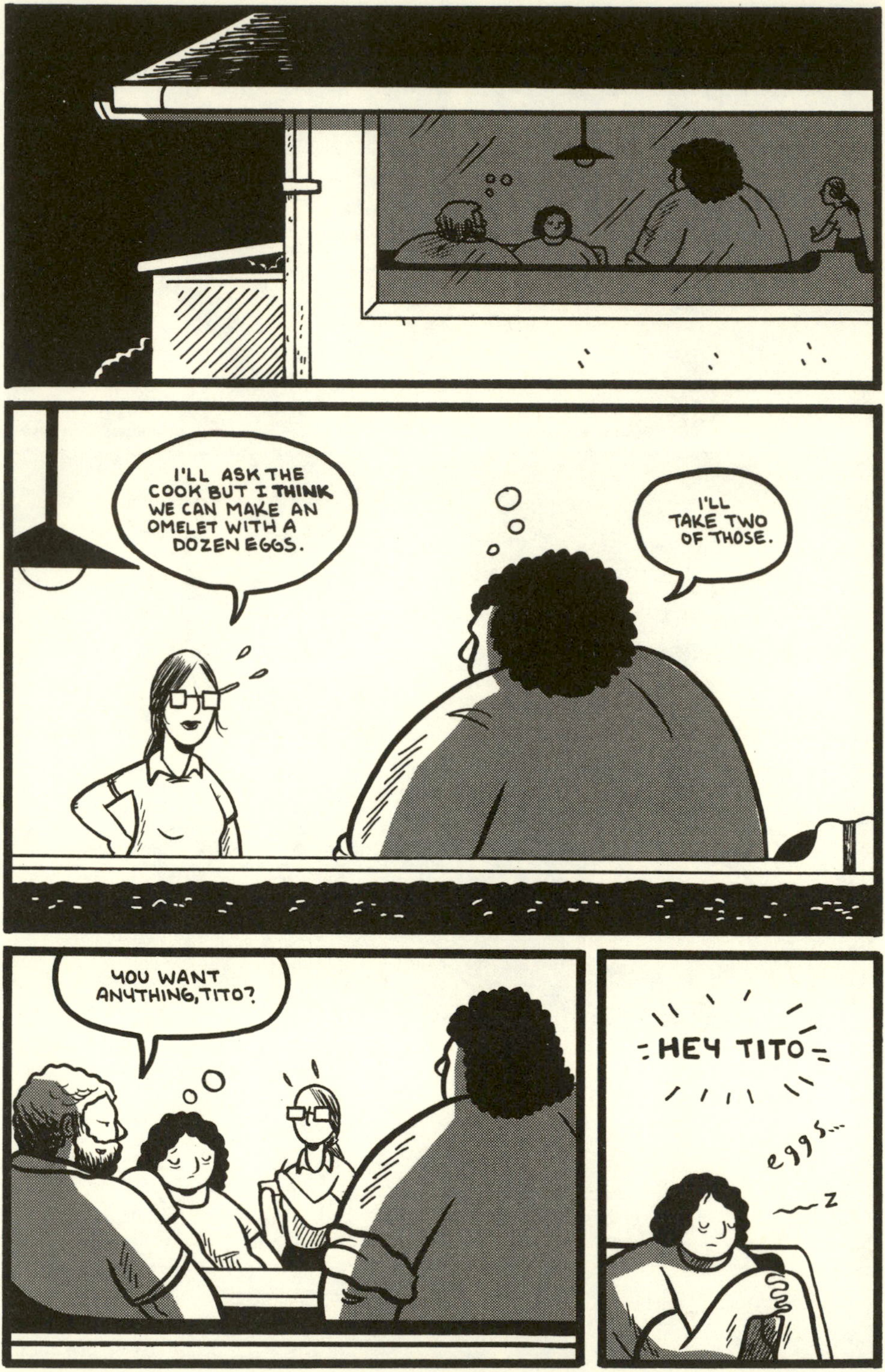
I'LL ASK THE COOK BUT I THINK WE CAN MAKE AN OMELET WITH A DOZEN EGGS.
I'LL TAKE TWO OF THOSE.
YOU WANT ANYTHING, TITO?
HEY TITO
eggs...
Z

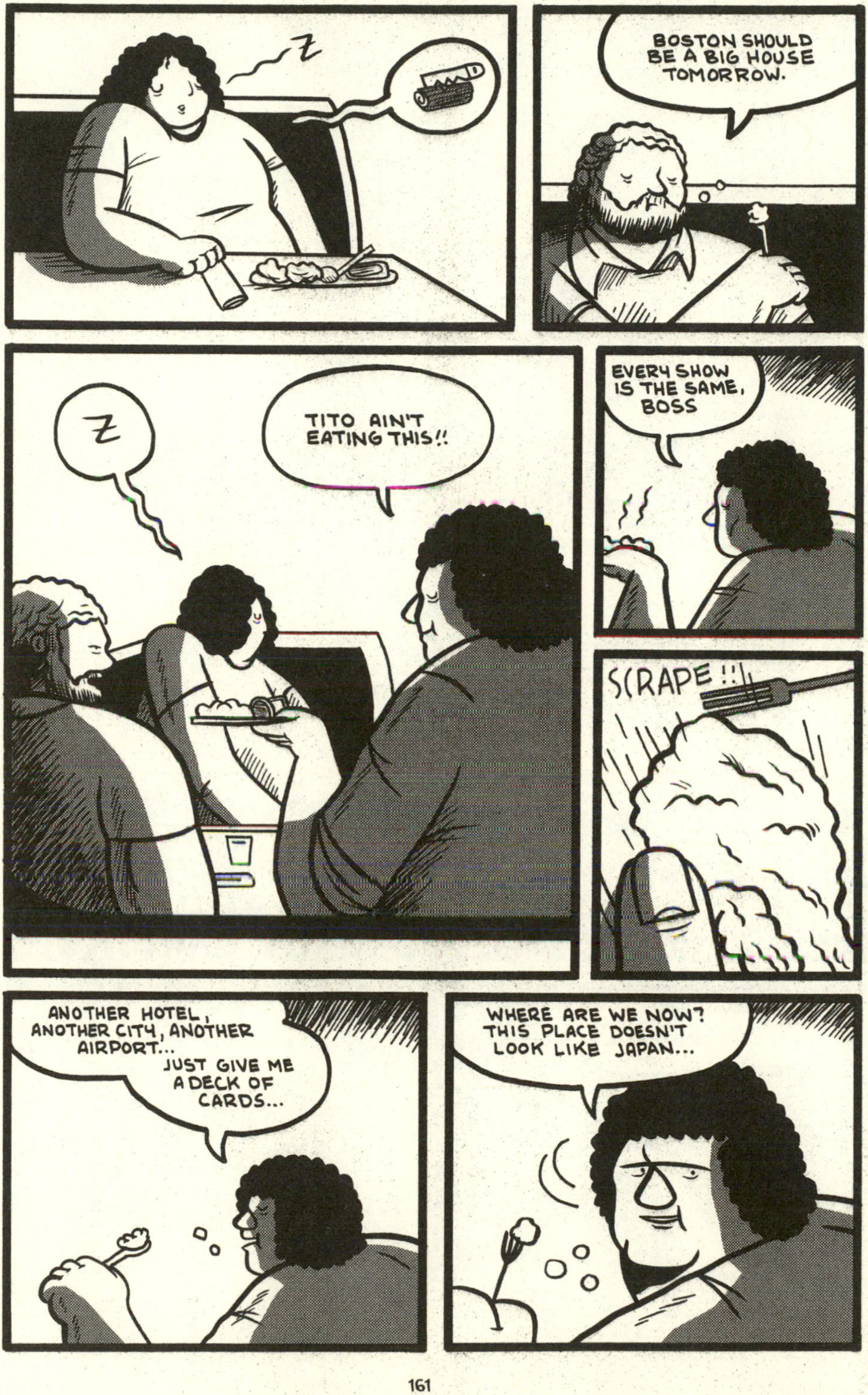
Z
BOSTON SHOULD BE A BIG HOUSE TOMORROW.
Z
TITO AIN'T EATING THIS!!
EVERY SHOW IS THE SAME, BOSS
SCRAPE!!
ANOTHER HOTEL, ANOTHER CITY, ANOTHER AIRPORT...
JUST GIVE ME A DECK OF CARDS...
WHERE ARE WE NOW? THIS PLACE DOESN'T LOOK LIKE JAPAN...

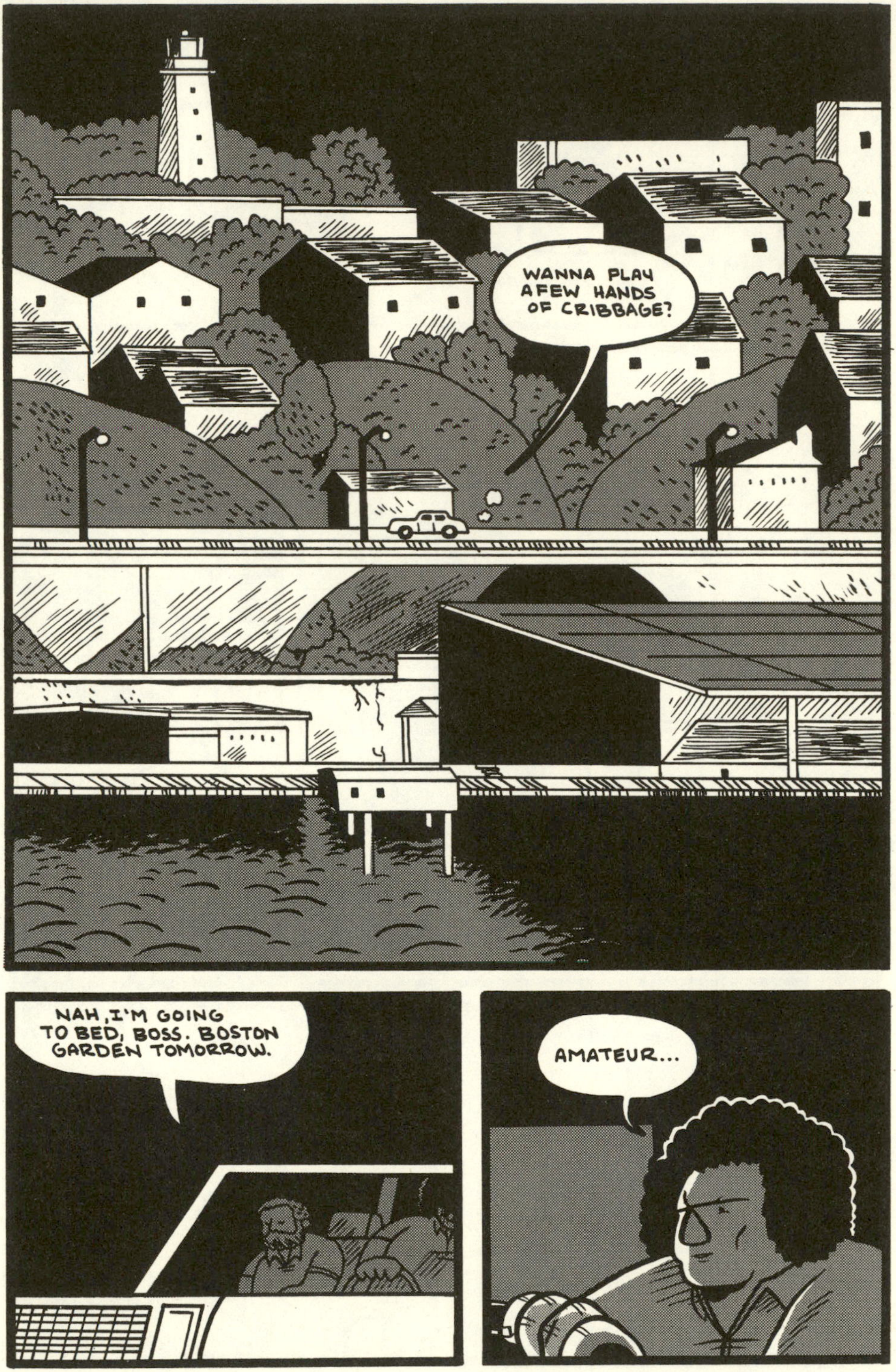
WANNA PLAY
A FEW HANDS
OF CRIBBAGE?
NAH, I'M GOING
TO BED, BOSS. BOSTON
GARDEN TOMORROW.
AMATEUR...

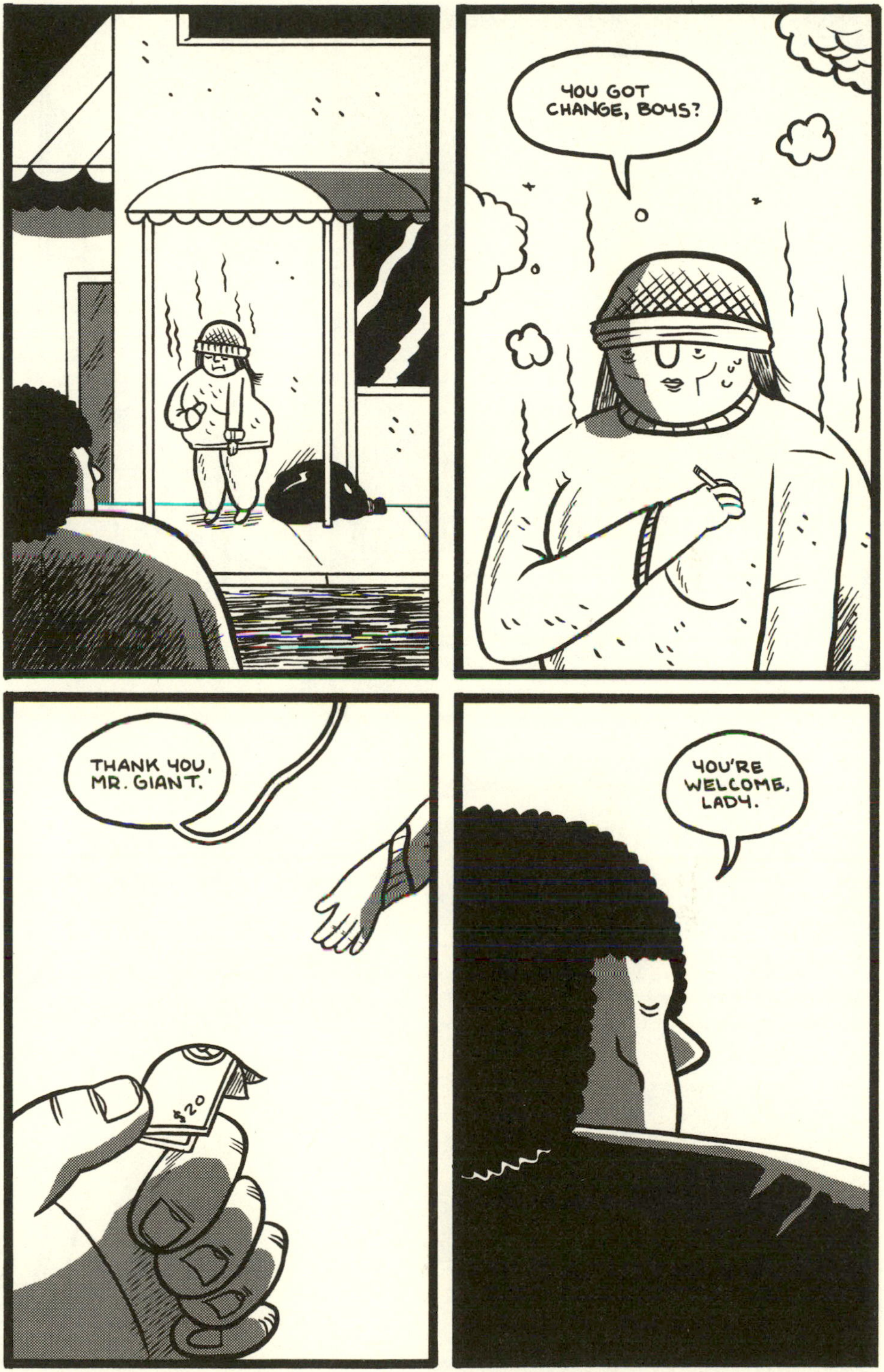
YOU GOT CHANGE, BOYS?
THANK YOU, MR. GIANT.
$20
YOU'RE WELCOME, LADY.

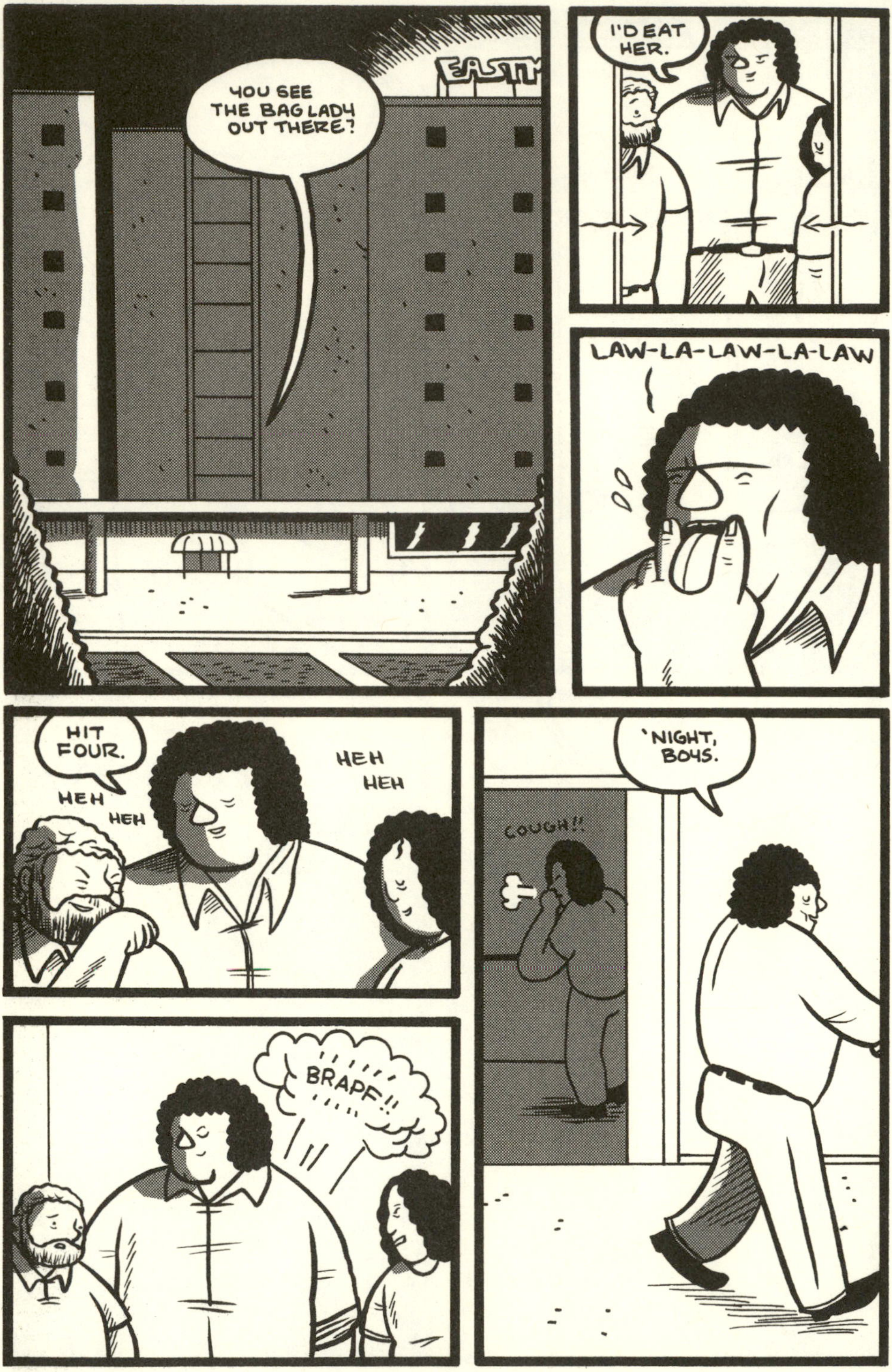
EASTM
YOU SEE THE BAG LADY OUT THERE?
I'D EAT HER.
LAW-LA-LAW-LA-LAW
HIT FOUR.
HEH HEH
HEH HEH
'NIGHT, BOYS.
COUGH!!
BRAPF!!

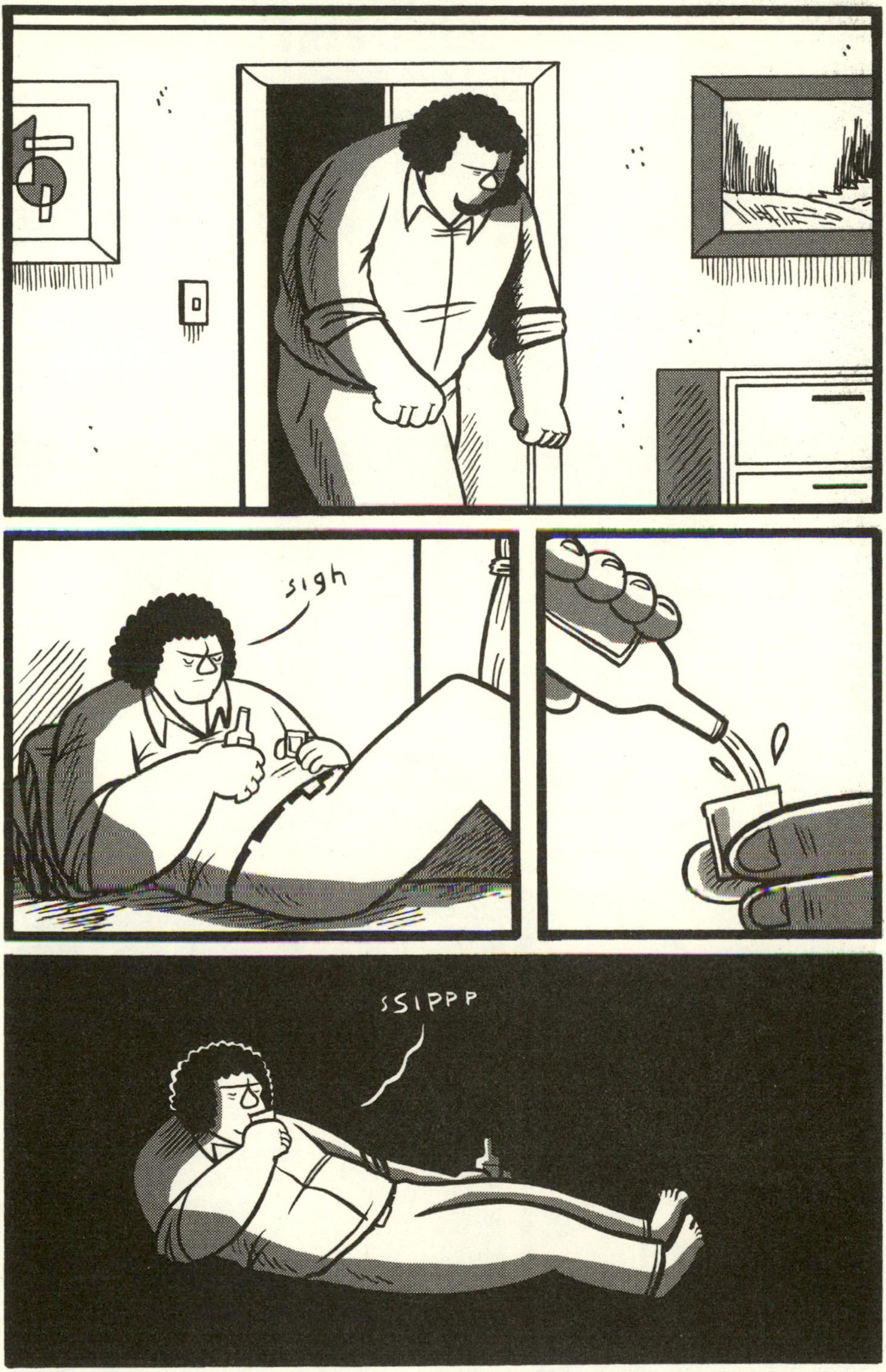
sigh
SSIPPP

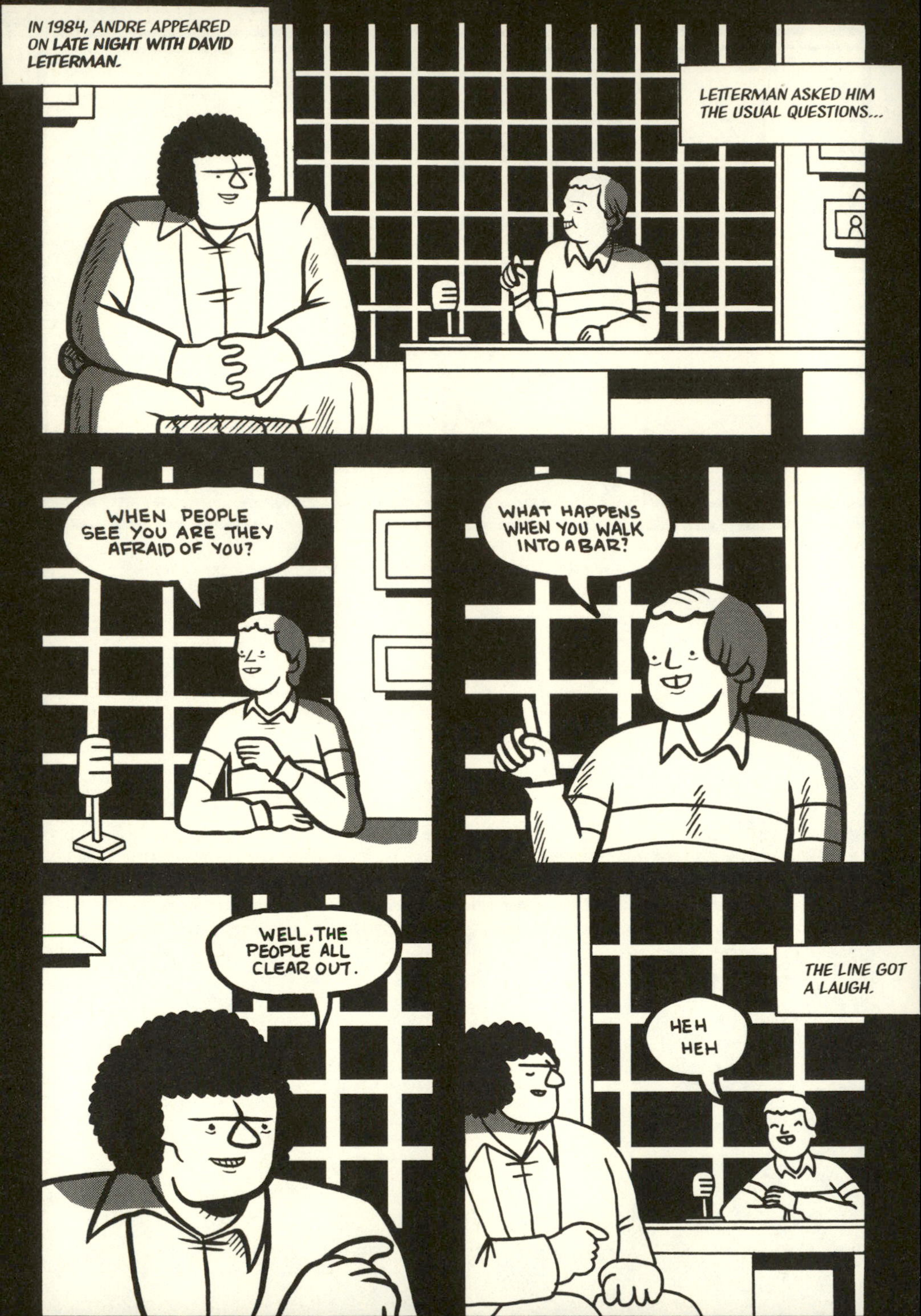
IN 1984, ANDRE APPEARED ON LATE NIGHT WITH DAVID LETTERMAN.
LETTERMAN ASKED HIM THE USUAL QUESTIONS...
WHEN PEOPLE SEE YOU ARE THEY AFRAID OF YOU?
WHAT HAPPENS WHEN YOU WALK INTO A BAR?
WELL, THE PEOPLE ALL CLEAR OUT.
THE LINE GOT A LAUGH.
HEH HEH

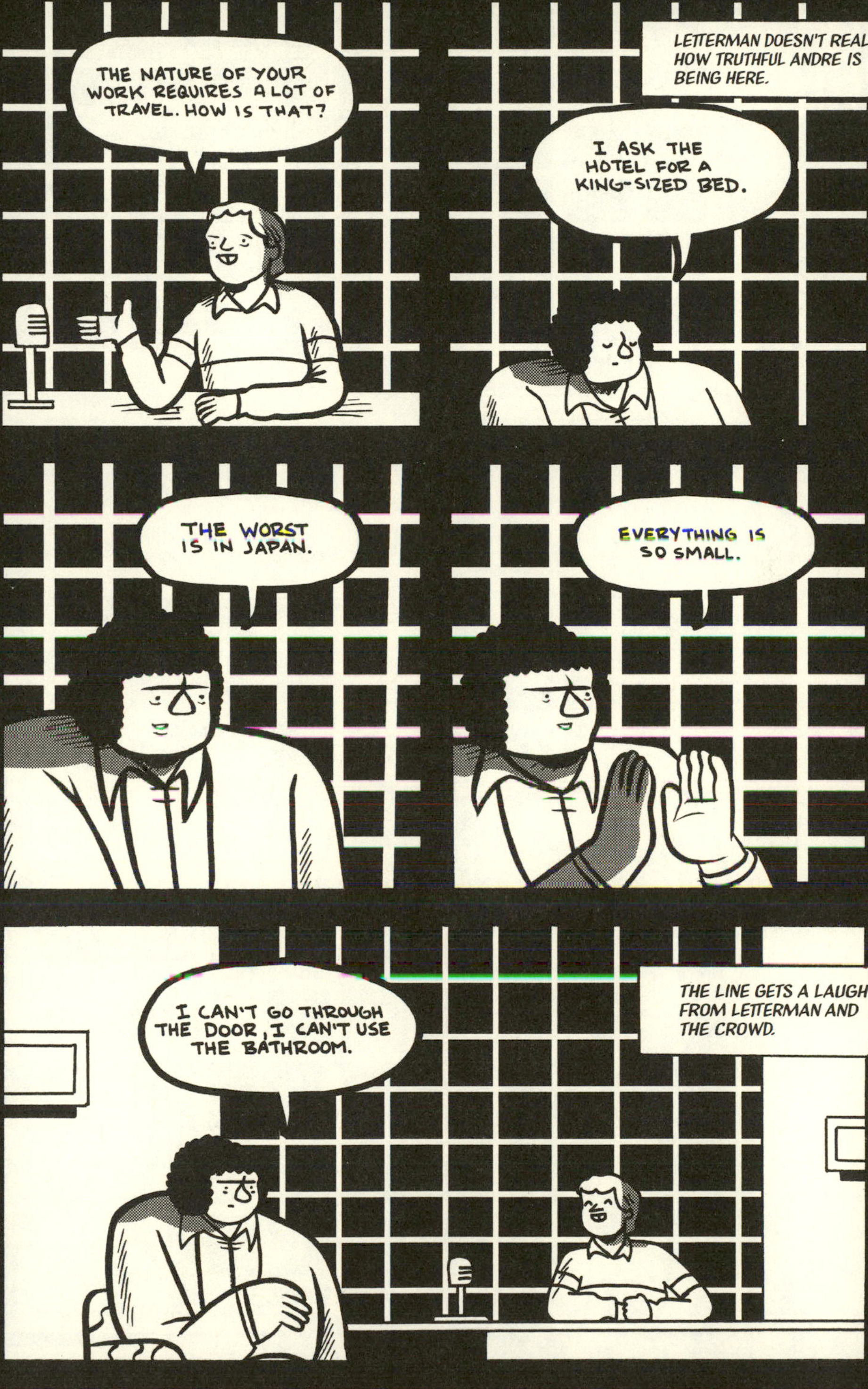
THE NATURE OF YOUR WORK REQUIRES A LOT OF TRAVEL. HOW IS THAT?
LETTERMAN DOESN'T REALIZE HOW TRUTHFUL ANDRE IS BEING HERE.
I ASK THE HOTEL FOR A KING-SIZED BED.
THE WORST IS IN JAPAN.
EVERYTHING IS SO SMALL.
I CAN'T GO THROUGH THE DOOR, I CAN'T USE THE BATHROOM.
THE LINE GETS A LAUGH FROM LETTERMAN AND THE CROWD.

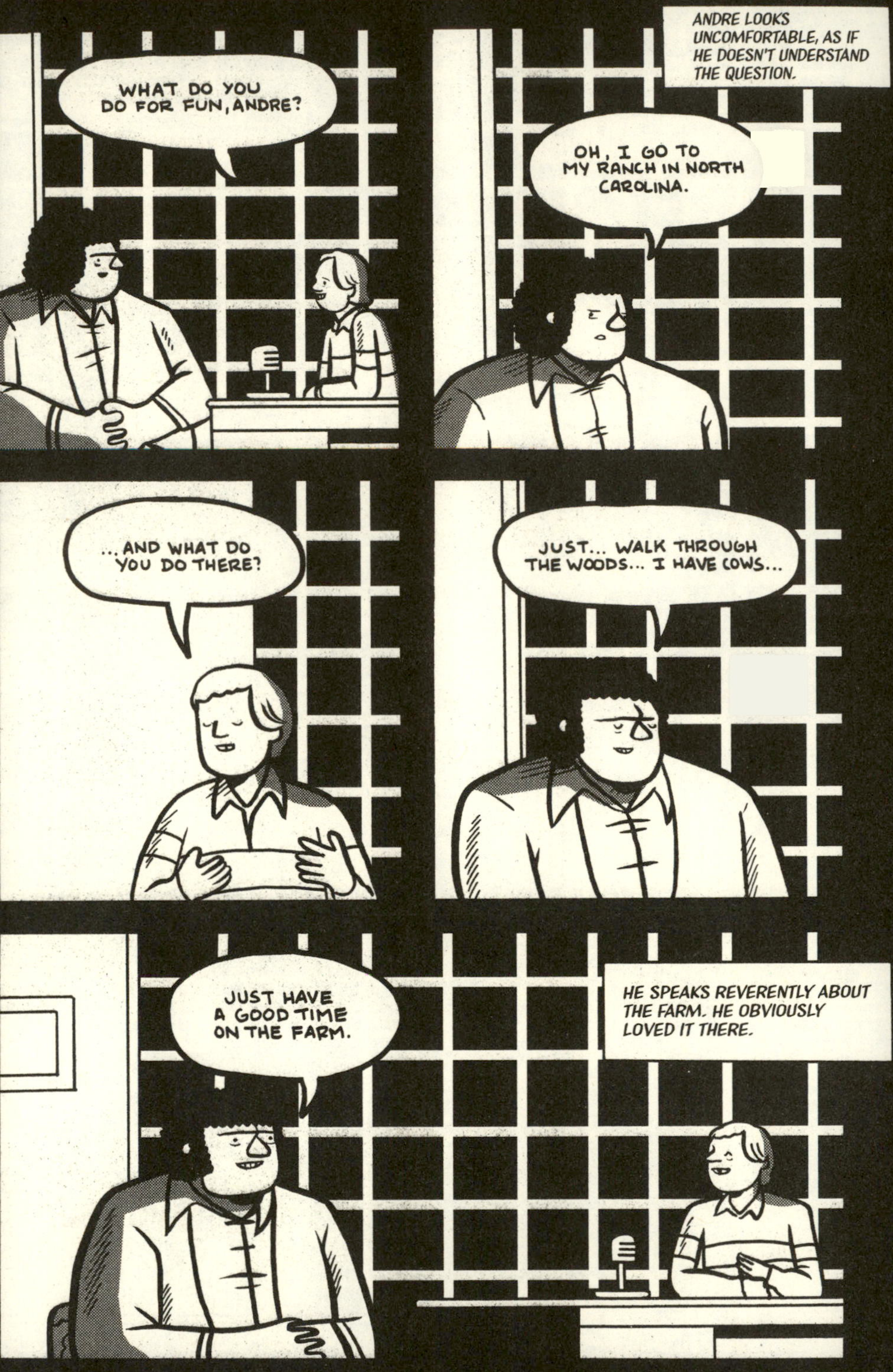
WHAT DO YOU DO FOR FUN, ANDRE?
ANDRE LOOKS UNCOMFORTABLE, AS IF HE DOESN'T UNDERSTAND THE QUESTION.
OH, I GO TO MY RANCH IN NORTH CAROLINA.
...AND WHAT DO YOU DO THERE?
JUST... WALK THROUGH THE WOODS... I HAVE COWS...
JUST HAVE A GOOD TIME ON THE FARM.
HE SPEAKS REVERENTLY ABOUT THE FARM. HE OBVIOUSLY LOVED IT THERE.

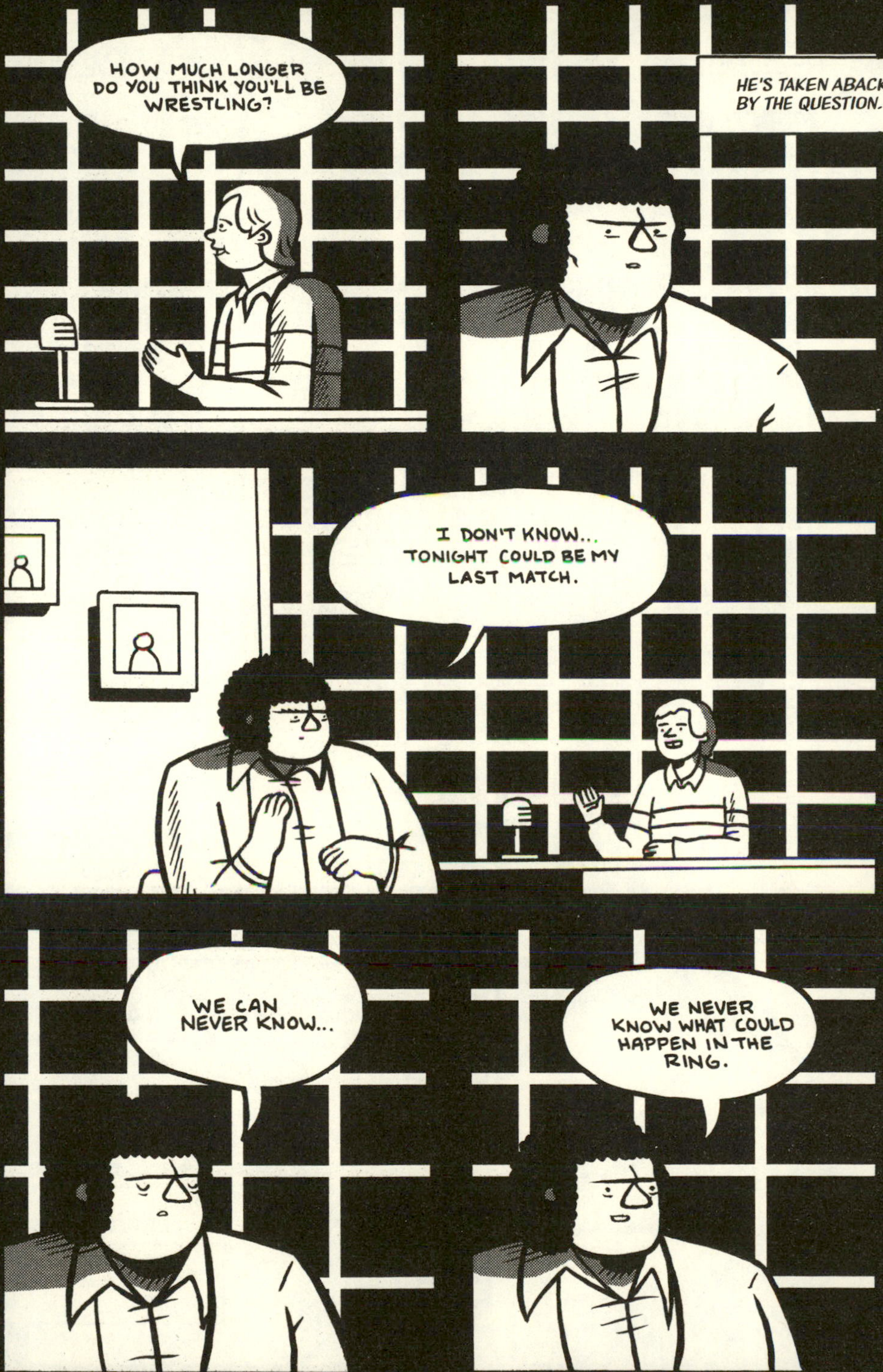
HOW MUCH LONGER DO YOU THINK YOU'LL BE WRESTLING?
HE'S TAKEN ABACK BY THE QUESTION.
I DON'T KNOW... TONIGHT COULD BE MY LAST MATCH.
WE CAN NEVER KNOW...
WE NEVER KNOW WHAT COULD HAPPEN IN THE RING.

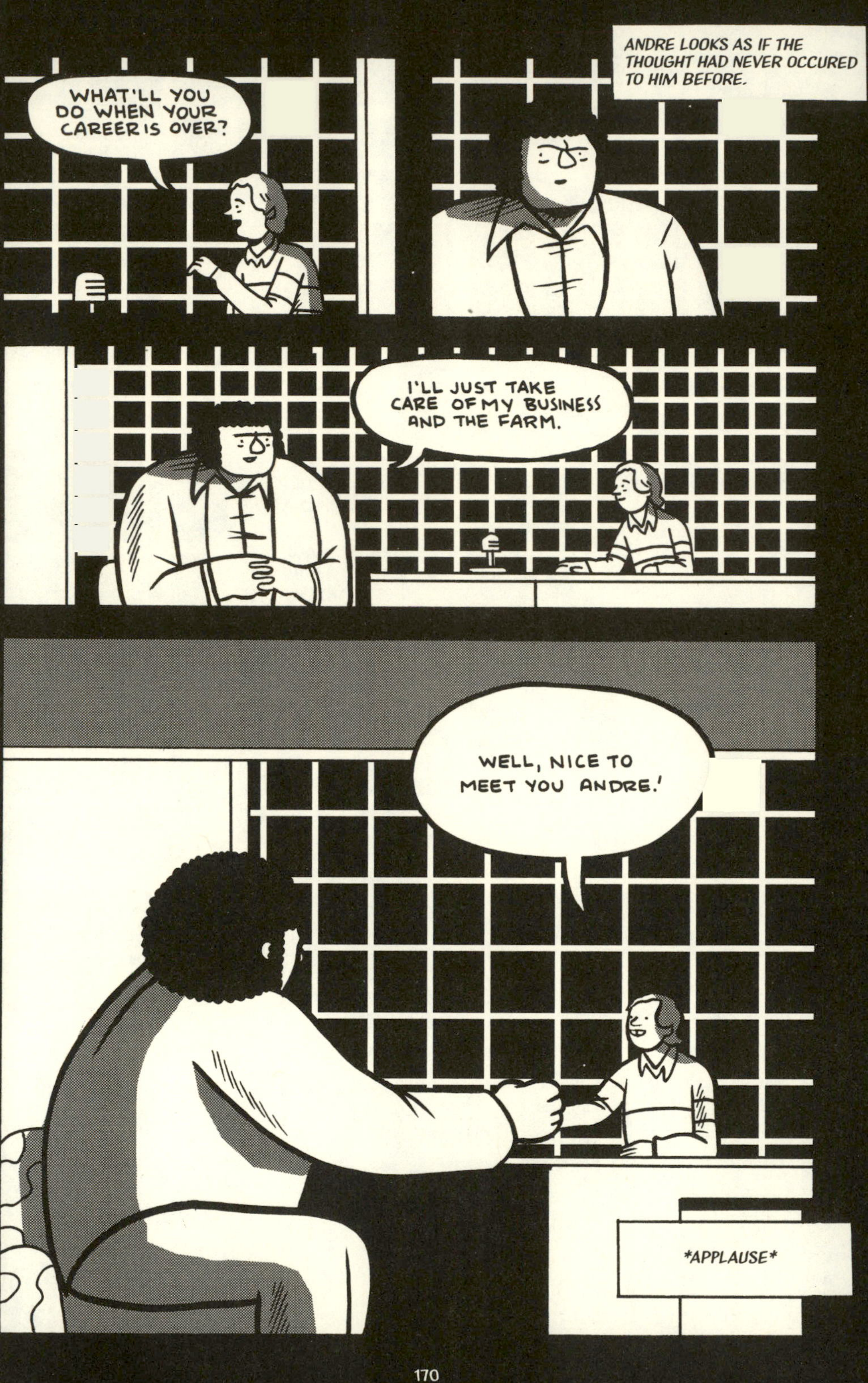
WHAT'LL YOU DO WHEN YOUR CAREER IS OVER?
ANDRE LOOKS AS IF THE THOUGHT HAD NEVER OCCURED TO HIM BEFORE.
I'LL JUST TAKE CARE OF MY BUSINESS AND THE FARM.
WELL, NICE TO MEET YOU ANDRE!
APPLAUSE

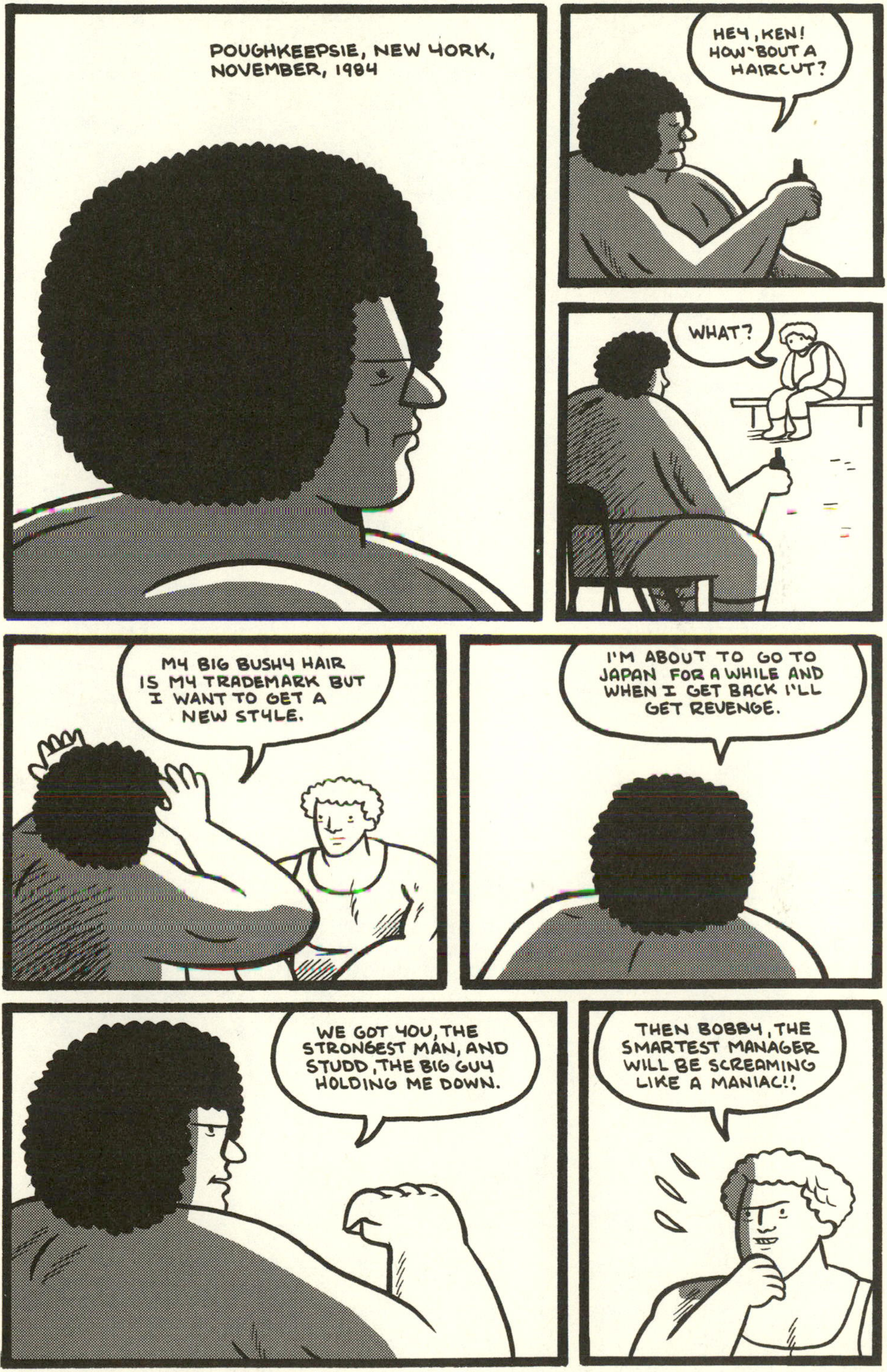
POUGHKEEPSIE, NEW YORK, NOVEMBER, 1984
HEY, KEN! HOW'BOUT A HAIRCUT?
WHAT?
MY BIG BUSHY HAIR IS MY TRADEMARK BUT I WANT TO GET A NEW STYLE.
I'M ABOUT TO GO TO JAPAN FOR A WHILE AND WHEN I GET BACK I'LL GET REVENGE.
WE GOT YOU, THE STRONGEST MAN, AND STUDD, THE BIG GUY HOLDING ME DOWN.
THEN BOBBY, THE SMARTEST MANAGER WILL BE SCREAMING LIKE A MANIAC!!

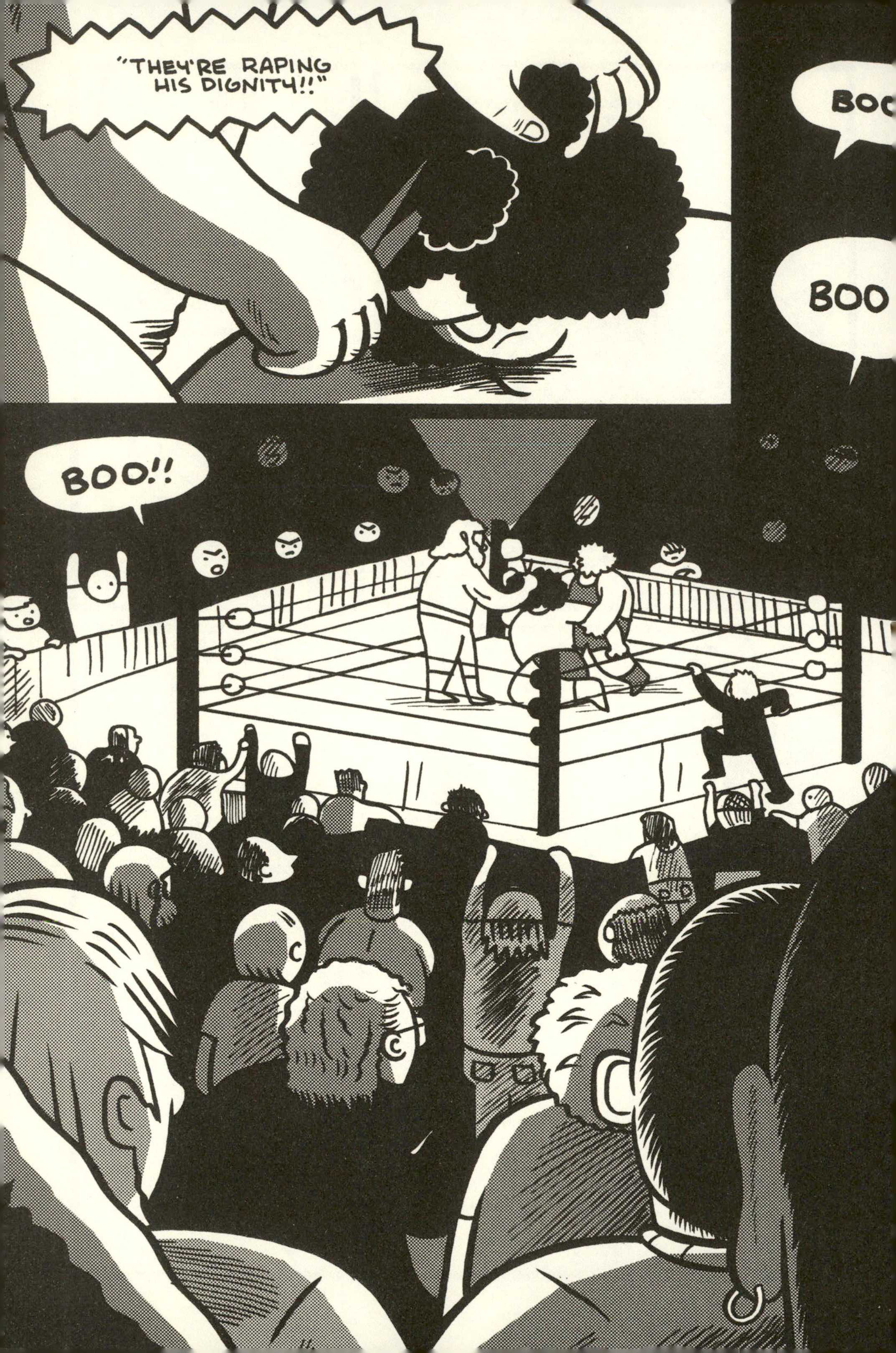
"THEY'RE RAPING HIS DIGNITY!!"
BOO
BOO
BOO!!

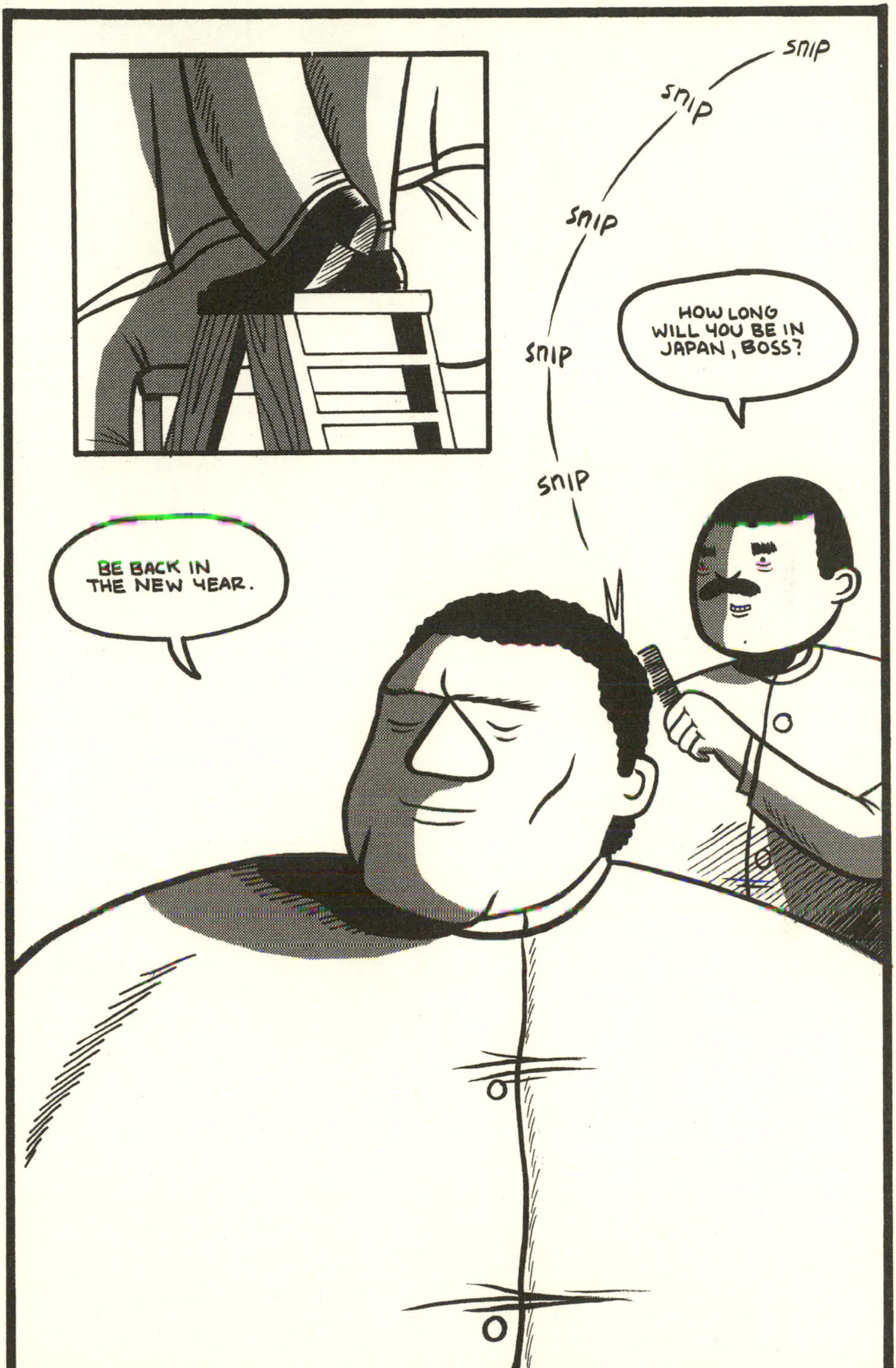
snip
snip
snip
snip
snip
HOW LONG WILL YOU BE IN JAPAN, BOSS?
BE BACK IN THE NEW YEAR.

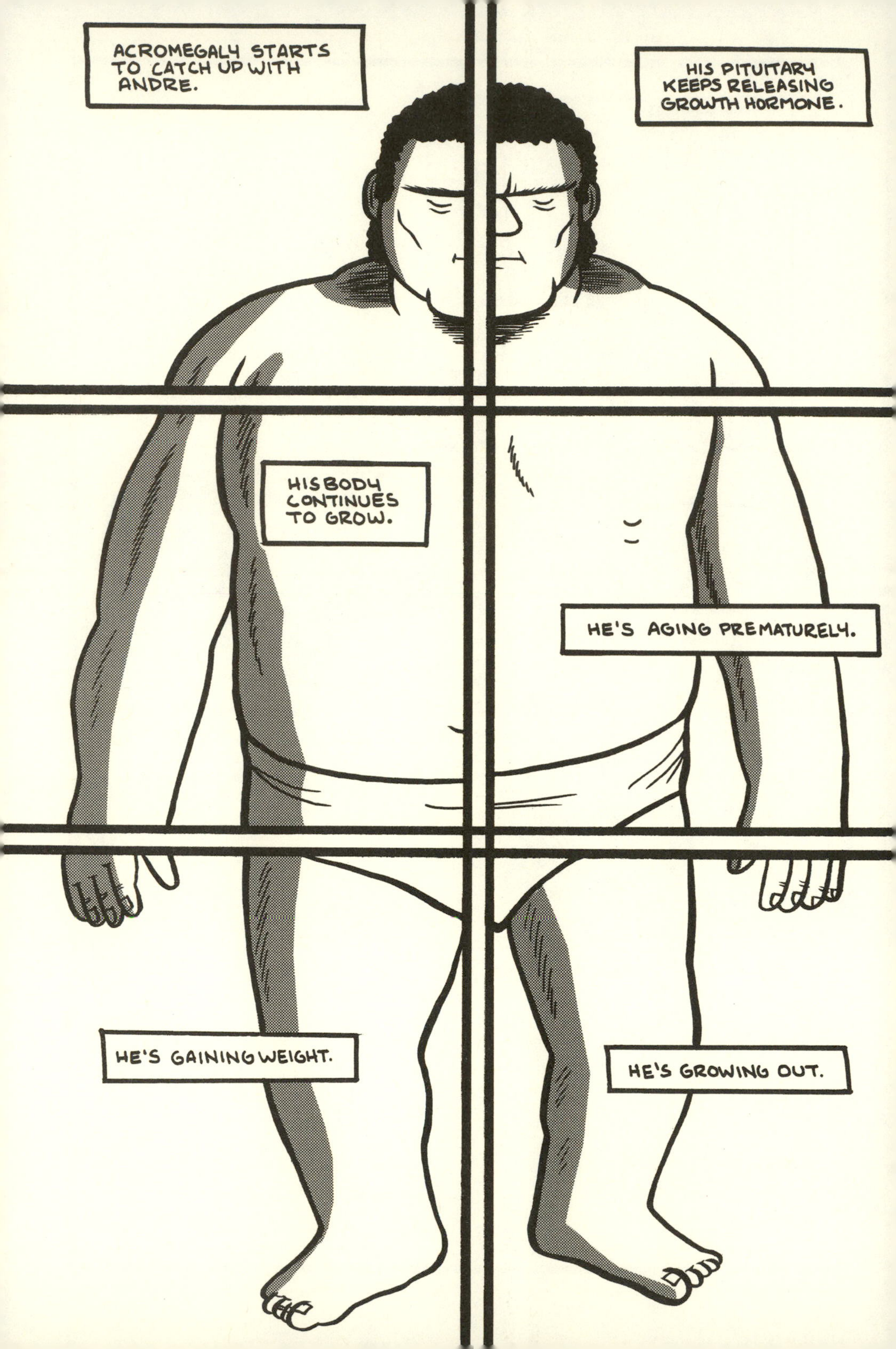
ACROMEGALY STARTS TO CATCH UP WITH ANDRE.
HIS PITUITARY KEEPS RELEASING GROWTH HORMONE.
HIS BODY CONTINUES TO GROW.
HE'S AGING PREMATURELY.
HE'S GAINING WEIGHT.
HE'S GROWING OUT.

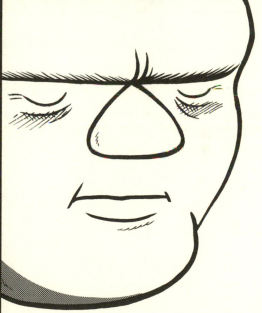

HE'S THIRTY-NINE.
THEY TOLD HIM HE
WOULDN'T SEE FORTY.

HIS BROW AND JAW
HAVE GROWN MORE PRONOUNCED.

HIS FACE IS RAPIDLY
STARTING TO SHOW AGE.

HE LOOKS LIKE A
MUCH OLDER MAN.

PAIN IS A PART OF DAILY LIFE.

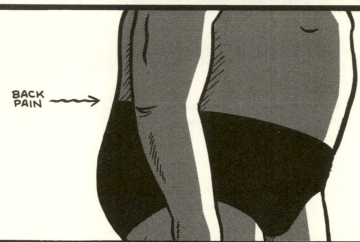

BACK PAIN →

HIS HEART OVERWORKING FROM JUST MOVING AROUND

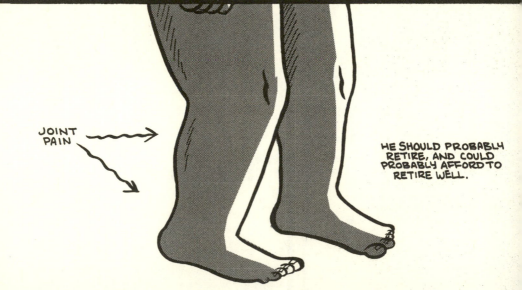

JOINT PAIN →

HE SHOULD PROBABLY RETIRE, AND COULD PROBABLY AFFORD TO RETIRE WELL.

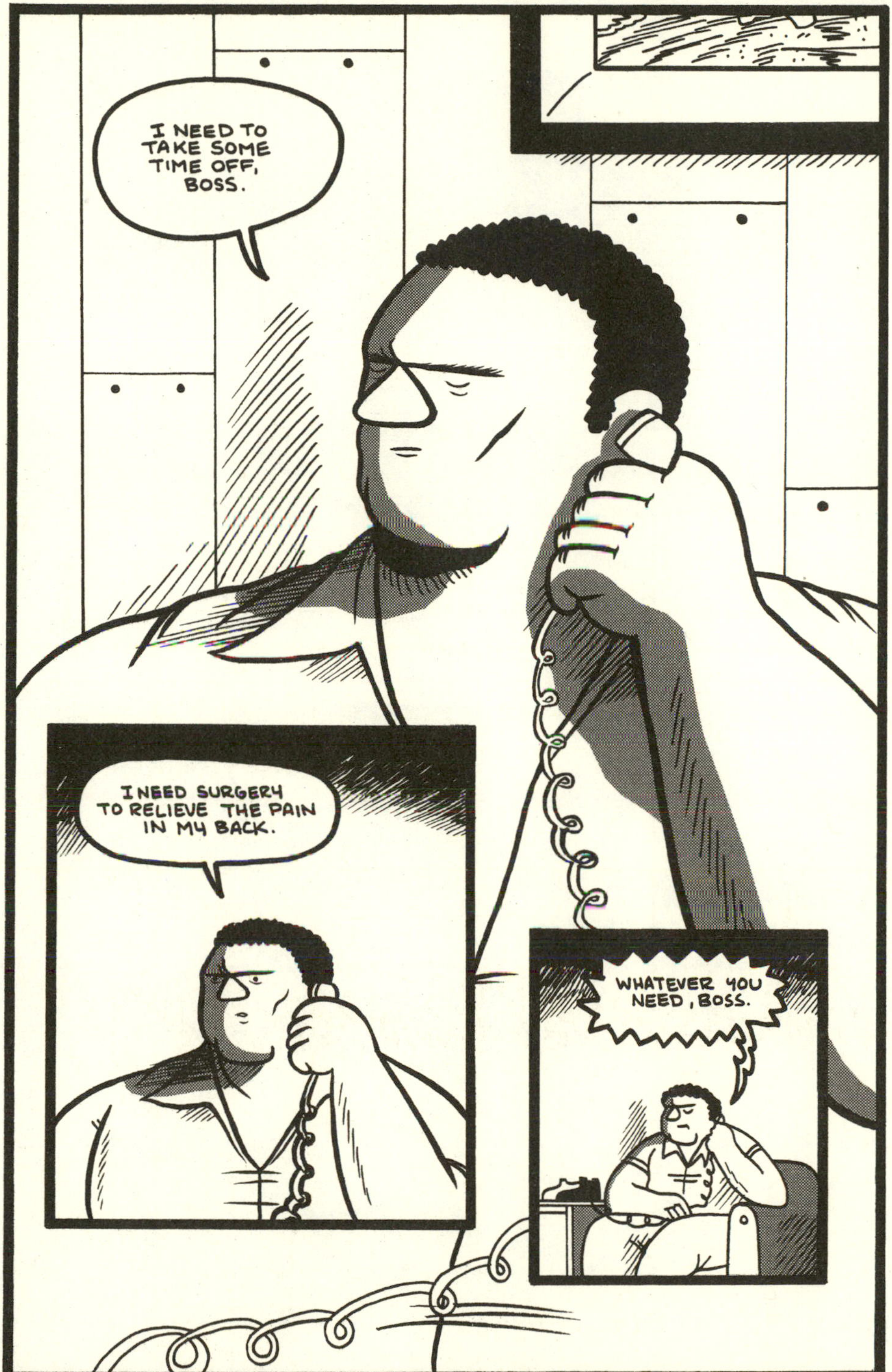
I NEED TO TAKE SOME TIME OFF, BOSS.
I NEED SURGERY TO RELIEVE THE PAIN IN MY BACK.
WHATEVER YOU NEED, BOSS.

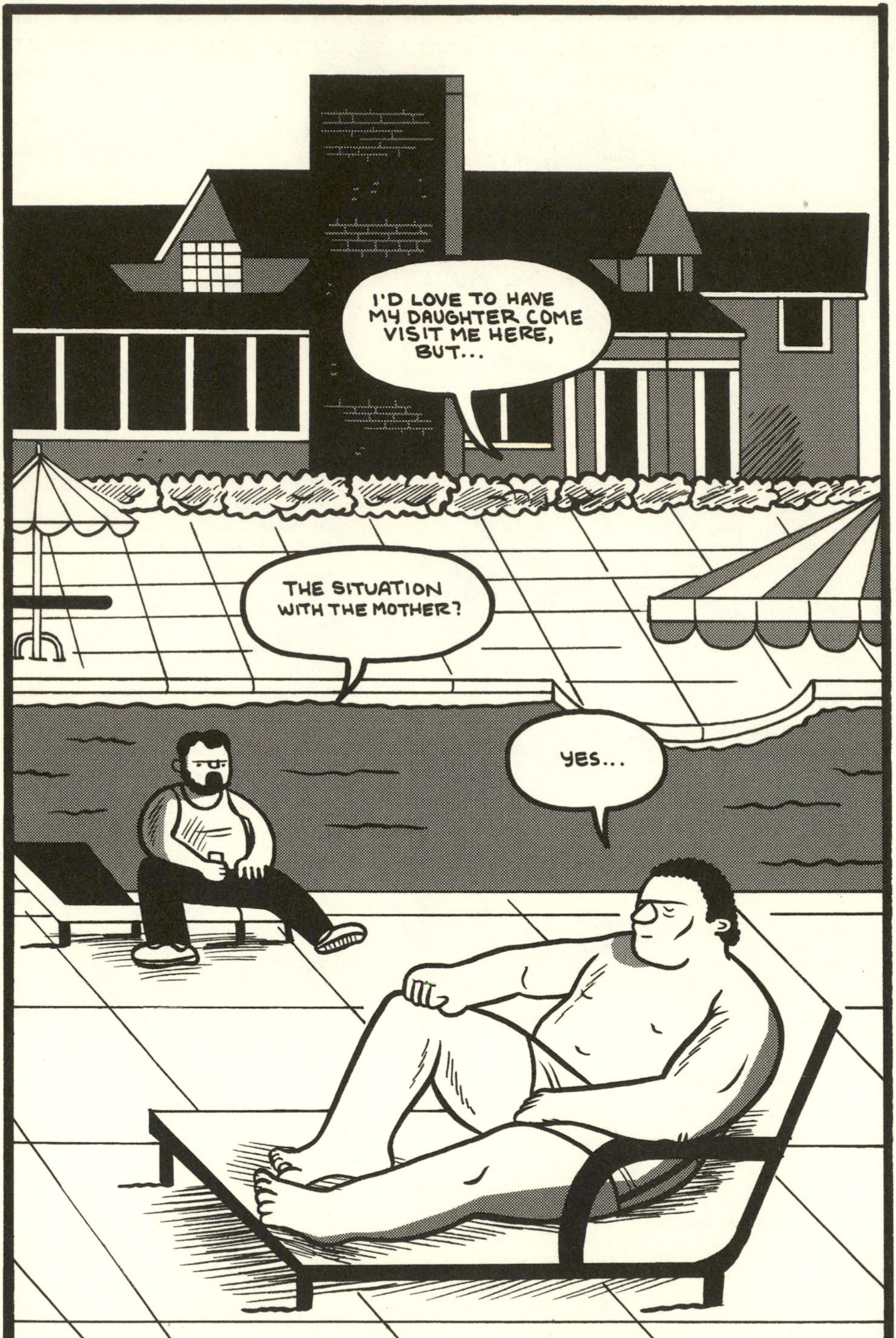
I'D LOVE TO HAVE MY DAUGHTER COME VISIT ME HERE, BUT...
THE SITUATION WITH THE MOTHER?
YES...

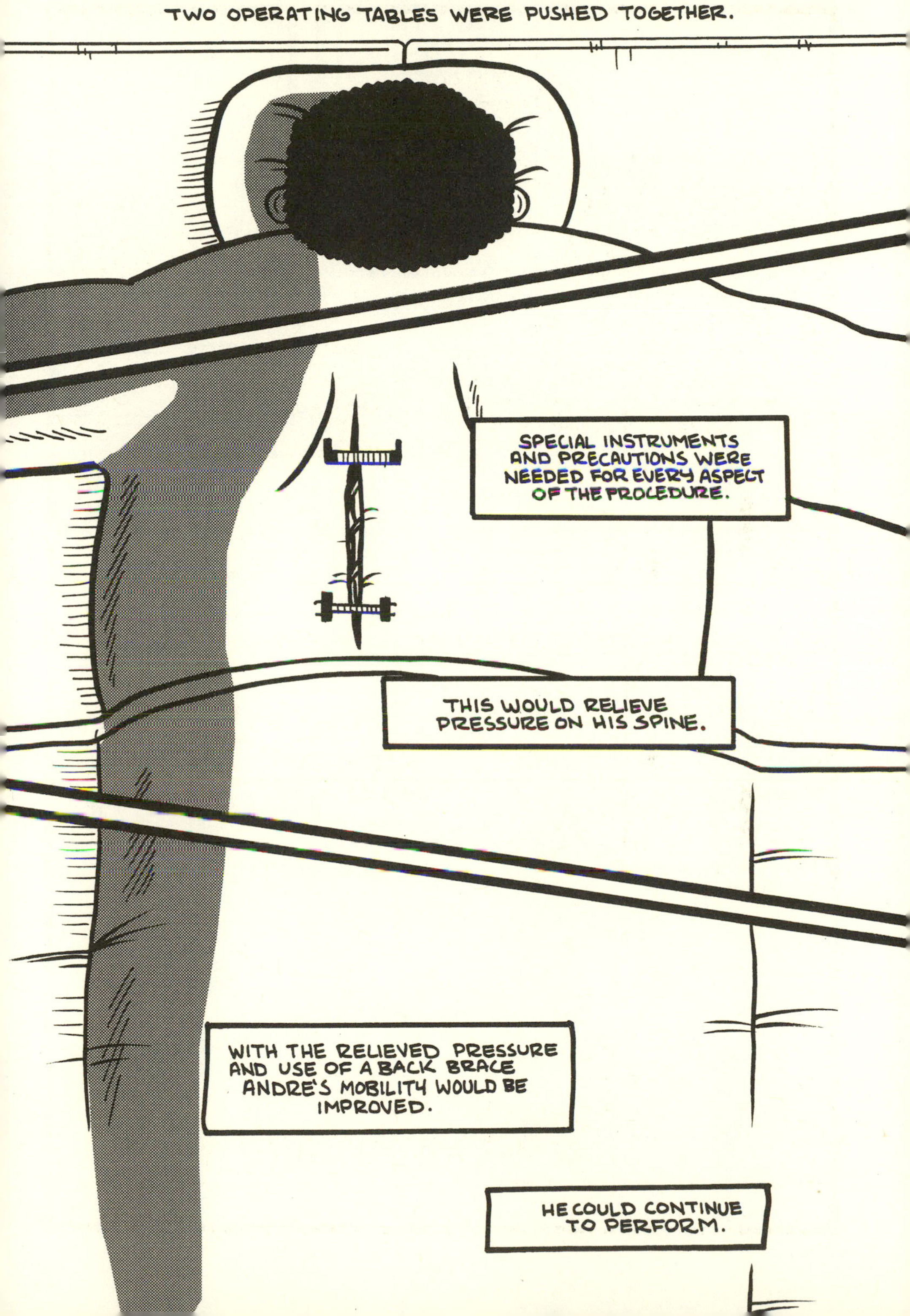
TWO OPERATING TABLES WERE PUSHED TOGETHER.
SPECIAL INSTRUMENTS AND PRECAUTIONS WERE NEEDED FOR EVERY ASPECT OF THE PROCEDURE.
THIS WOULD RELIEVE PRESSURE ON HIS SPINE.
WITH THE RELIEVED PRESSURE AND USE OF A BACK BRACE ANDRE'S MOBILITY WOULD BE IMPROVED.
HE COULD CONTINUE TO PERFORM.

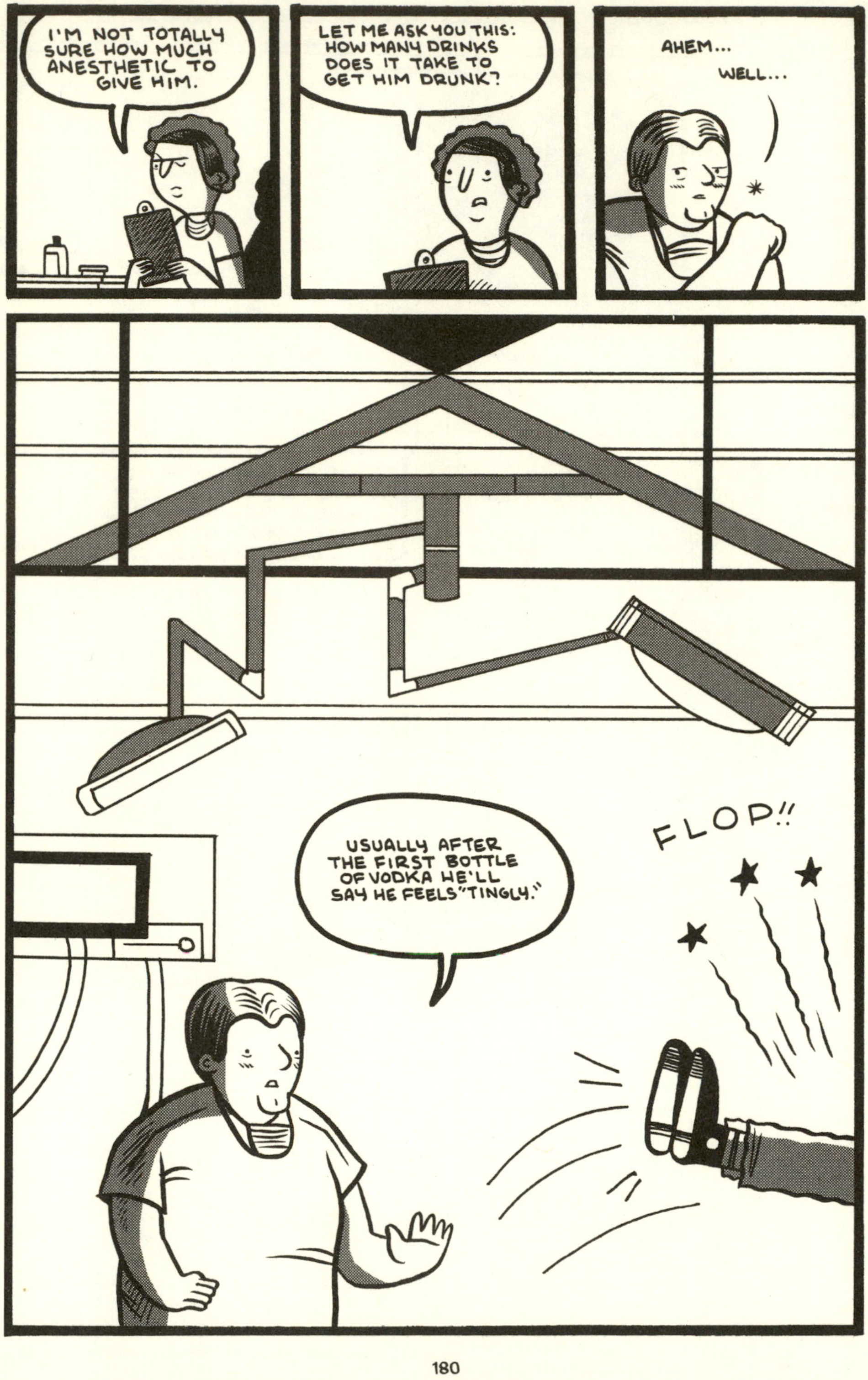
I'M NOT TOTALLY SURE HOW MUCH ANESTHETIC TO GIVE HIM.
LET ME ASK YOU THIS: HOW MANY DRINKS DOES IT TAKE TO GET HIM DRUNK?
AHEM...
WELL...
USUALLY AFTER THE FIRST BOTTLE OF VODKA HE'LL SAY HE FEELS "TINGLY."
FLOP!!

THE FILMING OF
THE PRINCESS BRIDE

SEPTEMBER TO DECEMBER
1986

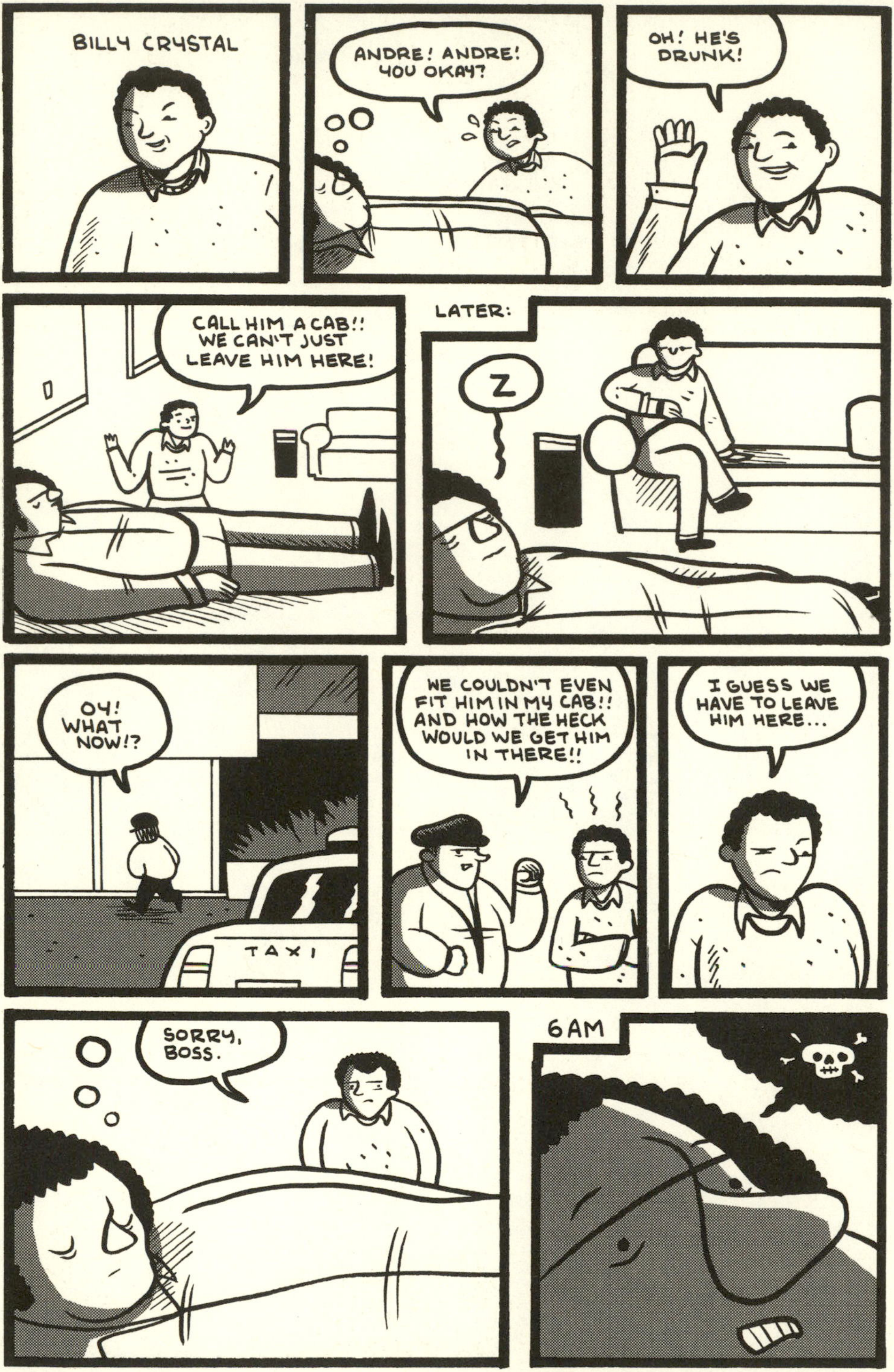
BILLY CRYSTAL
ANDRE! ANDRE! YOU OKAY?
OH! HE'S DRUNK!
CALL HIM A CAB!! WE CAN'T JUST LEAVE HIM HERE!
LATER:
Z
OY! WHAT NOW!?
TAXI
WE COULDN'T EVEN FIT HIM IN MY CAB!! AND HOW THE HECK WOULD WE GET HIM IN THERE!!
I GUESS WE HAVE TO LEAVE HIM HERE...
SORRY, BOSS.
6AM

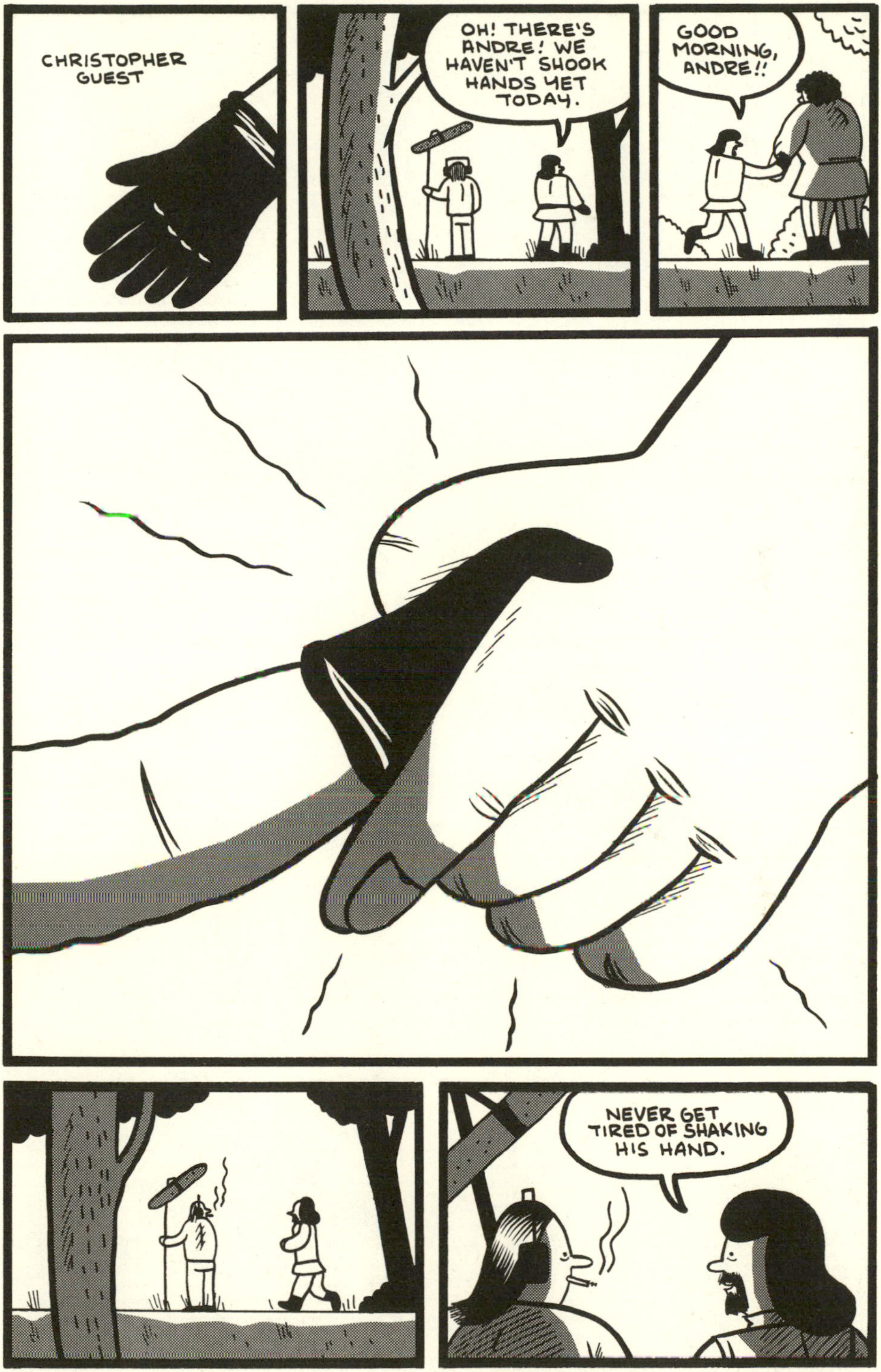

CHRISTOPHER GUEST
OH! THERE'S ANDRE! WE HAVEN'T SHOOK HANDS YET TODAY.
GOOD MORNING, ANDRE!!
NEVER GET TIRED OF SHAKING HIS HAND.

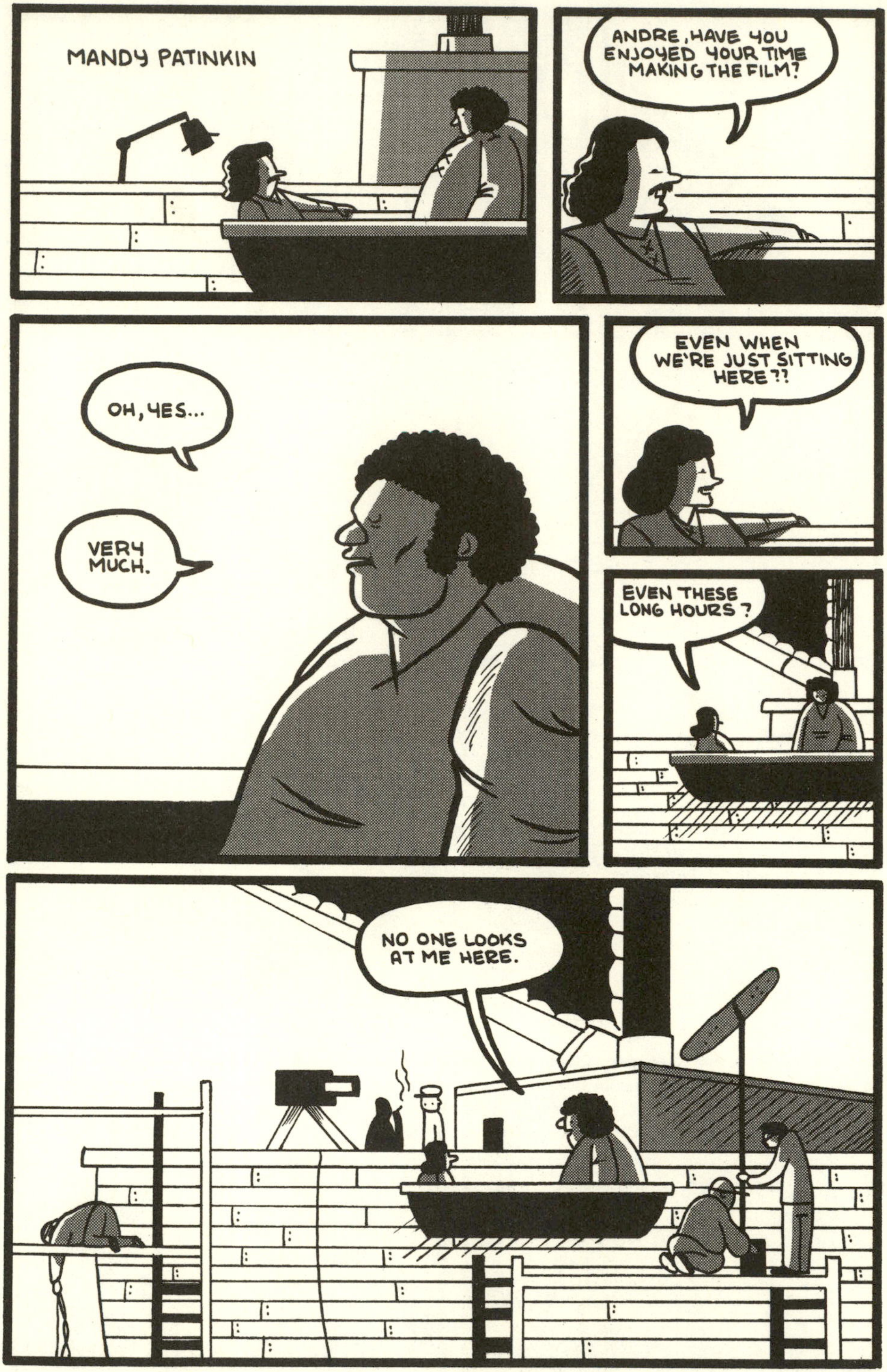
MANDY PATINKIN
ANDRE, HAVE YOU ENJOYED YOUR TIME MAKING THE FILM?
OH, YES...
VERY MUCH.
EVEN WHEN WE'RE JUST SITTING HERE??
EVEN THESE LONG HOURS?
NO ONE LOOKS AT ME HERE.

ROBIN WRIGHT

ACTION!

ARE YOU COLD, ROBIN?

YEAH! IT'S CHILLY THIS MORNING.

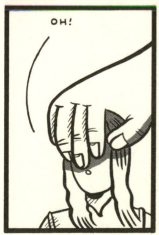

OH!

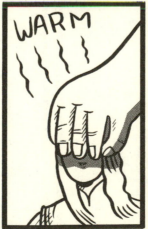

WARM

I AM NOT LEFT-HANDED EITHER!!

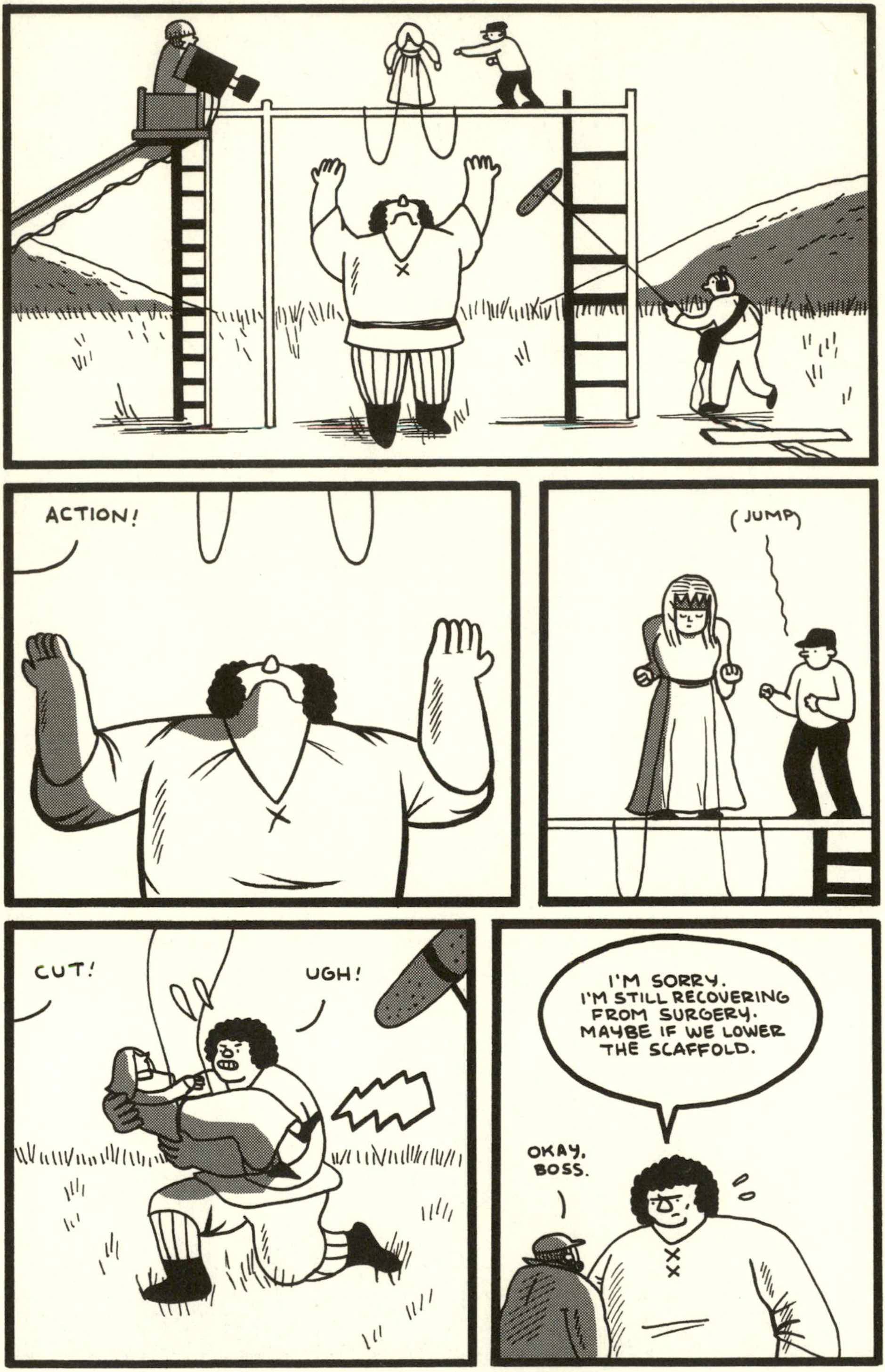
ACTION!
(JUMP)
CUT!
UGH!
I'M SORRY. I'M STILL RECOVERING FROM SURGERY. MAYBE IF WE LOWER THE SCAFFOLD.
OKAY, BOSS.

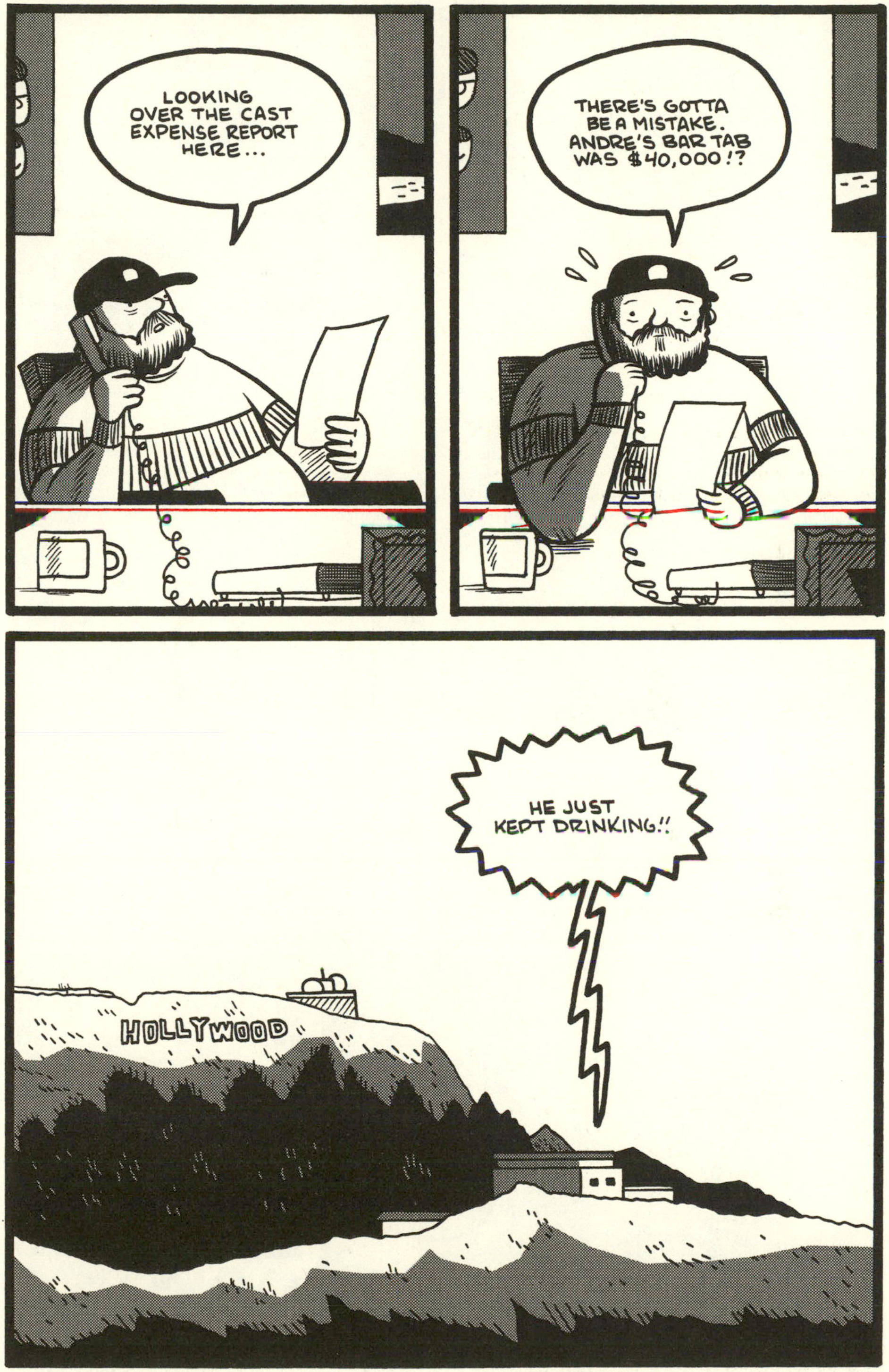
LOOKING OVER THE CAST EXPENSE REPORT HERE...
THERE'S GOTTA BE A MISTAKE. ANDRE'S BAR TAB WAS $40,000!?
HE JUST KEPT DRINKING!!
HOLLYWOOD

TERRY FUNK

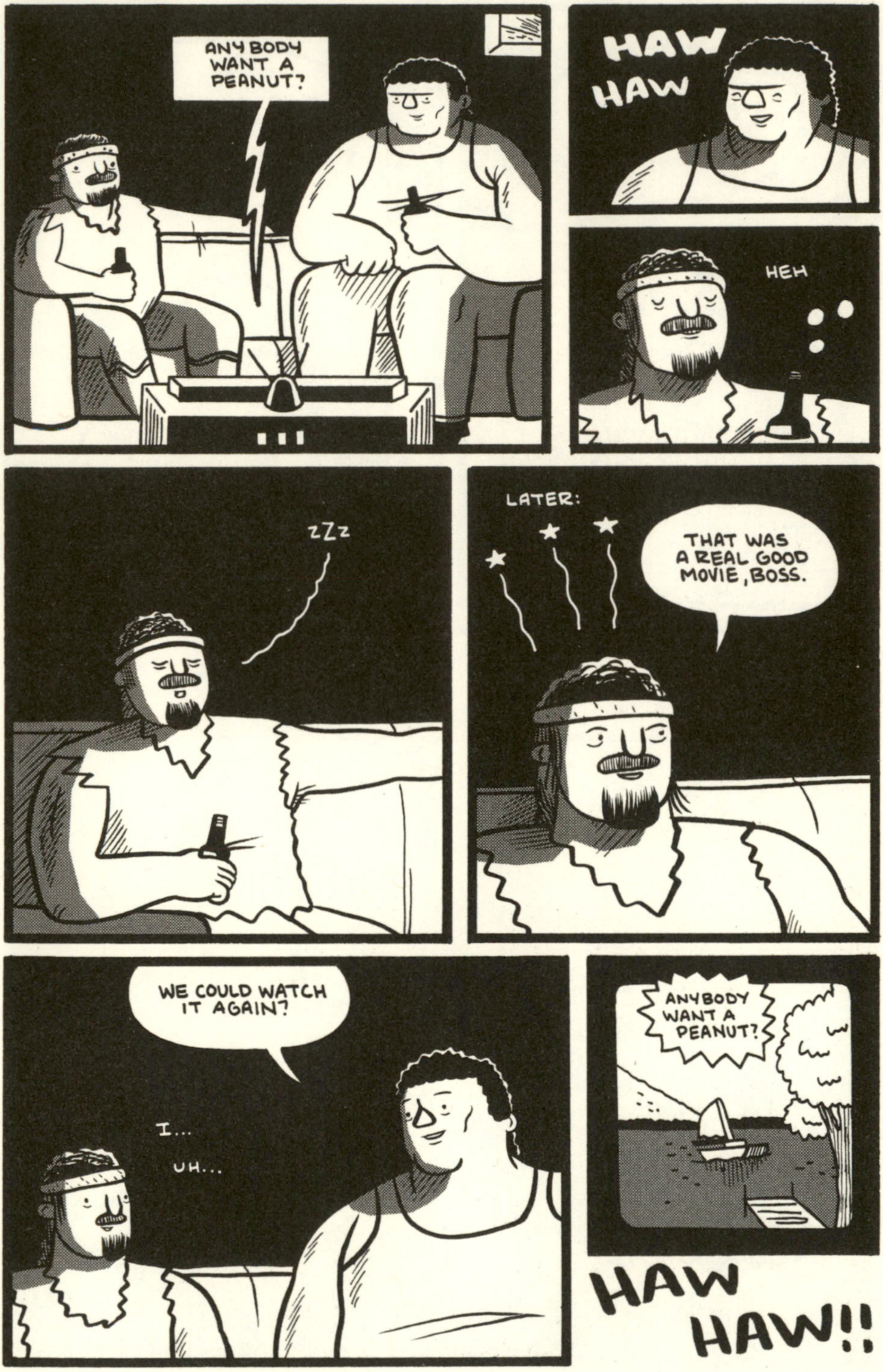
ANYBODY WANT A PEANUT?
HAW HAW
HEH
ZZZ
LATER:
THAT WAS A REAL GOOD MOVIE, BOSS.
WE COULD WATCH IT AGAIN?
I...
UH...
ANYBODY WANT A PEANUT?
HAW HAW!!

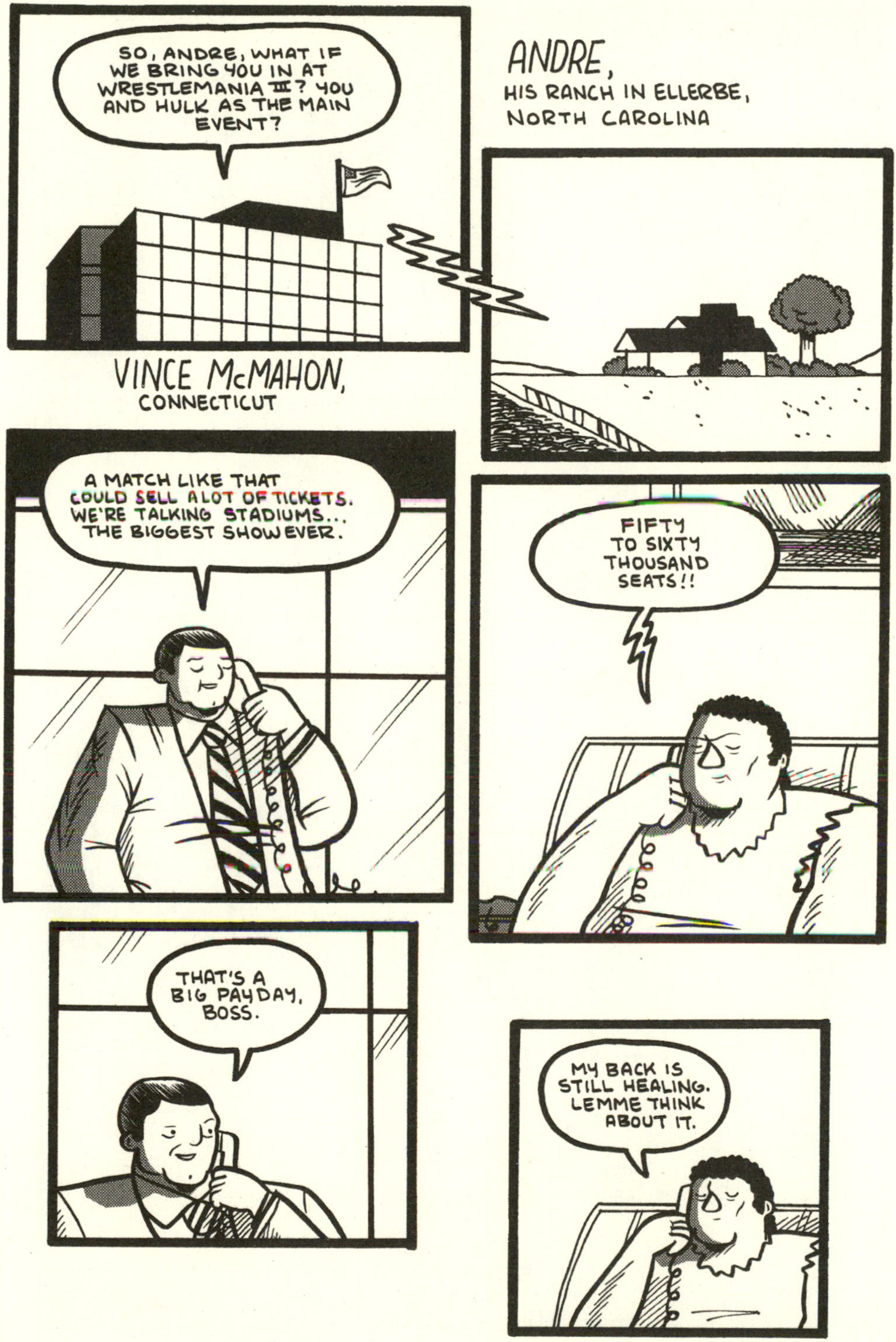
SO, ANDRE, WHAT IF WE BRING YOU IN AT WRESTLEMANIA III? YOU AND HULK AS THE MAIN EVENT?
ANDRE, HIS RANCH IN ELLERBE, NORTH CAROLINA
VINCE McMAHON, CONNECTICUT
A MATCH LIKE THAT COULD SELL A LOT OF TICKETS. WE'RE TALKING STADIUMS... THE BIGGEST SHOW EVER.
FIFTY TO SIXTY THOUSAND SEATS!!
THAT'S A BIG PAYDAY, BOSS.
MY BACK IS STILL HEALING. LEMME THINK ABOUT IT.

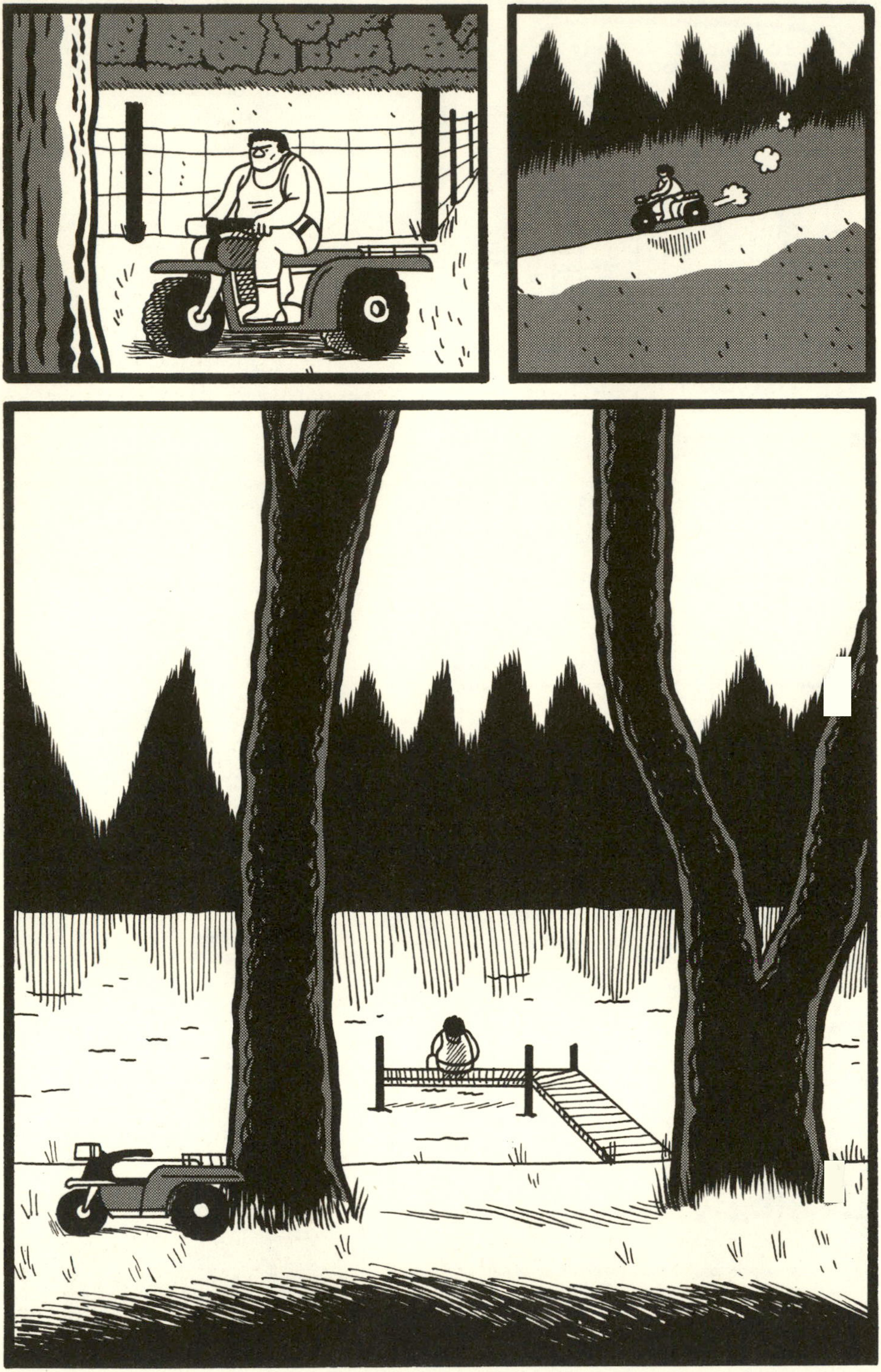

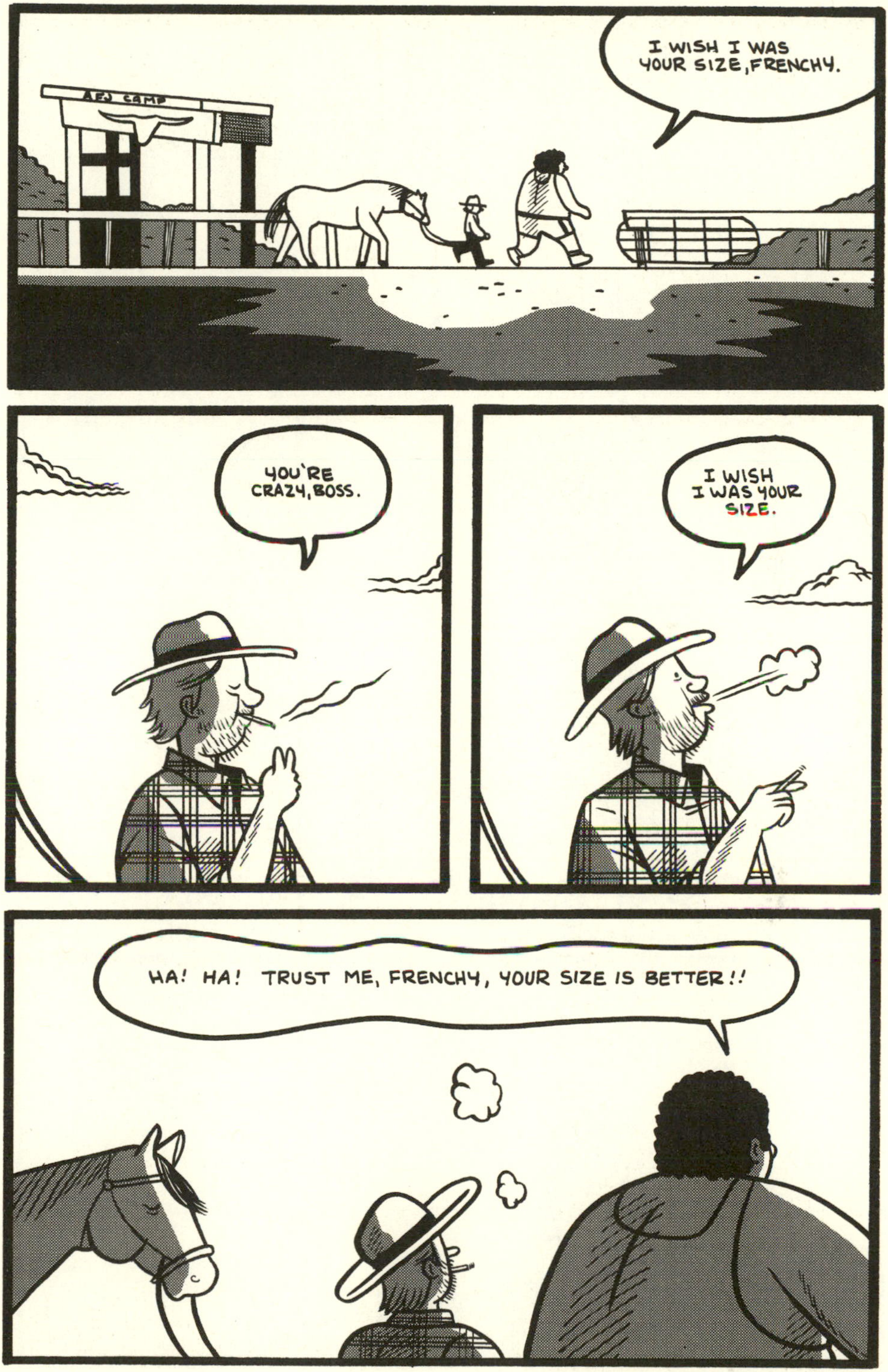
AEJ CAMP
I WISH I WAS YOUR SIZE, FRENCHY.
YOU'RE CRAZY, BOSS.
I WISH I WAS YOUR SIZE.
HA! HA! TRUST ME, FRENCHY, YOUR SIZE IS BETTER!!

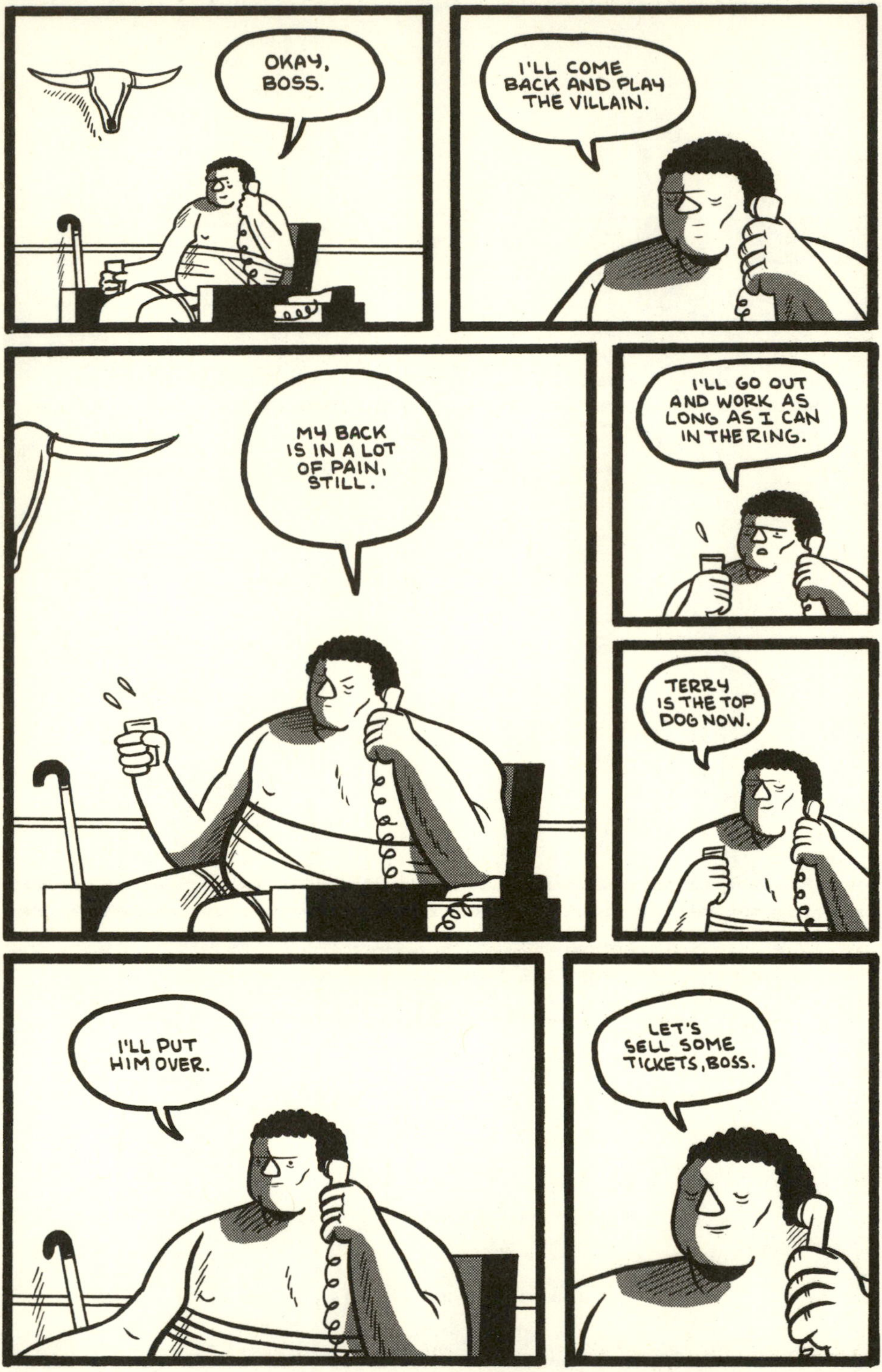
OKAY, BOSS.
I'LL COME BACK AND PLAY THE VILLAIN.
MY BACK IS IN A LOT OF PAIN, STILL.
I'LL GO OUT AND WORK AS LONG AS I CAN IN THE RING.
TERRY IS THE TOP DOG NOW.
I'LL PUT HIM OVER.
LET'S SELL SOME TICKETS, BOSS.

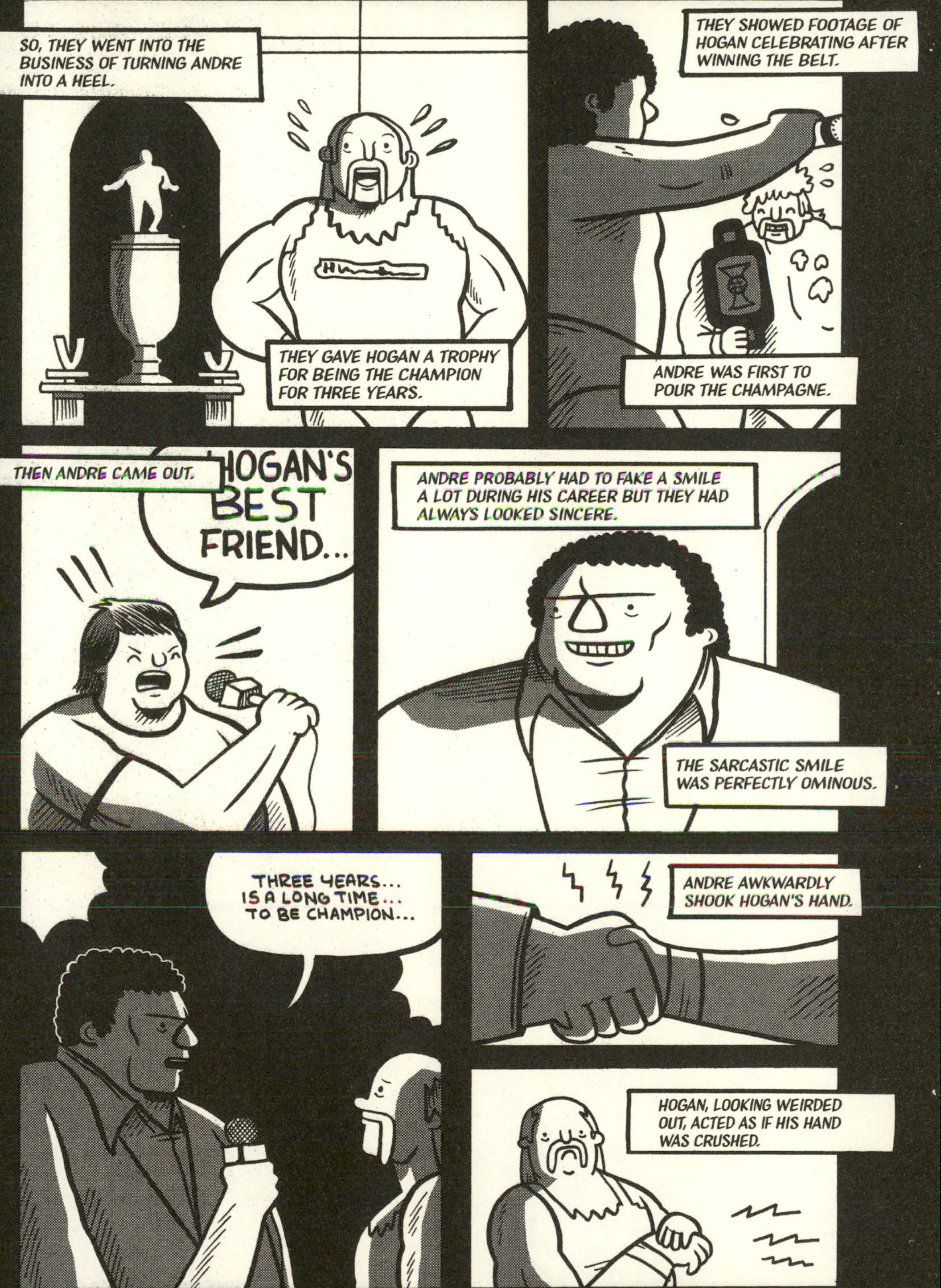

SO, THEY WENT INTO THE BUSINESS OF TURNING ANDRE INTO A HEEL.
THEY GAVE HOGAN A TROPHY FOR BEING THE CHAMPION FOR THREE YEARS.
THEY SHOWED FOOTAGE OF HOGAN CELEBRATING AFTER WINNING THE BELT.
ANDRE WAS FIRST TO POUR THE CHAMPAGNE.
THEN ANDRE CAME OUT.
HOGAN'S BEST FRIEND...
ANDRE PROBABLY HAD TO FAKE A SMILE A LOT DURING HIS CAREER BUT THEY HAD ALWAYS LOOKED SINCERE.
THE SARCASTIC SMILE WAS PERFECTLY OMINOUS.
THREE YEARS... IS A LONG TIME... TO BE CHAMPION...
ANDRE AWKWARDLY SHOOK HOGAN'S HAND.
HOGAN, LOOKING WEIRDED OUT, ACTED AS IF HIS HAND WAS CRUSHED.

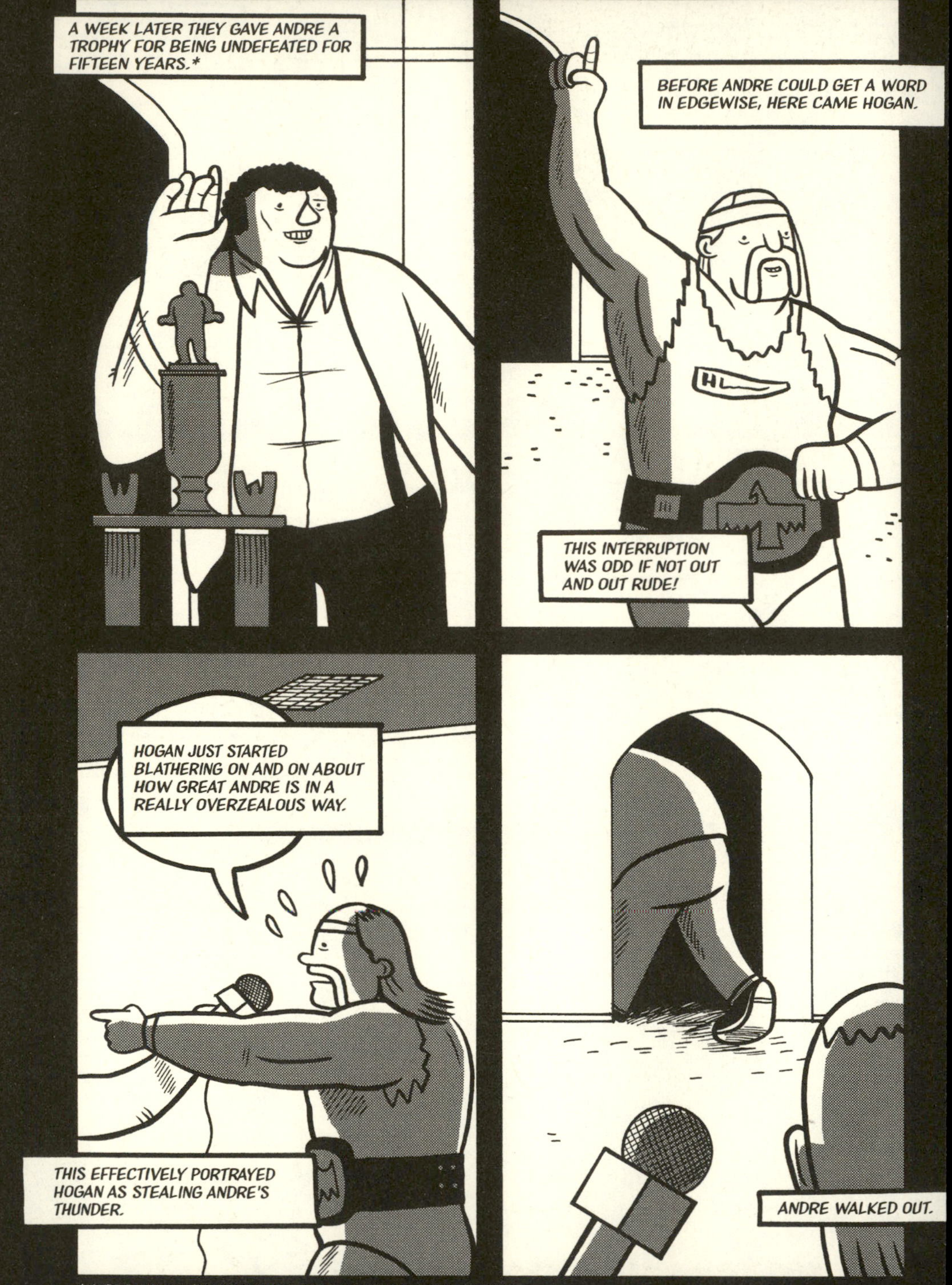
A WEEK LATER THEY GAVE ANDRE A TROPHY FOR BEING UNDEFEATED FOR FIFTEEN YEARS.*
BEFORE ANDRE COULD GET A WORD IN EDGEWISE, HERE CAME HOGAN.
HL
THIS INTERRUPTION WAS ODD IF NOT OUT AND OUT RUDE!
HOGAN JUST STARTED BLATHERING ON AND ON ABOUT HOW GREAT ANDRE IS IN A REALLY OVERZEALOUS WAY.
THIS EFFECTIVELY PORTRAYED HOGAN AS STEALING ANDRE'S THUNDER.
ANDRE WALKED OUT.

* ANDRE WAS NOT ACTUALLY UNDEFEATED BUT HIS LOSSES WERE FEW.

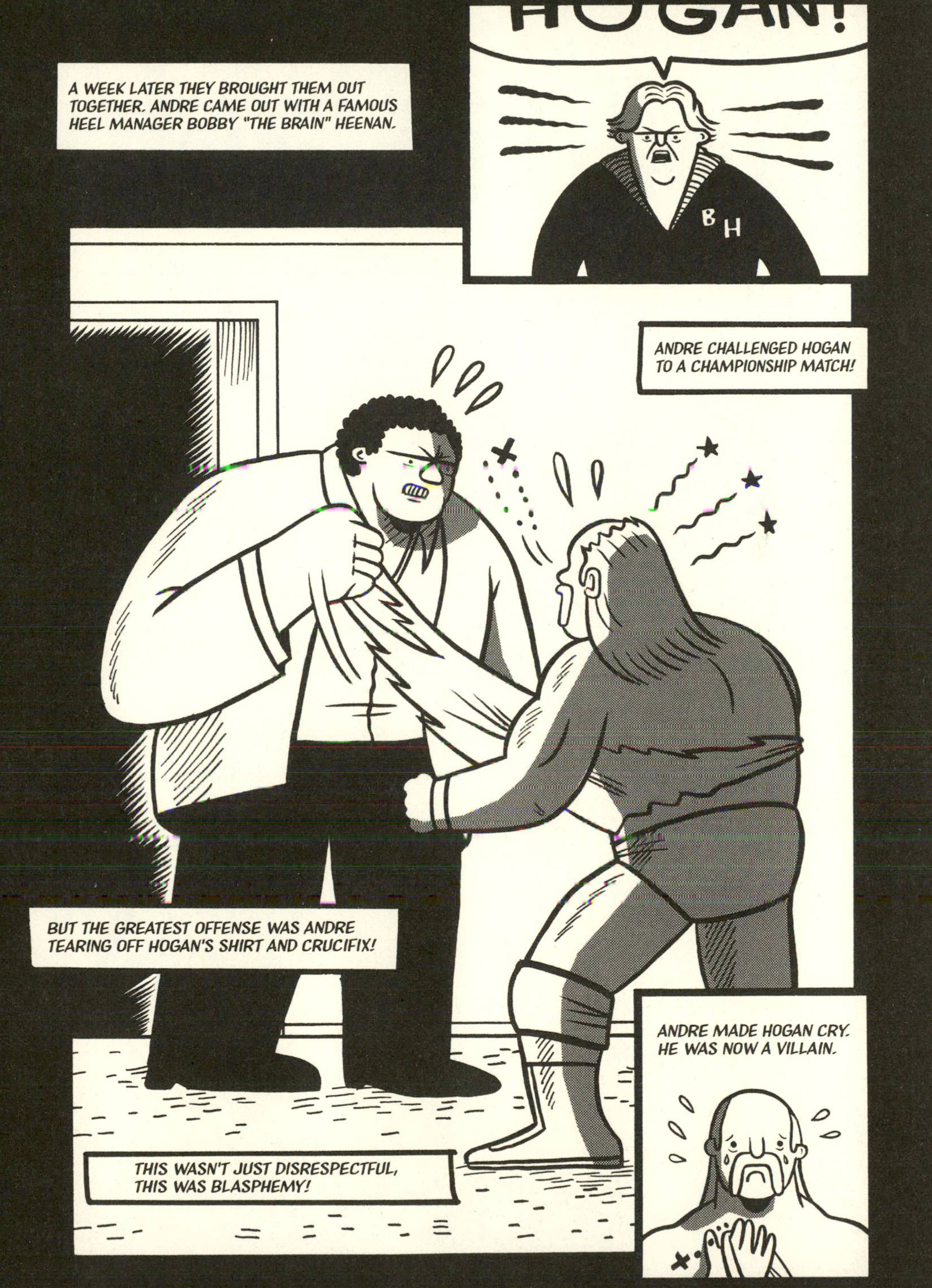
A WEEK LATER THEY BROUGHT THEM OUT TOGETHER. ANDRE CAME OUT WITH A FAMOUS HEEL MANAGER BOBBY "THE BRAIN" HEENAN.
HOGAN!
BH
ANDRE CHALLENGED HOGAN TO A CHAMPIONSHIP MATCH!
BUT THE GREATEST OFFENSE WAS ANDRE TEARING OFF HOGAN'S SHIRT AND CRUCIFIX!
ANDRE MADE HOGAN CRY. HE WAS NOW A VILLAIN.
THIS WASN'T JUST DISRESPECTFUL, THIS WAS BLASPHEMY!

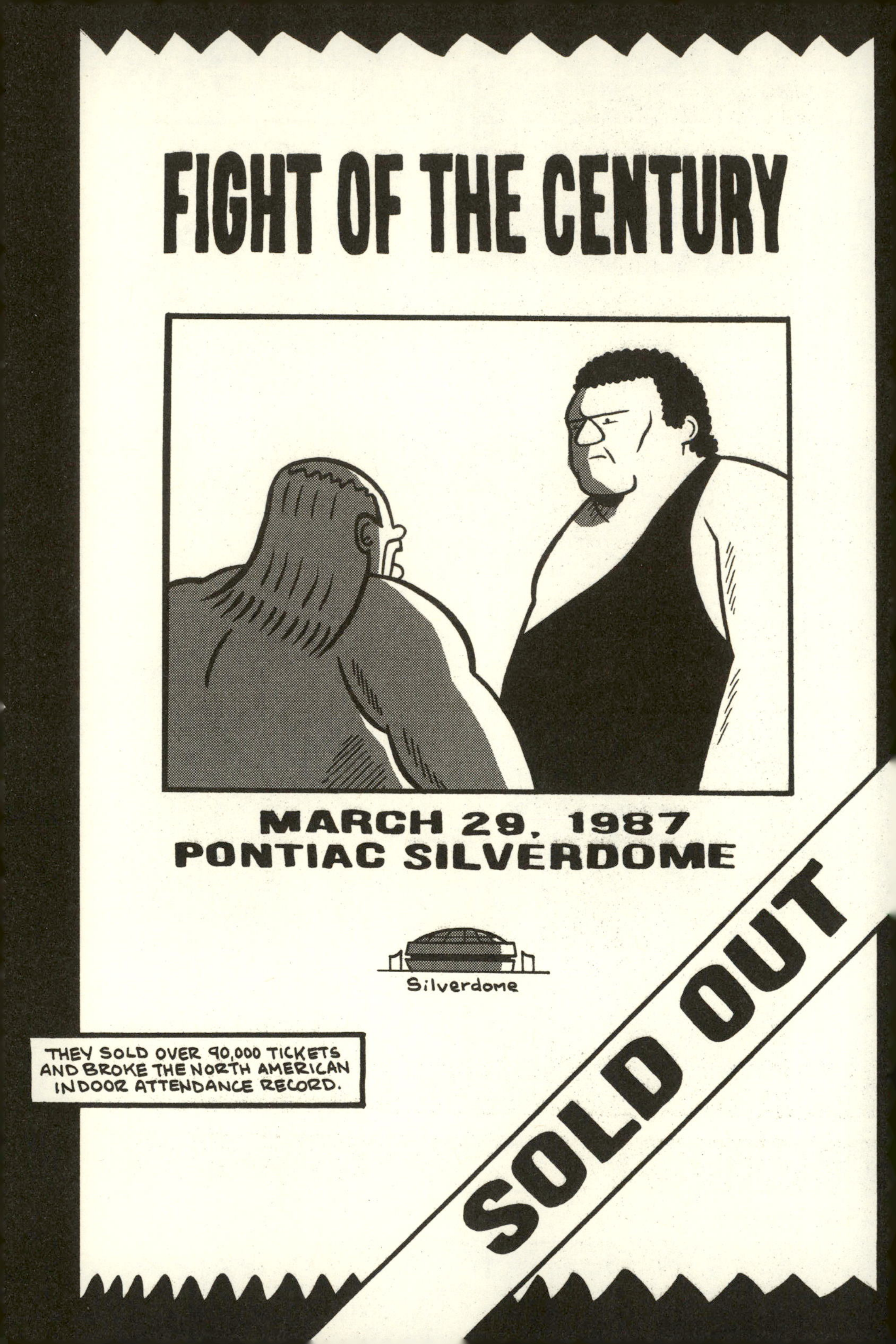
FIGHT OF THE CENTURY
MARCH 29, 1987
PONTIAC SILVERDOME
Silverdome
THEY SOLD OVER 90,000 TICKETS AND BROKE THE NORTH AMERICAN INDOOR ATTENDANCE RECORD.
SOLD OUT

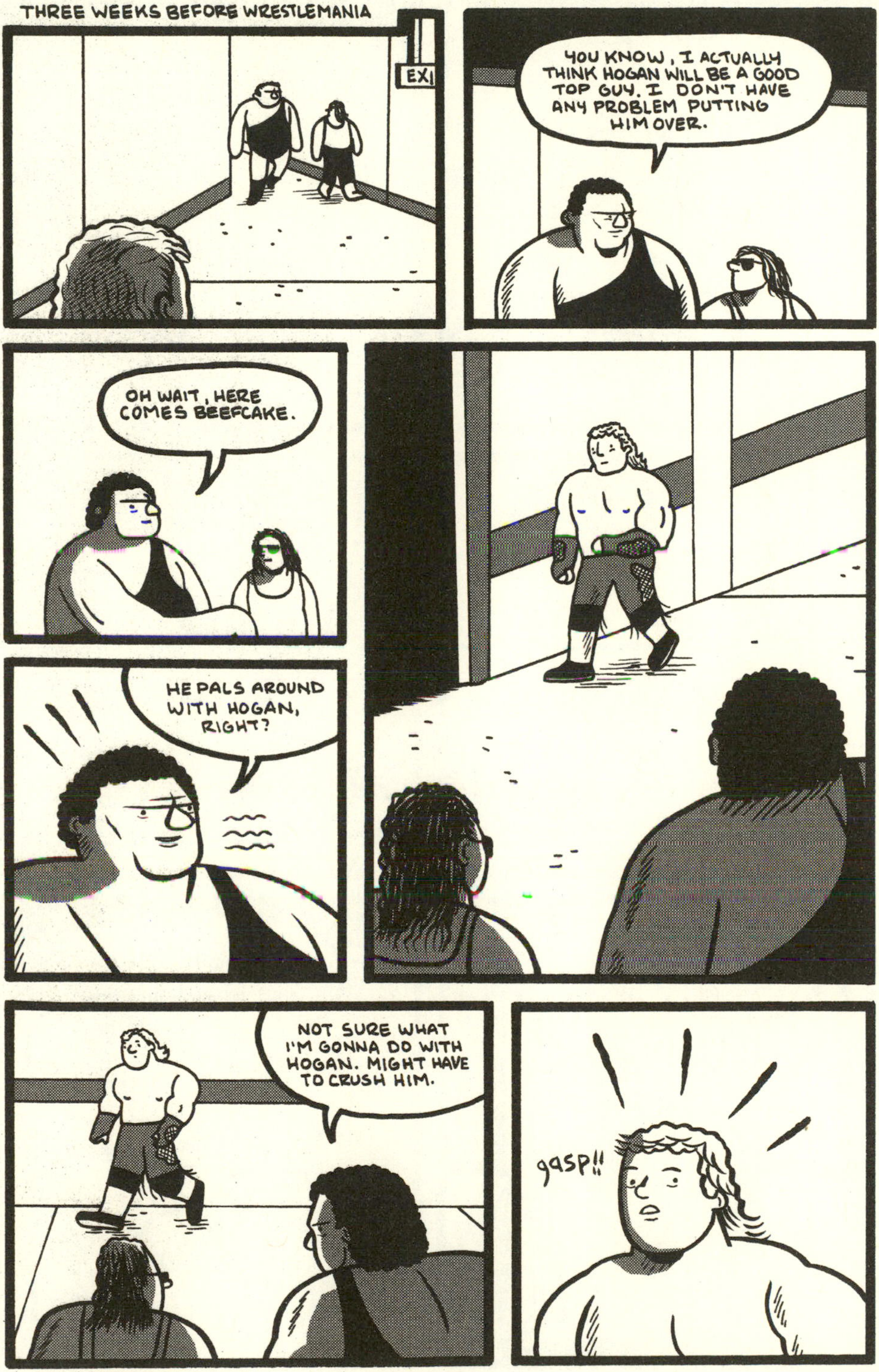
THREE WEEKS BEFORE WRESTLEMANIA
EXI
YOU KNOW, I ACTUALLY THINK HOGAN WILL BE A GOOD TOP GUY. I DON'T HAVE ANY PROBLEM PUTTING HIM OVER.
OH WAIT, HERE COMES BEEFCAKE.
HE PALS AROUND WITH HOGAN, RIGHT?
NOT SURE WHAT I'M GONNA DO WITH HOGAN. MIGHT HAVE TO CRUSH HIM.
gasp!!

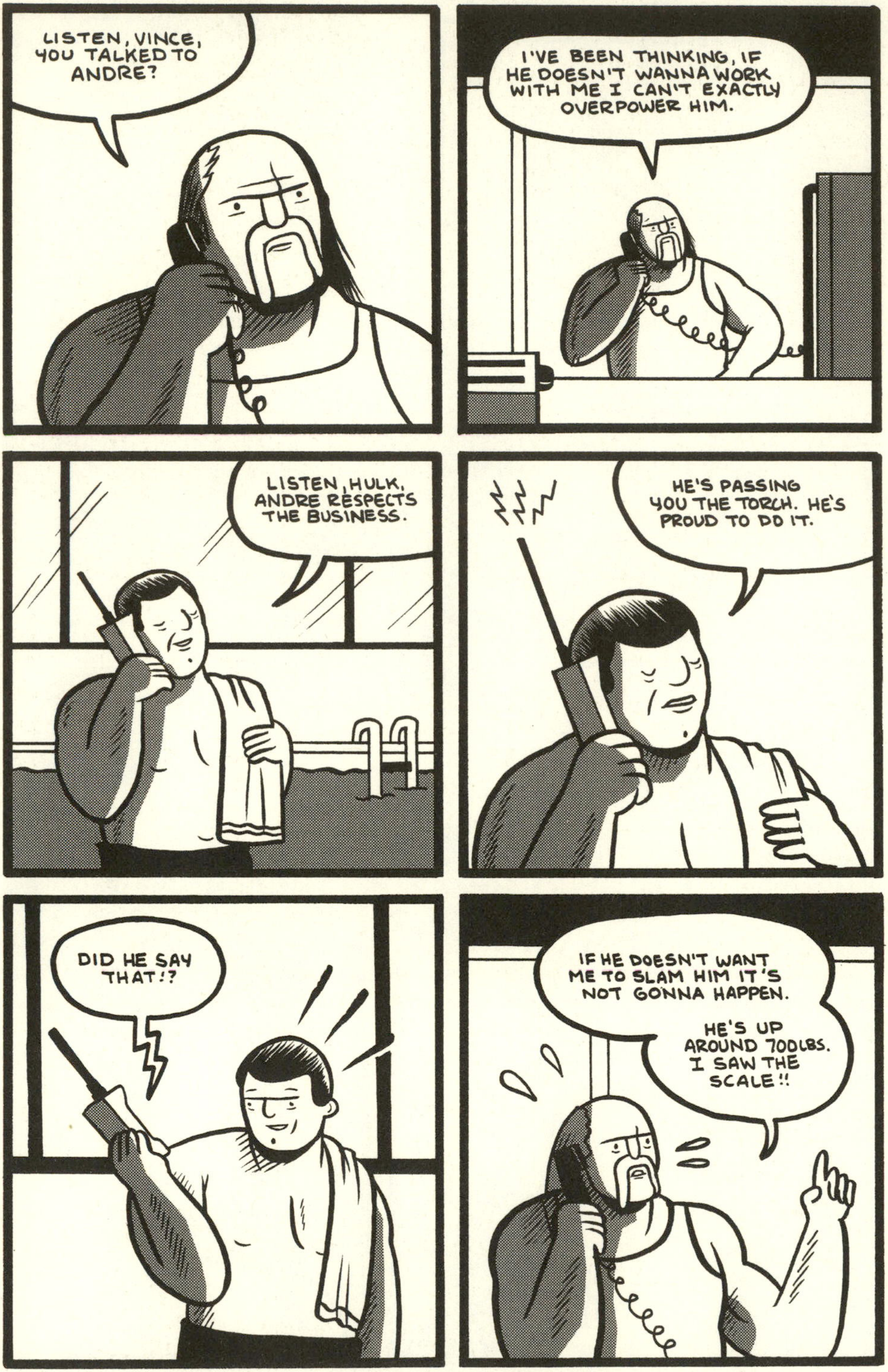
LISTEN, VINCE, YOU TALKED TO ANDRE?
I'VE BEEN THINKING, IF HE DOESN'T WANNA WORK WITH ME I CAN'T EXACTLY OVERPOWER HIM.
LISTEN, HULK, ANDRE RESPECTS THE BUSINESS.
HE'S PASSING YOU THE TORCH. HE'S PROUD TO DO IT.
DID HE SAY THAT!?
IF HE DOESN'T WANT ME TO SLAM HIM IT'S NOT GONNA HAPPEN.
HE'S UP AROUND 700LBS. I SAW THE SCALE!!

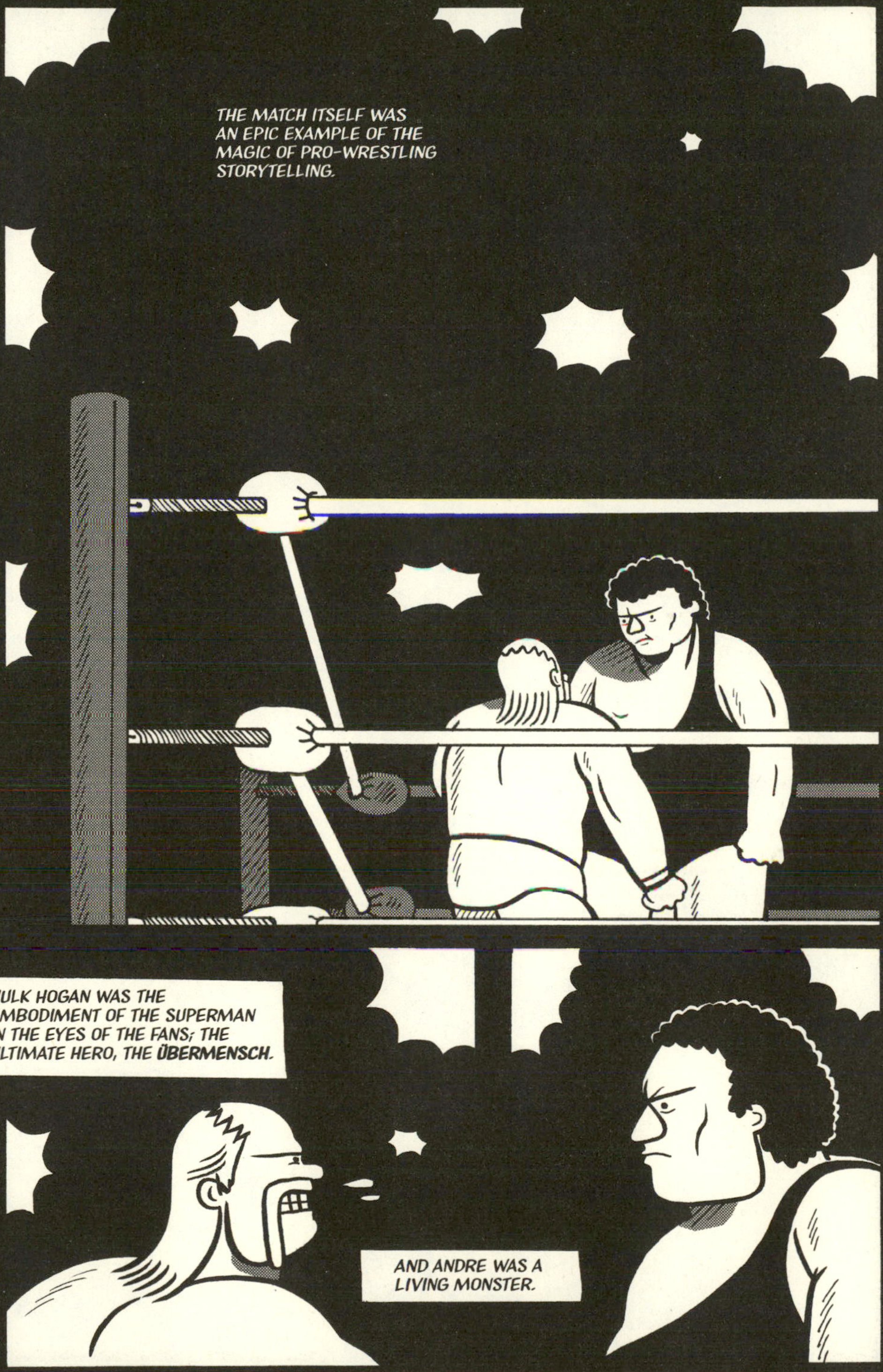
THE MATCH ITSELF WAS AN EPIC EXAMPLE OF THE MAGIC OF PRO-WRESTLING STORYTELLING.
HULK HOGAN WAS THE EMBODIMENT OF THE SUPERMAN IN THE EYES OF THE FANS; THE ULTIMATE HERO, THE ÜBERMENSCH.
AND ANDRE WAS A LIVING MONSTER.

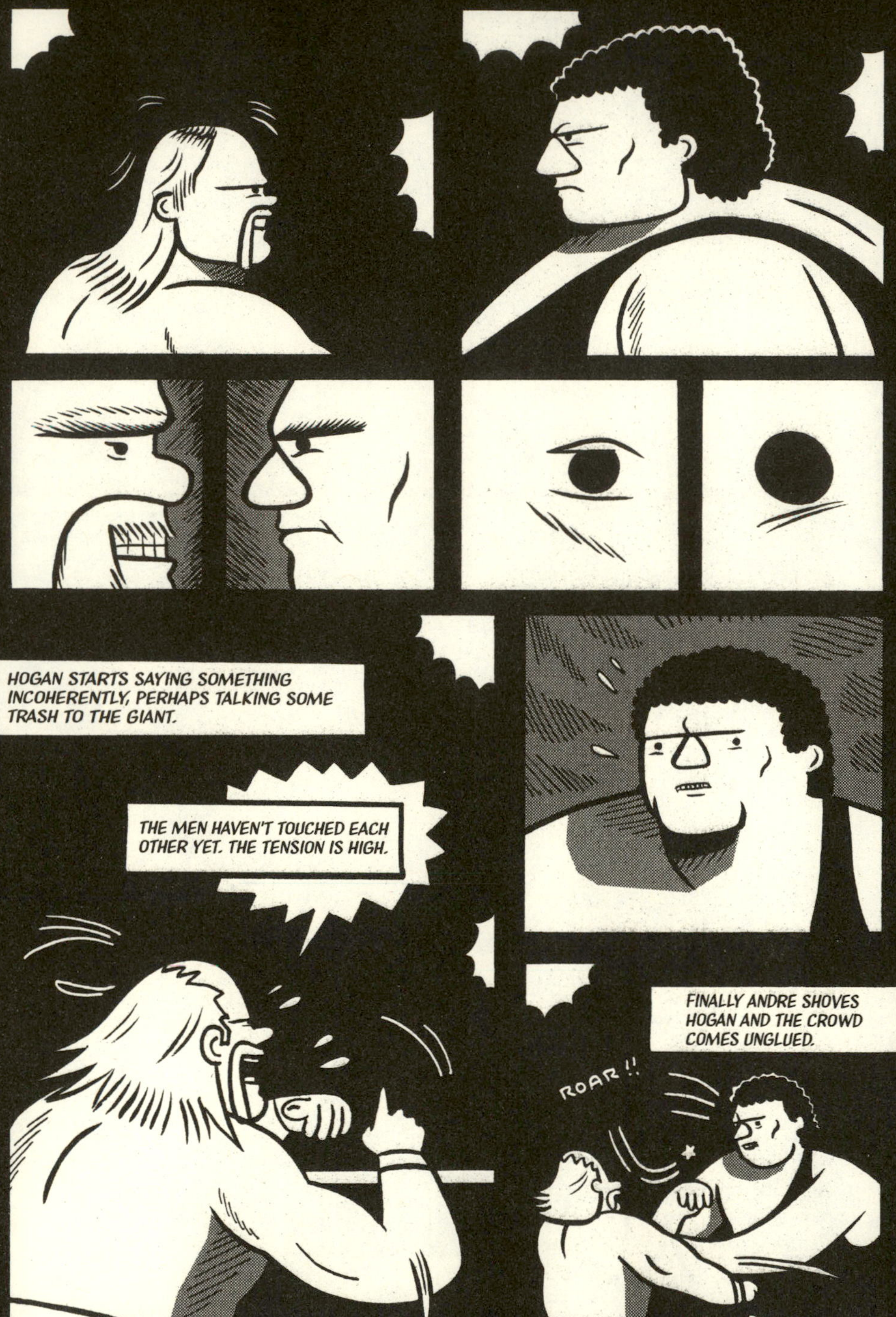
HOGAN STARTS SAYING SOMETHING INCOHERENTLY, PERHAPS TALKING SOME TRASH TO THE GIANT.
THE MEN HAVEN'T TOUCHED EACH OTHER YET. THE TENSION IS HIGH.
FINALLY ANDRE SHOVES HOGAN AND THE CROWD COMES UNGLUED.
ROAR!!

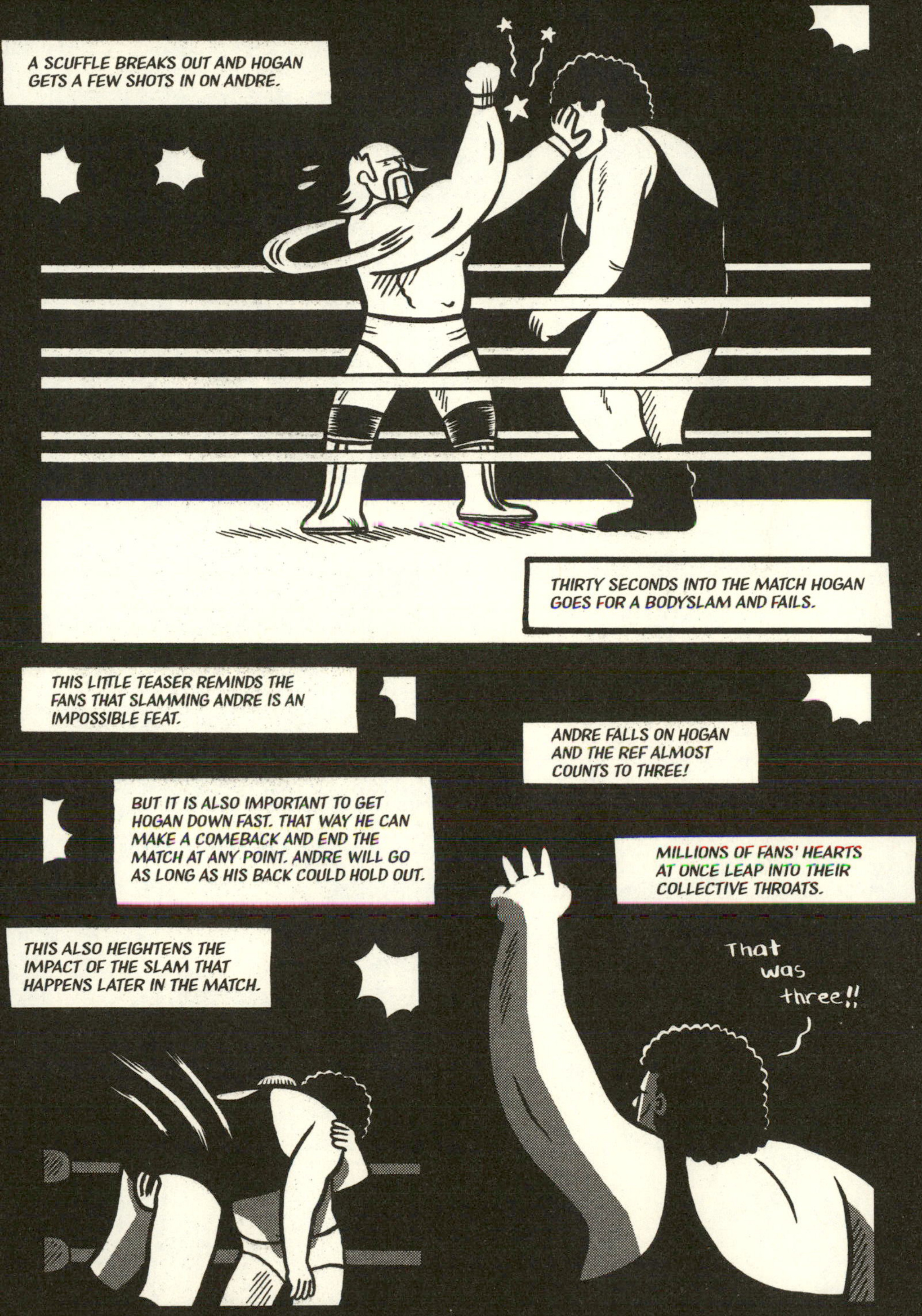
A SCUFFLE BREAKS OUT AND HOGAN GETS A FEW SHOTS IN ON ANDRE.
THIRTY SECONDS INTO THE MATCH HOGAN GOES FOR A BODYSLAM AND FAILS.
THIS LITTLE TEASER REMINDS THE FANS THAT SLAMMING ANDRE IS AN IMPOSSIBLE FEAT.
BUT IT IS ALSO IMPORTANT TO GET HOGAN DOWN FAST. THAT WAY HE CAN MAKE A COMEBACK AND END THE MATCH AT ANY POINT. ANDRE WILL GO AS LONG AS HIS BACK COULD HOLD OUT.
THIS ALSO HEIGHTENS THE IMPACT OF THE SLAM THAT HAPPENS LATER IN THE MATCH.
ANDRE FALLS ON HOGAN AND THE REF ALMOST COUNTS TO THREE!
MILLIONS OF FANS' HEARTS AT ONCE LEAP INTO THEIR COLLECTIVE THROATS.
That was three!!

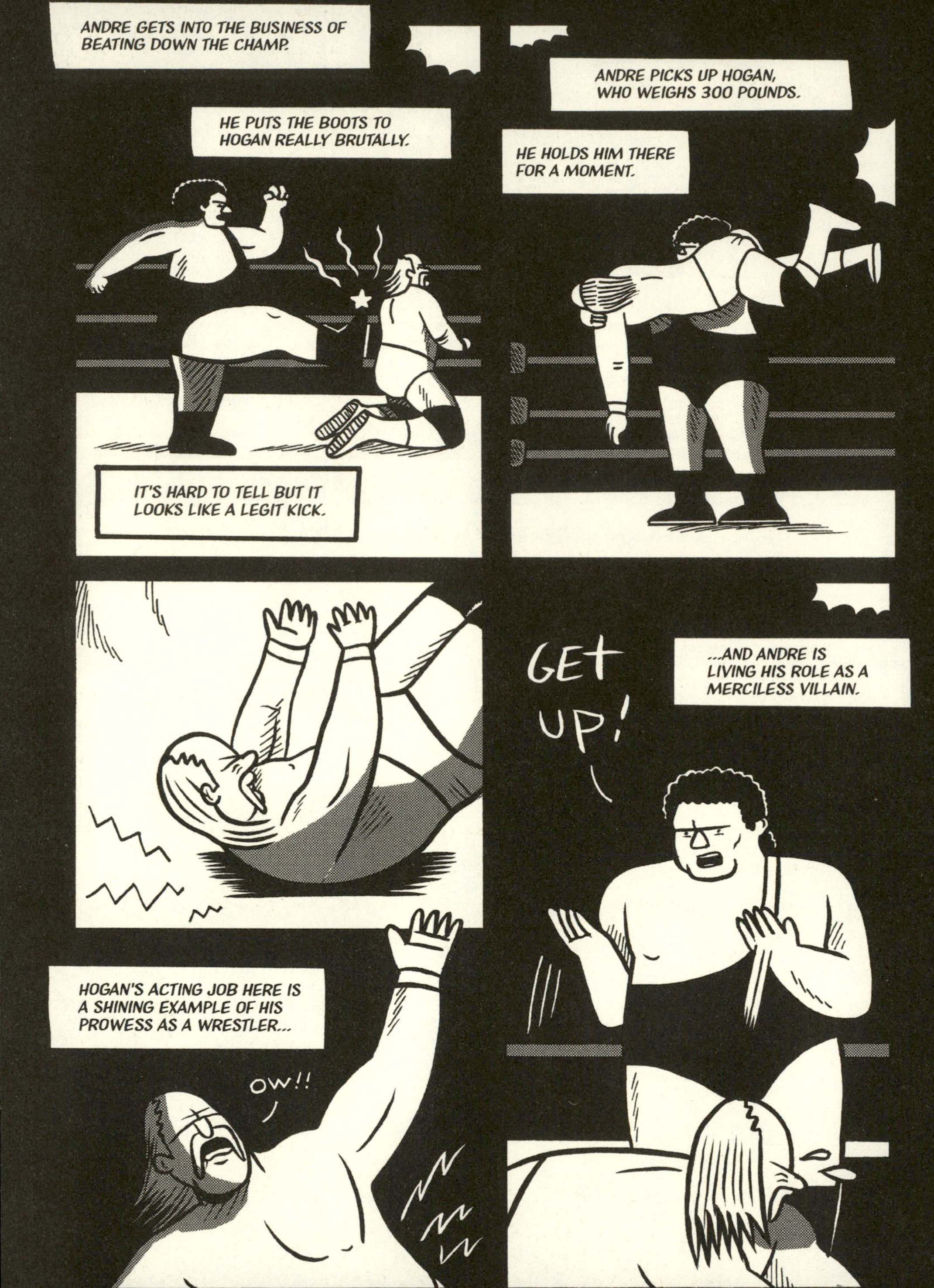
ANDRE GETS INTO THE BUSINESS OF BEATING DOWN THE CHAMP.
HE PUTS THE BOOTS TO HOGAN REALLY BRUTALLY.
IT'S HARD TO TELL BUT IT LOOKS LIKE A LEGIT KICK.
ANDRE PICKS UP HOGAN, WHO WEIGHS 300 POUNDS.
HE HOLDS HIM THERE FOR A MOMENT.
HOGAN'S ACTING JOB HERE IS A SHINING EXAMPLE OF HIS PROWESS AS A WRESTLER...
OW!!
...AND ANDRE IS LIVING HIS ROLE AS A MERCILESS VILLAIN.
GET UP!

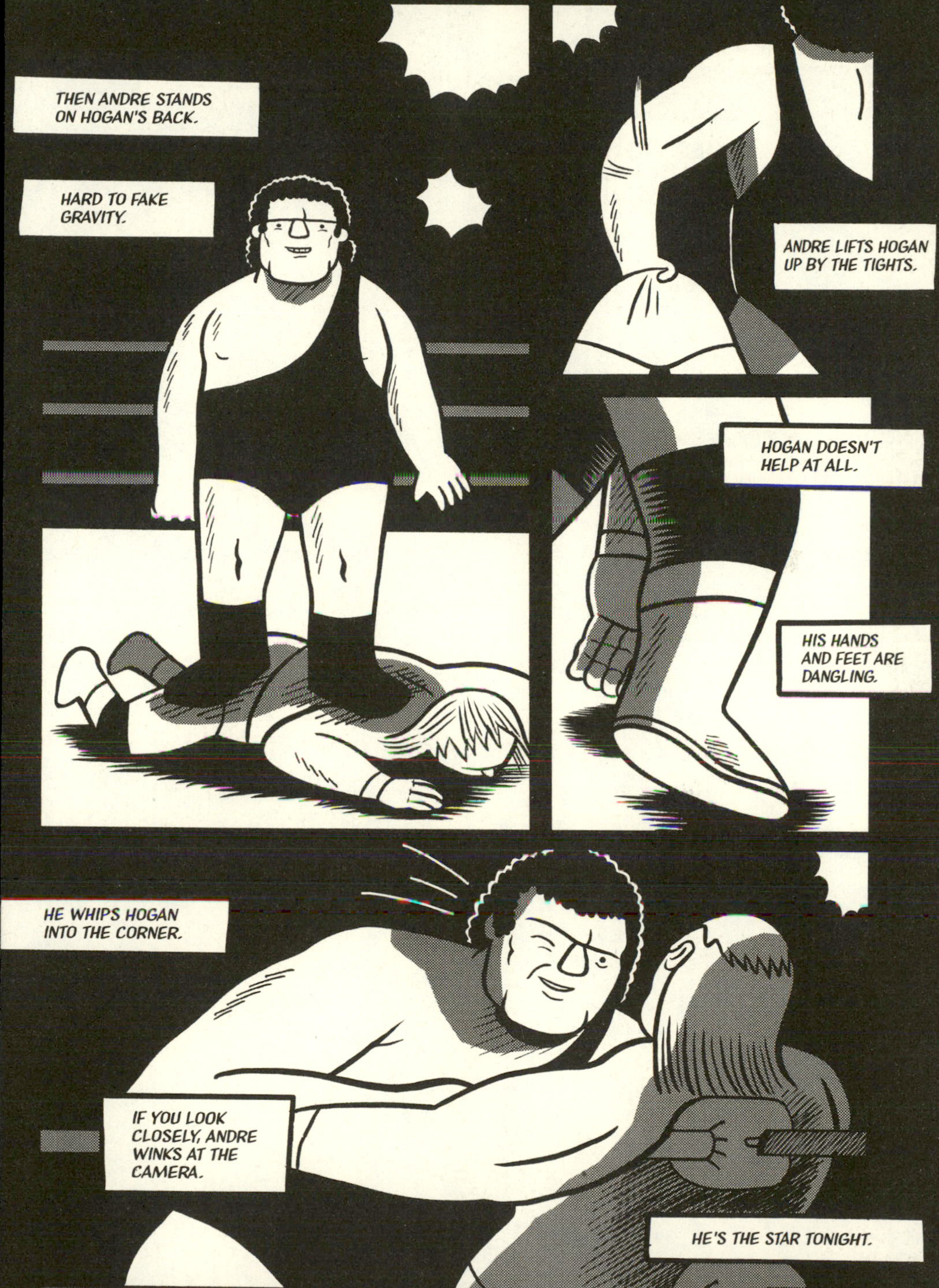
THEN ANDRE STANDS ON HOGAN'S BACK.
HARD TO FAKE GRAVITY.
ANDRE LIFTS HOGAN UP BY THE TIGHTS.
HOGAN DOESN'T HELP AT ALL.
HIS HANDS AND FEET ARE DANGLING.
HE WHIPS HOGAN INTO THE CORNER.
IF YOU LOOK CLOSELY, ANDRE WINKS AT THE CAMERA.
HE'S THE STAR TONIGHT.

ANDRE AD-LIBS HERE:

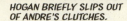
HOGAN BRIEFLY SLIPS OUT OF ANDRE'S CLUTCHES.

WHAT DO YOU THINK OF YOUR CHAMPION NOW!?

ANDRE SLAMS HIS OWN FACE INTO THE TURNBUCKLE TO MAKE HOGAN LOOK STRONG.

HE ACTS DAZED FOR A MOMENT.

HOGAN'S COMEBACK DOESN'T LAST LONG HERE.

HE RUNS FACE FIRST INTO ANDRE'S HUGE BOOT.

YOU CAN TELL ANDRE IS STARTING TO GET WINDED.

THE ANNOUNCERS CALL A BEAR HUG A "WEAR DOWN HOLD."

BUT A WRESTLER MIGHT CALL IT A REST HOLD.

THEY STAY IN THE HOLD FOR THREE OR FOUR MINUTES. THEN THE REF TESTS TO SEE IF HOGAN'S STILL CONSCIOUS.

LIFT

FALL!

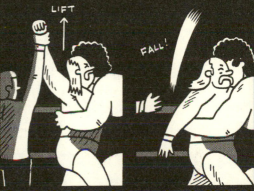

IF HIS HAND DROPS THREE TIMES HE'S CONSIDERED KNOCKED OUT AND ANDRE WILL WIN THE TITLE, BUT...

SQUEEZE

205

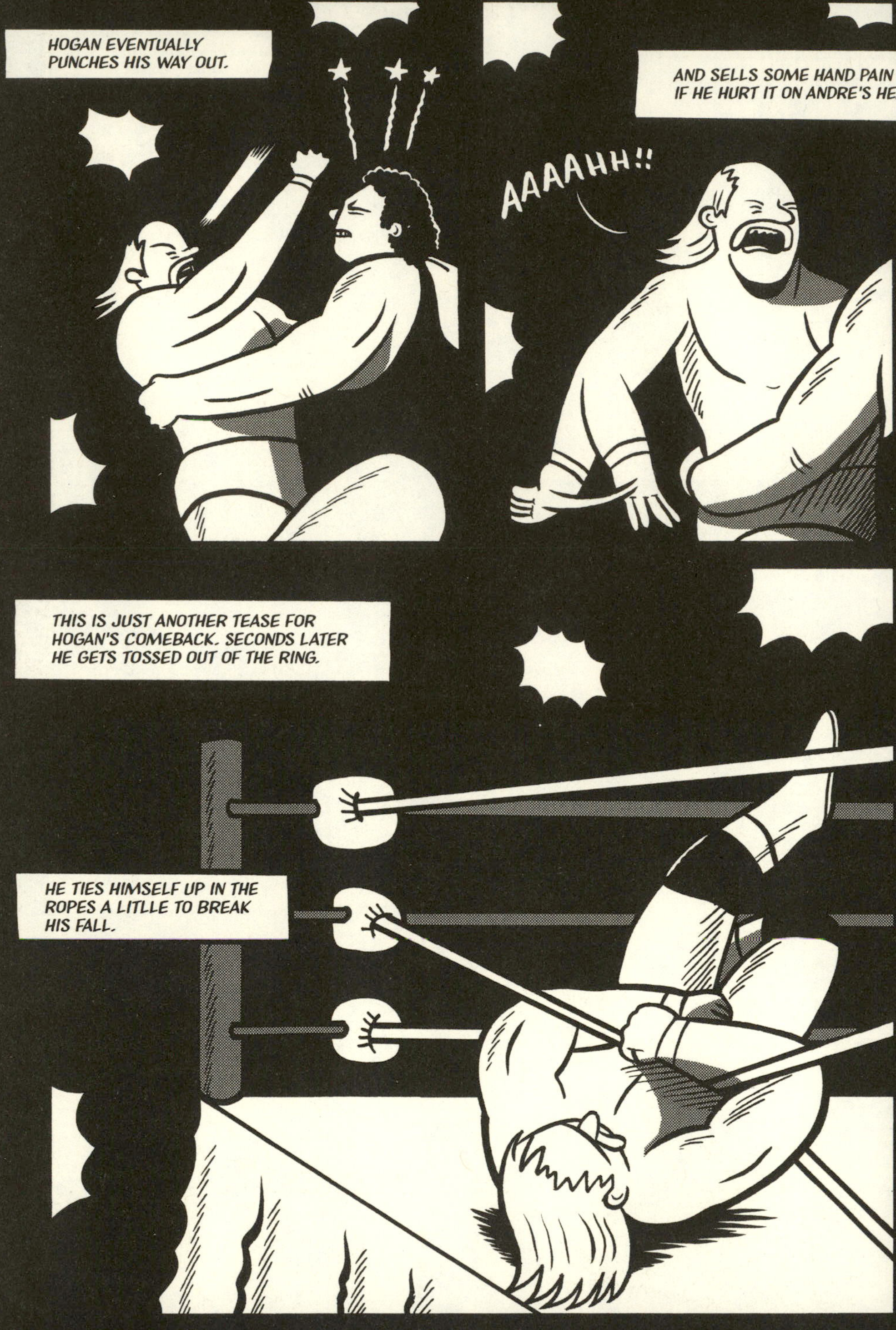
HOGAN EVENTUALLY PUNCHES HIS WAY OUT.
AND SELLS SOME HAND PAIN AS IF HE HURT IT ON ANDRE'S HEAD.
AAAAHH!!
THIS IS JUST ANOTHER TEASE FOR HOGAN'S COMEBACK. SECONDS LATER HE GETS TOSSED OUT OF THE RING.
HE TIES HIMSELF UP IN THE ROPES A LITLLE TO BREAK HIS FALL.

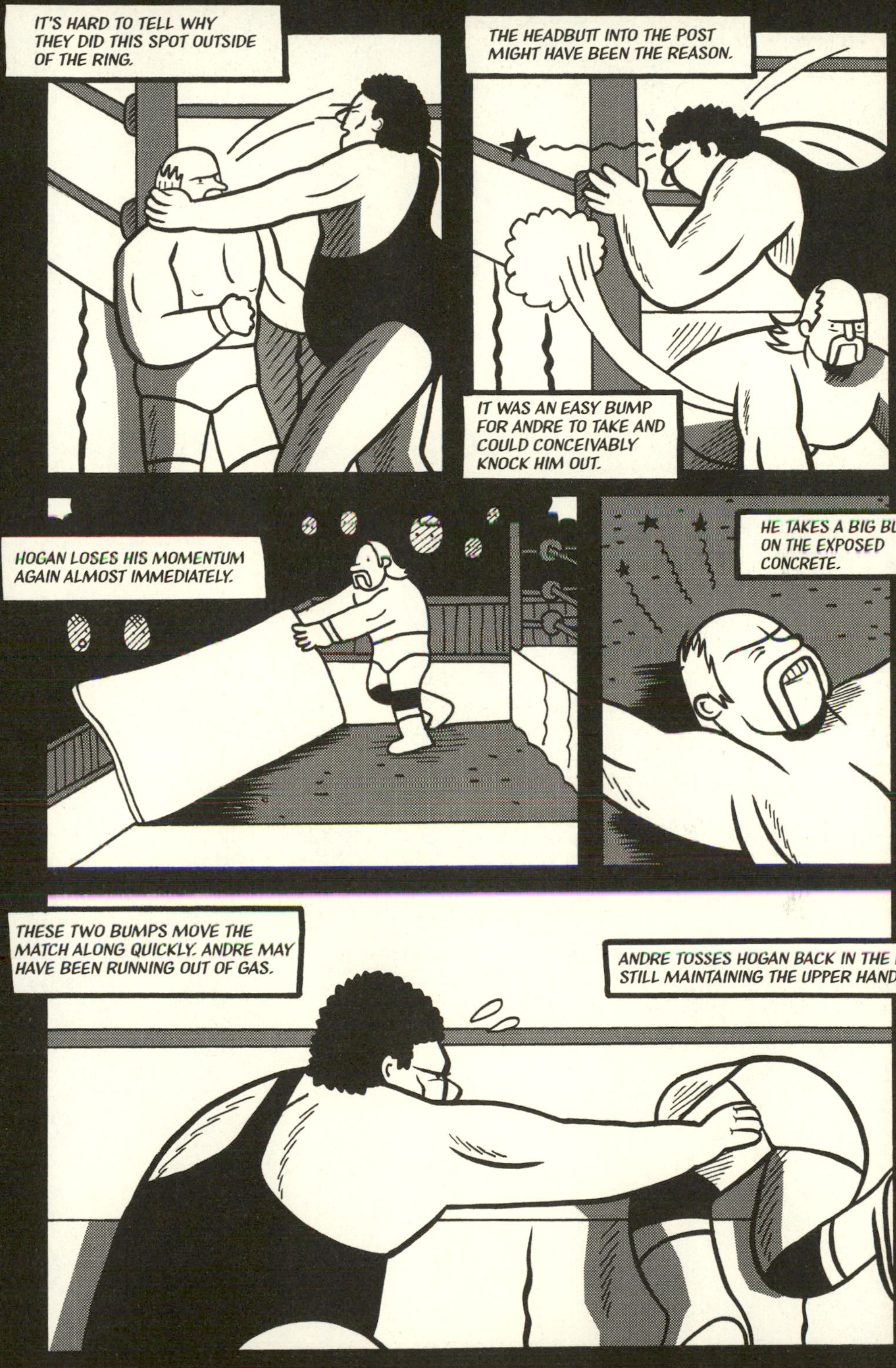
IT'S HARD TO TELL WHY THEY DID THIS SPOT OUTSIDE OF THE RING.
THE HEADBUTT INTO THE POST MIGHT HAVE BEEN THE REASON.
IT WAS AN EASY BUMP FOR ANDRE TO TAKE AND COULD CONCEIVABLY KNOCK HIM OUT.
HOGAN LOSES HIS MOMENTUM AGAIN ALMOST IMMEDIATELY.
HE TAKES A BIG BUMP ON THE EXPOSED CONCRETE.
THESE TWO BUMPS MOVE THE MATCH ALONG QUICKLY. ANDRE MAY HAVE BEEN RUNNING OUT OF GAS.
ANDRE TOSSES HOGAN BACK IN THE RING, STILL MAINTAINING THE UPPER HAND.

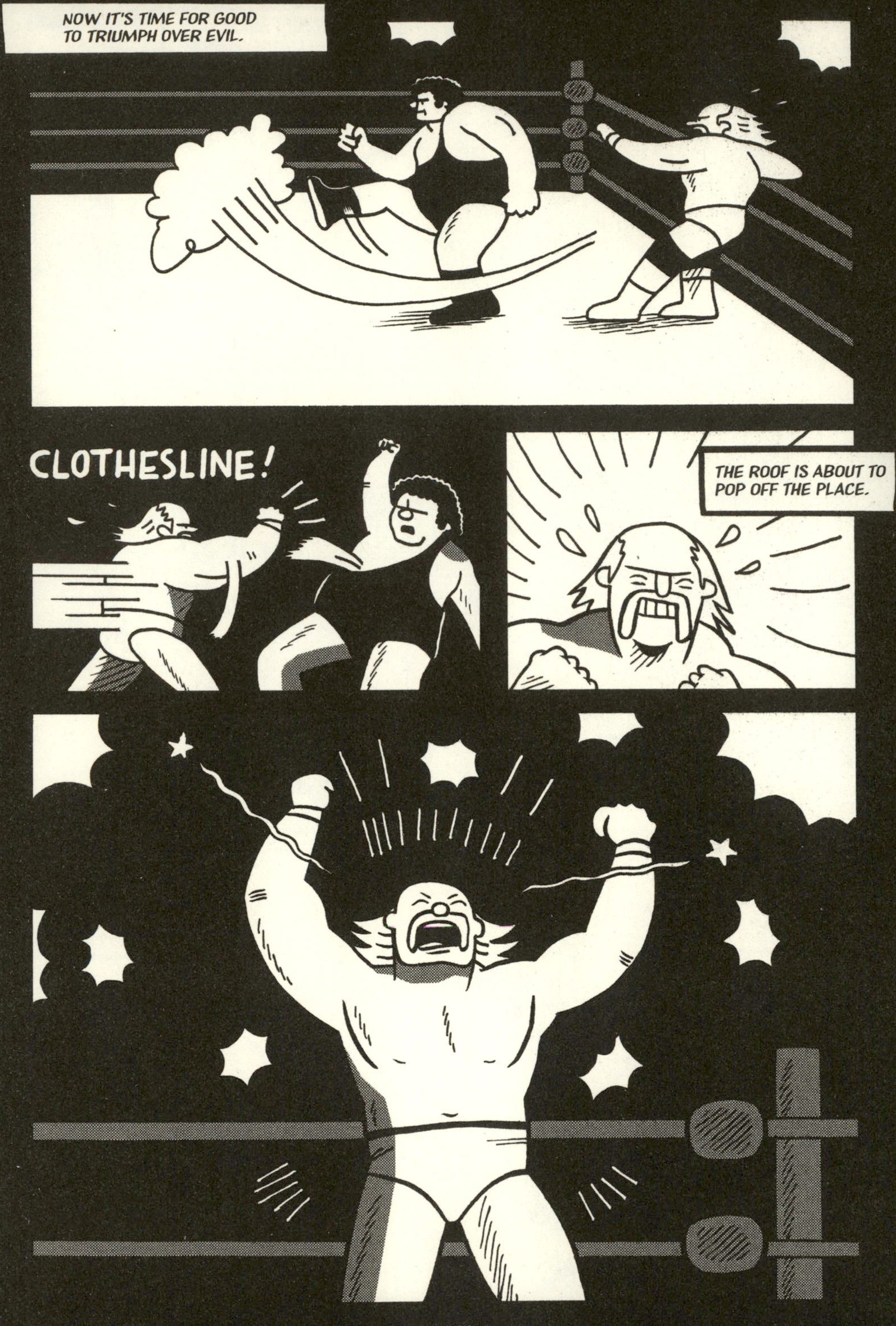
NOW IT'S TIME FOR GOOD TO TRIUMPH OVER EVIL.
CLOTHESLINE!
THE ROOF IS ABOUT TO POP OFF THE PLACE.

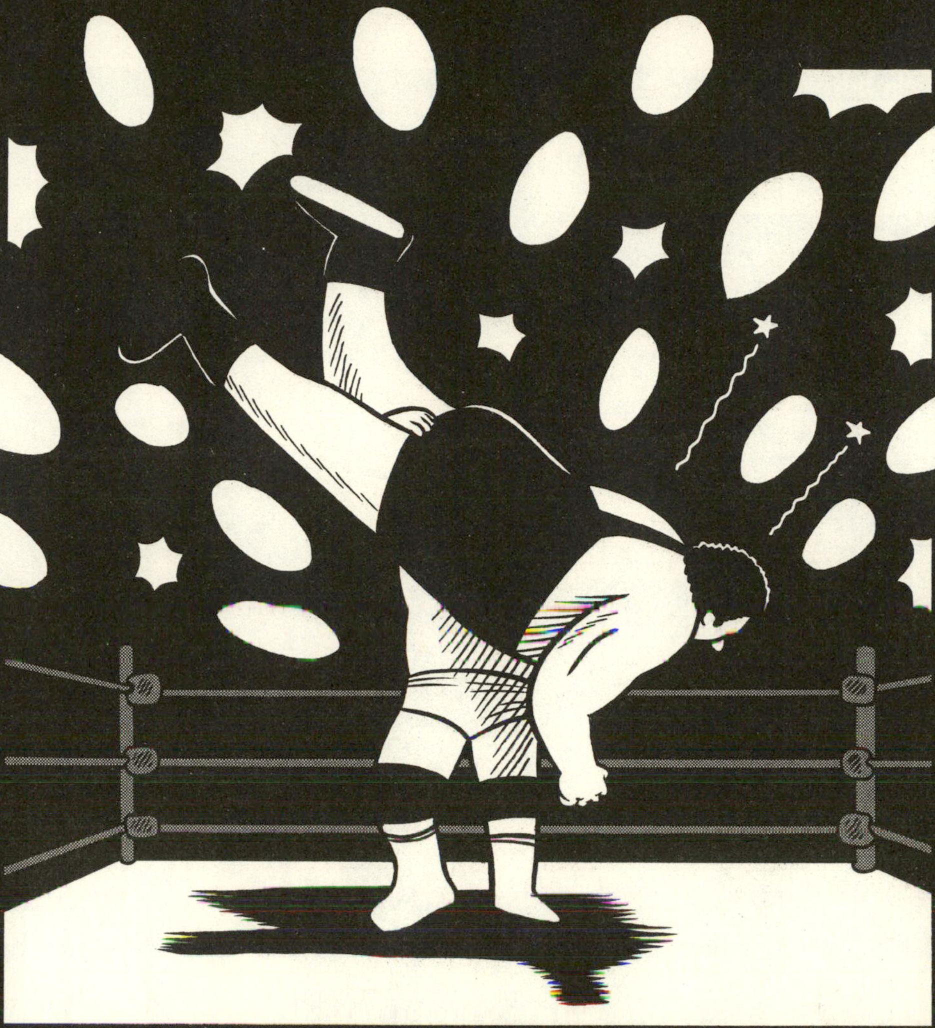

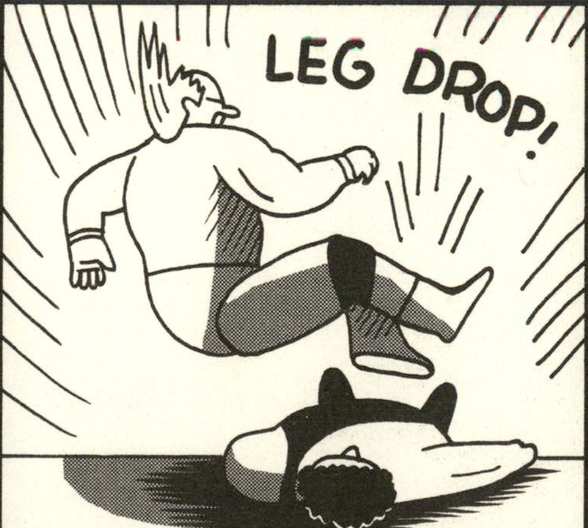
LEG DROP!

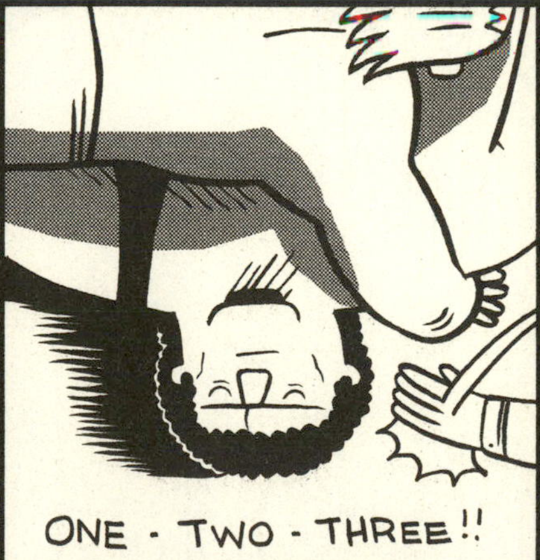
ONE - TWO - THREE!!

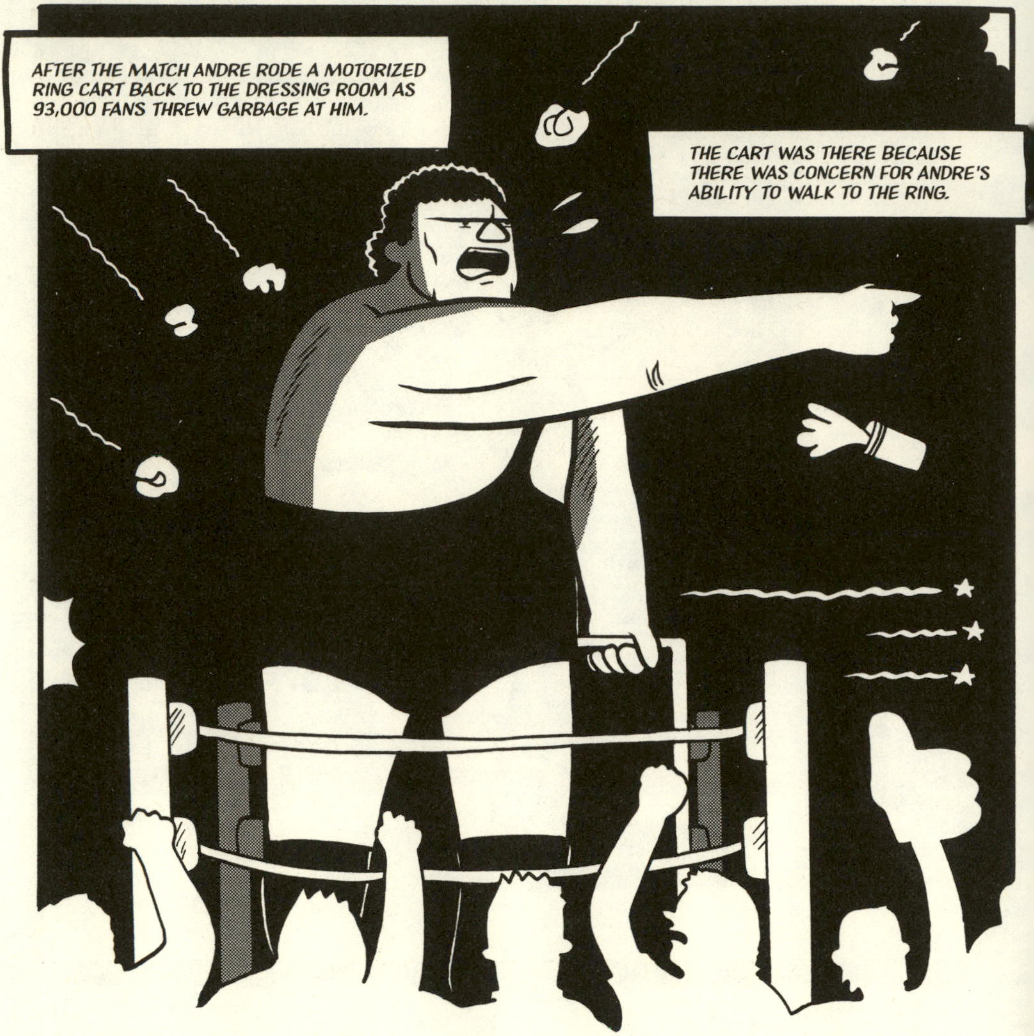
AFTER THE MATCH ANDRE RODE A MOTORIZED RING CART BACK TO THE DRESSING ROOM AS 93,000 FANS THREW GARBAGE AT HIM.
THE CART WAS THERE BECAUSE THERE WAS CONCERN FOR ANDRE'S ABILITY TO WALK TO THE RING.

STILL, THERE WAS ANDRE SCREAMING HIS HEAD OFF AS IF HE WAS ROBBED, LIKE A TRUE HEEL.

ANDRE IMMORTALIZED HULK HOGAN AND SENT THE WRESTLING BUSINESS INTO ORBIT.

THAT NIGHT, HOGAN BECAME A GOD...

...AND ANDRE MADE IT HAPPEN.

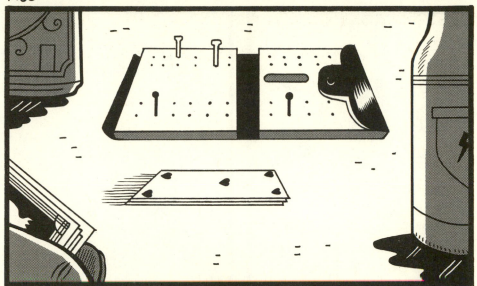

BAD NEWS BROWN ON THIS CARD?

HEY! BAD NEWS!

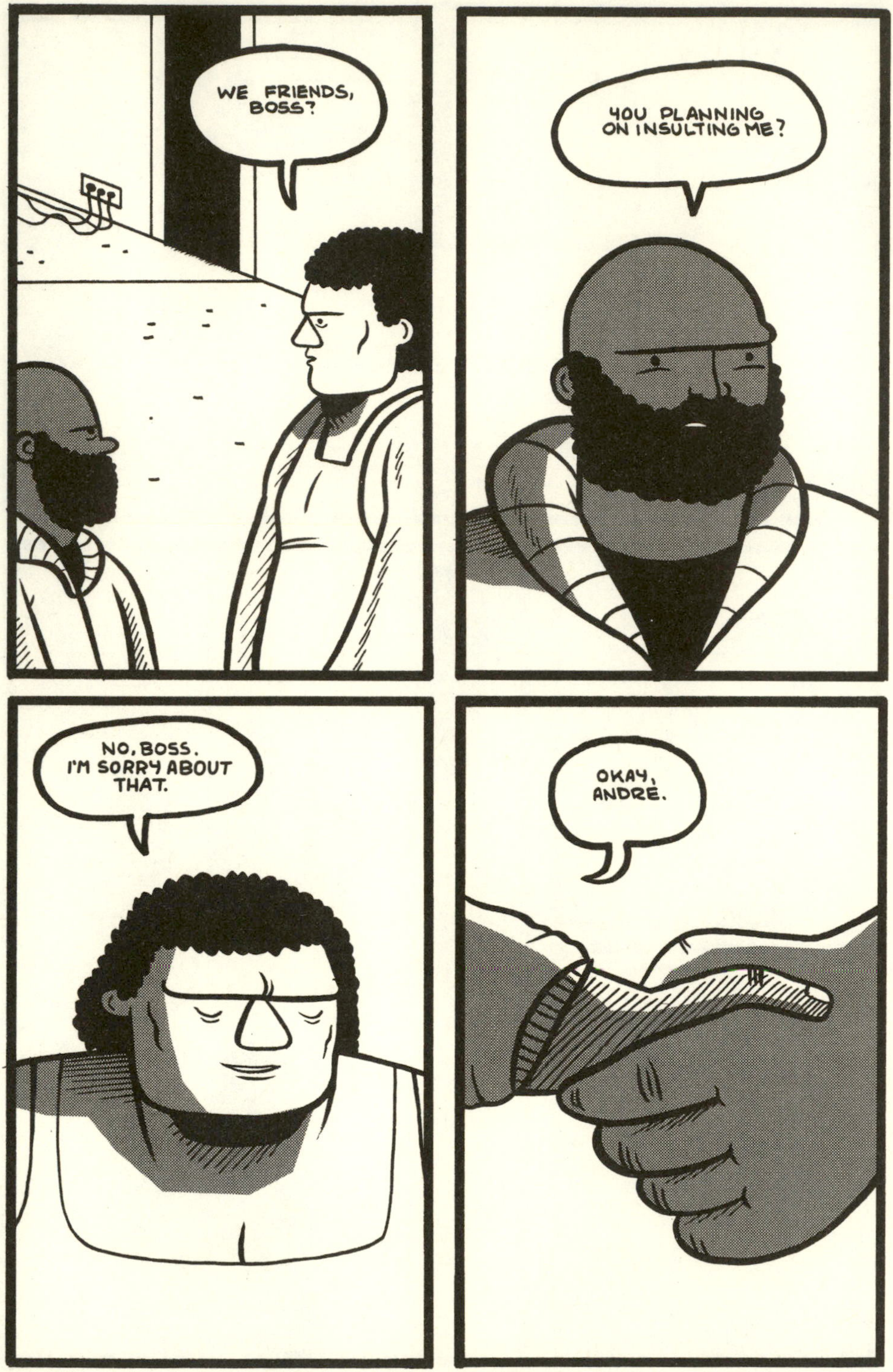
WE FRIENDS, BOSS?
YOU PLANNING ON INSULTING ME?
NO, BOSS. I'M SORRY ABOUT THAT.
OKAY, ANDRE.

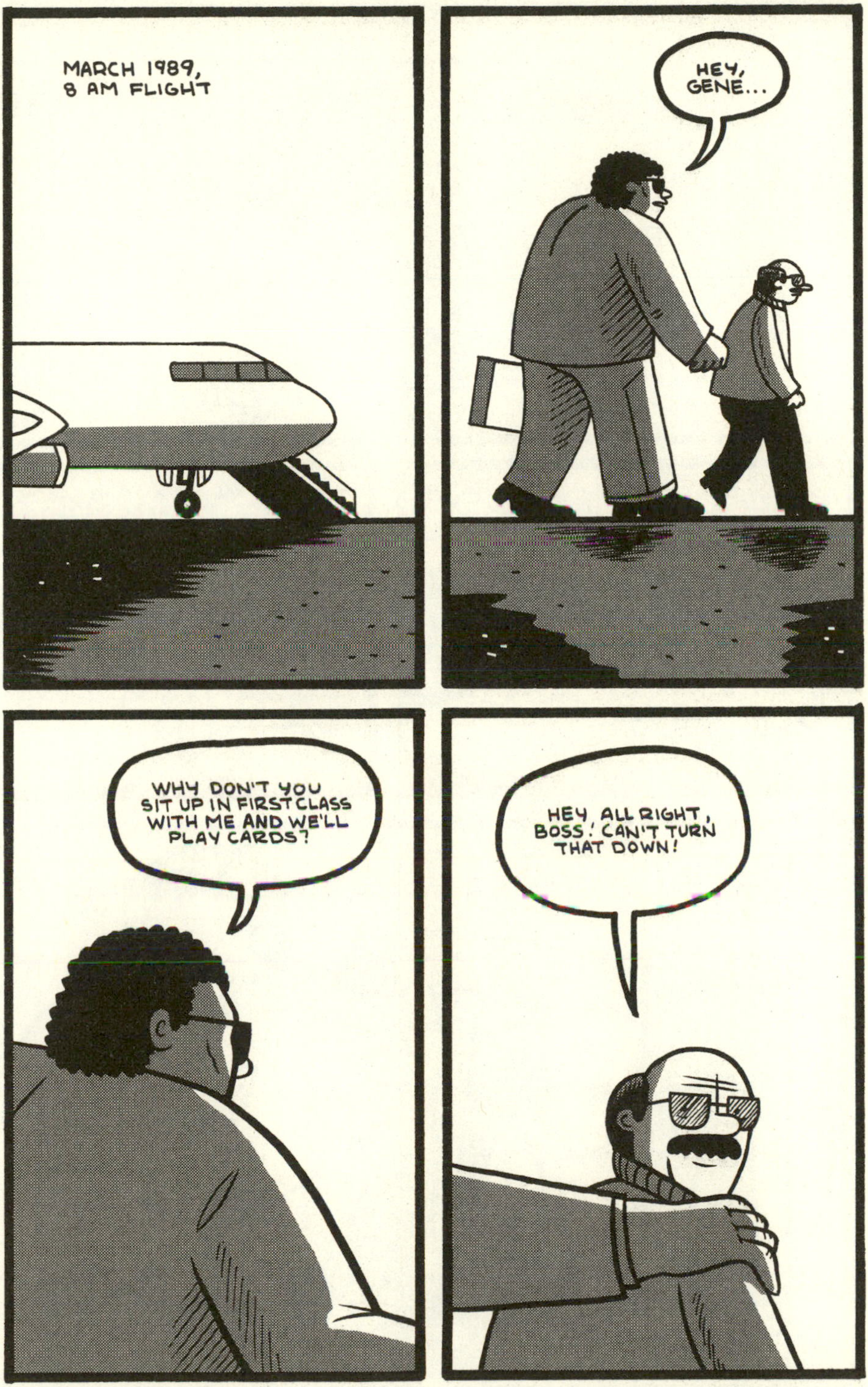
MARCH 1989, 8 AM FLIGHT
HEY, GENE...
WHY DON'T YOU SIT UP IN FIRSTCLASS WITH ME AND WE'LL PLAY CARDS?
HEY ALL RIGHT, BOSS! CAN'T TURN THAT DOWN!

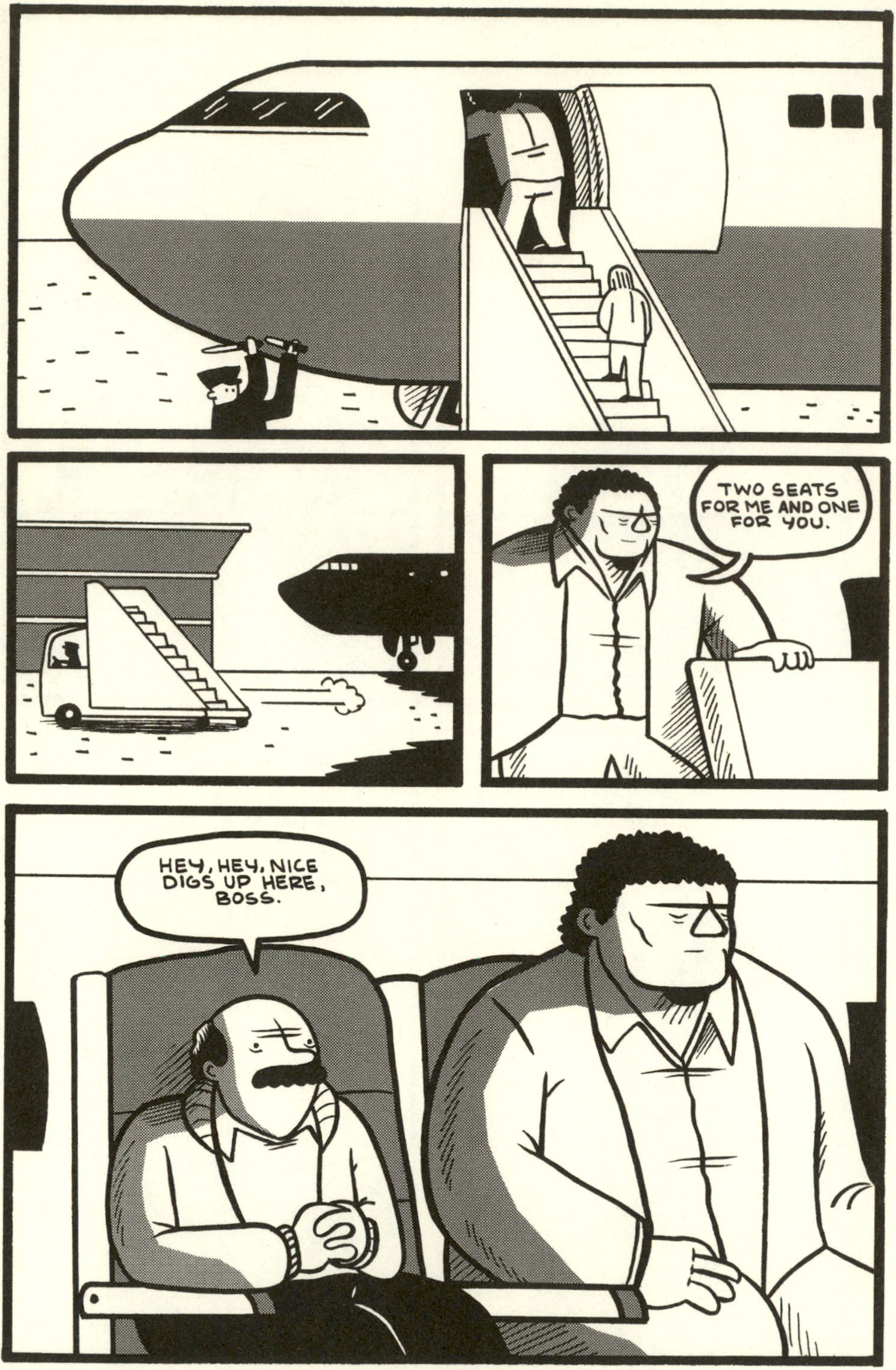
TWO SEATS FOR ME AND ONE FOR YOU.
HEY, HEY, NICE DIGS UP HERE, BOSS.

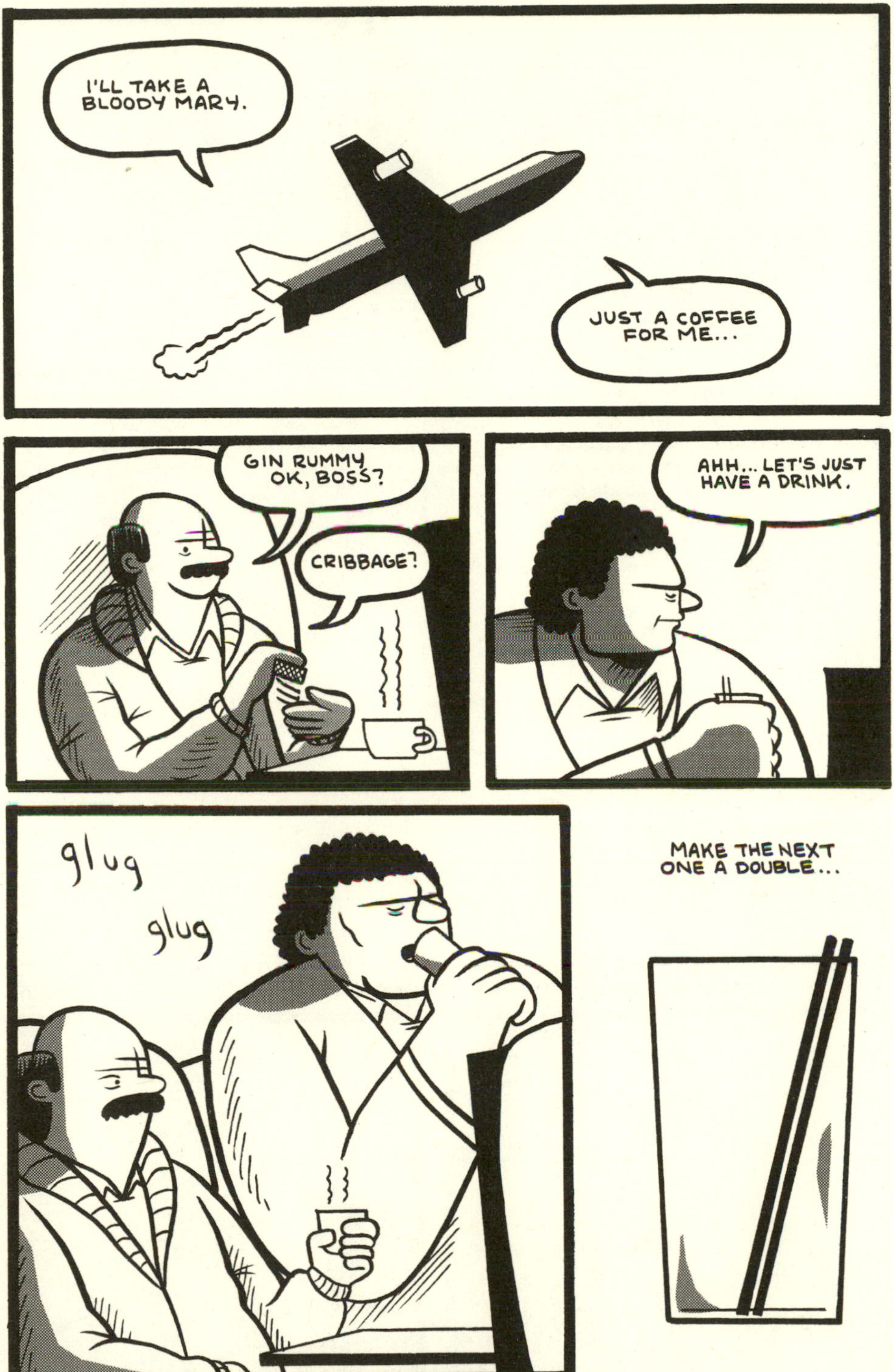
I'LL TAKE A BLOODY MARY.
JUST A COFFEE FOR ME...
GIN RUMMY OK, BOSS?
CRIBBAGE?
AHH... LET'S JUST HAVE A DRINK.
glug
glug
MAKE THE NEXT ONE A DOUBLE...

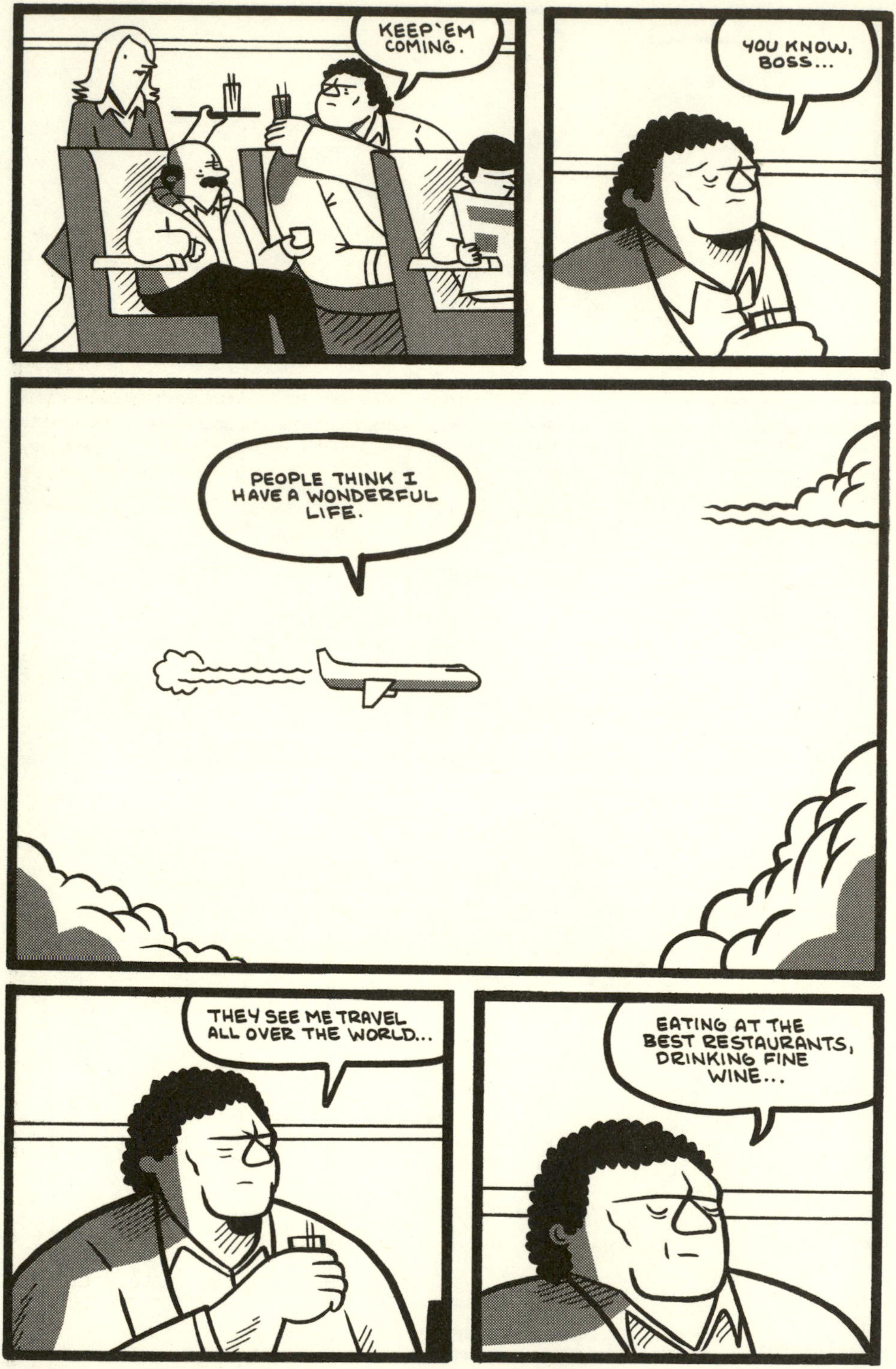
KEEP`EM COMING.
YOU KNOW, BOSS...
PEOPLE THINK I HAVE A WONDERFUL LIFE.
THEY SEE ME TRAVEL ALL OVER THE WORLD...
EATING AT THE BEST RESTAURANTS, DRINKING FINE WINE...

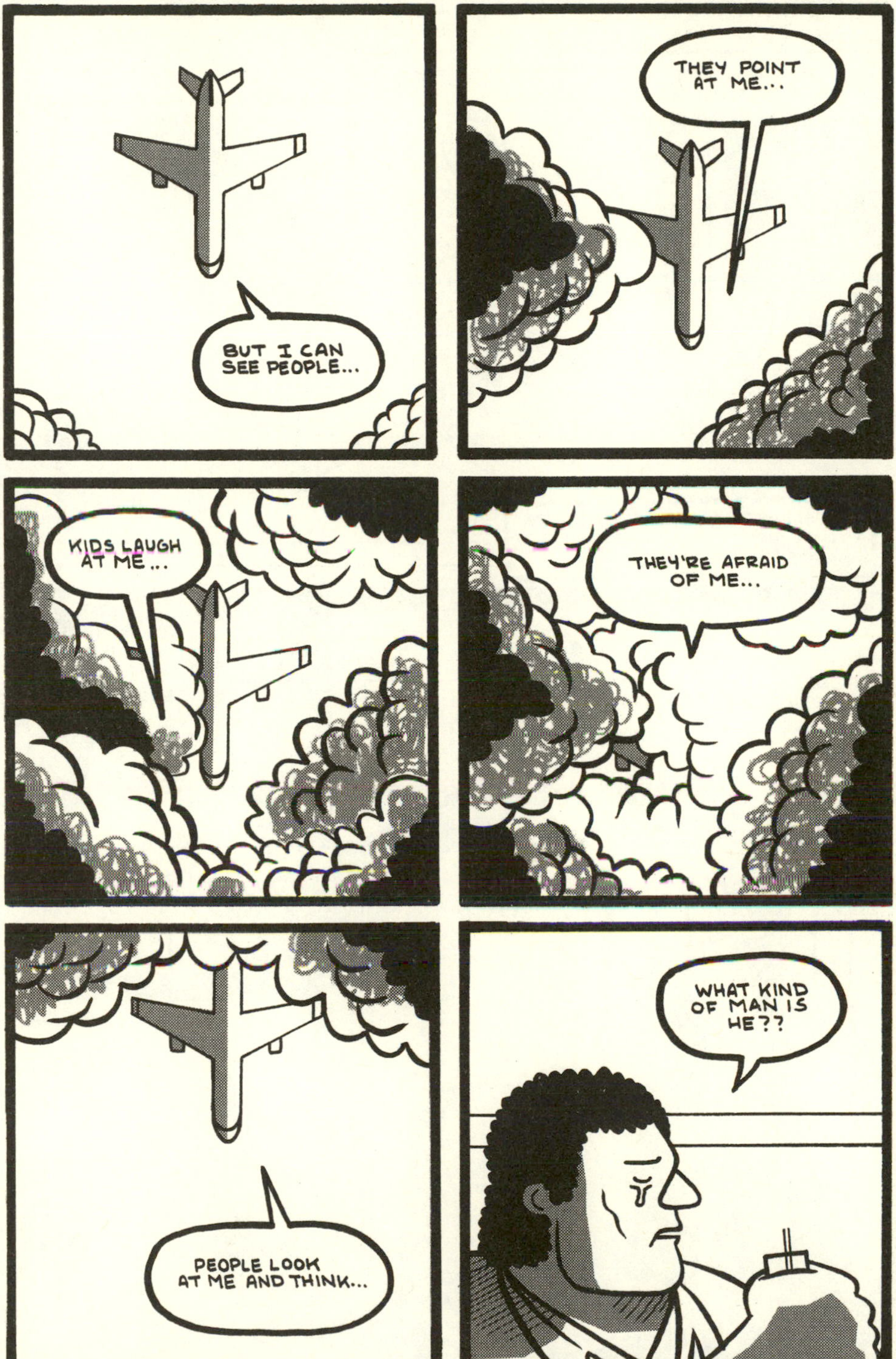
BUT I CAN SEE PEOPLE...
THEY POINT AT ME...
KIDS LAUGH AT ME...
THEY'RE AFRAID OF ME...
PEOPLE LOOK AT ME AND THINK...
WHAT KIND OF MAN IS HE??

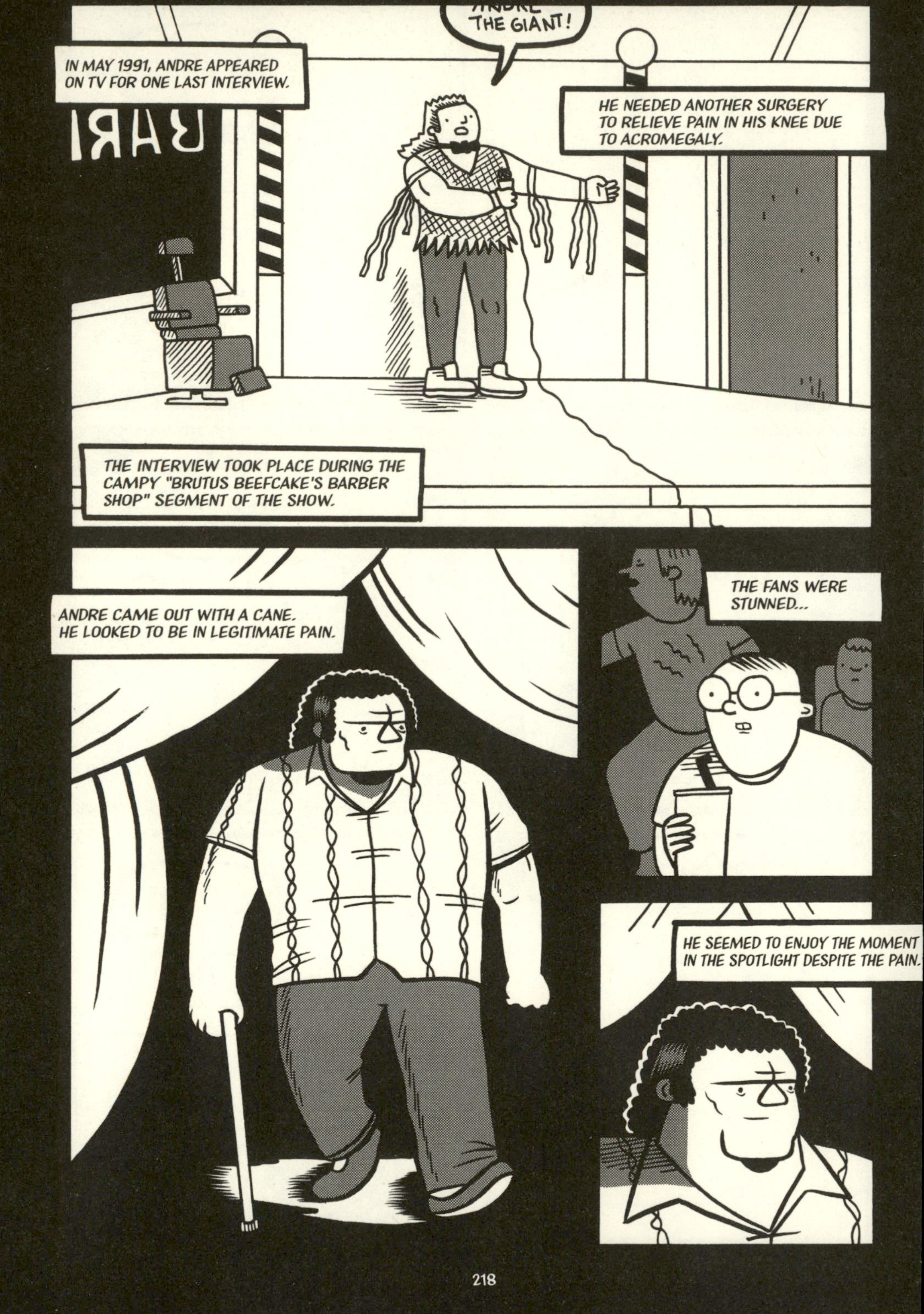
THE GIANT!
IN MAY 1991, ANDRE APPEARED ON TV FOR ONE LAST INTERVIEW.
HE NEEDED ANOTHER SURGERY TO RELIEVE PAIN IN HIS KNEE DUE TO ACROMEGALY.
THE INTERVIEW TOOK PLACE DURING THE CAMPY "BRUTUS BEEFCAKE'S BARBER SHOP" SEGMENT OF THE SHOW.
ANDRE CAME OUT WITH A CANE. HE LOOKED TO BE IN LEGITIMATE PAIN.
THE FANS WERE STUNNED...
HE SEEMED TO ENJOY THE MOMENT IN THE SPOTLIGHT DESPITE THE PAIN.

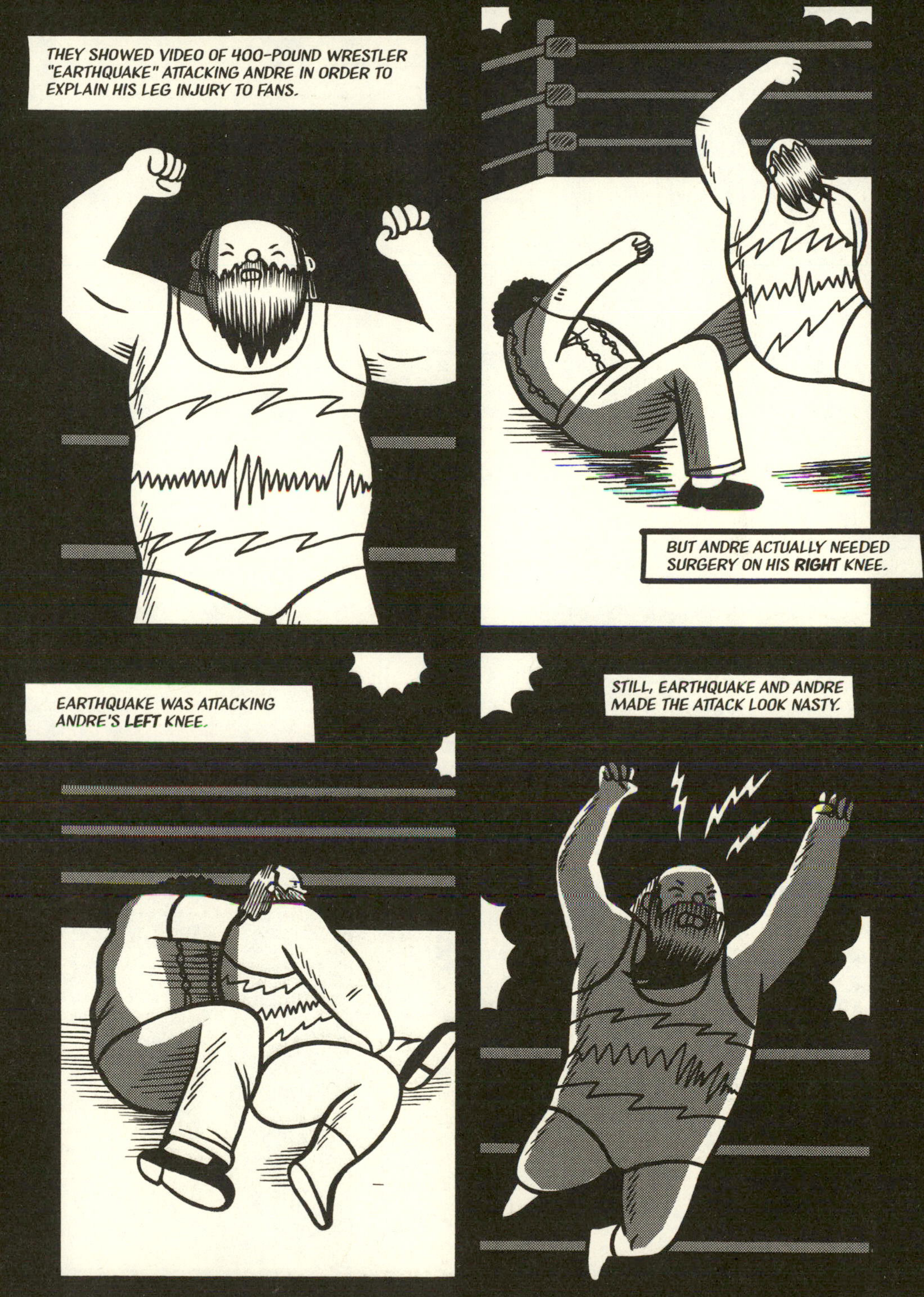
THEY SHOWED VIDEO OF 400-POUND WRESTLER "EARTHQUAKE" ATTACKING ANDRE IN ORDER TO EXPLAIN HIS LEG INJURY TO FANS.
BUT ANDRE ACTUALLY NEEDED SURGERY ON HIS **RIGHT** KNEE.
EARTHQUAKE WAS ATTACKING ANDRE'S **LEFT** KNEE.
STILL, EARTHQUAKE AND ANDRE MADE THE ATTACK LOOK NASTY.

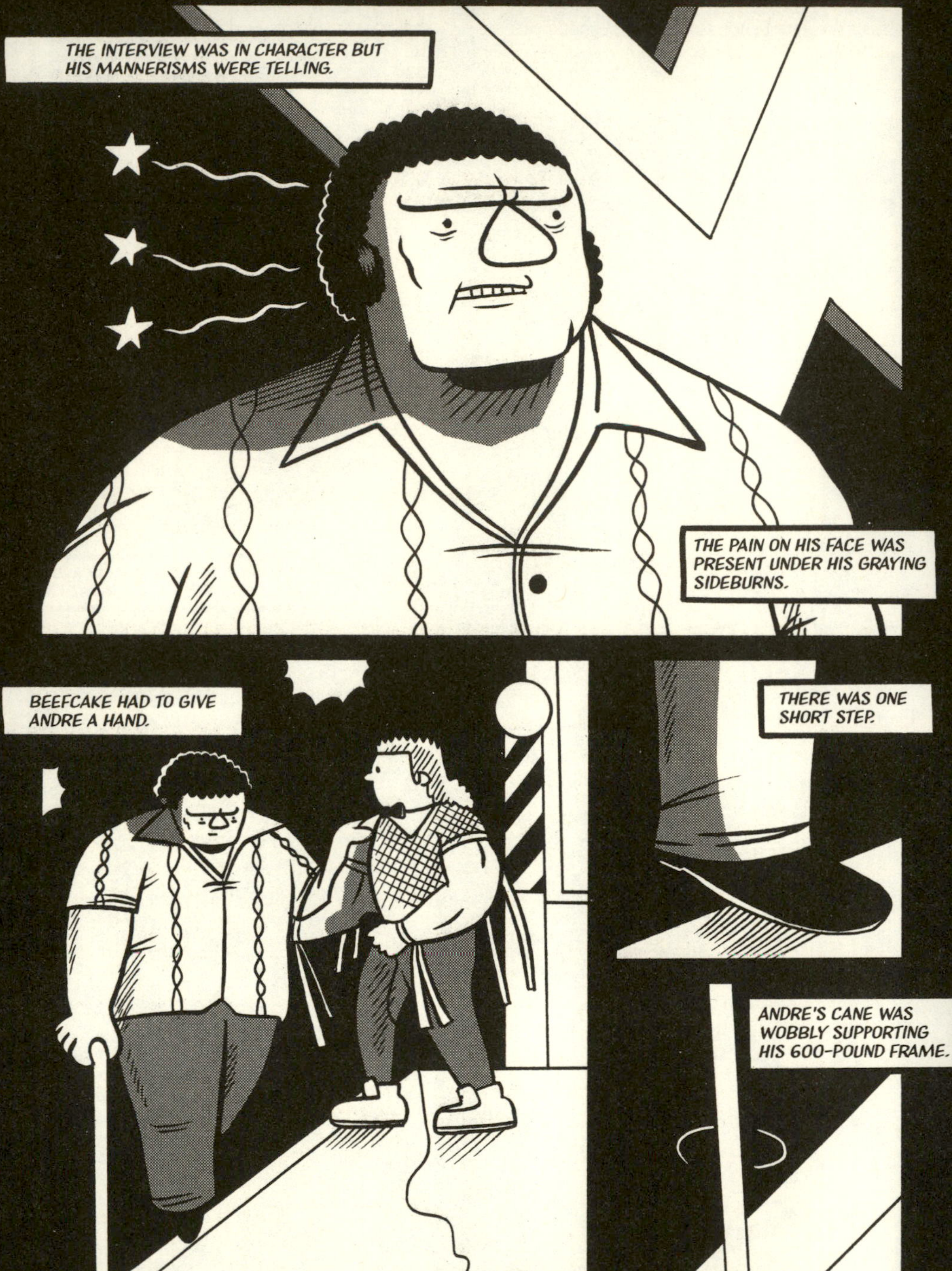

THE INTERVIEW WAS IN CHARACTER BUT HIS MANNERISMS WERE TELLING.
THE PAIN ON HIS FACE WAS PRESENT UNDER HIS GRAYING SIDEBURNS.
BEEFCAKE HAD TO GIVE ANDRE A HAND.
THERE WAS ONE SHORT STEP.
ANDRE'S CANE WAS WOBBLY SUPPORTING HIS 600-POUND FRAME.

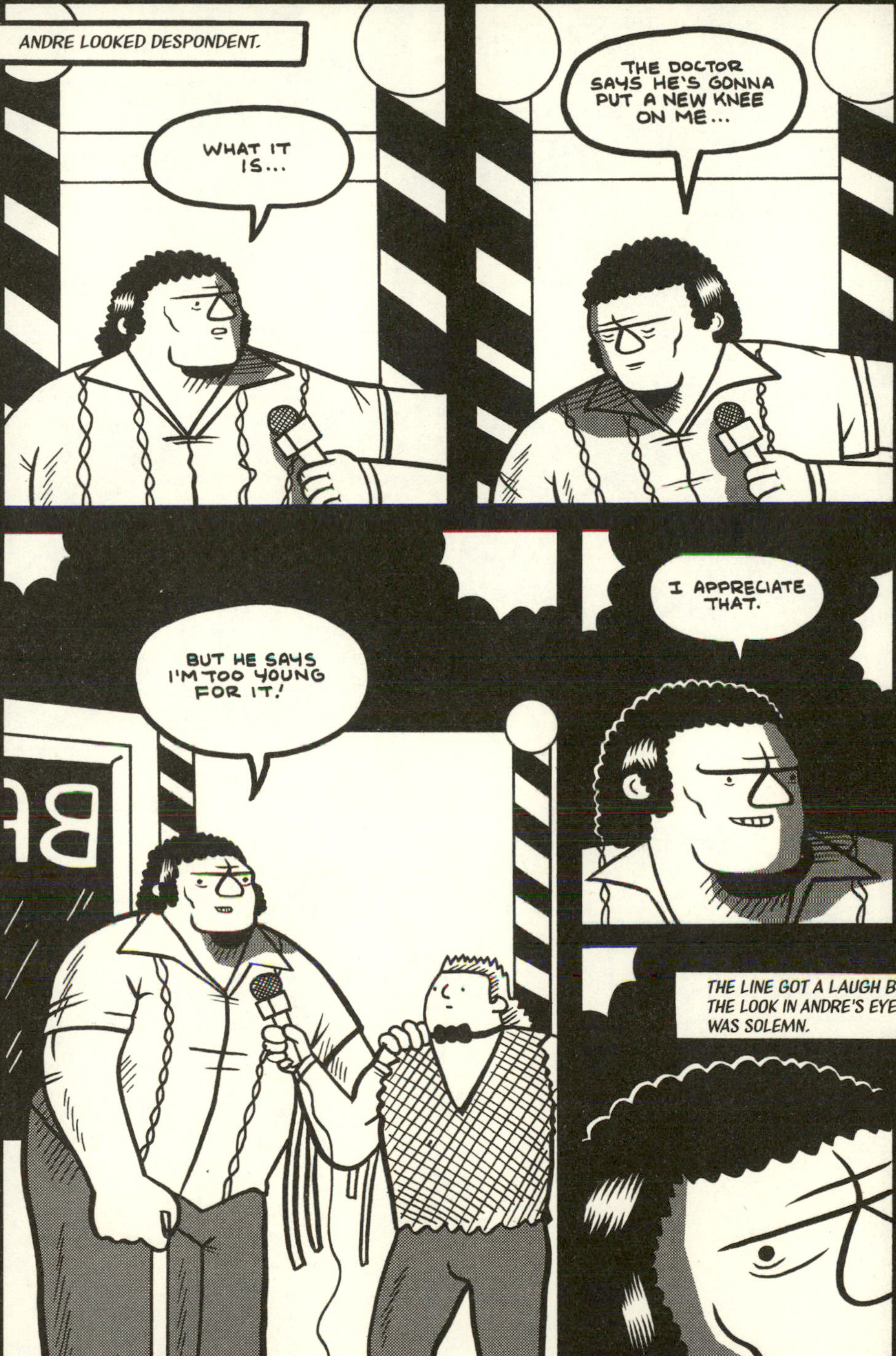
ANDRE LOOKED DESPONDENT.
WHAT IT IS...
THE DOCTOR SAYS HE'S GONNA PUT A NEW KNEE ON ME...
BUT HE SAYS I'M TOO YOUNG FOR IT!
I APPRECIATE THAT.
THE LINE GOT A LAUGH BUT THE LOOK IN ANDRE'S EYES WAS SOLEMN.

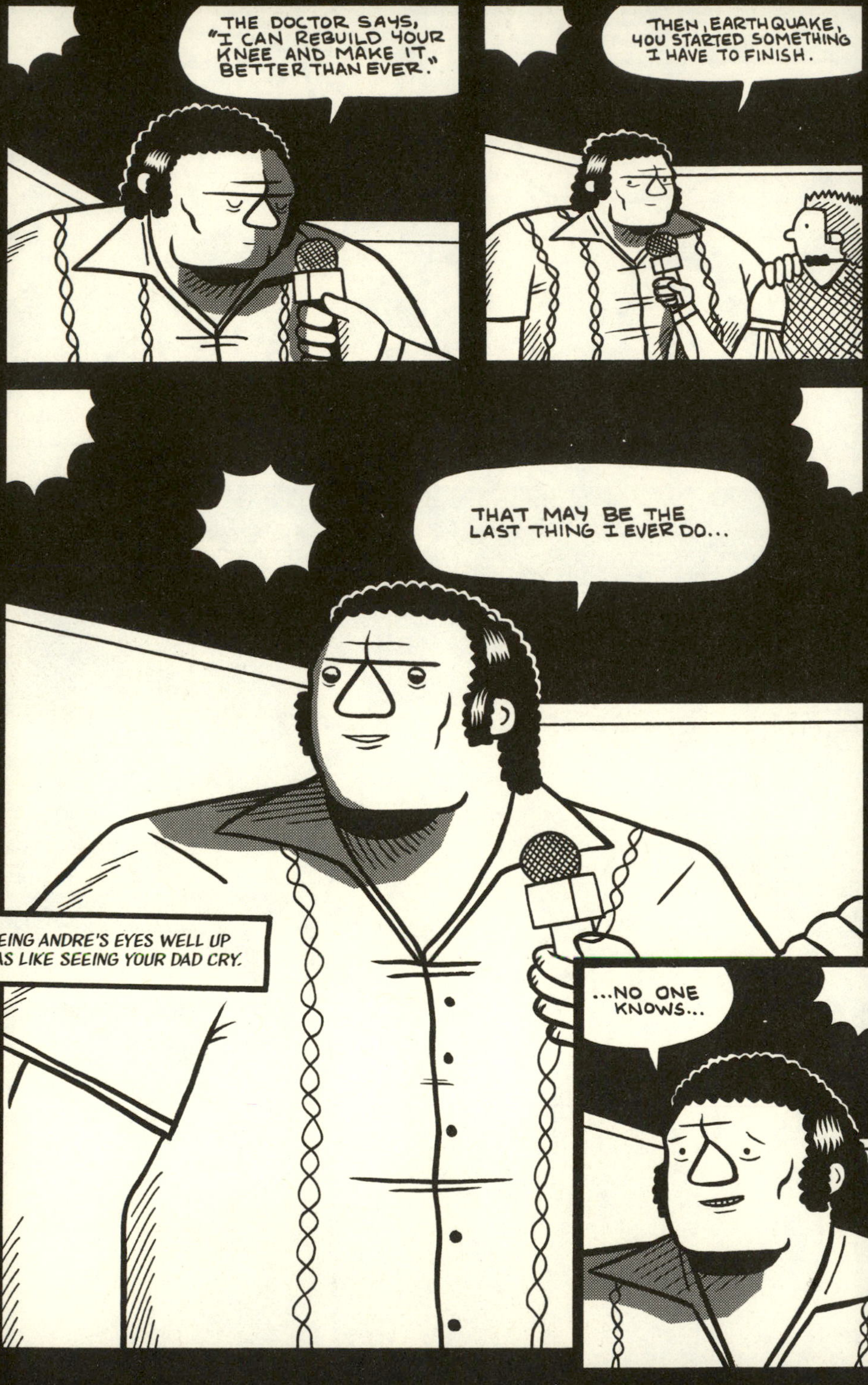
THE DOCTOR SAYS, "I CAN REBUILD YOUR KNEE AND MAKE IT BETTER THAN EVER."
THEN, EARTHQUAKE, YOU STARTED SOMETHING I HAVE TO FINISH.
THAT MAY BE THE LAST THING I EVER DO...
SEEING ANDRE'S EYES WELL UP WAS LIKE SEEING YOUR DAD CRY.
...NO ONE KNOWS...

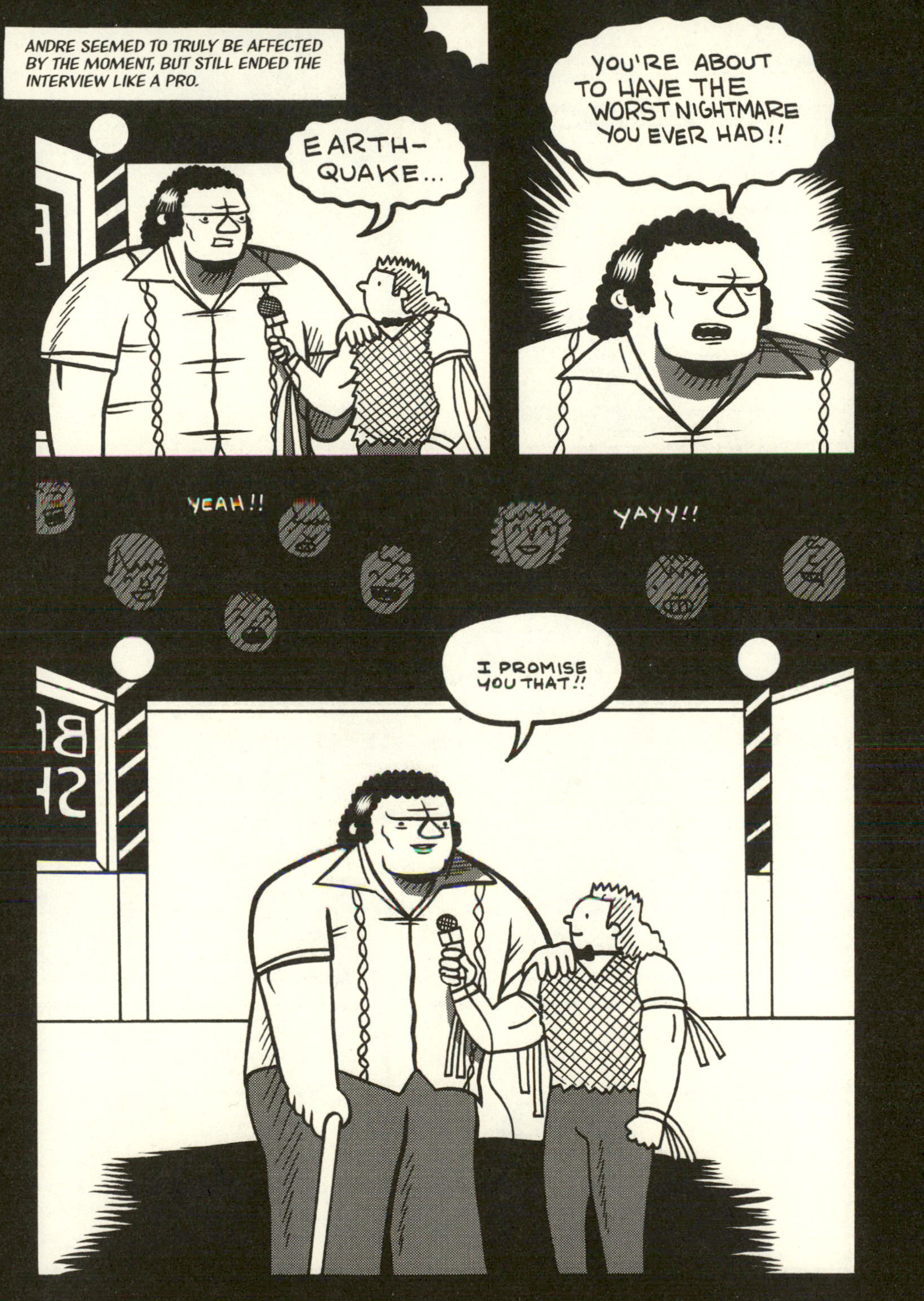
ANDRE SEEMED TO TRULY BE AFFECTED BY THE MOMENT, BUT STILL ENDED THE INTERVIEW LIKE A PRO.
EARTH-QUAKE...
YOU'RE ABOUT TO HAVE THE WORST NIGHTMARE YOU EVER HAD!!
YEAH!!
YAYY!!
I PROMISE YOU THAT!!

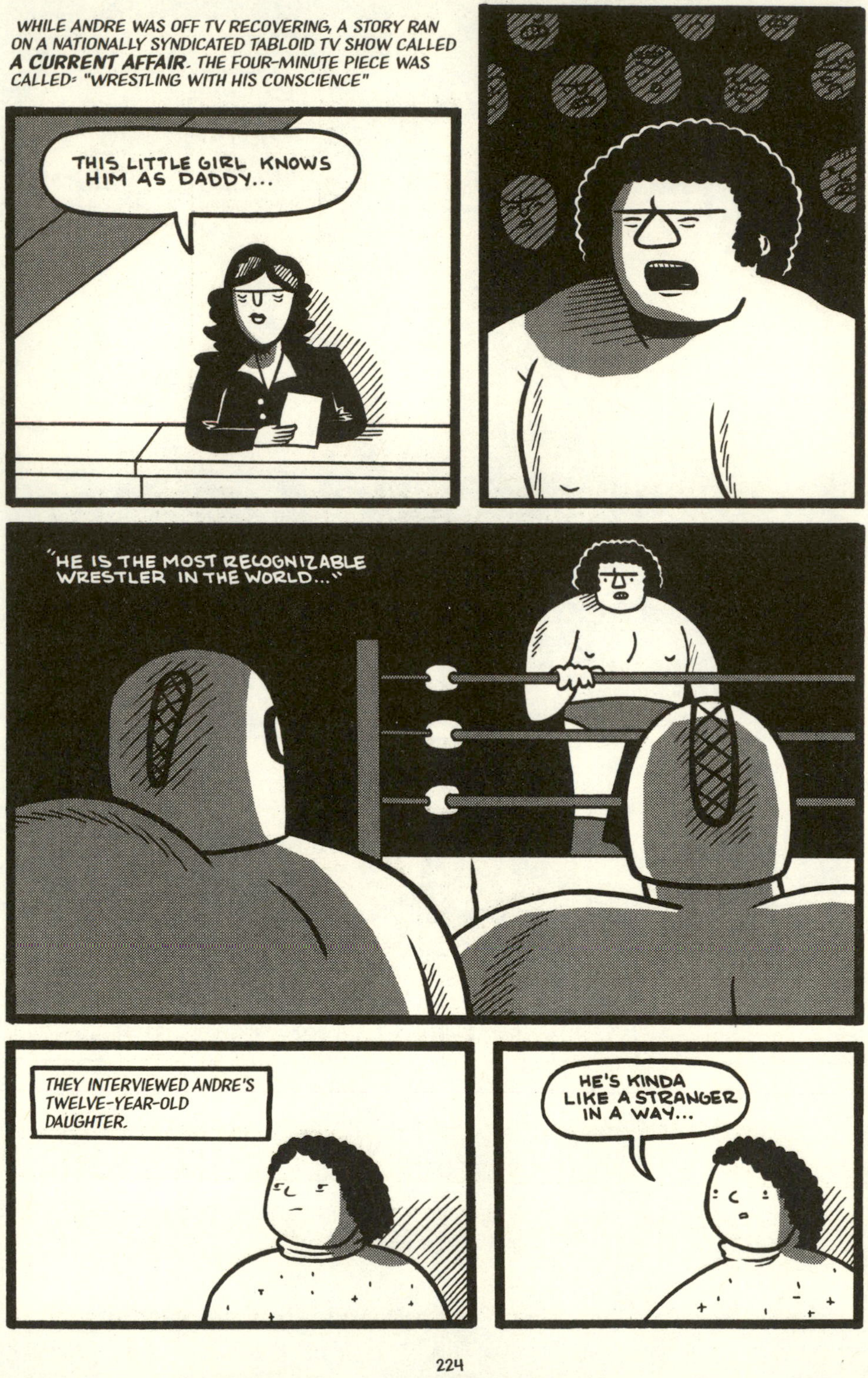
WHILE ANDRE WAS OFF TV RECOVERING, A STORY RAN ON A NATIONALLY SYNDICATED TABLOID TV SHOW CALLED **A CURRENT AFFAIR**. THE FOUR-MINUTE PIECE WAS CALLED: "WRESTLING WITH HIS CONSCIENCE"
THIS LITTLE GIRL KNOWS HIM AS DADDY...
"HE IS THE MOST RECOGNIZABLE WRESTLER IN THE WORLD..."
THEY INTERVIEWED ANDRE'S TWELVE-YEAR-OLD DAUGHTER.
HE'S KINDA LIKE A STRANGER IN A WAY...

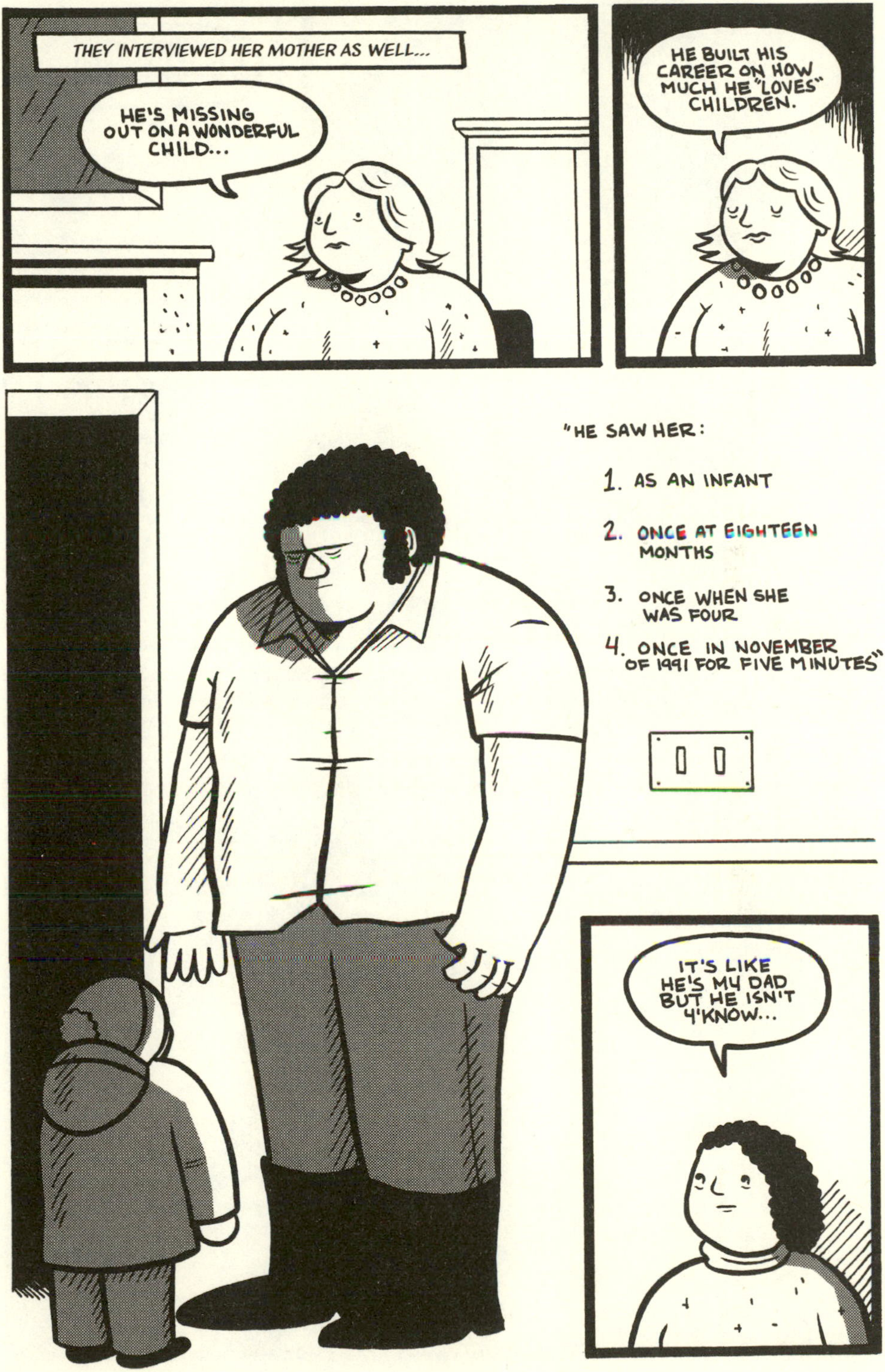
THEY INTERVIEWED HER MOTHER AS WELL...
HE'S MISSING OUT ON A WONDERFUL CHILD...
HE BUILT HIS CAREER ON HOW MUCH HE "LOVES" CHILDREN.
"HE SAW HER:
1. AS AN INFANT
2. ONCE AT EIGHTEEN MONTHS
3. ONCE WHEN SHE WAS FOUR
4. ONCE IN NOVEMBER OF 1991 FOR FIVE MINUTES"
IT'S LIKE HE'S MY DAD BUT HE ISN'T Y'KNOW...

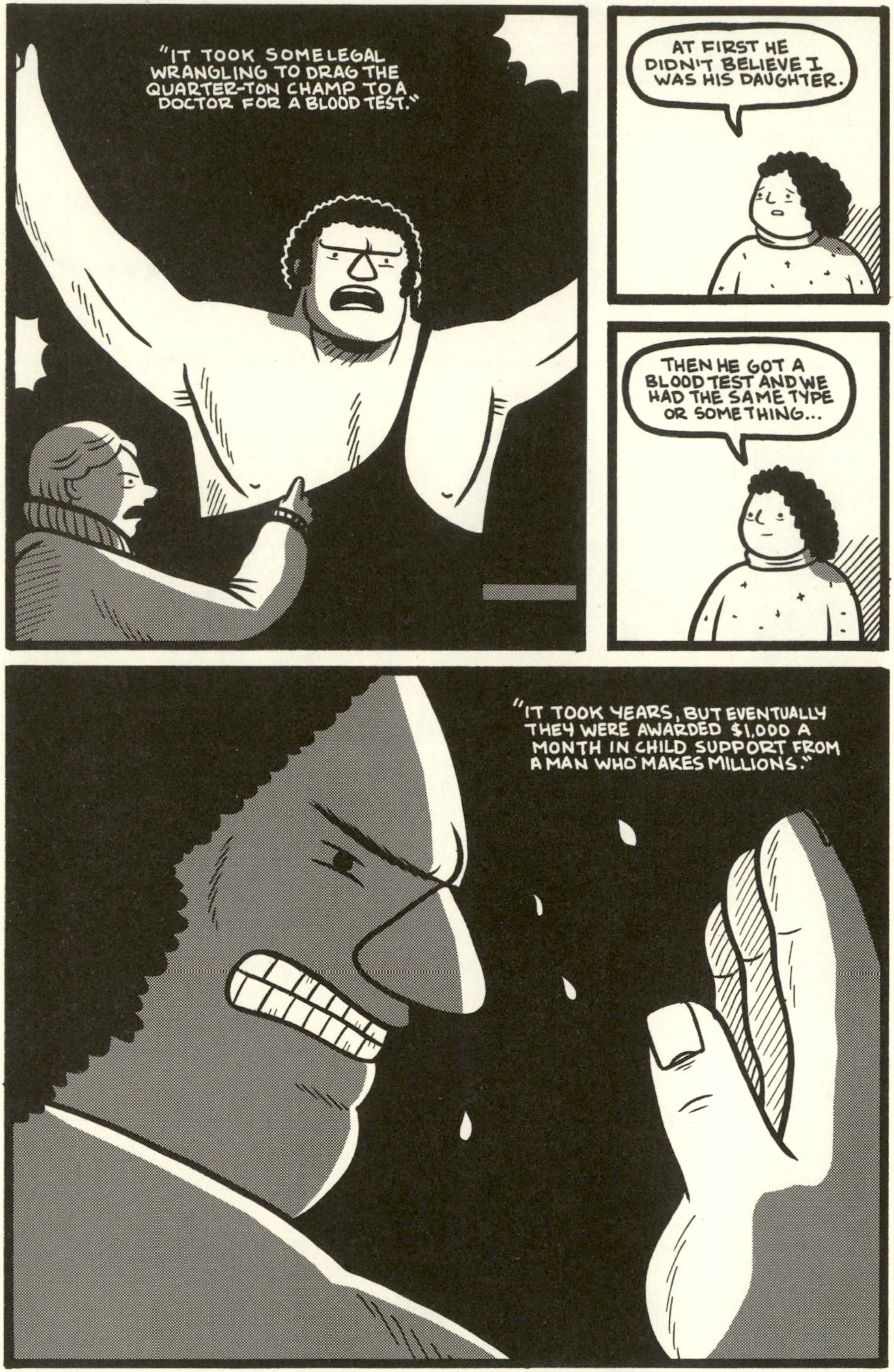
"IT TOOK SOME LEGAL WRANGLING TO DRAG THE QUARTER-TON CHAMP TO A DOCTOR FOR A BLOOD TEST."
AT FIRST HE DIDN'T BELIEVE I WAS HIS DAUGHTER.
THEN HE GOT A BLOOD TEST AND WE HAD THE SAME TYPE OR SOMETHING...
"IT TOOK YEARS, BUT EVENTUALLY THEY WERE AWARDED $1,000 A MONTH IN CHILD SUPPORT FROM A MAN WHO MAKES MILLIONS."

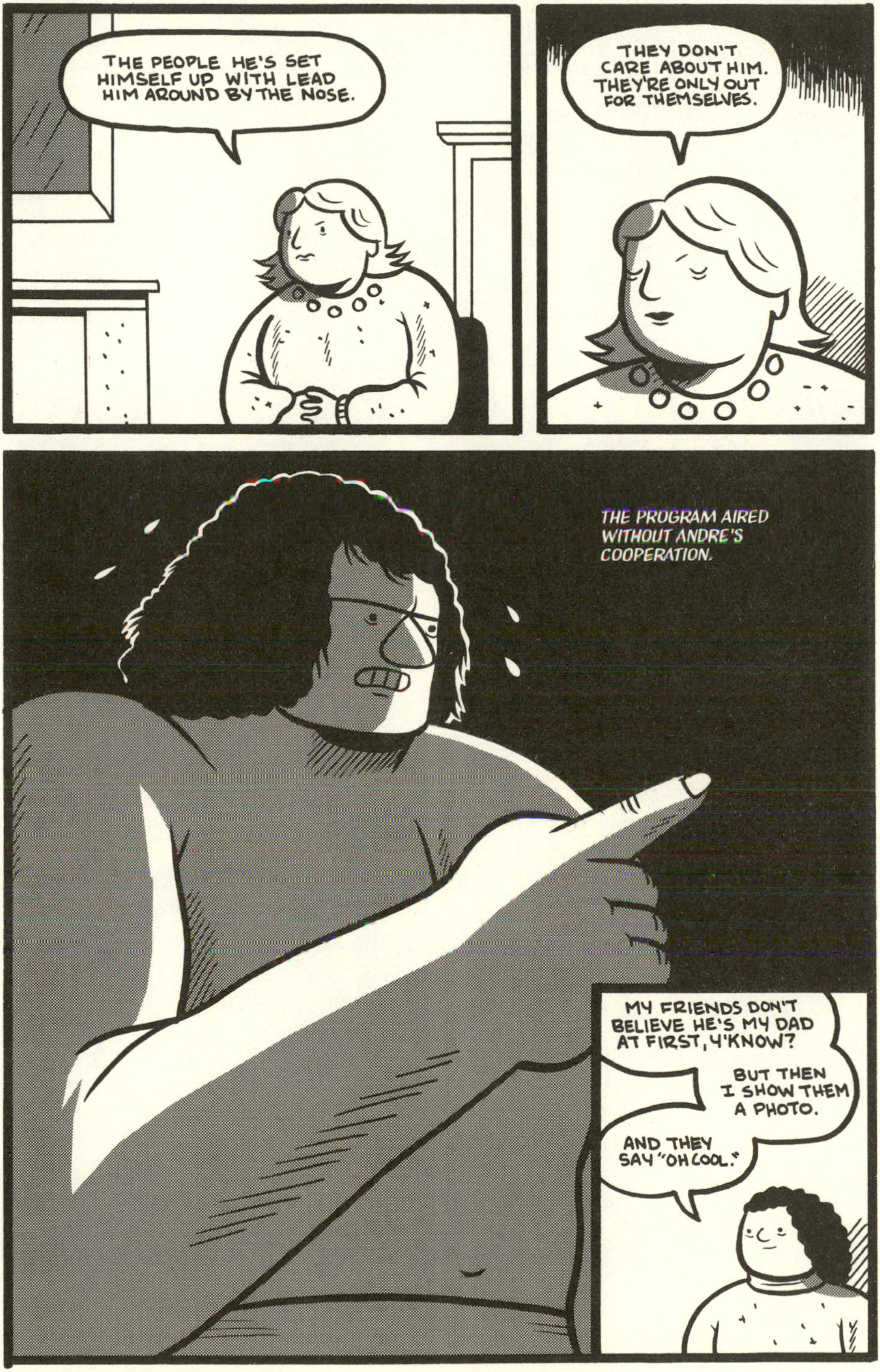

THE PEOPLE HE'S SET HIMSELF UP WITH LEAD HIM AROUND BY THE NOSE.
THEY DON'T CARE ABOUT HIM. THEY'RE ONLY OUT FOR THEMSELVES.
THE PROGRAM AIRED WITHOUT ANDRE'S COOPERATION.
MY FRIENDS DON'T BELIEVE HE'S MY DAD AT FIRST, Y'KNOW?
BUT THEN I SHOW THEM A PHOTO.
AND THEY SAY "OH COOL."

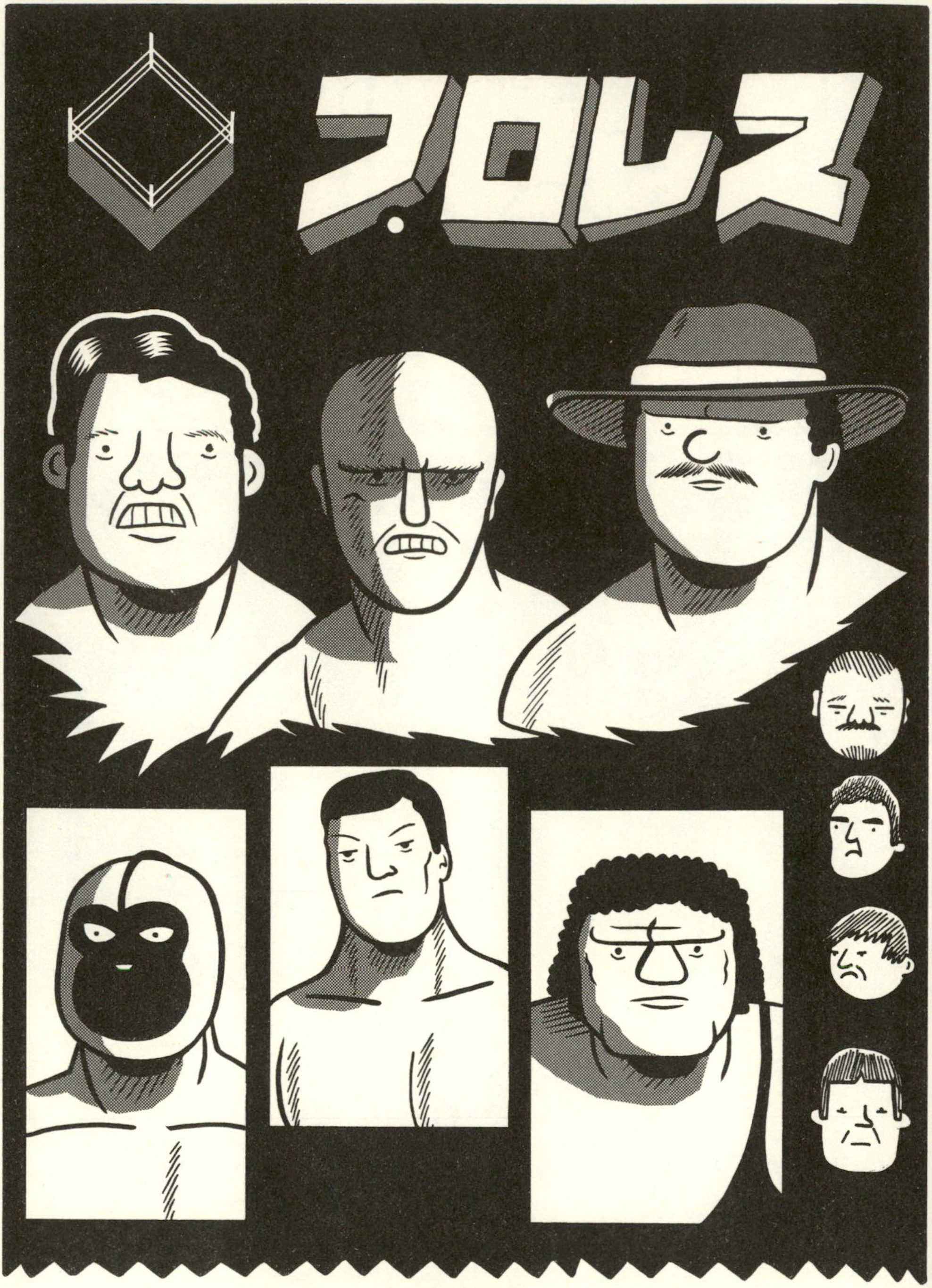
プロレス

ANDRE CONTINUED TO WRESTLE A REGULAR SCHEDULE IN JAPAN FROM LATE 1991 UNTIL LATE 1992.

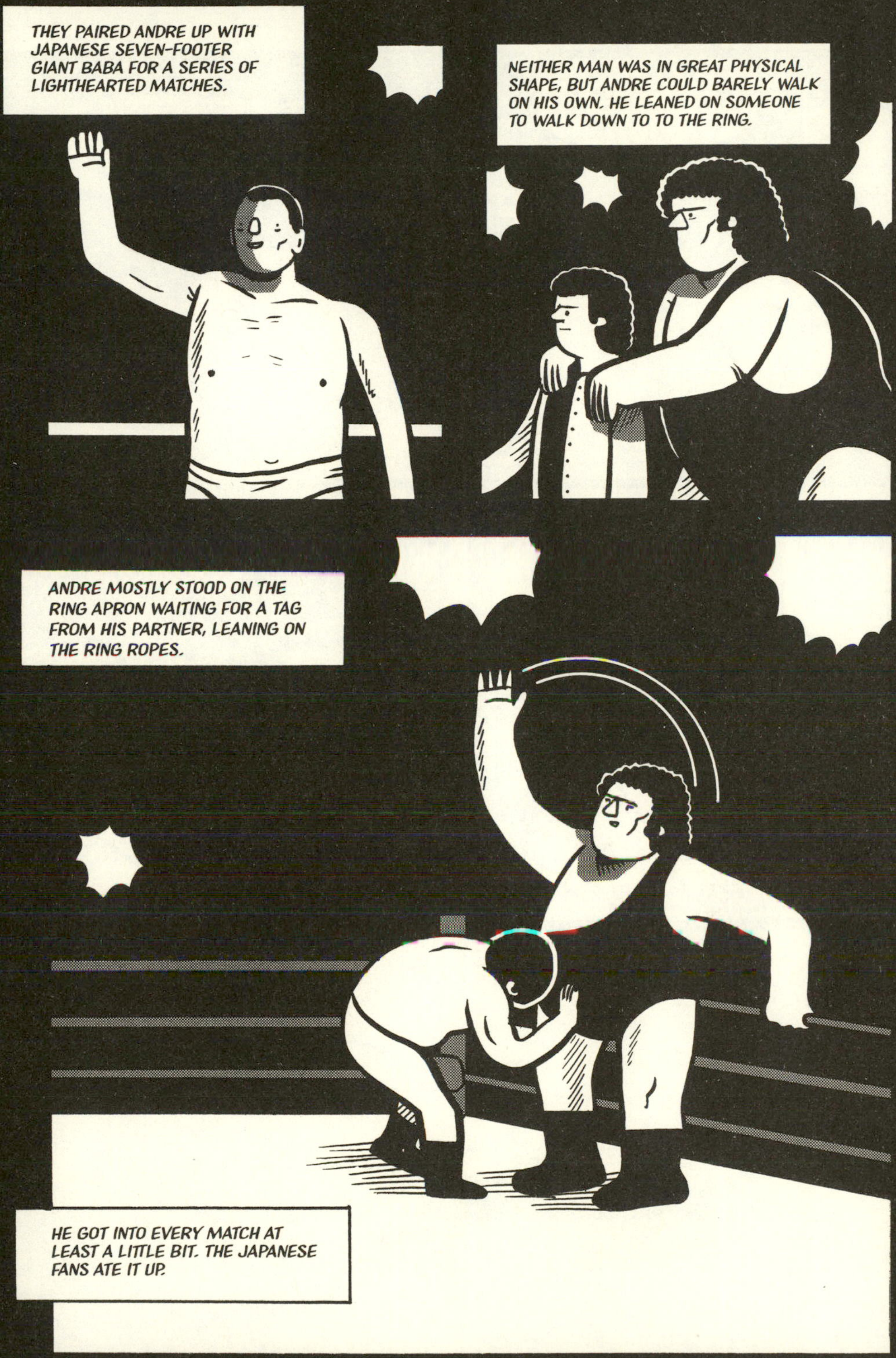
THEY PAIRED ANDRE UP WITH JAPANESE SEVEN-FOOTER GIANT BABA FOR A SERIES OF LIGHTHEARTED MATCHES.
NEITHER MAN WAS IN GREAT PHYSICAL SHAPE, BUT ANDRE COULD BARELY WALK ON HIS OWN. HE LEANED ON SOMEONE TO WALK DOWN TO TO THE RING.
ANDRE MOSTLY STOOD ON THE RING APRON WAITING FOR A TAG FROM HIS PARTNER, LEANING ON THE RING ROPES.
HE GOT INTO EVERY MATCH AT LEAST A LITTLE BIT. THE JAPANESE FANS ATE IT UP.

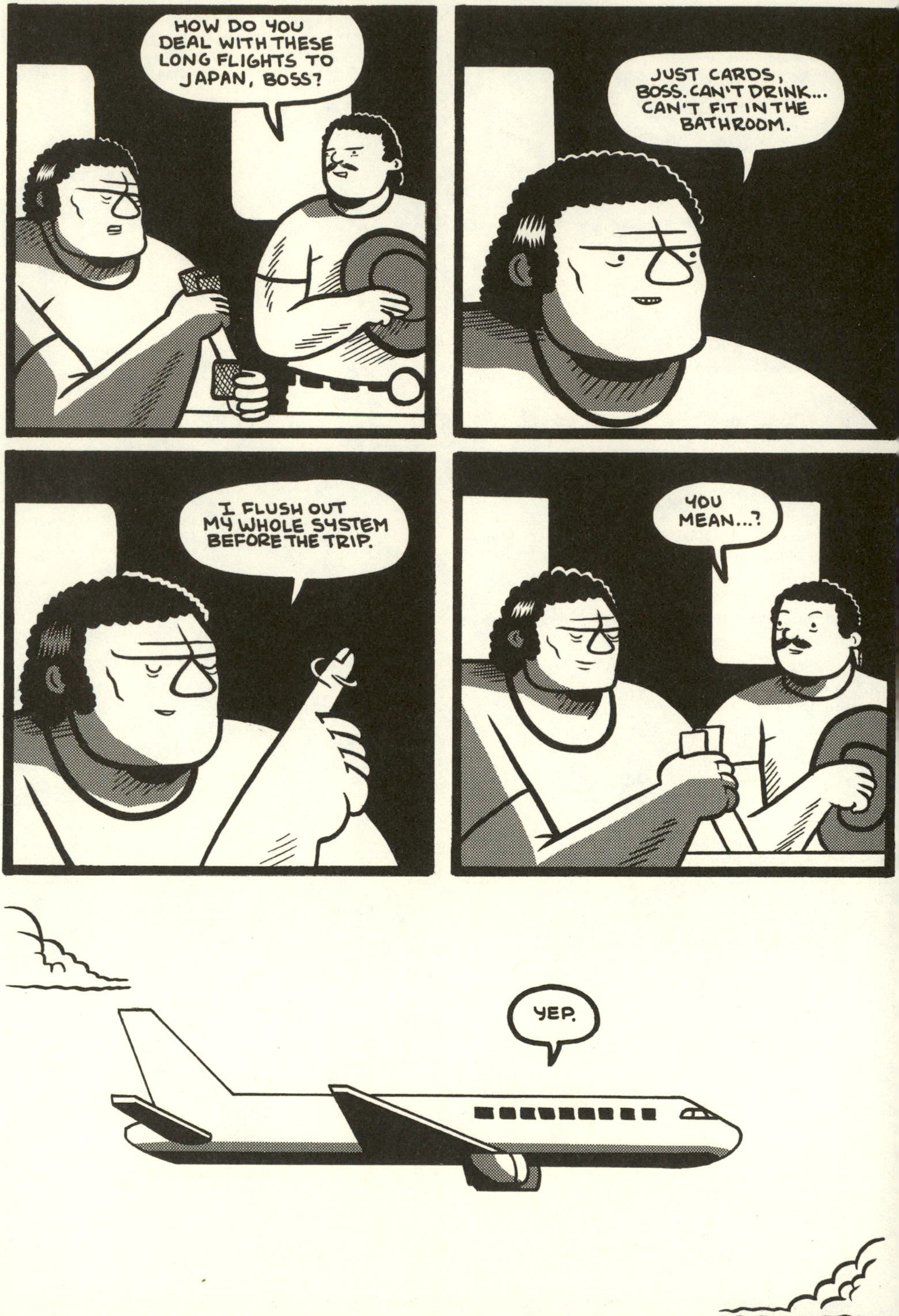
HOW DO YOU DEAL WITH THESE LONG FLIGHTS TO JAPAN, BOSS?
JUST CARDS, BOSS. CAN'T DRINK... CAN'T FIT IN THE BATHROOM.
I FLUSH OUT MY WHOLE SYSTEM BEFORE THE TRIP.
YOU MEAN...?
YEP.

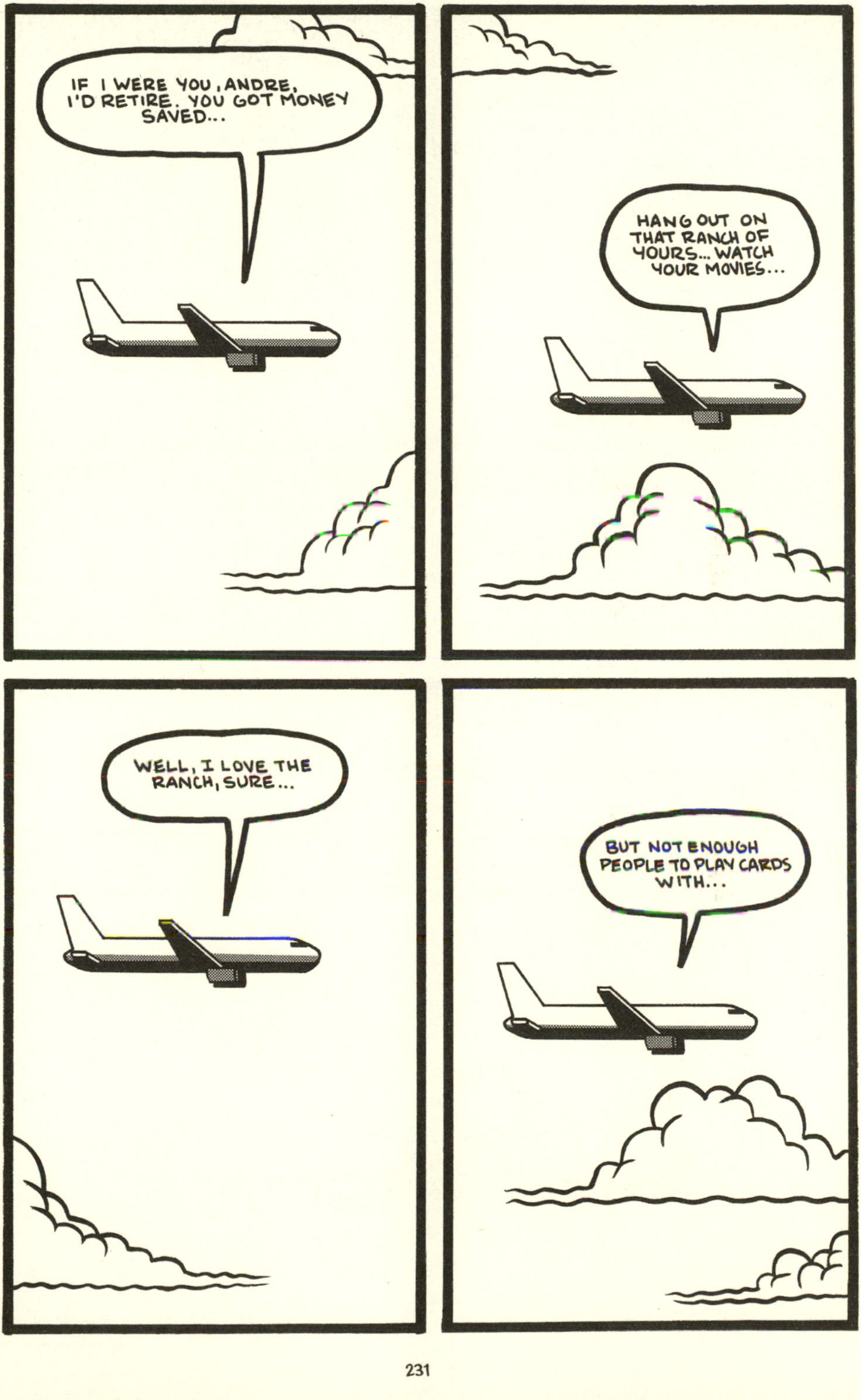
IF I WERE YOU, ANDRE, I'D RETIRE. YOU GOT MONEY SAVED...
HANG OUT ON THAT RANCH OF YOURS... WATCH YOUR MOVIES...
WELL, I LOVE THE RANCH, SURE...
BUT NOT ENOUGH PEOPLE TO PLAY CARDS WITH...

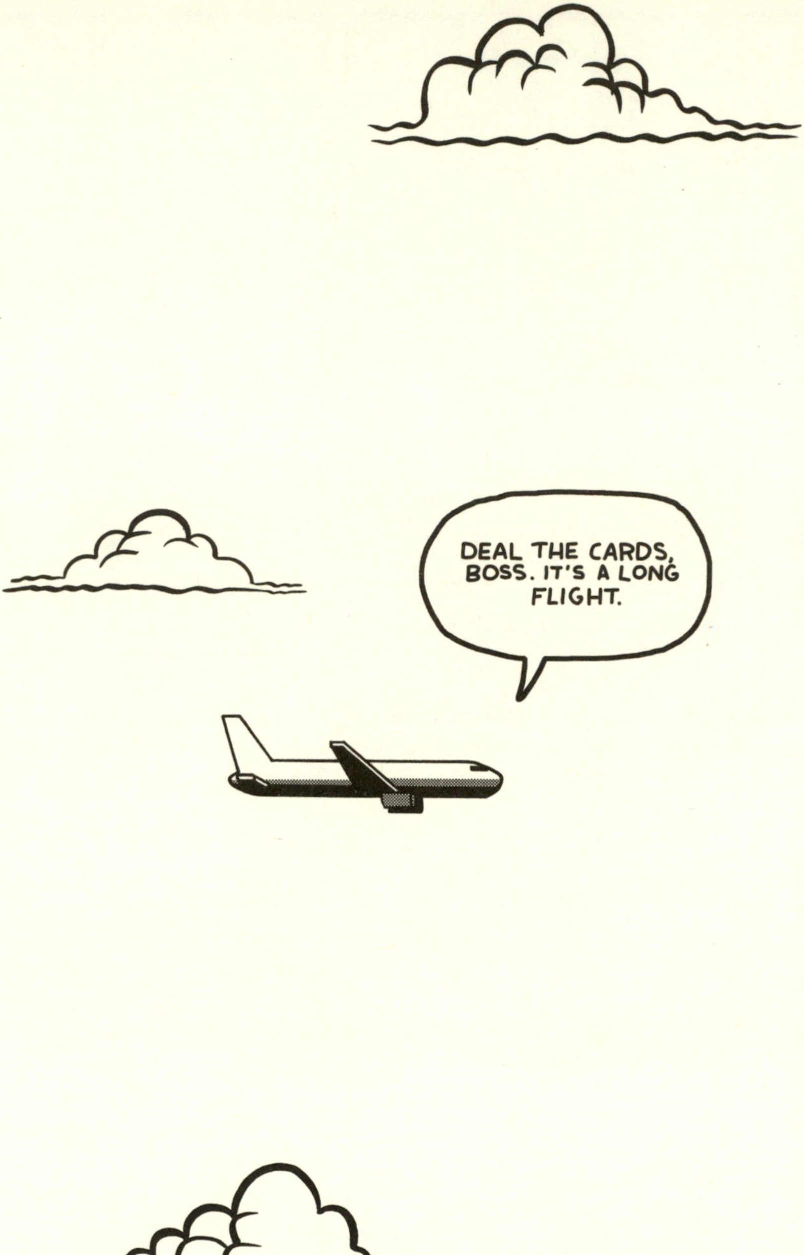
DEAL THE CARDS, BOSS. IT'S A LONG FLIGHT.

Andre died in his sleep in a Paris hotel room in late January of 1993. He was in town to attend the funeral of his father.

His ashes were scattered at his North Carolina ranch.

SOURCE NOTES

1 **Terry "Hulk Hogan" Bollea, Tampa, Florida, 2010** This is from a TV program called "The Voice Versus" hosted by Michael Schiavello. It aired on HDNet in 2010. The program was 60 minutes long. This part of the conversation is about two minutes long. I'm not sure how truthful Hogan is being throughout this interview. He tends to exaggerate all of his stories. Later in this same interview Hogan tells his version of the Bad News Brown bus incident. There are more than a few differences between Hulk Hogan's version of the incident and Bad News's own version. But he seems very sincere when talking about Andre here. The host asks a somewhat leading question and Hogan makes sure to set the record straight about Andre right off the bat. It's obvious that Hogan has the utmost respect for him.

6 **Molien, France, 1958** The story of the meeting between the writer Samuel Beckett and Andre the Giant is recounted in the book *One on One* by Craig Brown. According to Craig Brown, this is a true story.

18 **Molien, France, 1967** The story about Andre and the little car is told by his brother in the documentary *Larger Than Life* and in the obituary by Dave Meltzer.

22 **Paris, France, 1967** They mention how Andre worked as a mover in *Larger Than Life*. I found an audio recording of Andre on *Bill Apter Radio*. The year is unknown, but I'd place it in the mid 1970s. Andre is speaking French and Frank Valois is translating. Apter asks Andre about something published in a magazine that said Andre associated with prostitutes. Valois explains that he did but not in a sexual way. When he first came to Paris from his small town he didn't know anyone and sometimes "only the street people would help him." So, he did hang around with prostitutes but only to have coffee with or a drink and they enjoyed his company because he's a hard guy not to like.

   The Elysée Monmartre was a famous venue in Paris. I'm not sure if Andre ever actually wrestled there. He wrestled in Paris, though, in the late 1960s and that was one of the most popular venues in Paris at the time.

28 **The car flipping story** This story is told by Arnold Skaaland, one of Andre's first handlers, in *Larger Than Life*. But this story has been repeated

and retold by countless people, including Lee Majors, who I sincerely doubt got a first person recounting of the story, despite working with Andre on *The Six Million Dollar Man*. The details of the story often change. Was Andre picked on like this? Almost assuredly yes. Could Andre flip a car with two people in it? Most assuredly yes.

42 **Tokyo, 1970** It's mentioned in *Larger Than Life* that the first time he saw a doctor was in Japan, including the bit about them telling him he wouldn't live past forty.

50 **IWA World Series** Photos exist of this early event program. Not sure how many copies still remain, but it must be very few as there were none on eBay.

52 **Montreal, 1972** The description of events in Montreal comes from the obituary by Dave Meltzer.

57 **The Verne Gagne meeting** Verne was booking the AWA and the Montreal territory at the time. He's a legendary figure in wrestling but according to Dave Meltzer, Frank Valois (the other man in the scene with them) was the one who originally set up the meeting between Andre and McMahon, Sr.

58 **The Vince McMahon, Sr. meeting** The dialogue here is largely based on the description of how they booked Andre from Bobby Heenan's book *Bobby the Brain: Wrestling's Bad Boy Tells All*. He explains these tricks were intended to make Andre seem larger than life. Heenan attributes them all to McMahon, Sr.

65 **Los Angeles, 1974** This dissection of a wrestling match is from a WWE DVD, *Andre the Giant*. The analysis is my own.

72 ***The Tonight Show*** I had heard Vince McMahon talk about Andre being on *The Tonight Show* with Johnny Carson during a promotional interview. But I couldn't find any footage of Andre and Johnny Carson together. Eventually, I found out that Andre was on in the summer while Carson was on vacation. Sure enough, a search for Andre the Giant and Joey Bishop turned up the famous hand comparison photo.

73 **Dallas, 1975** This story is based on a retelling from *Bobby the Brain:*

Wrestling's Bad Boy Tells All. Bobby Heenan is a great storyteller but as with any story about Andre it's unknowable how stretched the truth is in this one.

81 Chuck Wepner match There is some commentary from Wepner's promoters in *Son of the Not So Great Moments in Sports*, an HBO documentary from the 1980s. The analysis of whether or not it was a real fight is my own.

90 Las Vegas, 1977 This is based on a story that Pat Patterson tells in the WWE-produced *Legends of Wrestling Roundtable.*

102 The Bad News Brown incident This is based on Bad News Brown's (Allen Coage) own recounting of this story from the *Bad News Brown Shoot Interview.*

116 Dick Murdoch's birthday party, 1980 This is based on Blackjack Mulligan's own recounting of this story in *Blackjack Mulligan On the Ranch*, a shoot interview conducted by Highspots. He talks about it in his book *True Lies and Alibis: The Blackjack Mulligan Story* as well. I actually conducted a personal interview with Blackjack myself, and he confirmed everything.

131 *Sports Illustrated* quote This was a long interview with Andre the Giant. It was really remarkable, especially at the time, that *Sports Illustrated* would devote that much attention to professional wrestling. I think it spoke to Andre's fame and respect as an athlete.

134 New Orleans, 1982 This is based on a story One Man Gang tells in the *One Man Gang Shoot Interview* DVD produced by RF Video.

139 Andre ankle break story This is from *Larger Than Life* and the obituary by Dave Meltzer.

143 Portland, Maine, 1983 This story is a mash-up of a bunch of different stories. Many people have commented on how Andre tended to treat the fans. This particular account is from Ted DiBiase's book *Ted DiBiase: The Million Dollar Man.* The story about the homeless woman is from "Classy" Freddie Blassie's book *Listen, You Pencil Neck Geeks.* Blassie also tells the story about Andre farting in the elevator, but so do a lot of other people, including Bobby Heenan in his book. The idea of him staying up after the others go to bed is based on a quote from Killer Kowalski in the book *Tributes II: Remembering More of the World's Greatest Wrestlers* by Dave Meltzer: "I remember the quantity he used to drink. He used to drink to numb himself from the reality that he wouldn't live long in this world."

158 **Letterman appearance** Based on the footage of that episode of *Late Night with David Letterman*. The analysis is my own.

163 **Poughkeepsie, New York, 1984** Ken Patera tells this story in *Ken Patera Shoot Interview*.

170 **"The situation with the mother"** This comes from a line Tim White said in *Larger Than Life*. Tim White was Andre's handler for a long time and one of his best friends.

171 **The information about the operation** This is from *Larger Than Life* and the obituary by Dave Meltzer.

173 ***The Princess Bride*** These stories are from the interview extras from *The Princess Bride* DVD except the notion of Andre's bar bill. That came from Bobby Heenan's book *Bobby the Brain: Wrestling's Bad Boy Tells All*. Terry Funk's part is from his book *Terry Funk: More Than Just Hardcore*.

181 ***Pre-WrestleMania III* sequence** This comes from two *Legends of Wrestling Roundtable* discussions: the Andre the Giant episode, the WrestleMania episode, and the Giants episode. Hogan's pre-match discussion with Vince McMahon comes from a story Vince tells on *The True Story of WrestleMania* video produced by WWE in 2011. The little story about Frenchy Bernard comes from *Larger Than Life*.

205 **March 1989** Based on *Gene Okerlund Shoot Interview*.

210 ***Brutus Beefcake's Barber Shop*** This was an interview on the WWF-produced show. The analysis is my own.

216 ***A Current Affair*** This piece aired in 1992 just a few months before Andre died.

222 **The flight home** This is mostly improvised. The part about the enema is from the *Gene Okerlund Shoot Interview*.

LIMITED GLOSSARY OF PROFESSIONAL WRESTLING TERMS

Babyface (n) the hero or "good-guy" in a wrestling match. Often abbreviated as "face."

The Business (n) refers to the pro-wrestling industry as a whole. Interestingly replaces reference to pro-wrestling as a "sport."

Blow-off (n) the last match in a series of matches between two wrestlers. Often used to decisively declare a winner and loser in the series.

Card (n) a list of matches that are to occur at an event.

Go Over (v) to beat an opponent.

Gimmick (n) 1. A foreign object used in a match 2. A wrestler's character. (v) To alter an object in order to manipulate how it is perceived by the fan (e.g., using a break-away chair or sugar glass).

Heel (n) the villain or "bad-guy" in a wrestling match.

Manager (n) a performer in a wrestling match who plays the role of a business associate of a wrestler. The manager will come to the ring and support his wrestler. The manager is many times used with a performer who is good in the ring but is not necessarily great on the microphone. The manager is almost never actually managing a wrestler's finances or accommodations.

Over (n) being popular with the intended audience. For heel wrestlers this actually means that they are hated. **Go over** (v) to beat an opponent. **Put over** (v) to allow an opponent to defeat you. **Putting over** (v) complimenting someone.

Promoter (n) the owner of a wrestling company.

Promotion (n) a wrestling company.

Sell (v) to act as if you have been injured or are in pain.

Shoot (n) an unscripted or unplanned occurrence in a wrestling match.

Spot (n) a specific series of moves or events in a wrestling match.

Squash (n) a wrestling match where one wrestler defeats the other wrestler without allowing their opponent any offensive moves.

Territory (n) an area where only a certain wrestling promotion could run shows and air their wrestling on local television.

Work (n) an event with a pre-determined outcome intended to deceive the audience. Pro-wrestling as a whole is considered to be a work. (v) 1. to set up an event or series of actions in order to deceive someone in wrestling 2. to lie.

BIBLIOGRAPHY

Apter, Bill. "All About Andre the Giant On Apter Pro Wrestling Classic Audio." *Classic ProWrestling Interviews on Wrestling.*

Bad News Brown Shoot Interview. Perf. Allen Coage. RF Video, DVD.

Biography: Andre the Giant: Larger Than Life. Perf. Andre the Giant. WWF Home Video, 1999, videocassette.

Blackjack Mulligan On the Ranch. Perf. Blackjack Mulligan. Highspots, 2006, DVD.

Blassie, Freddie, and Keith Elliot Greenberg. *Legends of Wrestling: "Classy" Freddie Blassie: Listen, You Pencil Neck Geeks.* New York, NY: Pocket, 2004.

Brown, Craig. *One on One.* London: Fourth Estate, 2011.

Clawmaster. "Andre the Giant Record Book." Online Posting in Sports and Wrestling. *Sports And Wrestling.*

Demain, Bill. "11 Peculiar Meetings Between Famous People." *Mental Floss.*

DiBiase, Ted, and Tom Caiazzo. *Ted DiBiase: The Million Dollar Man.* London: Simon & Schuster, 2008.

Funk, Terry, and Scott E. Williams. *Terry Funk: More Than Just Hardcore.* Champaign, IL: Sports Pub. L.L.C., 2005.

WITHDRAWN

Heenan, Bobby, and Steve Anderson. *Bobby the Brain: Wrestling's Bad Boy Tells All.* Chicago, IL: Triumph, 2002.

Ken Patera Shoot Interview. Highspots, DVD.

Legends of Wrestling 3: Andre the Giant & Iron Sheik. Perf. Andre the Giant. World Wrestling Entertainment, 2009, DVD.

"Legends of Wrestling: Giants." *Giants.* WWE Classics OnDemand. 2008.

Letterman, David. "Andre the Giant on Letterman." *Late Night with David Letterman.* NBC. New York, NY, 1984.

Mean Gene Okerlund Shoot Interview Wrestling DVD. Perf. Gene Okerlund. Highspots, DVD.

Meltzer, Dave, and Bret Hart. *Tributes II: Remembering More of the World's Greatest Professional Wrestlers.* Champaign, IL: Sports Pub., 2004.

Meltzer, Dave. "Death of Andre the Giant, Life and Times, Huge Bio." *Wrestling Observer Newsletter* , February 8, 1993.

Merchant, Larry. "Son of the Not-So-Great Moments in Sports." *Son of the Not-So-Great Moments in Sports.* HBO. 1986.

Mulligan, Blackjack, and Steve Buchanan. *True Lies and Alibis: The Blackjack Mulligan Story.* Omaha, NE: Headlock Ranch Pub., 2008.

O'Boyle, Maureen. "A Current Affair." *A Current Affair.* Prod. Peter Brennan. 20th Century Fox. 1992.

One Man Gang Shoot Interview. Perf. One Man Gang. RF Video, DVD.

The Princess Bride 20th Anniversary Edition (DVD Extras). Dir. Rob Reiner. Perf. Billy Crystal, Mandy Patinkin, Robin Wright, Christopher Guest. Twentieth Century Fox Film Corp., 2007, DVD.

Schiavello, Michael. "The Voice Versus." *Hulk Hogan.* HDNet. Dallas, Texas, 2010.

Stubbs, Dave. "Andre the Giant Obituary." *Montreal Gazette*, February 27, 1993.

Todd, Terry. "To the Giant Among Us." *Sports Illustrated,* December 21, 1981.

WWE Andre the Giant. Perf. Andre the Giant. WWE, 2005, DVD.

WWE: The True Story of WrestleMania. Dir. Vince McMahon, Jr. WWE, 2011, DVD.